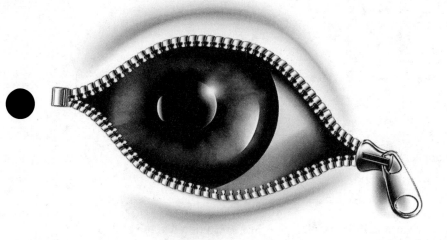

*my*Perspectives™
ENGLISH LANGUAGE ARTS

Pearson

NEW YORK, NEW YORK • BOSTON, MASSACHUSETTS
CHANDLER, ARIZONA • GLENVIEW, ILLINOIS

COVER: © Zffoto/Shutterstock

Acknowledgments of third-party content appear on page R77, which constitutes an extension of this copyright page.

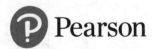

ISBN-13: 978-0-13-333878-2
ISBN-10: 0-13-333878-9

16 19

Welcome!

myPerspectives™ *English Language Arts* is a student-centered learning environment where you will analyze text, cite evidence, and respond critically about your learning. You will take ownership of your learning through goal-setting, reflection, independent text selection, and activities that allow you to collaborate with your peers.

Each unit of study includes selections of different genres—including multimedia—all related to a relevant and meaningful Essential Question. As you read, you will engage in activities that inspire thoughtful discussion and debate with your peers allowing you to formulate, and defend, your own perspectives.

myPerspectives ELA offers a variety of ways to interact directly with the text. You can annotate by writing in your print consumable, or you can annotate in your digital Student Edition. In addition, exciting technology allows you to access multimedia directly from your mobile device and communicate using an online discussion board!

We hope you enjoy using *myPerspectives ELA* as you develop the skills required to be successful throughout college and career.

Authors' Perspectives

myPerspectives is informed by a team of respected experts whose experiences working with students and study of instructional best practices have positively impacted education. From the evolving role of the teacher to how students learn in a digital age, our authors bring new ideas, innovations, and strategies that transform teaching and learning in today's competitive and interconnected world.

"The teaching of English needs to focus on engaging a new generation of learners. How do we get them excited about reading and writing? How do we help them to envision themselves as readers and writers? And, how can we make the teaching of English more culturally, socially, and technologically relevant? Throughout the curriculum, we've created spaces that enhance youth voice and participation and that connect the teaching of literature and writing to technological transformations of the digital age."

Ernest Morrell, Ph.D.

is the Macy professor of English Education at Teachers College, Columbia University, a class of 2014 Fellow of the American Educational Research Association, and the Past-President of the National Council of Teachers of English (NCTE). He is also the Director of Teachers College's Institute for Urban and Minority Education (IUME). He is an award-winning author and in his spare time he coaches youth sports and writes poems and plays. Dr. Morrell has influenced the development of *my*Perspectives in Assessment, Writing & Research, Student Engagement, and Collaborative Learning.

Elfrieda Hiebert, Ph.D.

is President and CEO of TextProject, a nonprofit that provides resources to support higher reading levels. She is also a research associate at the University of California, Santa Cruz. Dr. Hiebert has worked in the field of early reading acquisition for 45 years, first as a teacher's aide and teacher of primary-level students in California and, subsequently, as a teacher and researcher. Her research addresses how fluency, vocabulary, and knowledge can be fostered through appropriate texts. Dr. Hiebert has influenced the development of *my*Perspectives in Vocabulary, Text Complexity, and Assessment.

> " The signature of complex text is challenging vocabulary. In the systems of vocabulary, it's important to provide ways to show how concepts can be made more transparent to students. We provide lessons and activities that develop a strong vocabulary and concept foundation—a foundation that permits students to comprehend increasingly more complex text."

Kelly Gallagher, M.Ed.

teaches at Magnolia High School in Anaheim, California, where he is in his thirty-first year. He is the former co-director of the South Basin Writing Project at California State University, Long Beach. Mr. Gallagher has influenced the development of *my*Perspectives in Writing, Close Reading, and the Role of Teachers.

> " The *my*Perspectives classroom is dynamic. The teacher inspires, models, instructs, facilitates, and advises students as they evolve and grow. When teachers guide students through meaningful learning tasks and then pass them ownership of their own learning, students become engaged and work harder. This is how we make a difference in student achievement—by putting students at the center of their learning and giving them the opportunities to choose, explore, collaborate, and work independently."

> " It's critical to give students the opportunity to read a wide range of highly engaging texts and to immerse themselves in exploring powerful ideas and how these ideas are expressed. In *my*Perspectives, we focus on building up students' awareness of how academic language works, which is especially important for English language learners."

Jim Cummins, Ph.D.

is a Professor Emeritus in the Department of Curriculum, Teaching and Learning of the University of Toronto. His research focuses on literacy development in multilingual school contexts as well as on the potential roles of technology in promoting language and literacy development. In recent years, he has been working actively with teachers to identify ways of increasing the literacy engagement of learners in multilingual school contexts. Dr. Cummins has influenced the development of *my*Perspectives in English Language Learner and English Language Development support.

UNIT INTRODUCTION

WHOLE-CLASS LEARNING

COMPARE TEXT

PERFORMANCE TASK

SMALL-GROUP LEARNING

 PERFORMANCE TASK

INDEPENDENT LEARNING

These selections can be accessed via the Interactive Student Edition.

 PERFORMANCE-BASED ASSESSMENT PREP

 PERFORMANCE-BASED ASSESSMENT

UNIT REFLECTION

DIGITAL PERSPECTIVES

 SCAN FOR MULTIMEDIA

Use the BouncePage app whenever you see "Scan for Multimedia" to access:

- Unit Introduction Videos
- Media Selections
- Modeling Videos
- Selection Audio Recordings

Additional digital resources can be found in:

- Interactive Student Edition
- *my*Perspectives+

INDEPENDENT LEARNING

These selections can be accessed via the Interactive Student Edition.

PERFORMANCE-BASED
ASSESSMENT PREP

PERFORMANCE-BASED ASSESSMENT

UNIT REFLECTION

DIGITAL PERSPECTIVES

 SCAN FOR MULTIMEDIA

Use the BouncePage app whenever you see "Scan for Multimedia" to access:

- Unit Introduction Videos
- Media Selections
- Modeling Videos
- Selection Audio Recordings

Additional digital resources can be found in:

- Interactive Student Edition
- *my*Perspectives+

INDEPENDENT LEARNING

MEDIA: INFORMATIONAL TEXT

**Law and the Rule of Law:
The Role of Federal Courts**

Judicial Learning Center

ESSAY

Misrule of Law

Aung San Suu Kyi

SHORT STORY

Harrison Bergeron

Kurt Vonnegut, Jr.

PERSONAL ESSAY

Credo: What I Believe

Neil Gaiman

These selections can be accessed via the
Interactive Student Edition.

 **PERFORMANCE-BASED
ASSESSMENT PREP**

 PERFORMANCE-BASED
ASSESSMENT

Informative Text:

UNIT REFLECTION

DIGITAL ⌖
PERSPECTIVES

SCAN FOR
MULTIMEDIA

Use the BouncePage app
whenever you see "Scan
for Multimedia" to access:

• Unit Introduction Videos

• Media Selections

• Modeling Videos

• Selection Audio Recordings

Additional digital resources can be found in:

• Interactive Student Edition

• *my*Perspectives+

UNIT (4) All That Glitters

**DIGITAL
PERSPECTIVES**

 SCAN FOR
MULTIMEDIA

Use the BouncePage app
whenever you see "Scan
for Multimedia" to access:

- Unit Introduction Videos
- Media Selections
- Modeling Videos
- Selection Audio Recordings

Additional digital resources can be found in:

- Interactive Student Edition
- *my*Perspectives+

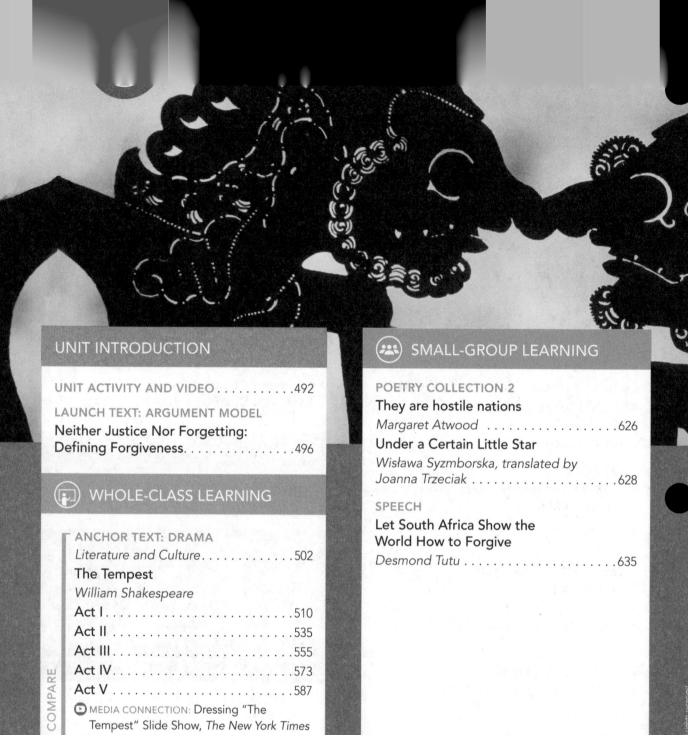

COMPARE

DIGITAL
PERSPECTIVES

SCAN FOR
MULTIMEDIA

Use the BouncePage app
whenever you see "Scan
for Multimedia" to access:

- Unit Introduction Videos
- Media Selections
- Modeling Videos
- Selection Audio Recordings

Additional digital resources can be found in:

- Interactive Student Edition
- *my*Perspectives+

UNIT **6** Blindness and Sight

INDEPENDENT LEARNING

These selections can be accessed via the Interactive Student Edition.

 PERFORMANCE-BASED
ASSESSMENT PREP

 PERFORMANCE-BASED
ASSESSMENT

UNIT REFLECTION

DIGITAL ⌕
PERSPECTIVES

 SCAN FOR
MULTIMEDIA

Use the BouncePage app whenever you see "Scan for Multimedia" to access:

- Unit Introduction Videos
- Media Selections
- Modeling Videos
- Selection Audio Recordings

Additional digital resources can be found in:

- Interactive Student Edition
- *my*Perspectives+

Interactive Student Edition

*my*Perspectives is completely interactive because you can work directly in your digital or print Student Edition.

All activities that you complete in your Interactive Student Edition are saved automatically. You can access your notes quickly so that reviewing work to prepare for tests and projects is easy!

Enter answers to prompts right in your digital Notebook and "turn it in" to your teacher.

The in-line annotation tool allows you to practice close reading by highlighting and adding comments about the text.

Interactivities are available for you to complete and submit directly to your teacher.

the shops in town lowered their shutters in preparation for the storm. Starting early in the morning, my father and brother went around the house nailing shut all the storm-doors, while my mother spent the day in the kitchen cooking emergency provisions. We filled bottles and canteens with water, and packed our most important possessions in rucksacks[2] for possible evacuation. To the adults, typhoons were an annoyance and a threat they had to face almost annually, but to the kids, removed as we were from such practical concerns, it was just a great big circus, a wonderful source of excitement.

12   Just after noon the color of the sky began to change all of a sudden. There was something strange and unreal about it. I stayed outside on the porch, watching the sky, until the wind began to howl and the rain began to beat against the house with a weird dry sound, like handfuls of sand. Then we closed the last storm-door and gathered together in one room of the darkened house, listening to the radio. This particular storm did not have a great deal of rain, it said, but the winds were doing a lot of damage, blowing roofs off houses and capsizing ships. Many people had been killed or injured by flying debris. Over and over again, they warned people against leaving their homes. Every once in a while, the house would creak and shudder as if a huge hand were shaking it, and sometimes there would be a great crash of some heavy-sounding object against a storm-door. My father guessed that these were tiles blowing off the neighbors' houses. For lunch we ate the rice and omelettes my mother had cooked, waiting for the typhoon to blow past.

13   But the typhoon gave no sign of blowing past. The radio said it had lost momentum[3] almost as soon as it came ashore at S. Province, and now it was moving north-east at the pace of a slow runner. The wind kept up its savage howling as it trie[...]
stood on land.

14   Perhaps an hour had gone by with the [...] when a hush fell over everything. All of a [...] could hear a bird crying in the distance. M[...] door a crack and looked outside. The win[...] rain had ceased to fall. Thick, gray clouds [...]

NOTES

This sentence is leading up to an exciting story.

CLOSE READ
ANNOTATE: In paragraph 12, annotate at least four vivid details about the storm. Underline those that compare one thing to another.

QUESTION: What is being compared? What picture does each detail create in the reader's mind?

CONCLUDE: How do these descriptions help you visualize the typhoon?

Typhoons are powerful, scary storms that can do a lot of damage.

Use the close-read prompts to guide you through an analysis of the text. You can highlight, circle, and underline the text right in your print Student Edition.

THE SEVENTH MAN

LANGUAGE DEVELOPMENT

Concept Vocabulary

desperate	hallucination	profound
entranced	premonition	meditative

Why These Words? These concept words help to reveal the emotional state of the seventh man. For example, when the wave approaches, the seventh man is *entranced*, waiting for it to attack. After the wave hits, the seventh man believes he sees his friend K. in the wave and claims that this experience was no *hallucination*. Notice that both words relate to experiences that occur only in the mind of the seventh man.

1. How does the concept vocabulary sharpen the reader's understanding of the mental or emotional state of the seventh man?
   These words are descriptive and precise.

2. What other words in the selection connect to this concept?
   ominous, overcome, nightmares

Practice

🔵 **Notebook** The concept vocabulary words appear in "The Seventh Man."

1. Use each concept word in a sentence that demonstrates your understanding of the word's meaning.

2. Challenge yourself to replace the concept word with one or two synonyms. How does the word change affect the meaning of your sentence? For example, which sentence is stronger? Which has a more positive meaning?

Word Study

Latin suffix: -tion The Latin suffix *-tion* often indicates that a word is a noun. Sometimes this suffix is spelled *-ion* or *-ation*. These related suffixes mean "act, state, or condition of." In "The Seventh Man," the word *premonition* means "the state of being forewarned."

1. Record a definition of *hallucination* based on your understanding of its root word and the meaning of the suffix *-tion*.
   The condition of seeing something that is not real

2. Look back at paragraphs 37–40 and find two other words that use the suffix *-tion*. Identify the root word that was combined with the suffix. Record a definition for each word.
   cooperate + -tion—the state of working together
   direct + -tion—the state of being guided

Respond to questions and activities directly in your book!

🔵 **WORD NETWORK**
Add interesting survival words from the text to your Word Network.

STANDARDS
Language
• Use various types of phrases and clauses to convey specific meanings and add variety and interest to writing or presentations.
• Identify and correctly use patterns of word changes that indicate different meanings or parts of speech, and continue to apply knowledge of Greek and Latin roots and affixes.
• Demonstrate understanding of figurative language, word relationships, and nuances in word meanings.

Digital Resources

You can access digital resources from your print Student Edition, or from Pearson Realize™.

To watch videos or listen to audio from your print Student Edition, all you need is a device with a camera and Pearson's BouncePages app!

ANCHOR TEXT | SHORT STORY

The Seventh Man

Haruki Murakami

BACKGROUND

Hurricanes that originate in the northwest Pacific Ocean are called typhoons. They can stretch up to 500 miles in diameter and produce high winds, heavy rains, enormous waves, and severe flooding. On average, Japan is hit by three severe typhoons each year due to its location and climatic conditions.

SCAN FOR MULTIMEDIA

1   "A huge wave nearly swept me away," said the seventh man, almost whispering. "It happened one September afternoon when I was ten years old."

2   The man was the last one to tell his story that night. The hands of the clock had moved past ten. The small group that huddled in

NOTES

CLOSE READ
ANNOTATE: Mark details in paragraph 2 that

How to watch a video or listen to audio:

1. Download Pearson's BouncePages App from the Apple App or Google Play Store.

2. Open the app on your mobile device.

3. Aim your camera so the page from your Student Edition is viewable on your screen.

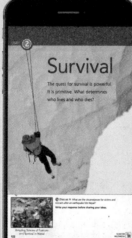

4. Tap the screen to scan the page.

5. Press the "Play" button on the page that appears on your device.

6. View the video or listen to the audio directly from your device!

Amazing Stories of Rescues and Survival in Nepal
122

Digital resources, including audio and video, can be accessed in the Interactive Student Edition. Your teacher might also assign activities for you to complete online.

Table of Contents

Interactive Student Edition

Unit 1: Immigrant Voices

Unit 2: Survival

Unit 3: The Literature of Civil Rights

Unit 4: Tragic Romances

Unit 5: Journeys of Transformation

Pearson eText 2.0 for Schools

Unit 2: Survival

UNIT 2
Survival

UNIT INTRODUCTION

WHOLE-CLASS LEARNING

SMALL-GROUP LEARNING

INDEPENDENT LEARNING

PERFORMANCE-BASED ASSESSMENT

UNIT REFLECTION

The quest for survival is powerful. It is primitive. What determines who lives and who dies?

You will also find digital novels, interactive lessons, and games!

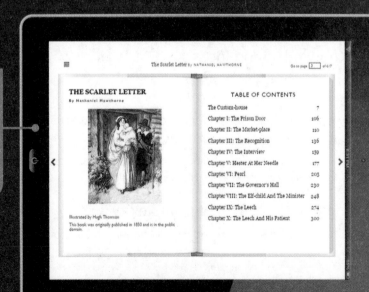

The Scarlet Letter By NATHANIEL HAWTHORNE

THE SCARLET LETTER
By Nathaniel Hawthorne

Illustrated by Hugh Thomson
This book was originally published in 1850 and is in the public domain.

TABLE OF CONTENTS

The Custom-house 7
Chapter I: The Prison Door 106
Chapter II: The Market-place 110
Chapter III: The Recognition 136
Chapter IV: The Interview 159
Chapter V: Hester At Her Needle 177
Chapter VI: Pearl 205
Chapter VII: The Governor's Hall 230
Chapter VIII: The Elf-child And The Minister ... 248
Chapter IX: The Leech 274
Chapter X: The Leech And His Patient 300

Standards Overview

The following English Language Arts standards will prepare you to succeed in college and your future career. The College and Career Readiness Anchor Standards define what you need to achieve by the end of high school, and the grade-specific Standards define what you need to know by the end of your current grade level.

The following provides an overview of the Standards.

Standards for Reading

College and Career Readiness Anchor Standards for Reading

Key Ideas and Details

1. Read closely to determine what the text says explicitly and to make logical inferences from it; cite specific textual evidence when writing or speaking to support conclusions drawn from the text.

2. Determine central ideas or themes of a text and analyze their development; summarize the key supporting details and ideas.

3. Analyze how and why individuals, events, and ideas develop and interact over the course of a text.

Craft and Structure

4. Interpret words and phrases as they are used in a text, including determining technical, connotative, and figurative meanings, and analyze how specific word choices shape meaning or tone.

5. Analyze the structure of texts, including how specific sentences, paragraphs, and larger portions of the text (e.g., a section, chapter, scene, or stanza) relate to each other and the whole.

6. Assess how point of view or purpose shapes the content and style of a text.

Integration of Knowledge and Ideas

7. Integrate and evaluate content presented in diverse formats and media, including visually and quantitatively, as well as in words.

8. Delineate and evaluate the argument and specific claims in a text, including the validity of the reasoning as well as the relevance and sufficiency of the evidence.

9. Analyze how two or more texts address similar themes or topics in order to build knowledge or to compare the approaches the authors take.

Range of Reading and Level of Text Complexity

10. Read and comprehend complex literary and informational texts independently and proficiently.

Grade 10 Reading Standards for Literature

Standard

Key Ideas and Details

Cite strong and thorough textual evidence to support analysis of what the text says explicitly as well as inferences drawn from the text.

Determine a theme or central idea of a text and analyze in detail its development over the course of the text, including how it emerges and is shaped and refined by specific details; provide an objective summary of the text.

Analyze how complex characters (e.g., those with multiple or conflicting motivations) develop over the course of a text, interact with other characters, and advance the plot or develop the theme.

Craft and Structure

Determine the meaning of words and phrases as they are used in the text, including figurative and connotative meanings; analyze the cumulative impact of specific word choices on meaning and tone (e.g., how the language evokes a sense of time and place; how it sets a formal or informal tone).

Analyze how an author's choices concerning how to structure a text, order events within it (e.g., parallel plots), and manipulate time (e.g., pacing, flashbacks) create such effects as mystery, tension, or surprise.

Analyze a particular point of view or cultural experience reflected in a work of literature from outside the United States, drawing on a wide reading of world literature.

Integration of Knowledge and Ideas

Analyze the representation of a subject or a key scene in two different artistic mediums, including what is emphasized or absent in each treatment (e.g., Auden's "Musée des Beaux Arts" and Breughel's *Landscape with the Fall of Icarus*).

Analyze how an author draws on and transforms source material in a specific work (e.g., how Shakespeare treats a theme or topic from Ovid or the Bible or how a later author draws on a play by Shakespeare).

Range of Reading and Level of Text Complexity

By the end of Grade 10, read and comprehend literature, including stories, dramas, and poems, at the high end of the grades 9–10 text complexity band independently and proficiently.

Standards Overview

Grade 10 Reading Standards for Informational Text
Standard
Key Ideas and Details
Cite strong and thorough textual evidence to support analysis of what the text says explicitly as well as inferences drawn from the text.
Determine a central idea of a text and analyze its development over the course of the text, including how it emerges and is shaped and refined by specific details; provide an objective summary of the text.
Analyze how the author unfolds an analysis or series of ideas or events, including the order in which the points are made, how they are introduced and developed, and the connections that are drawn between them.
Craft and Structure
Determine the meaning of words and phrases as they are used in a text, including figurative, connotative, and technical meanings; analyze the cumulative impact of specific word choices on meaning and tone (e.g., how the language of a court opinion differs from that of a newspaper).
Analyze in detail how an author's ideas or claims are developed and refined by particular sentences, paragraphs, or larger portions of a text (e.g., a section or chapter).
Determine an author's point of view or purpose in a text and analyze how an author uses rhetoric to advance that point of view or purpose.
Integration of Knowledge and Ideas
Analyze various accounts of a subject told in different mediums (e.g., a person's life story in both print and multimedia), determining which details are emphasized in each account.
Delineate and evaluate the argument and specific claims in a text, assessing whether the reasoning is valid and the evidence is relevant and sufficient; identify false statements and fallacious reasoning.
Analyze seminal U.S. documents of historical and literary significance (e.g., Washington's Farewell Address, the Gettysburg Address, Roosevelt's Four Freedoms speech, King's "Letter from Birmingham Jail"), including how they address related themes and concepts.
Range of Reading and Level of Text Complexity
By the end of Grade 10, read and comprehend literary nonfiction at the high end of the grades 9–10 text complexity band independently and proficiently.

Standards for Writing

College and Career Readiness Anchor Standards for Writing

Text Types and Purposes

1. Write arguments to support claims in an analysis of substantive topics or texts, using valid reasoning and relevant and sufficient evidence.

2. Write informative/explanatory texts to examine and convey complex ideas and information clearly and accurately through the effective selection, organization, and analysis of content.

3. Write narratives to develop real or imagined experiences or events using effective technique, well-chosen details, and well-structured event sequences

Production and Distribution of Writing

4. Produce clear and coherent writing in which the development, organization, and style are appropriate to task, purpose, and audience.

5. Develop and strengthen writing as needed by planning, revising, editing, rewriting, or trying a new approach.

6. Use technology, including the Internet, to produce and publish writing and to interact and collaborate with others.

Research to Build and Present Knowledge

7. Conduct short as well as more sustained research projects based on focused questions, demonstrating understanding of the subject under investigation.

8. Gather relevant information from multiple print and digital sources, assess the credibility and accuracy of each source, and integrate the information while avoiding plagiarism.

9. Draw evidence from literary or informational texts to support analysis, reflection, and research.

Range of Writing

10. Write routinely over extended time frames (time for research, reflection, and revision) and shorter time frames (a single sitting or a day or two) for a range of tasks, purposes, and audiences.

Grade 10 Writing Standards

Standard

Text Types and Purposes

Write arguments to support claims in an analysis of substantive topics or texts, using valid reasoning and relevant and sufficient evidence.

Introduce precise claim(s), distinguish the claim(s) from alternate or opposing claims, and create an organization that establishes clear relationships among claim(s), counterclaims, reasons, and evidence.

Standards Overview

Grade 10 Writing Standards
Standard
Text Types and Purposes (continued)
Develop claim(s) and counterclaims fairly, supplying evidence for each while pointing out the strengths and limitations of both in a manner that anticipates the audience's knowledge level and concerns.
Use words, phrases, and clauses to link the major sections of the text, create cohesion, and clarify the relationships between claim(s) and reasons, between reasons and evidence, and between claim(s) and counterclaims.
Establish and maintain a formal style and objective tone while attending to the norms and conventions of the discipline in which they are writing.
Provide a concluding statement or section that follows from and supports the argument presented.
Write informative/explanatory texts to examine and convey complex ideas, concepts, and information clearly and accurately through the effective selection, organization, and analysis of content.
Introduce a topic; organize complex ideas, concepts, and information to make important connections and distinctions; include formatting (e.g., headings), graphics (e.g., figures, tables), and multimedia when useful to aiding comprehension.
Develop the topic with well-chosen, relevant, and sufficient facts, extended definitions, concrete details, quotations, or other information and examples appropriate to the audience's knowledge of the topic.
Use appropriate and varied transitions to link the major sections of the text, create cohesion, and clarify the relationships among complex ideas and concepts.
Use precise language and domain-specific vocabulary to manage the complexity of the topic.
Establish and maintain a formal style and objective tone while attending to the norms and conventions of the discipline in which they are writing.
Provide a concluding statement or section that follows from and supports the information or explanation presented (e.g., articulating implications or the significance of the topic).
Write narratives to develop real or imagined experiences or events using effective technique, well-chosen details, and well-structured event sequences.
Engage and orient the reader by setting out a problem, situation, or observation, establishing one or multiple point(s) of view, and introducing a narrator and/or characters; create a smooth progression of experiences or events.
Use narrative techniques, such as dialogue, pacing, description, reflection, and multiple plot lines, to develop experiences, events, and/or characters.
Use a variety of techniques to sequence events so that they build on one another to create a coherent whole.

Grade 10 Writing Standards

Standard

Text Types and Purposes (continued)

Use precise words and phrases, telling details, and sensory language to convey a vivid picture of the experiences, events, setting, and/or characters.

Provide a conclusion that follows from and reflects on what is experienced, observed, or resolved over the course of the narrative.

Production and Distribution of Writing

Produce clear and coherent writing in which the development, organization, and style are appropriate to task, purpose, and audience.

Develop and strengthen writing as needed by planning, revising, editing, rewriting, or trying a new approach, focusing on addressing what is most significant for a specific purpose and audience.

Use technology, including the Internet, to produce, publish, and update individual or shared writing products, taking advantage of technology's capacity to link to other information and to display information flexibly and dynamically.

Research to Build and Present Knowledge

Conduct short as well as more sustained research projects to answer a question (including a self-generated question) or solve a problem; narrow or broaden the inquiry when appropriate; synthesize multiple sources on the subject, demonstrating understanding of the subject under investigation.

Gather relevant information from multiple authoritative print and digital sources, using advanced searches effectively; assess the usefulness of each source in answering the research question; integrate information into the text selectively to maintain the flow of ideas, avoiding plagiarism and following a standard format for citation.

Draw evidence from literary or informational texts to support analysis, reflection, and research.

Apply *grades 9–10 Reading standards* to literature (e.g., "Analyze how an author draws on and transforms source material in a specific work [e.g., how Shakespeare treats a theme or topic from Ovid or the Bible or how a later author draws on a play by Shakespeare]").

Apply *grades 9–10 Reading standards* to literary nonfiction (e.g., "Delineate and evaluate the argument and specific claims in a text, assessing whether the reasoning is valid and the evidence is relevant and sufficient; identify false statements and fallacious reasoning").

Range of Writing

Write routinely over extended time frames (time for research, reflection, and revision) and shorter time frames (a single sitting or a day or two) for a range of tasks, purposes, and audiences.

Standards Overview

Standards for Speaking and Listening

**College and Career Readiness
Anchor Standards for Speaking and Listening**

Comprehension and Collaboration

1. Prepare for and participate effectively in a range of conversations and collaborations with diverse partners, building on others' ideas and expressing their own clearly and persuasively.

2. Integrate and evaluate information presented in diverse media and formats, including visually, quantitatively, and orally.

3. Evaluate a speaker's point of view, reasoning, and use of evidence and rhetoric.

Presentation of Knowledge and Ideas

4. Present information, findings, and supporting evidence such that listeners can follow the line of reasoning and the organization, development, and style are appropriate to task, purpose, and audience.

5. Make strategic use of digital media and visual displays of data to express information and enhance understanding of presentations.

6. Adapt speech to a variety of contexts and communicative tasks, demonstrating command of formal English when indicated or appropriate.

Grade 10 Standards for Speaking and Listening

Standard

Comprehension and Collaboration

Initiate and participate effectively in a range of collaborative discussions (one-on-one, in groups, and teacher-led) with diverse partners on grades 9–10 topics, texts, and issues, building on others' ideas and expressing their own clearly and persuasively.

Come to discussions prepared, having read and researched material under study; explicitly draw on that preparation by referring to evidence from texts and other research on the topic or issue to stimulate a thoughtful, well-reasoned exchange of ideas.

Work with peers to set rules for collegial discussions and decision-making (e.g., informal consensus, taking votes on key issues, presentation of alternate views), clear goals and deadlines, and individual roles as needed.

Propel conversations by posing and responding to questions that relate the current discussion to broader themes or larger ideas; actively incorporate others into the discussion; and clarify, verify, or challenge ideas and conclusions.

Respond thoughtfully to diverse perspectives, summarize points of agreement and disagreement, and, when warranted, qualify or justify their own views and understanding and make new connections in light of the evidence and reasoning presented.

Integrate multiple sources of information presented in diverse media or formats (e.g., visually, quantitatively, orally) evaluating the credibility and accuracy of each source.

Evaluate a speaker's point of view, reasoning, and use of evidence and rhetoric, identifying any fallacious reasoning or exaggerated or distorted evidence.

Presentation of Knowledge and Ideas

Present information, findings, and supporting evidence clearly, concisely, and logically such that listeners can follow the line of reasoning and the organization, development, substance, and style are appropriate to purpose, audience, and task.

Make strategic use of digital media (e.g., textual, graphical, audio, visual, and interactive elements) in presentations to enhance understanding of findings, reasoning, and evidence and to add interest.

Adapt speech to a variety of contexts and tasks, demonstrating command of formal English when indicated or appropriate. (See grades 9–10 Language Standards 1 and 3 for specific expectations.)

Standards Overview

Standards for Language

College and Career Readiness Anchor Standards for Language

Conventions of Standard English

1. Demonstrate command of the conventions of standard English grammar and usage when writing or speaking.

2. Demonstrate command of the conventions of standard English capitalization, punctuation, and spelling when writing.

Knowledge of Language

3. Apply knowledge of language to understand how language functions in different contexts, to make effective choices for meaning or style, and to comprehend more fully when reading or listening.

Vocabulary Acquisition and Use

4. Determine or clarify the meaning of unknown and multiple-meaning words and phrases by using context clues, analyzing meaningful word parts, and consulting general and specialized reference materials, as appropriate.

5. Demonstrate understanding of figurative language, word relationships, and nuances in word meanings.

6. Acquire and use accurately a range of general academic and domain-specific words and phrases sufficient for reading, writing, speaking, and listening at the college and career readiness level; demonstrate independence in gathering vocabulary knowledge when considering a word or phrase important to comprehension or expression.

Grade 10 Standards for Language

Standard

Conventions of Standard English

Demonstrate command of the conventions of standard English grammar and usage when writing or speaking.

Use parallel structure.

Use various types of phrases (noun, verb, adjectival, adverbial, participial, prepositional, absolute) and clauses (independent, dependent; noun, relative, adverbial) to convey specific meanings and add variety and interest to writing or presentations.

Demonstrate command of the conventions of standard English capitalization, punctuation, and spelling when writing.

Use a semicolon (and perhaps a conjunctive adverb) to link two or more closely related independent clauses.

Grade 10 Standards for Language

Standard

Conventions of Standard English (continued)

Use a semicolon (and perhaps a conjunctive adverb) to link two or more closely related independent clauses.

Use a colon to introduce a list or quotation.

Spell correctly.

Knowledge of Language

Apply knowledge of language to understand how language functions in different contexts, to make effective choices for meaning or style, and to comprehend more fully when reading or listening.

Write and edit work so that it conforms to the guidelines in a style manual (e.g., *MLA Handbook*, Turabian's *Manual for Writers*) appropriate for the discipline and writing type.

Vocabulary Acquisition and Use

Determine or clarify the meaning of unknown and multiple-meaning words and phrases based on *grades 9–10 reading and content*, choosing flexibly from a range of strategies.

Use context (e.g., the overall meaning of a sentence, paragraph, or text; a word's position or function in a sentence) as a clue to the meaning of a word or phrase.

Identify and correctly use patterns of word changes that indicate different meanings or parts of speech (e.g., *analyze, analysis, analytical; advocate, advocacy*).

Consult general and specialized reference materials (e.g., dictionaries, glossaries, thesauruses), both print and digital, to find the pronunciation of a word or determine or clarify its precise meaning, its part of speech, or its etymology.

Verify the preliminary determination of the meaning of a word or phrase (e.g., by checking the inferred meaning in context or in a dictionary).

Demonstrate understanding of figurative language, word relationships, and nuances in word meanings.

Interpret figures of speech (e.g., euphemism, oxymoron) in context and analyze their role in the text.

Analyze nuances in the meaning of words with similar denotations.

Acquire and use accurately general academic and domain-specific words and phrases, sufficient for reading, writing, speaking, and listening at the college and career readiness level; demonstrate independence in gathering vocabulary knowledge when considering a word or phrase important to comprehension or expression.

Inside the Nightmare

Spine-tingling movies, books,
and experiences are everywhere.
What draws us to explore—and
to enjoy—frightening themes?

Spooky Business:
American Economy

⊘ Discuss It Why is Halloween big business?

Write your response before sharing your ideas.

SCAN FOR
MULTIMEDIA

UNIT INTRODUCTION

ESSENTIAL QUESTION:

What is the allure of fear?

LAUNCH TEXT
EXPLANATORY MODEL
My Introduction to
Gothic Literature

 ## WHOLE-CLASS LEARNING

 ## SMALL-GROUP LEARNING

 ## INDEPENDENT LEARNING

COMPARE

ANCHOR TEXT: SHORT STORY

The Fall of the House of Usher
Edgar Allan Poe

ANCHOR TEXT: SHORT STORY

House Taken Over
Julio Cortázar

MEDIA: INFORMATIONAL GRAPHIC

from **How to Tell You're Reading a Gothic Novel—In Pictures**
Adam Frost and Zhenia Vasiliev

SHORT STORY

Where Is Here?
Joyce Carol Oates

MEDIA: PHOTO GALLERY

from **The Dream Collector**
Arthur Tress

INTERVIEW

Why Do Some Brains Enjoy Fear?
Allegra Ringo

POETRY COLLECTION

beware: do not read this poem
Ishmael Reed

The Raven
Edgar Allan Poe

Windigo
Louise Erdrich

CRITICISM

How Maurice Sendak's "Wild Things" Moved Children's Books Toward Realism
Gloria Goodale

EXPLANATORY NONFICTION

Sleep Paralysis: A Waking Nightmare

SHORT STORY

The Feather Pillow
Horacio Quiroga, translated by Margaret Sayers Peden

NEWSPAPER ARTICLE

Stone Age Man's Terrors Still Stalk Modern Nightmares
Robin McKie

PERFORMANCE TASK

WRITING FOCUS:
Write an Explanatory Essay

PERFORMANCE TASK

SPEAKING AND LISTENING FOCUS:
Deliver an Explanatory Presentation

PERFORMANCE-BASED ASSESSMENT PREP

Review Evidence for an Explanatory Essay

PERFORMANCE-BASED ASSESSMENT

Explanatory Text: Essay and Informal Talk

PROMPT:

In what ways does transformation play a role in stories meant to scare us?

Unit Goals

Throughout this unit, you will deepen your understanding of scary literature by reading, writing, speaking, presenting, and listening. These goals will help you succeed on the Unit Performance-Based Assessment.

Rate how well you meet these goals right now. You will revisit your ratings later when you reflect on your growth during this unit.

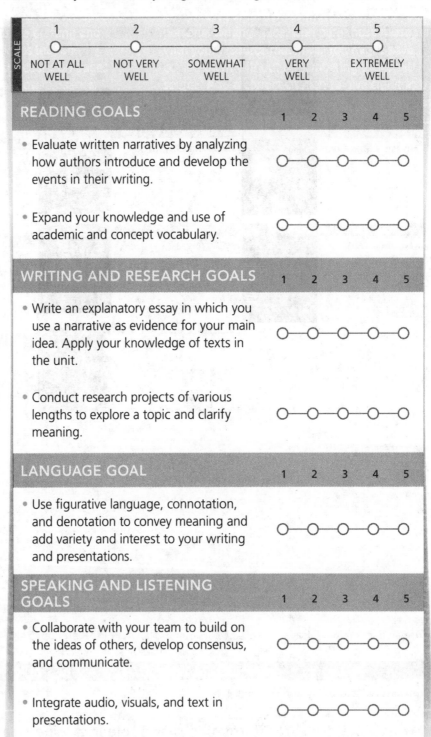

SCALE	1 NOT AT ALL WELL	2 NOT VERY WELL	3 SOMEWHAT WELL	4 VERY WELL	5 EXTREMELY WELL

READING GOALS	1	2	3	4	5
• Evaluate written narratives by analyzing how authors introduce and develop the events in their writing.	○	○	○	○	○
• Expand your knowledge and use of academic and concept vocabulary.	○	○	○	○	○

WRITING AND RESEARCH GOALS	1	2	3	4	5
• Write an explanatory essay in which you use a narrative as evidence for your main idea. Apply your knowledge of texts in the unit.	○	○	○	○	○
• Conduct research projects of various lengths to explore a topic and clarify meaning.	○	○	○	○	○

LANGUAGE GOAL	1	2	3	4	5
• Use figurative language, connotation, and denotation to convey meaning and add variety and interest to your writing and presentations.	○	○	○	○	○

SPEAKING AND LISTENING GOALS	1	2	3	4	5
• Collaborate with your team to build on the ideas of others, develop consensus, and communicate.	○	○	○	○	○
• Integrate audio, visuals, and text in presentations.	○	○	○	○	○

▤ STANDARDS

Language
Acquire and use accurately general academic and domain-specific words and phrases, sufficient for reading, writing, speaking, and listening at the college and career readiness level; demonstrate independence in gathering vocabulary knowledge when considering a word or phrase important to comprehension or expression.

SCAN FOR MULTIMEDIA

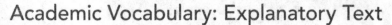

Academic Vocabulary: Explanatory Text

Academic terms appear in all subjects and can help you read, write, and discuss with more precision. Here are five academic words that will be useful to you in this unit as you analyze and write explanatory texts.

FOLLOW THROUGH
Study the words in this chart and mark them or their forms wherever they appear in the unit.

Complete the chart.

1. Review each word, its root, and the mentor sentences.

2. Use the information and your own knowledge to predict the meaning of each word.

3. For each word, list at least two related words.

4. Refer to a dictionary or other resources if needed.

WORD	MENTOR SENTENCES	PREDICT MEANING	RELATED WORDS
motivate ROOT: **-mot-** "move"	1. A mentor should try to *motivate* a student to perform well. 2. What might *motivate* a character to do something so deceitful?		motivation; unmotivated
dimension ROOT: **-mens-** "measure"	1. We have to consider every *dimension* of the problem before we can solve it. 2. That classic TV show told stories that explored another *dimension* of time, space, and imagination.		
manipulate ROOT: **-man-** "hand"	1. We watch as the sculptors *manipulate* the clay with great skill and speed. 2. People often become defensive when they believe others are trying to *manipulate* them.		
psychological ROOT: **-psych-** "mind"; "spirit"	1. The director's new film is a *psychological* thriller, and I found it extremely suspenseful. 2. The *psychological* effects of fear can last a long time.		
perspective ROOT: **-spec-** "look"; "see"	1. The narrator's *perspective* was limited and left readers wondering what other characters thought. 2. Living in another part of the country helped to broaden my *perspective* on the world.		

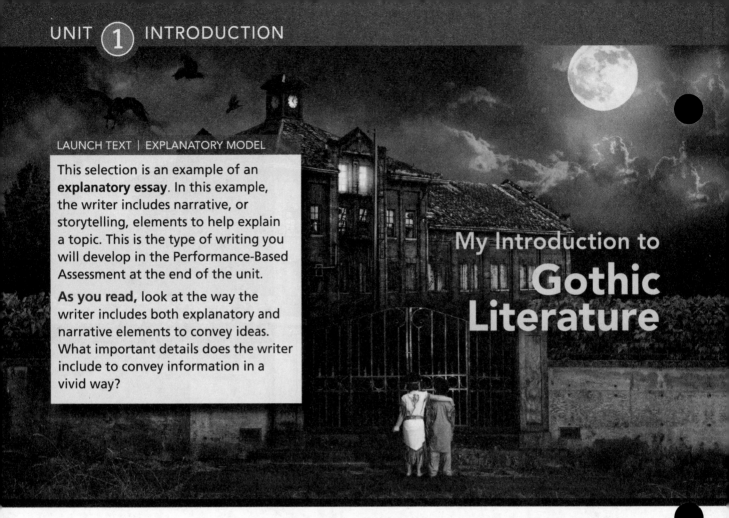

This selection is an example of an **explanatory essay**. In this example, the writer includes narrative, or storytelling, elements to help explain a topic. This is the type of writing you will develop in the Performance-Based Assessment at the end of the unit.

As you read, look at the way the writer includes both explanatory and narrative elements to convey ideas. What important details does the writer include to convey information in a vivid way?

My Introduction to Gothic Literature

NOTES

1   How does someone fall in love with a particular kind of writing or an author who has long departed this life? What draws us to find in words the echoes of our own fears or longings? For those of us lucky enough to have a literary passion, the story of how we met our first love is probably just like tales of other first meetings—funny or quirky, full of accident and coincidence. My literary passion is Edgar Allan Poe, and I met him—in print—when I was fourteen years old.

2   It was just after a huge storm that had featured an alarmingly beautiful display of lightning and wind. The power had been knocked out, and I was sitting at a window, watching the wet night grow darker. I had been living with my grandmother for a few weeks while my parents "figured things out." I loved my grandmother, but I couldn't shake the sadness and anxiety I was feeling. The storm had been a welcome diversion. As the clouds cleared, a fog rose and filtered the moonlight, casting a bluish hue over the yard. The scene was moody and solemn, but beautiful. My grandmother broke my reverie by bustling into the room, carrying two lit candles and a book. "It'll take hours for the electric company to get all the way out here to fix the power," she said. "Why don't you read? I'll go find some batteries for the flashlights."

3   She set the book and a candle on the floor, and rushed out as though she had to catch the batteries before they fled. I picked up the book she had left on the floor. It was a collection of old stories—just a paperback and not much to look at. I turned to one by

SCAN FOR MULTIMEDIA

Poe—"The Cask of Amontillado." Set during the carnival season in an unnamed European city, the story features an unhinged narrator named Montresor who plots revenge on an acquaintance. I liked the gruesome setting of a mysterious burial vault. In Poe's descriptions, I could practically smell the dust and mold. And I was stunned by the horrible ending. But what struck me most was how Montresor spoke directly to the reader—to me. He expected my sympathy as he brought his terrible revenge. Up to that point, all the stories I had ever read had set the criminal or lunatic at a distance. They didn't draw me into a mind that was a truly scary place to be. This one did.

4   I finished Poe's story and turned to another. My grandmother came back with a flashlight, and I kept reading. There were more stories by Poe and others by authors whom I had never heard of but who came to feel like friends—Amelia B. Edwards, Horace Walpole, Ann Radcliffe. I later learned that these stories were part of the Gothic tradition, but I didn't care about that. I fell into them and was carried away, like someone swimming in a river. In all of them, characters were driven by intense emotions of love or hate or jealousy. Some featured ghosts or monsters, but others featured regular people whose sorrow made them ghostly or monstrous. They were tales full of darkness and light, just like the storm I had enjoyed with its thunder and lightning. They were stories that made all I felt and feared seem less of a burden.

5   That evening spent in darkness both real and imaginary never left me. The stories helped me understand that life is not easy and people are complex—simultaneously strong and weak, wonderful and terrible. Though I could not articulate it then, I can now: The stories helped me see that life can be a mansion full of secrets and dark passages, but also of beauty and light. They helped me choose to embrace it all. After another week at my grandmother's, I went home, armed with stories to see me through whatever might come.

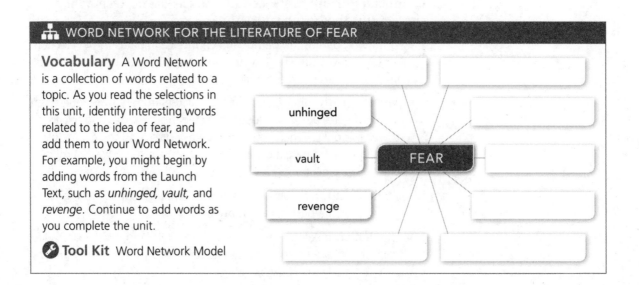

WORD NETWORK FOR THE LITERATURE OF FEAR

Vocabulary A Word Network is a collection of words related to a topic. As you read the selections in this unit, identify interesting words related to the idea of fear, and add them to your Word Network. For example, you might begin by adding words from the Launch Text, such as *unhinged, vault,* and *revenge.* Continue to add words as you complete the unit.

🔧 **Tool Kit** Word Network Model

unhinged

vault

revenge

FEAR

Summary

Write a summary of "My Introduction to Gothic Literature." A **summary** is a concise, complete, and accurate overview of a text. It should not include a statement of your opinion or an analysis.

Launch Activity

Conduct a Horror-Story Election Consider this question: Which character is the best horror-story hero?

- Form two "parties" to gather and choose candidates for an election. You will be voting on the best horror-story "hero." In this case, the heroes are the monsters and other villains.

- With your party, discuss the main characters from horror stories with which you are familiar. Include characters from movies and television, as well as books. When you feel you have discussed the characters thoroughly, nominate a candidate who will represent your party in a whole-class election.

- Choose a party member to deliver the campaign speech telling why your candidate is the best horror-story "hero."

- After both campaign speeches have been delivered, hold a class election. Then, tally the votes for each candidate. If you vote against your own party, be ready to explain why.

QuickWrite

Consider class discussions, presentations, the video, and the Launch Text as you think about the prompt. Record your first thoughts here.

PROMPT: **In what ways does transformation play a role in stories meant to scare us?**

EVIDENCE LOG FOR INSIDE THE NIGHTMARE

Review your QuickWrite. Summarize your initial position in one sentence to record in your Evidence Log. Then, record evidence from "My Introduction to Gothic Literature" that supports your position.

Prepare for the Performance-Based Assessment at the end of the unit by completing the Evidence Log after each selection.

Tool Kit
Evidence Log Model

Title of Text:		Date:
CONNECTION TO PROMPT	TEXT EVIDENCE/DETAILS	ADDITIONAL NOTES/IDEAS

How does this text change or add to my thinking? Date: _____

SCAN FOR MULTIMEDIA

ESSENTIAL QUESTION:

What is the allure of fear?

What is it that draws us to visit haunted houses on Halloween and read stories that keep us up all night startled by every strange noise we hear? The allure of fear is a powerful attraction. Similarly, the concept of "scary but fun" appeals to many of us. The selections you will read offer insight into why people enjoy stories that put them on the edges of their seats.

Whole-Class Learning Strategies

Throughout your life, in school, in your community, and in your career, you will continue to learn and work in large-group environments.

Review these strategies and the actions you can take to practice them as you work with your whole class. Add ideas of your own for each step. Get ready to use these strategies during Whole-Class Learning.

STRATEGY	ACTION PLAN
Listen actively	• Eliminate distractions. For example, put your cellphone away. • Keep your eyes on the speaker. •
Clarify by asking questions	• If you're confused, other people probably are, too. Ask a question to help your whole class. • If you see that you are guessing, ask a question instead. •
Monitor understanding	• Notice what information you already know, and be ready to build on it. • Ask for help if you are struggling. •
Interact and share ideas	• Share your ideas and answer questions, even if you are unsure. • Build on the ideas of others by adding details or making a connection. •

SCAN FOR MULTIMEDIA

CONTENTS

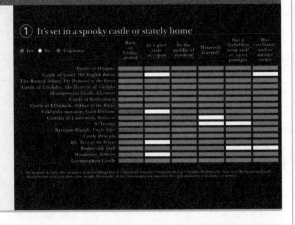

THE FALL OF THE HOUSE OF USHER

Comparing Texts

In this lesson, you will read and compare two stories: "The Fall of the House of Usher," by Edgar Allan Poe, and "House Taken Over," by Julio Cortázar. First, you will complete the first-read and close-read activities for Poe's story. Then, you will compare that story to the story Cortázar wrote a little more than a century later.

HOUSE TAKEN OVER

About the Author

Edgar Allan Poe (1809–1849) is regarded as the first American literary critic and the inventor of the detective story. Despite his literary success, Poe's life was almost as dark and dismal as the fiction he wrote. Shortly after his birth, his father deserted the family, and his mother died. He was raised by a wealthy yet miserly merchant and lived most of his adult life in extreme poverty. Poe died at the age of 40. The circumstances of his death remain a mystery.

 **Tool Kit**
First-Read Guide and Model Annotation

The Fall of the House of Usher

Concept Vocabulary

You will encounter the following words as you read "The Fall of the House of Usher." Before reading, note how familiar you are with each word. Rank the words in order from most familiar (1) to least familiar (6).

WORD	YOUR RANKING
annihilate	
antiquity	
fissure	
dissolution	
rending	
tumultuous	

After completing the first read, come back to the concept vocabulary and review your rankings. Mark changes to your original rankings as needed.

First Read FICTION

Apply these strategies as you conduct your first read. You will have an opportunity to complete the close-read notes after your first read.

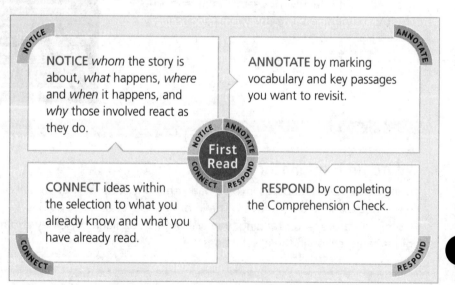

NOTICE *whom* the story is about, *what* happens, *where* and *when* it happens, and *why* those involved react as they do.

ANNOTATE by marking vocabulary and key passages you want to revisit.

First Read

CONNECT ideas within the selection to what you already know and what you have already read.

RESPOND by completing the Comprehension Check.

STANDARDS

Reading Literature
By the end of grade 10, read and comprehend literature, including stories, dramas, and poems, at the high end of the grades 9–10 text complexity band independently and proficiently.

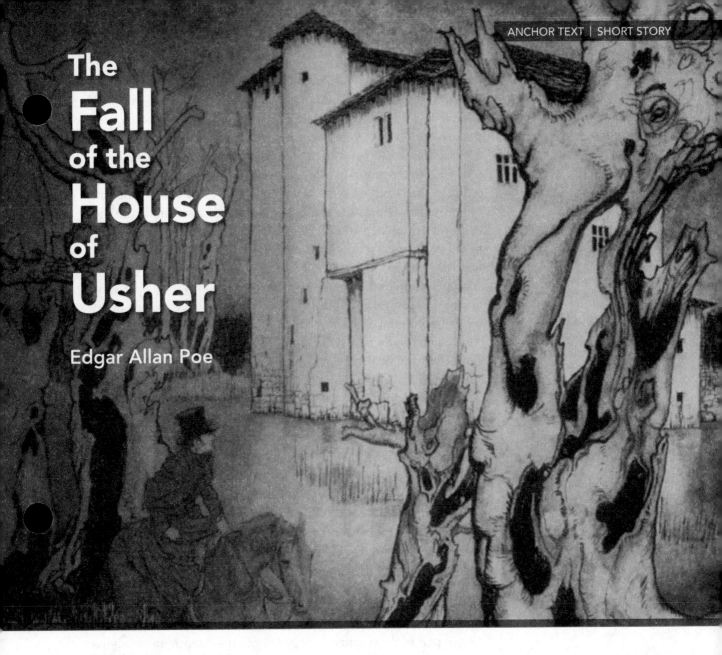

The Fall of the House of Usher

Edgar Allan Poe

BACKGROUND

In this story, Edgar Allan Poe shows his sympathy for the Romantic movement, which was at its height in Europe when he was writing, in the early nineteenth century. The Romantics explored themes of love and death, often with an intense interest in human psychology. For Poe, the darkest aspects of the mind and heart were most revealing of what it means to be human.

SCAN FOR MULTIMEDIA

1   During the whole of a dull, dark, and soundless day in the autumn of the year, when the clouds hung oppressively low in the heavens, I had been passing alone, on horseback, through a singularly dreary tract of country; and at length found myself, as the shades of the evening drew on, within view of the melancholy House of Usher. I know not how it was—but, with the first glimpse of the building, a sense of insufferable gloom pervaded my spirit. I say insufferable; for the feeling was unrelieved by any of that half-pleasurable, because poetic, sentiment, with which the mind usually receives even the sternest natural images of the desolate

NOTES

or terrible. I looked upon the scene before me—upon the mere house, and the simple landscape features of the domain—upon the bleak walls—upon the vacant eyelike windows—upon a few rank sedges[1]—and upon a few white trunks of decayed trees—with an utter depression of soul, which I can compare to no earthly sensation more properly than to the after-dream of the reveler upon opium—the bitter lapse into everyday life—the hideous dropping off of the veil. There was an iciness, a sinking, a sickening of the heart—an unredeemed dreariness of thought which no goading of the imagination could torture into aught[2] of the sublime. What was it—I paused to think—what was it that so unnerved me in the contemplation of the House of Usher? It was a mystery all insoluble; nor could I grapple with the shadowy fancies that crowded upon me as I pondered. I was forced to fall back upon the unsatisfactory conclusion, that while, beyond doubt, there are combinations of very simple natural objects which have the power of thus affecting us, still the analysis of this power lies among considerations beyond our depth. It was possible, I reflected, that a mere different arrangement of the particulars of the scene, of the details of the picture, would be sufficient to modify, or perhaps to **annihilate** its capacity for sorrowful impression; and, acting upon this idea, I reined my horse to the precipitous brink of a black and lurid tarn[3] that lay in unruffled luster by the dwelling, and gazed down—but with a shudder even more thrilling than before—upon the remodeled and inverted images of the gray sedge, and the ghastly tree-stems, and the vacant and eyelike windows.

2   Nevertheless, in this mansion of gloom I now proposed to myself a sojourn of some weeks. Its proprietor, Roderick Usher, had been one of my boon companions in boyhood; but many years had elapsed since our last meeting. A letter, however, had lately reached me in a distant part of the country—a letter from him—which, in its wildly importunate nature, had admitted of no other than a personal reply. The MS[4] gave evidence of nervous agitation. The writer spoke of acute bodily illness—of a mental disorder which oppressed him—and of an earnest desire to see me, as his best and indeed his only personal friend, with a view of attempting, by the cheerfulness of my society, some alleviation of his malady. It was the manner in which all this, and much more, was said—it was the apparent *heart* that went with his request—which allowed me no room for hesitation; and I accordingly obeyed forthwith what I still considered a very singular summons.

3   Although, as boys, we had been even intimate associates, yet I really knew little of my friend. His reserve had been always excessive and habitual. I was aware, however, that his very ancient family had been noted, time out of mind, for a peculiar sensibility

---

1. **sedges** *n.* grasslike plants.
2. **aught** (awt) *n.* anything.
3. **tarn** *n.* small lake.
4. **MS** *abbr.* manuscript; document written by hand.

of temperament, displaying itself, through long ages, in many works of exalted art, and manifested, of late, in repeated deeds of munificent yet unobtrusive charity, as well as in a passionate devotion to the intricacies, perhaps even more than to the orthodox and easily recognizable beauties, of musical science. I had learned, too, the very remarkable fact, that the stem of the Usher race, all time-honored as it was, had put forth, at no period, any enduring branch: in other words, that the entire family lay in the direct line of descent, and had always, with very trifling and very temporary variation, so lain. It was this deficiency, I considered, while running over in thought the perfect keeping of the character of the premises with the accredited character of the people, and while speculating upon the possible influence which the one, in the long lapse of centuries, might have exercised upon the other—it was this deficiency, perhaps of collateral issue,[5] and the consequent undeviating transmission, from sire to son, of the patrimony[6] with the name, which had, at length, so identified the two as to merge the original title of the estate in the quaint and equivocal appellation of the "House of Usher"—an appellation which seemed to include, in the minds of the peasantry who used it, both the family and the family mansion.

4   I have said that the sole effect of my somewhat childish experiment—that of looking down within the tarn—had been to deepen the first singular impression. There can be no doubt that the consciousness of the rapid increase of my superstition—for why should I not so term it?—served mainly to accelerate the increase itself. Such, I have long known, is the paradoxical law of all sentiments having terror as a basis. And it might have been for this reason only, that, when I again uplifted my eyes to the house itself, from its image in the pool, there grew in my mind a strange fancy—a fancy so ridiculous, indeed, that I but mention it to show the vivid force of the sensations which oppressed me. I had so worked upon my imagination as really to believe that about the whole mansion and domain there hung an atmosphere peculiar to themselves and their immediate vicinity—an atmosphere which had no affinity with the air of heaven, but which had reeked up from the decayed trees, and the gray wall, and the silent tarn—a pestilent and mystic vapor, dull, sluggish, faintly discernible, and leaden-hued.

5   Shaking off from my spirit what *must* have been a dream, I scanned more narrowly the real aspect of the building. Its principal feature seemed to be that of an excessive **antiquity**. The discoloration of ages had been great. Minute fungi overspread the whole exterior, hanging in a fine tangled web-work from the eaves. Yet all this was apart from any extraordinary dilapidation. No portion of the masonry had fallen; and there appeared to be

antiquity (an TIHK wuh tee) *n.* very great age

5. **of collateral issue** descended from the same ancestors but in a different line.
6. **patrimony** (PA truh moh nee) *n.* property inherited from one's father.

fissure (FIHSH uhr) *n.* long, narrow crack or opening

a wild inconsistency between its still perfect adaptation of parts, and the crumbling condition of the individual stones. In this there was much that reminded me of the specious totality of old woodwork which has rotted for long years in some neglected vault, with no disturbance from the breath of the external air. Beyond this indication of extensive decay, however, the fabric gave little token of instability. Perhaps the eye of a scrutinizing observer might have discovered a barely perceptible **fissure**, which, extending from the roof of the building in front, made its way down the wall in a zigzag direction, until it became lost in the sullen waters of the tarn.

6   Noticing these things, I rode over a short causeway to the house. A servant in waiting took my horse, and I entered the Gothic[7] archway of the hall. A valet, of stealthy step, thence conducted me, in silence, through many dark and intricate passages in my progress to the studio of his master. Much that I encountered on the way contributed, I know not how, to heighten the vague sentiments of which I have already spoken. While the objects around me—while the carvings of the ceilings, the somber tapestries of the walls, the ebon blackness of the floors, and the phantasmagoric[8] armorial trophies which rattled as I strode, were but matters to which, or to such as which, I had been accustomed from my infancy—while I hesitated not to acknowledge how familiar was all this—I still wondered to find how unfamiliar were the fancies which ordinary images were stirring up. On one of the staircases, I met the physician of the family. His countenance, I thought, wore a mingled expression of low cunning and perplexity. He accosted me with trepidation and passed on. The valet now threw open a door and ushered me into the presence of his master.

7   The room in which I found myself was very large and lofty. The windows were long, narrow, and pointed, and at so vast a distance from the black oaken floor as to be altogether inaccessible from within. Feeble gleams of encrimsoned light made their way through the trellised panes, and served to render sufficiently distinct the more prominent objects around; the eye, however, struggled in vain to reach the remoter angles of the chamber, or the recesses of the vaulted and fretted[9] ceiling. Dark draperies hung upon the walls. The general furniture was profuse, comfortless, antique, and tattered. Many books and musical instruments lay scattered about, but failed to give any vitality to the scene. I felt that I breathed an atmosphere of sorrow. An air of stern, deep, and irredeemable gloom hung over and pervaded all.

8   Upon my entrance, Usher arose from a sofa on which he had been lying at full length, and greeted me with a vivacious warmth which had much in it, I at first thought, of an overdone

---

7. **Gothic** *adj.* high and ornate.
8. **phantasmagoric** (fan taz muh GAWR ihk) *adj.* fantastic or dreamlike.
9. **fretted** *adj.* ornamented with a pattern of small, straight, intersecting bars.

cordiality—of the constrained effort of the *ennuyé*[10] man of the world. A glance, however, at his countenance convinced me of his perfect sincerity. We sat down; and for some moments, while he spoke not, I gazed upon him with a feeling half of pity, half of awe. Surely, man had never before so terribly altered, in so brief a period, as had Roderick Usher! It was with difficulty that I could bring myself to admit the identity of the wan being before me with the companion of my early boyhood. Yet the character of his face had been at all times remarkable. A cadaverousness[11] of complexion; an eye large, liquid, and luminous beyond comparison; lips somewhat thin and very pallid, but of a surpassingly beautiful curve; a nose of a delicate Hebrew model, but with a breadth of nostril unusual in similar formations; a finely molded chin, speaking, in its want of prominence, of a want of moral energy; hair of a more than weblike softness and tenuity— these features, with an inordinate expansion above the regions of the temple, made up altogether a countenance not easily to be forgotten. And now in the mere exaggeration of the prevailing character of these features, and of the expression they were wont to convey, lay so much of change that I doubted to whom I spoke. The now ghastly pallor of the skin, and the now miraculous luster of the eye, above all things startled and even awed me. The silken hair, too, had been suffered to grow all unheeded, and as, in its wild gossamer[12] texture, it floated rather than fell about the face, I could not, even with effort, connect its Arabesque[13] expression with any idea of simple humanity.

9. In the manner of my friend I was at once struck with an incoherence—an inconsistency; and I soon found this to arise from a series of feeble and futile struggles to overcome an habitual trepidancy—an excessive nervous agitation. For something of this nature I had indeed been prepared, no less by his letter, than by reminiscences of certain boyish traits, and by conclusions deduced from his peculiar physical conformation and temperament. His action was alternately vivacious and sullen. His voice varied rapidly from a tremulous indecision (when the animal spirits seemed utterly in abeyance) to that species of energetic concision—that abrupt, weighty, unhurried, and hollow-sounding enunciation—that leaden, self-balanced, and perfectly modulated guttural utterance, which may be observed in the lost drunkard, or the irreclaimable eater of opium, during the periods of his most intense excitement.

10. It was thus that he spoke of the object of my visit, of his earnest desire to see me, and of the solace he expected me to afford him. He entered, at some length, into what he conceived to be the nature of his malady. It was, he said, a constitutional and a family evil, and one

CLOSE READ
ANNOTATE: Mark details in paragraph 8 that relate to the absence of color and force.

QUESTION: What portrait of Usher do these details create?

CONCLUDE: What does this portrayal of Usher help the reader understand?

---

10. ***ennuyé*** (on wee AY) *adj.* French for "bored."
11. **cadaverousness** (kuh DAV uhr uhs nihs) *n.* quality of being like a dead body.
12. **gossamer** (GOS uh muhr) *adj.* very delicate and light, like a cobweb.
13. **Arabesque** (ar uh BEHSK) *adj.* of complex and elaborate design.

© Pearson Education, Inc., or its affiliates. All rights reserved.

The Fall of the House of Usher **17**

for which he despaired to find a remedy—a mere nervous affection,[14] he immediately added, which would undoubtedly soon pass off. It displayed itself in a host of unnatural sensations. Some of these, as he detailed them, interested and bewildered me; although, perhaps, the terms and the general manner of the narration had their weight. He suffered much from a morbid acuteness of the senses; the most insipid food was alone endurable; he could wear only garments of certain texture; the odors of all flowers were oppressive; his eyes were tortured by even a faint light; and there were but peculiar sounds, and these from stringed instruments, which did not inspire him with horror.

11   To an anomalous species of terror I found him a bounden slave. "I shall perish:" said he, "I *must* perish in this deplorable folly. Thus, thus, and not otherwise, shall I be lost. I dread the events of the future, not in themselves, but in their results. I shudder at the thought of any, even the most trivial, incident, which may operate upon this intolerable agitation of soul. I have, indeed, no abhorrence of danger, except in its absolute effect—in terror. In this unnerved, in this pitiable, condition I feel that the period will sooner or later arrive when I must abandon life and reason together, in some struggle with the grim phantasm, FEAR."

---

14. **affection** *n.* affliction; illness.

12   I learned, moreover, at intervals, and through broken and equivocal hints, another singular feature of his mental condition. He was enchained by certain superstitious impressions in regard to the dwelling which he tenanted, and whence, for many years, he had never ventured forth—in regard to an influence whose supposititious[15] force was conveyed in terms too shadowy here to be restated—an influence which some peculiarities in the mere form and substance of his family mansion, had, by dint of long sufferance, he said, obtained over his spirit—an effect which the physique of the gray walls and turrets, and of the dim tarn into which they all looked down, had at length, brought about upon the morale of his existence.

13   He admitted, however, although with hesitation, that much of the peculiar gloom which thus afflicted him could be traced to a more natural and far more palpable origin—to the severe and long-continued illness—indeed to the evidently approaching **dissolution**—of a tenderly beloved sister—his sole companion for long years, his last and only relative on earth. "Her decease," he said, with a bitterness which I can never forget, "would leave him (him, the hopeless and the frail) the last of the ancient race of the Ushers." While he spoke, the lady Madeline (for so was she called) passed slowly through a remote portion of the apartment, and, without having noticed my presence, disappeared. I regarded her with an utter astonishment not unmingled with dread; and yet I found it impossible to account for such feelings. A sensation of stupor oppressed me, as my eyes followed her retreating steps. When a door, at length, closed upon her, my glance sought instinctively and eagerly the countenance of the brother; but he had buried his face in his hands, and I could only perceive that a far more than ordinary wanness had overspread the emaciated fingers through which trickled many passionate tears.

14   The disease of the lady Madeline had long baffled the skill of her physicians. A settled apathy, a gradual wasting away of the person, and frequent although transient affections of a partially cataleptical[16] character were the unusual diagnosis. Hitherto she had steadily borne up against the pressure of her malady, and had not betaken herself finally to bed; but on the closing in of the evening of my arrival at the house, she succumbed (as her brother told me at night with inexpressible agitation) to the prostrating power of the destroyer; and I learned that the glimpse I had obtained of her person would thus probably be the last I should obtain—that the lady, at least while living, would be seen by me no more.

15   For several days ensuing, her name was unmentioned by either Usher or myself; and during this period I was busied in earnest endeavors to alleviate the melancholy of my friend. We painted

---

15. **supposititious** (suh poz uh TIHSH uhs) *adj.* supposed.
16. **cataleptical** (kat uh LEHP tihk uhl) *adj.* in a state in which consciousness and feeling are suddenly and temporarily lost and the muscles become rigid.

NOTES

dissolution (dihs uh LOO shuhn) *n.* ending or downfall

CLOSE READ
ANNOTATE: In the first two sentences of paragraph 13, mark the sections that are set off by dashes or parentheses.

QUESTION: Why does the author structure these sentences in this way?

CONCLUDE: What do these fragmented sentences suggest about the way Usher speaks and behaves?

and read together, or I listened, as if in a dream, to the wild improvisations of his speaking guitar. And thus, as a closer and still closer intimacy admitted me more unreservedly into the recesses of his spirit, the more bitterly did I perceive the futility of all attempt at cheering a mind from which darkness, as if an inherent positive quality, poured forth upon all objects of the moral and physical universe, in one unceasing radiation of gloom.

16   I shall ever bear about me a memory of the many solemn hours I thus spent alone with the master of the House of Usher. Yet I should fail in any attempt to convey an idea of the exact character of the studies, or of the occupations, in which he involved me, or led me the way. An excited and highly distempered ideality[17] threw a sulfureous luster over all. His long improvised dirges will ring forever in my ears. Among other things, I hold painfully in mind a certain singular perversion and amplification of the wild air of the last waltz of von Weber.[18] From the paintings over which his elaborate fancy brooded, and which grew, touch by touch, into vaguenesses at which I shuddered the more thrillingly, because I shuddered knowing not why—from these paintings (vivid as their images now are before me) I would in vain endeavor to educe more than a small portion which should lie within the compass of merely written words. By the utter simplicity, by the nakedness of his designs, he arrested and overawed attention. If ever mortal painted an idea, that mortal was Roderick Usher. For me at least, in the circumstances then surrounding me, there arose out of the pure abstractions which the hypochondriac contrived to throw upon his canvas, an intensity of intolerable awe, no shadow of which felt I ever yet in the contemplation of the certainly glowing yet too concrete reveries of Fuseli.[19]

17   One of the phantasmagoric conceptions of my friend, partaking not so rigidly of the spirit of abstraction, may be shadowed forth, although feebly, in words. A small picture presented the interior of an immensely long and rectangular vault or tunnel, with low walls, smooth, white and without interruption or device. Certain accessory points of the design served well to convey the idea that this excavation lay at an exceeding depth below the surface of the earth. No outlet was observed in any portion of its vast extent, and no torch, or other artificial source of light was discernible; yet a flood of intense rays rolled throughout, and bathed the whole in a ghastly and inappropriate splendor.

18   I have just spoken of that morbid condition of the auditory nerve which rendered all music intolerable to the sufferer, with the exception of certain effects of stringed instruments. It was, perhaps,

---

17. **ideality** (y dee AL uh tee) *n.* something that is ideal or has no reality.
18. **von Weber** (fon VAY buhr) Carl Maria von Weber (1786–1826), German Romantic composer whose music was highly emotional and dramatic.
19. **Fuseli** (FYOO zuh lee) Johann Heinrich Füssli (1741–1825), also known as Henry Fuseli, Swiss-born painter who lived in England and was noted for his depictions of dreamlike and sometimes nightmarish images.

the narrow limits to which he thus confined himself upon the guitar, which gave birth, in great measure, to the fantastic character of his performances. But the fervid facility of his impromptus could not be so accounted for. They must have been, and were, in the notes, as well as in the words of his wild fantasias (for he not unfrequently accompanied himself with rhymed verbal improvisations), the result of that intense mental collectedness and concentration to which I have previously alluded as observable only in particular moments of the highest artificial excitement. The words of one of these rhapsodies I have easily remembered. I was, perhaps, the more forcibly impressed with it, as he gave it because, in the under or mystic current of its meaning, I fancied that I perceived, and for the first time, a full consciousness on the part of Usher of the tottering of his lofty reason upon her throne. The verses, which were entitled "The Haunted Palace," ran very nearly, if not accurately, thus:

I

19
In the greenest of our valleys,
  By good angels tenanted,
Once a fair and stately palace—
  Radiant palace—reared its head.
In the monarch Thought's dominion—
  It stood there!
Never seraph[20] spread a pinion[21]
  Over fabric half so fair.

II

20
Banners yellow, glorious, golden,
  On its roof did float and flow
(This—all this—was in the olden
  Time long ago)
And every gentle air that dallied,
  In that sweet day,
Along the ramparts plumed and pallid,
  A winged odor went away.

III

21
Wanderers in that happy valley
  Through two luminous windows saw
Spirits moving musically
  To a lute's well-tuned law;
Round about a throne, where sitting
  (Porphyrogene!)[22]
In state his glory well befitting,
  The ruler of the realm was seen.

---

20. **seraph** (SEHR uhf) *n.* angel.
21. **pinion** (PIHN yuhn) *n.* wing.
22. **Porphyrogene** (pawr fehr oh JEEN) *adj.* born to royalty or "the purple."

IV

22

And all with pearl and ruby glowing
*   Was the fair palace door,*
Through which came flowing, flowing, flowing
*   And sparkling evermore.*
A troop of Echoes whose sweet duty
*   Was but to sing,*
In voices of surpassing beauty,
*   The wit and wisdom of their king.*

V

23

But evil things, in robes of sorrow,
*   Assailed the monarch's high estate;*
(Ah, let us mourn, for never morrow
*   Shall dawn upon him, desolate!)*
And, round about his home, the glory
*   That blushed and bloomed*
Is but a dim-remembered story
*   Of the old time entombed.*

VI

24

And travelers now within that valley,
*   Through the red-litten[23] windows, see*
Vast forms that move fantastically
*   To a discordant melody;*
While, like a rapid ghastly river,
*   Through the pale door,*
A hideous throng rush out forever,
*   And laugh—but smile no more.*

25   I well remember that suggestions arising from this ballad led us into a train of thought wherein there became manifest an opinion of Usher's which I mention not so much on account of its novelty (for other men have thought thus), as on account of the pertinacity[24] with which he maintained it. This opinion, in its general form, was that of the sentience of all vegetable things. But, in his disordered fancy the idea had assumed a more daring character, and trespassed, under certain conditions, upon the kingdom of inorganization.[25] I lack words to express the full extent, or the earnest abandon of his persuasion. The belief, however, was connected (as I have previously hinted) with the gray stones of the home of his forefathers. The conditions of the sentience had been here, he imagined, fulfilled in the method of collocation of these stones—in the order of their arrangement, as well as in that of the many fungi which overspread them, and of the decayed trees which stood around—above all, in the long undisturbed endurance of

---

23. *litten* adj. lighted.
24. **pertinacity** (purt uhn AS uh tee) n. determined stubbornness.
25. **inorganization** n. inanimate objects.

this arrangement, and in its reduplication in the still waters of the tarn. Its evidence—the evidence of the sentience—was to be seen, he said (and I here started as he spoke), in the gradual yet certain condensation of an atmosphere of their own about the waters and the walls. The result was discoverable, he added, in that silent, yet importunate and terrible influence which for centuries had molded the destinies of his family, and which made him what I now saw him—what he was. Such opinions need no comment, and I will make none.

26   Our books—the books which, for years, had formed no small portion of the mental existence of the invalid—were, as might be supposed, in strict keeping with this character of phantasm. We pored together over such works as the *Ververt et Chartreuse* of Gresset; the *Belphegor* of Machiavelli; the *Heaven and Hell* of Swedenborg; the *Subterranean Voyage of Nicholas Klimm* by Holberg; the *Chiromancy* of Robert Flud, of Jean D'Indaginé, and of De la Chambre; the *Journey into the Blue Distance* of Tieck; and the *City of the Sun* of Campanella.[26] One favorite volume was a small octavo edition of the *Directorium Inquisitorium*, by the Dominican Eymeric de Gironne; and there were passages in Pomponius Mela, about the old African Satyrs and Œgipans, over which Usher would sit dreaming for hours. His chief delight, however, was found in the perusal of an exceedingly rare and curious book in quarto Gothic— the manual of a forgotten church—the *Vigiliae Mortuorum secundum Chorum Ecclesiae Maguntinae*.

27   I could not help thinking of the wild ritual of this work, and of its probable influence upon the hypochondriac, when, one evening, having informed me abruptly that the lady Madeline was no more, he stated his intention of preserving her corpse for a fortnight (previously to its final interment), in one of the numerous vaults within the main walls of the building. The worldly reason, however, assigned for this singular proceeding, was one which I did not feel at liberty to dispute. The brother had been led to his resolution (so he told me) by consideration of the unusual character of the malady of the deceased, of certain obtrusive and eager inquiries on the part of her medical men, and of the remote and exposed situation of the burial ground of the family. I will not deny that when I called to mind the sinister countenance of the person whom I met upon the staircase, on the day of my arrival at the house, I had no desire to oppose what I regarded as at best but a harmless, and by no means an unnatural precaution.

28   At the request of Usher, I personally aided him in the arrangements for the temporary entombment. The body having been encoffined, we two alone bore it to its rest. The vault in which we placed it (and which had been so long unopened that our torches, half smothered in its oppressive atmosphere, gave us little

---

26. ***Ververt et Chartreuse* of Gresset . . . *City of the Sun* of Campanella** All the books listed deal with magic or mysticism.

opportunity for investigation) was small, damp, and entirely without means of admission for light; lying, at great depth, immediately beneath that portion of the building in which was my own sleeping apartment. It had been used, apparently, in remote feudal times, for the worst purposes of a donjon-keep,[27] and, in later days, as a place of deposit for powder, or some other highly combustible substance, as a portion of its floor, and the whole interior of a long archway through which we reached it, were carefully sheathed with copper. The door, of massive iron, had been, also, similarly protected. Its immense weight caused an unusually sharp, grating sound, as it moved upon its hinges.

29   Having deposited our mournful burden upon trestles within this region of horror, we partially turned aside the yet unscrewed lid of the coffin, and looked upon the face of the tenant. A striking similitude between the brother and sister now first arrested my attention; and Usher, divining, perhaps, my thoughts, murmured out some few words from which I learned that the deceased and himself had been twins, and that sympathies of a scarcely intelligible nature had always existed between them. Our glances, however, rested not long upon the dead—for we could not regard her unawed. The disease which had thus entombed the lady in the maturity of youth, had left, as usual in all maladies of a strictly cataleptical character, the mockery of a faint blush upon the bosom and the face, and that suspiciously lingering smile upon the lip which is so terrible in death. We replaced and screwed down the lid, and, having secured the door of iron, made our way, with toil, into the scarcely less gloomy apartments of the upper portion of the house.

30   And now, some days of bitter grief having elapsed, an observable change came over the features of the mental disorder of my friend. His ordinary manner had vanished. His ordinary occupations were neglected or forgotten. He roamed from chamber to chamber with hurried, unequal, and object-less step. The pallor of his countenance had assumed, if possible, a more ghastly hue—but the luminousness of his eye had utterly gone out. The once occasional huskiness of his tone was heard no more; and a tremulous quaver, as if of extreme terror, habitually characterized his utterance. There were times, indeed, when I thought his unceasingly agitated mind was laboring with some oppressive secret, to divulge which he struggled for the necessary courage. At times, again, I was obliged to resolve all into the mere inexplicable vagaries[28] of madness, for I beheld him gazing upon vacancy for long hours, in an attitude of the profoundest attention, as if listening to some imaginary sound. It was no wonder that his condition terrified—that it infected me. I felt creeping upon me, by

---

CLOSE READ

ANNOTATE: In paragraph 30, mark words that relate to physical actions and behavior.

QUESTION: What do these physical details show about Usher's mental state and emotions?

CONCLUDE: What is the effect of these descriptive details?

---

27. **donjon-keep** (DUHN juhn keep) *n.* inner storage room of a castle; dungeon.
28. **vagaries** (VAY guhr eez) *n.* odd, unexpected actions or notions.

slow yet certain degrees, the wild influences of his own fantastic yet impressive superstitions.

31   It was, especially, upon retiring to bed late in the night of the seventh or eighth day after the placing of the lady Madeline within the donjon, that I experienced the full power of such feelings. Sleep came not near my couch—while the hours waned and waned away. I struggled to reason off the nervousness which had dominion over me. I endeavored to believe that much, if not all of what I felt, was due to the bewildering influence of the gloomy furniture of the room—of the dark and tattered draperies, which, tortured into motion by the breath of a rising tempest, swayed fitfully to and fro upon the walls, and rustled uneasily about the decorations of the bed. But my efforts were fruitless. An irrepressible tremor gradually pervaded my frame; and, at length, there sat upon my very heart an incubus[29] of utterly causeless alarm. Shaking this off with a gasp and a struggle, I uplifted myself upon the pillows, and, peering earnestly

29. **incubus** (IHN kyuh buhs) *n.* something nightmarishly burdensome.

within the intense darkness of the chamber, hearkened—I know not why, except that an instinctive spirit prompted me—to certain low and indefinite sounds which came, through the pauses of the storm, at long intervals, I knew not whence. Overpowered by an intense sentiment of horror, unaccountable yet unendurable, I threw on my clothes with haste (for I felt that I should sleep no more during the night), and endeavored to arouse myself from the pitiable condition into which I had fallen, by pacing rapidly to and fro through the apartment.

32   I had taken but few turns in this manner, when a light step on an adjoining staircase arrested my attention. I presently recognized it as that of Usher. In an instant afterward he rapped, with a gentle touch, at my door, and entered, bearing a lamp. His countenance was, as usual, cadaverously wan—but, moreover, there was a species of mad hilarity in his eyes—an evidently restrained hysteria in his whole demeanor. His air appalled me—but anything was preferable to

the solitude which I had so long endured, and I even welcomed his presence as a relief.

33   "And you have not seen it?" he said abruptly, after having stared about him for some moments in silence—"you have not then seen it?—but, stay! you shall." Thus speaking, and having carefully shaded his lamp, he hurried to one of the casements, and threw it freely open to the storm.

34   The impetuous fury of the entering gust nearly lifted us from our feet. It was, indeed, a tempestuous yet sternly beautiful night, and one wildly singular in its terror and its beauty. A whirlwind had apparently collected its force in our vicinity; for there were frequent and violent alterations in the direction of the wind; and the exceeding density of the clouds (which hung so low as to press upon the turrets of the house) did not prevent our perceiving the lifelike velocity with which they flew careering from all points against each other, without passing away into the distance. I say that even their exceeding density did not prevent our perceiving this—yet we had no glimpse of the moon or stars, nor was there any flashing forth of the lightning. But the under surfaces of the huge masses of agitated vapor, as well as all terrestrial objects immediately around us, were glowing in the unnatural light of a faintly luminous and distinctly visible gaseous exhalation which hung about and enshrouded the mansion.

35   "You must not—you shall not behold this!" said I, shudderingly, to Usher, as I led him, with a gentle violence, from the window to a seat. "These appearances, which bewilder you, are merely electrical phenomena not uncommon—or it may be that they have their ghastly origin in the rank miasma[30] of the tarn. Let us close this casement:— the air is chilling and dangerous to your frame. Here is one of your favorite romances. I will read, and you shall listen:—and so we will pass away this terrible night together."

36   The antique volume which I had taken up was the *Mad Trist* of Sir Launcelot Canning;[31] but I had called it a favorite of Usher's more in sad jest than in earnest; for, in truth, there is little in its uncouth and unimaginative prolixity which could have had interest for the lofty and spiritual ideality of my friend. It was, however, the only book immediately at hand; and I indulged a vague hope that the excitement which now agitated the hypochondriac, might find relief (for the history of mental disorder is full of similar anomalies) even in the extremeness of the folly which I should read. Could I have judged, indeed, by the wild overstrained air of vivacity with which he harkened, or apparently harkened, to the words of the tale, I might well have congratulated myself upon the success of my design.

37   I had arrived at that well-known portion of the story where Ethelred, the hero of the Trist, having sought in vain for peaceable admission into the dwelling of the hermit, proceeds to make good

© Pearson Education, Inc., or its affiliates. All rights reserved.

NOTES

CLOSE READ

ANNOTATE: In paragraph 34, mark words and phrases that suggest extremes, whether of emotion, action, or size.

QUESTION: What is noteworthy about this storm?

CONCLUDE: What greater meaning do these details give to the storm?

---

30. **miasma** (my AZ muh) *n.* unwholesome atmosphere.
31. ***Mad Trist* of Sir Launcelot Canning** fictional book and author.

an entrance by force. Here, it will be remembered, the words of the narrative run thus:

38   "And Ethelred, who was by nature of a doughty[32] heart, and who was now mighty withal, on account of the powerfulness of the wine which he had drunken, waited no longer to hold parley[33] with the hermit, who, in sooth, was of an obstinate and maliceful turn, but, feeling the rain upon his shoulders, and fearing the rising of the tempest, uplifted his mace outright, and, with blows, made quickly room in the plankings of the door for his gauntleted hand; and now pulling therewith sturdily, he so cracked, and ripped, and tore all asunder, that the noise of the dry and hollow-sounding wood alarumed and reverberated throughout the forest."

39   At the termination of this sentence I started and, for a moment, paused; for it appeared to me (although I at once concluded that my excited fancy had deceived me)—it appeared to me that, from some very remote portion of the mansion, there came, indistinctly, to my ears, what might have been, in its exact similarity of character, the echo (but a stifled and dull one certainly) of the very cracking and ripping sound which Sir Launcelot had so particularly described. It was, beyond doubt, the coincidence alone which had arrested my attention; for, amid the rattling of the sashes of the casements, and the ordinary commingled noises of the still increasing storm, the sound, itself, had nothing, surely, which should have interested or disturbed me. I continued the story:

40   "But the good champion Ethelred, now entering within the door, was sore enraged and amazed to perceive no signal of the maliceful hermit; but, in the stead thereof, a dragon of a scaly and prodigious demeanor, and of a fiery tongue, which sate in guard before a palace of gold, with a floor of silver; and upon the wall there hung a shield of shining brass with this legend enwritten—

Who entereth herein, a conqueror hath bin;

Who slayeth the dragon, the shield he shall win.

41   And Ethelred uplifted his mace, and struck upon the head of the dragon, which fell before him, and gave up his pesty breath, with a shriek so horrid and harsh, and withal so piercing, that Ethelred had fain to close his ears with his hands against the dreadful noise of it, the like whereof was never before heard."

42   Here again I paused abruptly, and now with a feeling of wild amazement—for there could be no doubt whatever that, in this instance, I did actually hear (although from what direction it proceeded I found it impossible to say) a low and apparently distant, but harsh, protracted, and most unusual screaming or grating sound—the exact counterpart of what my fancy had already conjured up for the dragon's unnatural shriek as described by the romancer.

43   Oppressed, as I certainly was, upon the occurrence of this second and most extraordinary coincidence, by a thousand conflicting

---

32. **doughty** (DOWT ee) *adj.* brave.
33. **parley** (pahr LEE) *n.* conference; discussion.

sensations, in which wonder and extreme terror were predominant, I still retained sufficient presence of mind to avoid exciting, by any observation, the sensitive nervousness of my companion. I was by no means certain that he had noticed the sounds in question; although, assuredly, a strange alteration had, during the last few minutes, taken place in his demeanor. From a position fronting my own, he had gradually brought round his chair, so as to sit with his face to the door of the chamber; and thus I could but partially perceive his features, although I saw that his lips trembled as if he were murmuring inaudibly. His head had dropped upon his breast—yet I knew that he was not asleep, from the wide and rigid opening of the eye as I caught a glance of it in profile. The motion of his body, too, was at variance with this idea—for he rocked from side to side with a gentle yet constant and uniform sway. Having rapidly taken notice of all this, I resumed the narrative of Sir Launcelot, which thus proceeded:

44   "And now, the champion, having escaped from the terrible fury of the dragon, bethinking himself of the brazen shield, and of the breaking up of the enchantment which was upon it, removed the carcass from out of the way before him, and approached valorously over the silver pavement of the castle to where the shield was upon the wall; which in sooth tarried not for his full coming, but fell down at his feet upon the silver floor, with a mighty great and terrible ringing sound."

45   No sooner had these syllables passed my lips, than—as if a shield of brass had indeed, at the moment, fallen heavily upon a floor of silver—I became aware of a distinct, hollow, metallic, and clangorous, yet apparently muffled, reverberation. Completely unnerved, I leaped to my feet; but the measured rocking movement of Usher was undisturbed. I rushed to the chair in which he sat. His eyes were bent fixedly before him, and throughout his whole countenance there reigned a stony rigidity. But, as I placed my hand upon his shoulder, there came a strong shudder over his whole person; a sickly smile quivered about his lips; and I saw that he spoke in a low, hurried, and gibbering murmur, as if unconscious of my presence. Bending closely over him I at length drank in the hideous import of his words.

46   "Not hear it?—yes, I hear it, and have heard it. Long—long— long—many minutes, many hours, many days, have I heard it— yet I dared not—oh, pity me, miserable wretch that I am!—I *dared not*—I dared not speak! *We have put her living in the tomb!* Said I not that my senses were acute? I *now* tell you that I heard her first feeble movements in the hollow coffin. I heard them—many, many days ago—yet I dared not—*I dared not speak!* and now—tonight— Ethelred—ha! ha!—the breaking of the hermit's door, and the death cry of the dragon, and the clangor of the shield—say, rather, the rending of her coffin, and the grating of the iron hinges of her prison, and her struggles within the coppered archway of the vault! Oh! wither shall I fly? Will she not be here anon? Is she not hurrying to

NOTES

CLOSE READ
ANNOTATE: Mark examples of repeated words in paragraph 46.

QUESTION: Why do these words merit being repeated?

CONCLUDE: What is the effect of these repeated words?

rending (REHN dihng) *n.* violent or forceful pulling apart of something

upbraid me for my haste? Have I not heard her footstep on the stair? Do I not distinguish that heavy and horrible beating of her heart? Madman!"—here he sprang furiously to his feet, and shrieked out his syllables, as if in the effort he were giving up his soul—"*Madman! I tell you that she now stands without the door!*"

47   As if in the superhuman energy of his utterance there had been found the potency of a spell, the huge antique panels to which the speaker pointed, threw slowly back, upon the instant, their ponderous and ebony jaws. It was the work of the rushing gust—but then without those doors there *did* stand the lofty and enshrouded figure of the lady Madeline of Usher. There was blood upon her white robes, and the evidence of some bitter struggle upon every portion of her emaciated frame. For a moment she remained trembling and reeling to and fro upon the threshold—then, with a low moaning cry, fell heavily inward upon the person of her brother, and in her violent and now final death agonies, bore him to the floor a corpse, and a victim to the terrors he had anticipated.

48   From that chamber, and from that mansion, I fled aghast. The storm was still abroad in all its wrath as I found myself crossing the old causeway. Suddenly there shot along the path a wild light, and I turned to see whence a gleam so unusual could have issued; for the vast house and its shadows were alone behind me. The radiance was that of the full, setting, and bloodred moon, which now shone vividly through that once barely discernible fissure, of which I have before spoken as extending from the roof of the building, in a zigzag direction, to the base. While I gazed, this fissure rapidly widened— there came a fierce breath of the whirlwind—the entire orb of the satellite burst at once upon my sight—my brain reeled as I saw the mighty walls rushing asunder—there was a long tumultuous shouting sound like the voice of a thousand waters—and the deep and dank tarn at my feet closed sullenly and silently over the fragments of the *"House of Usher."* ❧

tumultuous (too MUHL choo uhs) *adj.* loud, excited, and emotional

Comprehension Check

Complete the following items after you finish your first read.

1. Why does the narrator go to visit Usher?

2. Early in the story, what flaw in the front of the house does the narrator observe?

3. What forms of artistic expression does Usher share with the narrator?

4. What does the narrator learn about the relationship between Usher and Madeline after her death?

5. What confession does Usher make to the narrator during the final storm?

6. 📓 **Notebook** Draw a storyboard that summarizes the events of "The Fall of the House of Usher" to confirm your understanding of the story.

- -

RESEARCH

Research to Clarify Choose at least one unfamiliar detail from the text. Briefly research that detail. In what way does the information you learned shed light on an aspect of the story?

Research to Explore Choose a detail or reference in the text that interests you, and formulate a research question.

THE FALL OF THE HOUSE
OF USHER

Close Read the Text

This model, from paragraph 11 of the text, shows two sample annotations, along with questions and conclusions. Close read the passage, and find another detail to annotate. Then, write a question and your conclusion.

ANNOTATE: Poe begins this passage with two long, complex sentences.

QUESTION: Why does Poe pack so many ideas into these sentences?

CONCLUDE: These complex sentences suggest that Usher's thoughts are racing, that he is being swept away with fear.

ANNOTATE: Poe ends two sentences with the synonyms *terror* and *FEAR*.

QUESTION: Why does Poe emphasize these words—one with a dash, one with capitals?

CONCLUDE: Poe is conveying the idea that Usher is not afraid of danger; rather, he is afraid of fear itself.

> I shudder at the thought of any, even the most trivial, incident, which may operate upon this intolerable agitation of soul. I have, indeed, no abhorrence of danger, except in its absolute effect—in terror. In this unnerved, in this pitiable condition, I feel that the period will sooner or later arrive when I must abandon life and reason together, in some struggle with the grim phantasm, FEAR.

🔧 Tool Kit
Close-Read Guide and
Model Annotation

Analyze the Text

CITE TEXTUAL EVIDENCE
to support your answers.

📓 Notebook Respond to these questions.

1. **(a) Interpret** Which descriptive details of the interior of the house suggest that the narrator has entered a realm that is very different from the ordinary world? **(b) Make Inferences** In what ways is the appearance of the interior of the house related to Usher's appearance and the condition of his mind?

2. **(a) Connect** How do the works of art described in the story reflect the story's events? **(b) Interpret** What idea about the relationship between art and life is supported by these elements of the story? Explain.

3. **(a) Analyze** In what ways is the narrator affected by Usher's condition? **(b) Evaluate** Do you think the narrator is a reliable witness to the events he describes? Explain.

4. **Make a Judgment** Is Usher responsible for the death of his sister and the collapse of his home? Explain.

5. **Essential Question:** *What is the allure of fear?* What have you learned from this story about portrayals of fear in literature?

STANDARDS
Reading Literature
• Cite strong and thorough textual evidence to support analysis of what the text says explicitly as well as inferences drawn from the text.
• Analyze how an author's choices concerning how to structure a text, order events within it, and manipulate time create such effects as mystery, tension, or surprise.

Analyze Craft and Structure

Literary Style "The Fall of the House of Usher" is an example of **Gothic literature**, a literary genre that began in England in the late 1700s. The term *Gothic* was originally used as an architectural term. It refers to medieval buildings, such as castles and cathedrals, that were seen as dark and gloomy by later generations. When writers began to set their stories in those buildings of the past, the term for the architecture was applied to the literature. The Gothic style, which has the following elements, appealed to Edgar Allan Poe's dark view of the world:

- Bleak or remote settings
- Characters in psychological and/or physical torment
- Plots that involve weird or violent incidents and supernatural or otherworldly occurrences
- Strongly dramatic and intensely descriptive language
- A gloomy, melancholy, or eerie mood
- Symbolism that evokes ideas and feelings through repeated images

Practice

CITE TEXTUAL EVIDENCE
to support your answers.

Use the chart to record passages from the story that exemplify elements of the Gothic literary tradition. Explain each choice.

GOTHIC ELEMENT	PASSAGE	EXPLANATION
bleak setting		
tortured characters		
strange or violent plot		
dramatic description		
gloomy mood		
recurring symbolism		

THE FALL OF THE HOUSE
OF USHER

Concept Vocabulary

annihilate	fissure	rending
antiquity	dissolution	tumultuous

Why These Words? These concept vocabulary words convey decay and destruction. For example, the narrator talks about a *fissure* in the wall, a long crack from the roof down, as evidence of the house's decay.

1. How does the concept vocabulary contribute to the sense of finality suggested by the title of the story?

2. What other words in the selection connect to the concepts of decay and destruction?

Practice

Notebook The concept vocabulary words appear in "The Fall of the House of Usher."

1. Use the concept words to complete the paragraph.

The black and suffocating night air hung close as _____ winds threatened to snap tree trunks and toss them aloft. Seeking shelter from the raging storm, I approached the gloomy mansion. The _____ of the home was obvious from the style, which had not been popular for a century. When my initial knocking produced no result, I began to bang harder and harder. A thin _____ in the wooden panel shuddered with each blow of my hand. Would my pounding lead to _____ this ancient slab in two? In my desperation to enter, I cared little that I might _____ the door. I had arrived to prevent the _____ of the family Usher.

2. Explain the context clues that help you determine the correct words.

Word Study

Denotation and Connotation A word's **denotation** is its literal definition that you would find in a dictionary. The associations or feelings that a word suggests are its **connotations**. Words can have connotations that express the extreme nature of an act or a quality. *Annihilate* means "to destroy completely." Its connotations suggest an extreme form of destruction in which something is not merely destroyed but utterly wiped out or obliterated. Complete these activities, using a thesaurus or college-level dictionary as needed.

1. Provide the denotation and connotations of *dissolution, antiquity,* and *tumultuous*.

2. Name a synonym for each concept vocabulary word, and tell how its connotations differ.

🔧 WORD NETWORK

Add words related to fear from the text to your Word Network.

⊞ STANDARDS

Language
• Demonstrate command of the conventions of standard English grammar and usage when writing or speaking.
• Use various types of phrases and clauses to convey specific meanings and add variety and interest to writing or presentations.
• Demonstrate understanding of figurative language, word relationships, and nuances in word meanings.
• Analyze nuances in the meaning of words with similar denotations.

Conventions

Sentence Structure Sentences can be classified by the number of independent and dependent clauses they contain. An **independent clause** has a subject and a verb and can stand alone as a complete thought. A **dependent**, or **subordinate**, **clause** also has a subject and a verb, but it cannot stand alone as a complete thought.

CLARIFICATION
Refer to the Grammar Handbook to learn more about these terms.

This chart shows examples from "The Fall of the House of Usher" of the four basic sentence structures.

SENTENCE STRUCTURE	ELEMENTS	EXAMPLE
simple	a single <u>independent</u> clause	*The general furniture was profuse, comfortless, antique, and tattered.* (paragraph 7)
compound	two or more <u>independent</u> clauses, joined either by a comma and a coordinating conjunction or by a semicolon	*A servant in waiting took my horse, and I entered the Gothic archway of the hall.* (paragraph 6)
complex	one <u>independent</u> clause and one or more <u>dependent</u> clauses	*Although, as boys, we had been even intimate associates, . . . I really knew little of my friend.* (paragraph 3)
compound-complex	two or more <u>independent</u> clauses and one or more <u>dependent</u> clauses	*We sat down[,] and . . . , while he spoke not, I gazed upon him with a feeling half of pity, half of awe.* (paragraph 8)

Read It

1. Reread paragraph 2 of "The Fall of the House of Usher." Mark independent and dependent clauses. Then, classify each sentence as simple, compound, complex, or compound-complex.

2. Reread the final paragraph of the story. Identify the structure of each sentence.

Write It

📓 **Notebook** In the example, a simple sentence has been expanded to create other types of sentences. Expand the simple sentences below by adding details to create compound, complex, and compound-complex sentences.

> Example
> **Simple:** The house collapses.
> **Compound:** The house collapses, and the lake seems to swallow it whole.
> **Complex:** The house collapses as I flee in terror.
> **Compound-Complex:** The house collapses, and the lake seems to swallow it whole, as I flee in terror.

1. Madeline wanders in a distant hallway.

2. Usher sings a melancholy song.

EVIDENCE LOG

Before moving on to a new selection, go to your Evidence Log and record what you learned from "The Fall of the House of Usher."

THE FALL OF THE HOUSE OF USHER

Comparing Texts

You will now read "House Taken Over." First, complete the first-read and close-read activities. Then, compare the literary styles of "The Fall of the House of Usher" and "House Taken Over."

HOUSE TAKEN OVER

About the Author

Julio Cortázar (1914–1984) grew up in a suburb of Buenos Aires, in Argentina. Because he had health problems as a child, he spent much of his time in bed, reading, but he grew to be an impressive man, about six feet six inches tall. His talents were impressive, too. After teaching for several years in Argentina, he moved to Paris, where he lived out his days writing and translating distinguished English-language literature, particularly that of Edgar Allan Poe, into Spanish. Cortázar remained connected to his Argentinian roots throughout his life.

 **Tool Kit**
First-Read Guide and Model Annotation

House Taken Over
Concept Vocabulary

You will encounter the following words as you read "House Taken Over." Before reading, note how familiar you are with each word. Then, rank the words in order from most familiar (1) to least familiar (6).

WORD	YOUR RANKING
spacious	
unvoiced	
obscure	
recessed	
vestibule	
muffled	

After completing the first read, come back to the concept vocabulary and review your rankings. Mark changes to your original rankings as needed.

First Read FICTION

Apply these strategies as you conduct your first read. You will have an opportunity to complete the close-read notes after your first read.

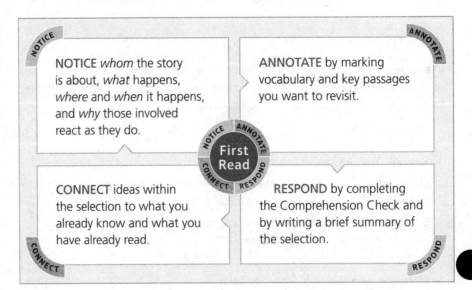

NOTICE *whom* the story is about, *what* happens, *where* and *when* it happens, and *why* those involved react as they do.

ANNOTATE by marking vocabulary and key passages you want to revisit.

CONNECT ideas within the selection to what you already know and what you have already read.

RESPOND by completing the Comprehension Check and by writing a brief summary of the selection.

First Read

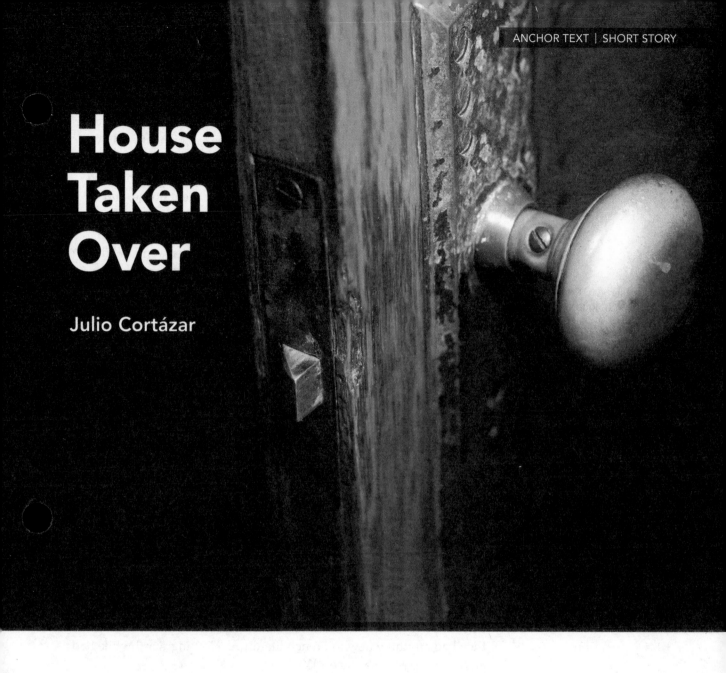

House Taken Over

Julio Cortázar

BACKGROUND

In 1946, when this story was written, Julio Cortázar lived in Buenos Aires, Argentina. World War II had only recently ended, and Argentina was in a state of political turmoil. Young people, including Cortázar, were critical of a conservative element in the government that had refused to join the Allied cause against Adolf Hitler until late in the war, by which time communication with Europe had all but stopped. The young author left Buenos Aires five years after writing this story, in protest against the policies of Juan Peron, who was increasingly dominating Argentinian politics.

1   We liked the house because, apart from its being old and **spacious** (in a day when old houses go down for a profitable auction of their construction materials), it kept the memories of great-grandparents, our paternal grandfather, our parents and the whole of childhood.

SCAN FOR
MULTIMEDIA

NOTES

spacious (SPAY shuhs) *adj.*
large; roomy

unvoiced (uhn VOYST) *adj.*
not spoken out loud or
expressed

obscure (uhb SKYAWR) *adj.*
not well-known

CLOSE READ

ANNOTATE: Mark details
in paragraphs 3 and 4 that
relate to the idea of being
necessary or unnecessary,
useful or useless.

QUESTION: Why might
concepts of necessity and
uselessness be important?

CONCLUDE: What do these
details show about the
characters and their lives?

2 Irene and I got used to staying in the house by ourselves, which was crazy, eight people could have lived in that place and not have gotten in each other's way. We rose at seven in the morning and got the cleaning done, and about eleven I left Irene to finish off whatever rooms and went to the kitchen. We lunched at noon precisely; then there was nothing left to do but a few dirty plates. It was pleasant to take lunch and commune with the great hollow, silent house, and it was enough for us just to keep it clean. We ended up thinking, at times, that that was what had kept us from marrying. Irene turned down two suitors for no particular reason, and María Esther went and died on me before we could manage to get engaged. We were easing into our forties with the **unvoiced** concept that the quiet, simple marriage of sister and brother was the indispensable end to a line established in this house by our grandparents. We would die here someday, **obscure** and distant cousins would inherit the place, have it torn down, sell the bricks and get rich on the building plot; or more justly and better yet, we would topple it ourselves before it was too late.

3 Irene never bothered anyone. Once the morning housework was finished, she spent the rest of the day on the sofa in her bedroom, knitting. I couldn't tell you why she knitted so much; I think women knit when they discover that it's a fat excuse to do nothing at all. But Irene was not like that, she always knitted necessities, sweaters for winter, socks for me, handy morning robes and bedjackets for herself. Sometimes she would do a jacket, then unravel it the next moment because there was something that didn't please her; it was pleasant to see a pile of tangled wool in her knitting basket fighting a losing battle for a few hours to retain its shape. Saturdays I went downtown to buy wool; Irene had faith in my good taste, was pleased with the colors and never a skein[1] had to be returned. I took advantage of these trips to make the rounds of the bookstores, uselessly asking if they had anything new in French literature. Nothing worthwhile had arrived in Argentina since 1939.

4 But it's the house I want to talk about, the house and Irene, I'm not very important. I wonder what Irene would have done without her knitting. One can reread a book, but once a pullover is finished you can't do it over again, it's some kind of disgrace. One day I found that the drawer at the bottom of the chiffonier, replete with mothballs, was filled with shawls, white, green, lilac. Stacked amid a great smell of camphor—it was like a shop; I didn't have the nerve to ask her what she planned to do with them. We didn't have to earn our living, there was plenty coming in from the farms each month, even piling up. But

---

1. **skein** (skayn) *n.* quantity of thread or yarn wound in a coil.

Irene was only interested in the knitting and showed a wonderful dexterity, and for me the hours slipped away watching her, her hands like silver sea urchins, needles flashing, and one or two knitting baskets on the floor, the balls of yarn jumping about. It was lovely.

5   How not to remember the layout of that house. The dining room, a living room with tapestries, the library and three large bedrooms in the section most **recessed**, the one that faced toward Rodríguez Peña.[2] Only a corridor with its massive oak door separated that part from the front wing, where there was a bath, the kitchen, our bedrooms and the hall. One entered the house through a **vestibule** with enameled tiles, and a wrought-iron grated door opened onto the living room. You had to come in through the vestibule and open the gate to go into the living room; the doors to our bedrooms were on either side of this, and opposite it was the corridor leading to the back section; going down the passage, one swung open the oak door beyond which was the other part of the house; or just before the door, one could turn to the left and go down a narrower passageway which led to the kitchen and the bath. When the door was open, you became aware of the size of the house; when it was closed, you had the impression of an apartment, like the ones they build today, with barely enough room to move around in. Irene and I always lived in this part of the house and hardly ever went beyond the oak door except to do the cleaning. Incredible how much dust collected on the furniture. It may be Buenos Aires[3] is a clean city, but she owes it to her population and nothing else. There's too much dust in the air, the slightest breeze and it's back on the marble console tops and in the diamond patterns of the tooled-leather desk set. It's a lot of work to get it off with a feather duster; the motes[4] rise and hang in the air, and settle again a minute later on the pianos and the furniture.

6   I'll always have a clear memory of it because it happened so simply and without fuss. Irene was knitting in her bedroom, it was eight at night, and I suddenly decided to put the water up for *mate*.[5] I went down the corridor as far as the oak door, which was ajar, then turned into the hall toward the kitchen, when I heard something in the library or the dining room. The sound came through muted and indistinct, a chair being knocked over onto the carpet or the **muffled** buzzing of a conversation. At the same time or a second later, I heard it at the end of the passage which led from those two rooms toward the door. I hurled myself against the door before it was too late and

---

2. **Rodríguez Peña** fashionable street in Buenos Aires.
3. **Buenos Aires** capital of Argentina.
4. **motes** *n.* specks of dust or other tiny particles.
5. *mate* (MAH tay) *n.* beverage made from the dried leaves of a South American evergreen tree.

NOTES

recessed (rih SEHST) *adj.* remote; set back

vestibule (VEHS tuh byool) *n.* entrance room

muffled (MUH fuhld) *adj.* difficult to hear because something is covering and softening the sound

CLOSE READ
ANNOTATE: In paragraphs 8–13, mark the short sentences.

QUESTION: Why does the author use so many shorter sentences?

CONCLUDE: How do these short sentences add to the portrayal of the characters' reactions?

shut it, leaned on it with the weight of my body; luckily, the key was on our side; moreover, I ran the great bolt into place, just to be safe.

7   I went down to the kitchen, heated the kettle, and when I got back with the tray of *mate*, I told Irene:

8   "I had to shut the door to the passage. They've taken over the back part."

9   She let her knitting fall and looked at me with her tired, serious eyes.

10   "You're sure?"

11   I nodded.

12   "In that case," she said, picking up her needles again, "we'll have to live on this side."

13   I sipped at the *mate* very carefully, but she took her time starting her work again. I remember it was a gray vest she was knitting. I liked that vest.

14   The first few days were painful, since we'd both left so many things in the part that had been taken over. My collection of French literature, for example, was still in the library. Irene had left several folios of stationery and a pair of slippers that she used a lot in the winter. I missed my briar pipe, and Irene, I think, regretted the loss of an ancient bottle of Hesperidin.[6] It happened repeatedly (but only in the first few days) that we would close some drawer or cabinet and look at one another sadly.

15   "It's not here."

16   One thing more among the many lost on the other side of the house.

17   But there were advantages, too. The cleaning was so much simplified that, even when we got up late, nine thirty for instance, by eleven we were sitting around with our arms folded. Irene got into the habit of coming to the kitchen with me to help get lunch. We thought about it and decided on this: while I prepared the lunch, Irene would cook up dishes that could be eaten cold in the evening. We were happy with the arrangement because it was always such a bother to have to leave our bedrooms in the evening and start to cook. Now we made do with the table in Irene's room and platters of cold supper.

18   Since it left her more time for knitting, Irene was content. I was a little lost without my books, but so as not to inflict myself on my sister, I set about reordering papa's stamp collection; that killed some time. We amused ourselves sufficiently, each with his own thing, almost always getting together in Irene's bedroom, which was the more comfortable. Every once in a while, Irene might say:

19   "Look at this pattern I just figured out, doesn't it look like clover?"

6. **Hesperidin** substance that comes from the rind of certain citrus fruits and is used for various medicinal purposes.

20   After a bit it was I, pushing a small square of paper in front of her so that she could see the excellence of some stamp or another from Eupen-et-Malmédy.[7] We were fine, and little by little we stopped thinking. You can live without thinking.

21   (Whenever Irene talked in her sleep, I woke up immediately and stayed awake. I never could get used to this voice from a statue or a parrot, a voice that came out of the dreams, not from a throat. Irene said that in my sleep I flailed about enormously and shook the blankets off. We had the living room between us, but at night you could hear everything in the house. We heard each other breathing, coughing, could even feel each other reaching for the light switch when, as happened frequently, neither of us could fall asleep.

22   Aside from our nocturnal rumblings, everything was quiet in the house. During the day there were the household sounds, the metallic click of knitting needles, the rustle of stamp-album pages turning. The oak door was massive, I think I said that. In the kitchen or the bath, which adjoined the part that was taken over, we managed to talk loudly, or Irene sang lullabies. In a kitchen there's always too much noise, the plates and glasses, for there to be interruptions from other sounds. We seldom allowed ourselves silence there, but when we went back to our rooms or to the living room, then the house grew quiet, half-lit, we ended by stepping around more slowly so as not to disturb one another. I think it was because of this that I woke up irremediably[8] and at once when Irene began to talk in her sleep.)

23   Except for the consequences, it's nearly a matter of repeating the same scene over again. I was thirsty that night, and before we went to sleep, I told Irene that I was going to the kitchen for a glass of water. From the door of the bedroom (she was knitting) I heard the noise in the kitchen; if not the kitchen, then the bath, the passage off at that angle dulled the sound. Irene noticed how brusquely I had paused, and came up beside me without a word. We stood listening to the noises, growing more and more sure that they were on our side of the oak door, if not the kitchen then the bath, or in the hall itself at the turn, almost next to us.

24   We didn't wait to look at one another. I took Irene's arm and forced her to run with me to the wrought-iron door, not waiting to look back. You could hear the noises, still muffled but louder, just behind us. I slammed the grating and we stopped in the vestibule. Now there was nothing to be heard.

25   "They've taken over our section," Irene said. The knitting had reeled off from her hands and the yarn ran back toward the door and

---

7. **Eupen-et-Malmédy** (yoo PEHN ay mahl may DEE) districts in eastern Belgium.
8. **irremediably** (ihr ih MEE dee uh blee) *adv.* in a way that cannot be helped or corrected.

disappeared under it. When she saw that the balls of yarn were on the other side, she dropped the knitting without looking at it.

26   "Did you have time to bring anything?" I asked hopelessly.

27   "No, nothing."

28   We had what we had on. I remembered fifteen thousand pesos[9] in the wardrobe in my bedroom. Too late now.

29   I still had my wrist watch on and saw that it was 11 P.M. I took Irene around the waist (I think she was crying) and that was how we went into the street. Before we left, I felt terrible; I locked the front door up tight and tossed the key down the sewer. It wouldn't do to have some poor devil decide to go in and rob the house, at that hour and with the house taken over. ❧

---

9. **fifteen thousand pesos** large sum of money at the time of the story.

Comprehension Check

Complete the following items after you finish your first read.

1. Briefly describe the house in which the narrator and his sister live.

2. What is the source of the siblings' income?

3. How do Irene and the narrator occupy their time?

4. What decision do Irene and the narrator make when they realize the back part of the house has been taken over?

5. What happens to the brother and sister at the end of the story?

6. ▣ **Notebook** Write a summary of "House Taken Over" to confirm your understanding of the story.

- -

RESEARCH

Research to Clarify Choose at least one unfamiliar detail from the text. Briefly research that detail. In what way does the information you learned shed light on an aspect of the story.

Research to Explore Research the origin of the story. Discover information about the home in Buenos Aires Province that inspired it.

HOUSE TAKEN OVER

Close Read the Text

1. This model, from paragraph 6 of the text, shows two sample annotations, along with questions and conclusions. Close read the passage, and find another detail to annotate. Then, write a question and your conclusion.

ANNOTATE: The words describing the sounds the intruders make seem intentionally vague.

QUESTION: Why does the writer give so little detail about the intruders?

CONCLUDE: By providing only vague hints, the writer makes the invaders seem more frightening and mysterious.

ANNOTATE: The writer includes a series of action verbs in one sentence.

QUESTION: Why does the writer pack all of these actions into a single sentence?

CONCLUDE: Packed into one sentence, this series of urgent actions shows the narrator's intense fear.

> . . . I heard something in the library or the dining room. The sound came through muted and indistinct, a chair being knocked over onto the carpet or the muffled buzzing of a conversation. . . . I hurled myself against the door before it was too late and shut it, leaned on it with the weight of my body; luckily, the key was on our side; moreover, I ran the great bolt into place, just to be safe.

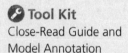

Tool Kit
Close-Read Guide and Model Annotation

2. For more practice, go back into the text and complete the close-read notes.

3. Revisit a section of the text you found important during your first read. Read this section closely, and **annotate** what you notice. Ask yourself **questions** such as "Why did the author make this choice?" What can you **conclude**?

Analyze the Text

CITE TEXTUAL EVIDENCE to support your answers.

Notebook Respond to these questions.

1. (a) Interpret To what social class do the brother and sister belong? How do you know? **(b) Connect** How are the characters' hobbies evidence of their social class?

2. (a) Compare and Contrast How is the behavior the siblings exhibit during sleep different from their behavior while awake? **(b) Analyze** What does this difference suggest about their true reactions to the invasion of the house?

3. Extend Cortázar wrote this story after having a nightmare. In what ways does this story resemble a nightmare? Explain.

4. Essential Question: *What is the allure of fear?* What have you learned from this story about portrayals of fear in literature?

STANDARDS
Reading Literature
• Analyze how an author's choices concerning how to structure a text, order events within it, and manipulate time create such effects as mystery, tension, or surprise.
• Analyze a particular point of view or cultural experience reflected in a work of literature from outside the United States, drawing on a wide reading of world literature.

Analyze Craft and Structure

Literary Style "House Taken Over" is an example of **Magical Realism**, a literary genre closely associated with some Latin American twentieth-century authors. Magical Realism combines two seemingly contrasting elements: reality and fantasy. By introducing supernatural or unreal elements into carefully observed depictions of real life, writers in this genre shock and surprise readers while also providing insightful commentary on human nature and perceptions. Elements of magical realism include:

- Recognizable characters who feel, act, and react in customary ways
- Realistic settings that include ordinary details of everyday life
- Fantastic events that coexist with realistic characters and actions
- An accepting or unimpressed narrative **tone,** or attitude, that presents fantastic events as logical parts of life

Cortázar balances these elements carefully, creating a unique representation of a realistic world where dreamlike events can still happen.

Practice

CITE TEXTUAL EVIDENCE to support your answers.

Use the chart to record passages from the story that exemplify elements of Magical Realism. Explain each choice.

MAGICAL REALIST ELEMENT	PASSAGE(S)	EXPLANATION
Recognizable Characters		
Realistic Setting and Details		
Fantastic Events		
Unimpressed Tone		

HOUSE TAKEN OVER

Concept Vocabulary

spacious	obscure	vestibule
unvoiced	recessed	muffled

Why These Words? These concept vocabulary words express different types of emptiness, including those of emotion, sound, and space. For example, the narrator describes one part of his home as being "the most recessed." Something *recessed* is set back or remote.

1. How does the author use the concept vocabulary to describe the house vividly and precisely?

2. What other words in the selection connect to the idea of emptiness?

Practice

📓 **Notebook** The concept vocabulary words appear in "House Taken Over." Tell whether each sentence is true or false, and explain why.

1. A *spacious* home would probably be cheaper than a cramped one.
2. People's loud, persistent complaints are usually *unvoiced*.
3. You should consider visiting *obscure* places if you want to avoid crowds.
4. A *recessed* set of shelves sticks out into a room.
5. A *vestibule* is a small building that stands at a distance from a house.
6. It is easy to understand a *muffled* announcement over a PA system.

Word Study

Patterns of Word Changes Suffixes and prefixes can be added to base words to change their meanings. Often, suffixes change a word's part of speech. The base word *space*, a noun—from the Latin *spatium*—becomes *spacious*, an adjective, when the suffix *-ious* is added.

1. The word *voice*, when it is used as a verb, means "to speak out loud." Explain how this word is changed by the addition of the prefix *un-* and the suffix *-ed*.

2. Find two other examples in the story of words that contain either a prefix or a suffix. Explain how the meaning of the base word is changed by the addition of the prefix or suffix.

🔗 **WORD NETWORK**

Add words related to fear from the text to your Word Network.

STANDARDS

Language
• Demonstrate command of the conventions of standard English grammar and usage when writing or speaking.
• Use various types of phrases and clauses to convey specific meanings and add variety and interest to writing or presentations.
• Identify and correctly use patterns of word changes that indicate different meanings or parts of speech.
• Demonstrate understanding of figurative language, word relationships, and nuances in word meanings.

Conventions

Types of Phrases A **preposition** connects a noun or a pronoun to another word in the sentence. A **prepositional phrase** is made up of a preposition, the object of the preposition, and any modifiers of the object. Prepositional phrases modify other words by functioning either as adjectives or as adverbs. In these examples from "House Taken Over," the prepositions are underlined once, and the objects of the prepositions are underlined twice.

CLARIFICATION
Refer to the Grammar Handbook to learn more about these terms.

_in_ the _house_	_by_ _ourselves_	_at_ _seven_
_of_ the _day_	_from_ the front _wing_	_through_ a _vestibule_
into the _living room_	_before_ the _door_	_with_ a _feather duster_
_on_ the _sofa_	_down_ the _corridor_	_against_ the _door_

Read It

1. Mark all of the prepositional phrases in each sentence. Then, label each preposition and its object.

   a. I lived in this part of the house and rarely went beyond the oak door.

   b. A chair was knocked onto the carpet and dragged along the floor.

   c. I hurried toward the door and pushed the heavy bolt into place.

2. Reread paragraph 24 of the story. Mark the prepositional phrases, and tell how these phrases help to clarify the action.

Write It

📓 **Notebook** In the example, the second sentence in each pair contains prepositional phrases that help clarify, describe, or explain. Revise the paragraph below. Add prepositional phrases to make the paragraph more interesting and detailed.

> **EXAMPLE**
> I tossed the key. I tossed the key _down the drain_ _in the gutter_.
> I heard a noise. _At midnight_, I heard a noise _behind the door_.

We heard a noise that was impossible to describe. When the noise grew louder, we decided to run. We didn't have time to grab anything. We found ourselves outside. We looked but could see nothing.

THE FALL OF THE HOUSE
OF USHER

HOUSE TAKEN OVER

Writing to Compare

You have read "The Fall of the House of Usher" and "House Taken Over," two short stories that have similarities but represent two different literary styles, or genres. Now, deepen your understanding of both stories by comparing and writing about them.

Assignment

Write an **explanatory essay** in which you compare and contrast Gothic style and Magical Realism as seen in the stories by Poe and Cortázar. Include the following elements in your essay:

- definitions of the two genres

- a discussion of how each story is a good example of its genre

- effective use of evidence from the stories

- an evaluation of the effect each story has on the reader

Make sure you are clear about the qualities that define the Gothic style and Magical Realism. If necessary, do a little research or reread the instruction about the genres.

Planning and Prewriting

Analyze the Texts When you are analyzing complex works, a smaller focus can help you see the bigger picture more clearly. For example, instead of analyzing all the elements of both stories, you might focus on the siblings, the supernatural elements, or another specific aspect of each story. For this assignment, compare and contrast the settings—the two houses and the worlds they occupy. Use the chart to gather story details that relate to that focus.

FOCUS: DETAILS RELATED TO SETTING	
THE FALL OF THE HOUSE OF USHER	HOUSE TAKEN OVER

Notebook Respond to these questions.

1. How are the settings of the two stories similar? How are they different?

2. In each story, how does the setting affect the characters and the choices they make?

STANDARDS

Reading Literature
Analyze how an author's choices concerning how to structure a text, order events within it, and manipulate time create such effects as mystery, tension, or surprise.

Writing
• Write informative/explanatory texts to examine and convey complex ideas, concepts, and information clearly and accurately through the effective selection, organization, and analysis of content.
• Draw evidence from literary or informational texts to support analysis, reflection, and research.
• Apply *grades 9–10 Reading standards* to literature.

Drafting

Synthesize Ideas Review your Prewriting notes. Decide how setting reveals Gothic sensibilities in Poe's story and Magical Realist ideas in Cortázar's story, and how those styles are both similar and different. Record your ideas using these sentence frames:

In both stories, the setting _____

_____

_____.

However, in Poe's story "The Fall of the House of Usher," the setting: _____

_____

_____.

Similarly/By contrast, in Cortázar's story "House Taken Over," the setting ___

_____

_____.

Identify Supporting Details Identify passages to use as examples for your ideas. Make sure each passage presents a clear similarity or difference, and demonstrates either a Gothic or a Magical Realist approach. Note the passages you will use and the ideas each one will support.

PASSAGE	IDEA

Organize Ideas Make some organizational decisions before you begin to write. Consider using one of these two structures:

Grouping Ideas: discuss all the similarities between the settings and genres of the two stories and then all the differences

Grouping Texts: discuss the setting and genre of one story and then the setting and genre of the other story

Review, Revise, and Edit

Once you are done drafting, review your essay. Because your essay is about multiple subjects—two different settings and two different genres—clarity and balance are critical. Reread your draft, and mark the points at which you discuss Poe's story and the Gothic. Use a different mark to identify the points at which you discuss Cortázar's story and Magical Realism. Check your draft to see if you have addressed the two stories in a balanced way. Add more analysis or examples as needed. Then, proofread and edit your essay for grammatical and spelling errors.

EVIDENCE LOG

Before moving on to a new selection, go to your Evidence Log and record what you learned from "House Taken Over."

About the Designers

Adam Frost is a designer of websites, games, books, and exhibitions. His children's books include such titles as *Stop, There's a Snake in Your Suitcase!* Frost currently works as the Data Visualization Manager at the *Guardian* newspaper and specializes in creating infographic articles such as this one.

Zhenia Vasiliev is a London-based designer and graphic artist. His clients include Sony, Google, the *Guardian*, NBC Universal, and others. He has been featured in several art shows and is a recipient of the Macmillan Children's Books Prize.

📇 STANDARDS
Reading Informational Text
• By the end of grade 10, read and comprehend literary nonfiction at the high end of the grades 9–10 text complexity band independently and proficiently.

from How to Tell You're Reading a Gothic Novel—In Pictures

Concept Vocabulary

You will encounter the following words as you read and view these informational graphics.

WORD	PRONUNCIATION AND MEANING
reclusive	(rih KLOO sihv) *adj.* solitary; avoiding the company of others
sinister	(SIHN uh stuhr) *adj.* giving the impression that something harmful or evil is happening or will happen
ethereal	(ih THIHR ee uhl) *adj.* extremely delicate and light in a way that seems too perfect for this world

First Read MEDIA: INFORMATIONAL GRAPHIC

Apply these strategies as you conduct your first read. You will have an opportunity to complete a close read after your first read.

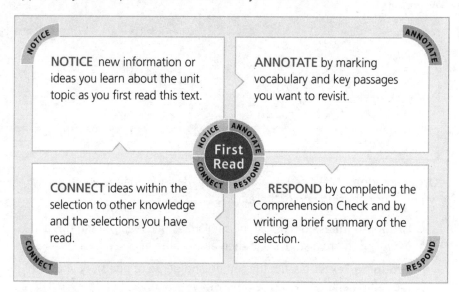

NOTICE new information or ideas you learn about the unit topic as you first read this text.

ANNOTATE by marking vocabulary and key passages you want to revisit.

CONNECT ideas within the selection to other knowledge and the selections you have read.

RESPOND by completing the Comprehension Check and by writing a brief summary of the selection.

Reading Strategy: Text and Graphics

As you encounter each screen of the informational graphic, read all of the text, and note how the different visuals support the text.

from How to Tell You're Reading a Gothic Novel—In Pictures

Adam Frost and Zhenia Vasiliev

BACKGROUND

The Gothic literary genre began in 1764 with Horace Walpole's novel *The Castle of Otranto*. The term *Gothic* came from the Visigoths, a Germanic people who once ruled land that includes what is now Spain, parts of Portugal, and France. The Visigoths contributed to the fall of the Roman Empire and were regarded as barbaric and wild. To this day, Gothic ideas, such as madness, horror, and the supernatural, remain popular in literature, movies, and television.

SCAN FOR MULTIMEDIA

1 It's set in a spooky castle or stately home

● Yes ● No ● Unknown

	Built in Gothic period	In a poor state of repair	In the middle of nowhere	Haunted/Cursed[1]	Has a forbidden wing and/or secret passages	Has reclusive and/or sinister owner
Castle of Otranto						
Castle of Lovel, *Old English Baron*		☐				☐
The Ruined Abbey, *The Romance of the Forest*						
Castle of Udolpho, *The Mysteries of Udolpho*						
Montmorenci Castle, *Clermont*						
Castle of Wolfenbach						
Castle of Elfinbach, *Orphan of the Rhine*						
Falkland's mansion, *Caleb Williams*		☐				
Castella di Laurentini, *Zastrozzi*				☐		
St Irvyne				☐	☐	
Bartram-Haugh, *Uncle Silas*						
Castle Dracula						
Bly, *Turn of the Screw*		☐				
Baskerville Hall					☐	☐
Manderley, *Rebecca*		☐				
Gormenghast Castle						

1 By haunted, we have also included castles/buildings that are mistakenly believed to be haunted (e.g. Udolpho, Wolfenbach). Note that the haunting should ideally be linked to a terrible crime, usually the murder of the castle's legitimate owner or the current owner's wife, father or brother.

NOTES

2 There is (probably) a ghost or monster[1]

GHOST	MONSTER	WITCH/ SORCERESS	VAMPIRE	THE DEVIL	NOT REALLY A GHOST AT ALL[2]
The Old English Baron	Frankenstein	Vathek	The Vampyre	The Monk	The Mysteries of Udolpho
A Christmas Carol	Wagner the Wehr-Wolf	The Lancashire Witches	Varney the Vampire	Zofloya	Wieland
The Uninhabited House	Dr Jekyll and Mr Hyde	She	'Carmilla'	Confessions of a Justified Sinner	The Castle of Wolfenbach
The Turn of the Screw	Lair of the White Worm	'The Withered Arm'	Dracula	Melmoth the Wanderer	The Italian

1 We focussed on eighteenth and nineteenth century Gothic here. After that, Gothic splits into innumerable sub-categories, 'weird fiction', 'horror', 'Southern Gothic', 'Southern Ontario Gothic' etc. Also, after 1900, it is film rather than prose that produces the most notable Gothic monsters. In addition, we focussed on English-language Gothic (so no Hoffman, Gogol etc) and 'serious' Gothic only – so no satires (e.g. Northanger Abbey). We had to impose some limits as Gothic is such a potentially gigantic subject – sorry if we missed any of your favourites.

2 In these stories, the groans, clankings and/or strange ethereal music end up being caused by dastardly humans. Think *Scooby Doo*.

NOTES

3 It's set in the olden days[1]

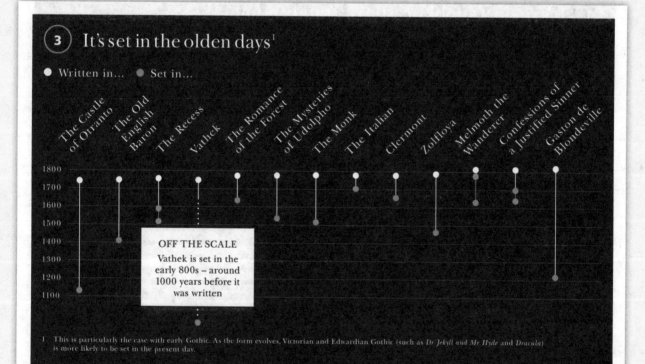

● Written in...   ● Set in...

OFF THE SCALE
Vathek is set in the early 800s – around 1000 years before it was written

1 This is particularly the case with early Gothic. As the form evolves, Victorian and Edwardian Gothic (such as *Dr Jekyll and Mr Hyde* and *Dracula*) is more likely to be set in the present day.

NOTES

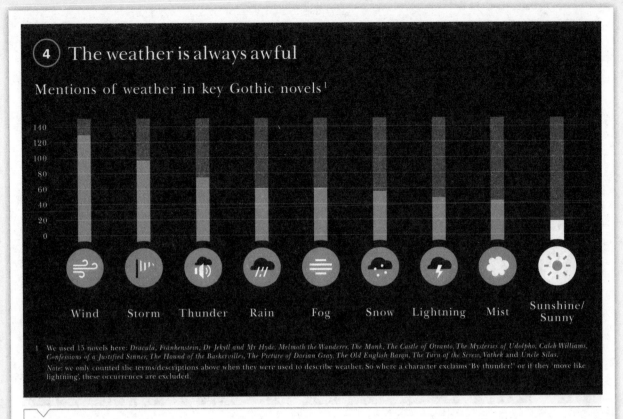

4 The weather is always awful

Mentions of weather in key Gothic novels[1]

Wind · Storm · Thunder · Rain · Fog · Snow · Lightning · Mist · Sunshine/Sunny

1 We used 15 novels here: *Dracula, Frankenstein, Dr Jekyll and Mr Hyde, Melmoth the Wanderer, The Monk, The Castle of Otranto, The Mysteries of Udolpho, Caleb Williams, Confessions of a Justified Sinner, The Hound of the Baskervilles, The Picture of Dorian Gray, The Old English Baron, The Turn of the Screw, Vathek* and *Uncle Silas*.
   Note: we only counted the terms/descriptions above when they were used to describe weather. So where a character exclaims 'By thunder!' or if they 'move like lightning', these occurrences are excluded.

NOTES

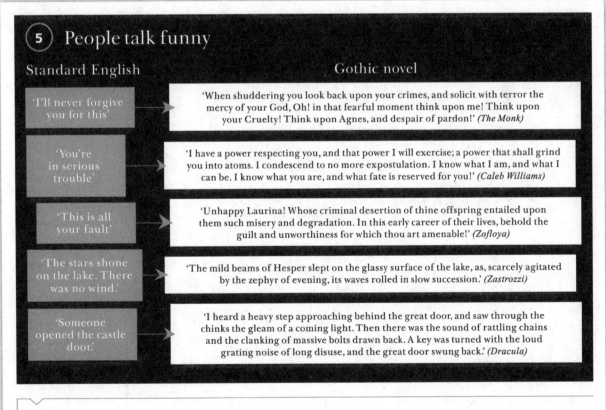

5 People talk funny

Standard English	Gothic novel
'I'll never forgive you for this'	'When shuddering you look back upon your crimes, and solicit with terror the mercy of your God, Oh! in that fearful moment think upon me! Think upon your Cruelty! Think upon Agnes, and despair of pardon!' *(The Monk)*
'You're in serious trouble'	'I have a power respecting you, and that power I will exercise; a power that shall grind you into atoms. I condescend to no more expostulation. I know what I am, and what I can be. I know what you are, and what fate is reserved for you!' *(Caleb Williams)*
'This is all your fault'	'Unhappy Laurina! Whose criminal desertion of thine offspring entailed upon them such misery and degradation. In this early career of their lives, behold the guilt and unworthiness for which thou art amenable!' *(Zofloya)*
'The stars shone on the lake. There was no wind.'	'The mild beams of Hesper slept on the glassy surface of the lake, as, scarcely agitated by the zephyr of evening, its waves rolled in slow succession.' *(Zastrozzi)*
'Someone opened the castle door.'	'I heard a heavy step approaching behind the great door, and saw through the chinks the gleam of a coming light. Then there was the sound of rattling chains and the clanking of massive bolts drawn back. A key was turned with the loud grating noise of long disuse, and the great door swung back.' *(Dracula)*

NOTES

6 So which Gothic novels are the best?

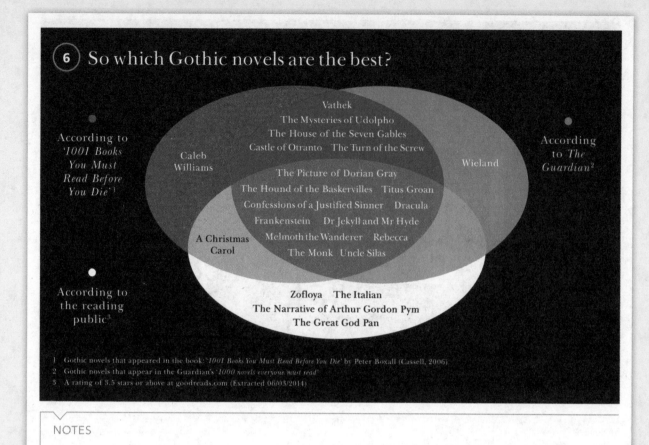

According to '1001 Books You Must Read Before You Die'[1]

According to the reading public[3]

According to The Guardian[2]

Vathek
The Mysteries of Udolpho
The House of the Seven Gables
Castle of Otranto   The Turn of the Screw

Caleb Williams

Wieland

The Picture of Dorian Gray
The Hound of the Baskervilles   Titus Groan
Confessions of a Justified Sinner   Dracula
Frankenstein   Dr Jekyll and Mr Hyde
A Christmas Carol
Melmoth the Wanderer   Rebecca
The Monk   Uncle Silas

Zofloya   The Italian
The Narrative of Arthur Gordon Pym
The Great God Pan

1 Gothic novels that appeared in the book: '*1001 Books You Must Read Before You Die*' by Peter Boxall (Cassell, 2006)
2 Gothic novels that appear in the Guardian's '*1000 novels everyone must read*'
3 A rating of 3.5 stars or above at goodreads.com (Extracted 06/03/2014)

NOTES

NOTES

Comprehension Check

Complete the following items after you finish your first read.

1. Where do many Gothic novels take place?

2. What is the weather like in many Gothic novels?

3. What are some types of characters you might encounter in a Gothic novel?

4. When do most Gothic novels take place?

5. ▣ **Notebook** Write a three- or four-sentence summary that describes the basic elements of Gothic literature.

- -

RESEARCH

Research to Clarify Choose at least one unfamiliar detail from the informational graphics. Briefly research that detail. In what way does the information you learned add to your understanding of the topic?

Research to Explore Choose something that interests you from the text, and formulate a research question.

HOW TO TELL YOU'RE READING A
GOTHIC NOVEL—IN PICTURES

Close Read the Text

Review the informational graphics again. **Annotate** details that you notice. What **questions** do you have? What can you **conclude**?

Analyze the Text

Notebook Respond to these questions.

1. **Make a Judgment** Consider the types of places in which the authors say Gothic novels are set. Do these places support the idea, presented in graphic 1, that all Gothic novels are set "in the middle of nowhere"? Explain.

2. **Infer** What types of events and moods would you expect to find in any Gothic novel?

3. **(a) Describe** What **tone**, or attitude, do these writers seem to take toward Gothic novels? Explain. **(b) Analyze** How does the tone add to the impact of the informational graphics?

4. **Essential Question:** *What is the allure of fear?* What have you learned about portrayals of fear in literature by reading this text?

STANDARDS

Reading Informational Text
Cite strong and thorough textual evidence to support analysis of what the text says explicitly as well as inferences drawn from the text.

Speaking and Listening
• Integrate multiple sources of information presented in diverse media or formats evaluating the credibility and accuracy of each source.
• Present information, findings, and supporting evidence clearly, concisely, and logically such that listeners can follow the line of reasoning and the organization, development, substance, and style are appropriate to purpose, audience, and task.
• Make strategic use of digital media in presentations to enhance understanding of findings, reasoning, and evidence and to add interest.

LANGUAGE DEVELOPMENT

Concept Vocabulary

reclusive	sinister	ethereal

Why These Words? The three concept vocabulary words relate to different elements of Gothic literature.

1. How does the concept vocabulary help readers understand the elements of Gothic literature?

2. What other words in the informational graphics capture the essence of Gothic literature?

Practice

Notebook Confirm your understanding of the concept vocabulary words by using them in sentences. Be sure to include context clues that signal the meanings of the words.

Speaking and Listening

> **Assignment**
>
> Informational graphics, such as those presented in "How to Tell You're Reading A Gothic Novel—In Pictures," are an effective way to communicate ideas. The use of images, symbols, graphs, and text allows writers to explain and depict the complexities of a topic in a clear, engaging, and sometimes funny way. Create and present your own **informational graphic,** in which you show how elements of "The Fall of the House of Usher" combine to create a Gothic tale.

1. **Organize Your Content**
   - Use words, images, and symbols to create an informational graphic.
   - Sketch your ideas on a sheet of paper. Plan each element of your graphic separately.
   - Use symbols or icons to represent ideas. For example, you could use a small picture of a lightning bolt and clouds to represent stormy weather.
   - Consider using the concept vocabulary words (*reclusive, sinister, ethereal*) in your informational graphic.

2. **Prepare Your Presentation** When you have completed a draft of your informational graphic, review it to make sure it is accurate and visually engaging. Revise it as necessary to make it clearer or more interesting. Present your work to the class. As you share your graphic, keep these presentation techniques in mind:
   - Speak clearly and naturally, and avoid rushing.
   - Refer to your graphic, but try not to read from it. Instead, glance at it, and then make eye contact with your listeners.
   - Do your best to avoid standing in a stiff, uncomfortable way.

3. **Evaluate Presentations** As your classmates deliver their presentations, listen attentively. Use a presentation evaluation guide to analyze their presentations.

PRESENTATION EVALUATION GUIDE

Rate each statement on a scale of 1 (not demonstrated) to 6 (demonstrated).

- [ ] The speaker used examples from Poe's story effectively.
- [ ] The speaker maintained eye contact with the audience.
- [ ] The speaker seemed comfortable and at ease.
- [ ] The information was presented logically and effectively.

☑ EVIDENCE LOG

Before moving on to a new selection, go to your Evidence Log and record what you learned from "How to Tell You're Reading a Gothic Novel—In Pictures."

WRITING TO SOURCES

- THE FALL OF THE HOUSE OF USHER

- HOUSE TAKEN OVER

- HOW TO TELL YOU'RE READING A GOTHIC NOVEL—IN PICTURES

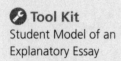 **Tool Kit**
Student Model of an Explanatory Essay

ACADEMIC VOCABULARY

As you craft your essay, consider using some of the academic vocabulary you learned in the beginning of the unit.

dimension
motivate
manipulate
perspective
psychological

STANDARDS
Writing
- Write informative/explanatory texts to examine and convey ideas, concepts, and information clearly and accurately through the effective selection, organization, and analysis of content.
- Write narratives to develop real or imagined experiences or events using effective technique, well-chosen details, and well-structured event sequences.
- Produce clear and coherent writing in which the development, organization, and style are appropriate to task, purpose, and audience.
- Draw evidence from literary or informational texts to support analysis, reflection, and research.
- Write routinely over extended time frames and shorter time frames for a range of tasks, purposes, and audiences.

Write an Explanatory Essay

You have just read three selections having to do with the literature of fear. In "The Fall of the House of Usher," Edgar Allan Poe creates a chilling Gothic tale in which a brother and sister seem to be decaying along with their house. In "House Taken Over," another brother and sister are driven from their home when it is invaded by unwelcome visitors—or is it? The creators of "How to Tell You're Reading a Gothic Novel—In Pictures" play infographic games with some scary elements of the Gothic tradition. Now, use your knowledge of the topic to write an explanatory essay about fear in life and literature. In addition to references to the texts, you will incorporate an anecdote, or brief story, as evidence to support your central idea.

Assignment

Use your knowledge of these texts and your own experience or observations to write an **explanatory essay** that answers this question:

> **How and when does imagination overcome reason?**

Support your ideas with references to the selections in Whole-Class Learning, as well as an anecdote—or brief narrative—from your own experience, that of someone you know, film or TV, or another literary work. Present the narrative as a specific example of a general idea.

Elements of an Explanatory Essay with Narrative Evidence

An **explanatory essay** explains a topic by presenting information and insights in a logical, well-ordered sequence. An effective explanatory essay includes the following elements:

- a central point that will increase readers' knowledge of the subject or help readers understand the subject better

- varied evidence that engages readers and clarifies ideas—An anecdote, or brief narrative, is one type of evidence; facts examples, and textual details from literary works are other types of evidence.

- the use of transitions that clarify relationships among ideas

- precise language and correct grammar

- a tone appropriate to the audience and the subject

Analyze Writing Model

Explanatory Essay Model For a model of a well-crafted explanatory essay that incorporates nonfiction narrative, see the Launch Text, "My Introduction to Gothic Literature."

Challenge yourself to find all the elements of an explanatory text that uses narrative evidence in the text. You will have the opportunity to review these elements as you start to write your essay.

Prewriting / Planning

Focus Your Ideas Think about the texts you've read. Consider how imagination works in "The Fall of the House of Usher" and "House Taken Over." Consider other examples in literature, popular culture, and your own life.

- What does imagination make the characters feel?

- What does it make them do?

- What happens when people "let their imaginations run away with them"?

Now, decide on your central point. What would you like to explain? Your central point should be an insight into how and when imagination can overcome reason and create mindless fear. Write a sentence that states the idea you want to explain to your readers.

Central Idea: _____

_____ .

Gather Evidence You have now given a lot of thought to your central idea. It's time to get specific. What evidence can you use to support your point? Think about these possibilities:

- Situations and events from "The Fall of the House of Usher," "House Taken Over," and other works of fiction

- Quotations from experts in psychology or sociology—people who study fear

- A brief narrative based on your own experience or your observations of others

Including thoughts and feelings about a relevant text will help make your essay stronger. For example, in the Launch Text, the writer explains what it was like to first read Poe's "The Cask of Amontillado."

But what struck me most was how Montresor spoke directly to the reader—to me. He expected my sympathy as he brought his terrible revenge. Up to that point, all the stories I had ever read had set the criminal or the lunatic at a distance. They didn't draw me into a mind that was a truly scary place to be. This one did.
                                        —from "My Introduction to Gothic Literature"

Connect Across Texts As you write your essay, consider how the authors of the selections in Whole-Class Learning explore the relationships among imagination, reason, and fear. Make sure that you are conveying the ideas of the original text accurately.

✐ EVIDENCE LOG

Review your Evidence Log and identify key details you may want to cite in your essay.

▤ STANDARDS

Writing
• Introduce a topic; organize complex ideas, concepts, and information to make important connections and distinctions; include formatting, graphics and multimedia when useful to aiding comprehension.
• Develop a topic with well-chosen, relevant, and sufficient facts, extended definitions, concrete details, quotations, or other information and examples appropriate to the audience's knowledge of the topic.

Drafting

Identify Sources of Narrative Evidence The selections in Whole-Class Learning will provide most of your supporting evidence. However, you also need to incorporate an anecdote as a specific example of a general idea. Consider these types of sources for narrative evidence.

- **Real Life** Do you have friends who imagine dangers on amusement park rides to make them scarier? Have you ever been at a sleepover where people were trying to scare themselves and one another? These sorts of experiences may provide strong narrative evidence for your essay.

- **Movies** Have you seen movies about people who were in spooky situations? How did they behave? How did their imaginations affect their decisions?

- **Books** Have you read books in which people faced similar dangers but reacted in different ways? Who approached fear with reason? Who didn't? How did their reactions affect the outcome of events?

Use the chart to gather your ideas for different types of evidence you will use in this essay.

EVIDENCE	WHAT IT SHOWS ABOUT IMAGINATION, REASON, FEAR
example from real life	
example from media	
example from literature	

Connect Ideas and Evidence Use your insights from the selections in Whole-Class Learning to connect to your other evidence. For example, you might write, "In 'House Taken Over,' the brother and sister are afraid, but the source of that fear is mysterious. The unknown can be terrifying." You might support this point with a real-life example, such as this: "Last year, raccoons nested in our attic. At night, we heard murmurs and scurrying sounds. It was terrifying, until we learned what was causing it."

Maintain a Formal Style and Tone Throughout the essay, your style and tone should be appropriately formal, even during the section (or sections) in which you relate an anecdote. Avoid the use of slang and exclamations, and follow grammatical rules. Consider these examples.

Casual Style and Tone: I figured the sounds couldn't be anything that serious, but those raccoons totally freaked me out!

Appropriate Style and Tone: Reason told me there was no real danger, but the sounds of the raccoons terrified me anyway.

Use Appropriate Structure Begin your essay with a paragraph that draws the reader in and states your central point. Then, in a few paragraphs, present your evidence, including your narrative. Finish the essay with a conclusion that briefly summarizes your ideas and evidence. You may add a clever or thought-provoking last sentence.

STANDARDS

Writing
- Develop the topic with well-chosen, relevant, and sufficient facts, extended definitions, concrete details, quotations, or other information and examples appropriate to the audience's knowledge of the topic.
- Establish and maintain a formal style and objective tone while attending to the norms and conventions of the discipline in which they are writing.
- Write narratives to develop real or imagined experiences or events using effective technique, well-chosen details, and wellstructured event sequences.

LANGUAGE DEVELOPMENT: AUTHOR'S STYLE

Descriptive Details

Descriptive details give readers precise information about people, settings, events, and ideas. These details often appeal to the senses—sight, hearing, smell, touch, and taste. For example, in the Launch Text, instead of writing, "The power went out," the author writes: "The power had been knocked out, and I was sitting at a window, watching the wet night grow darker." Descriptive details in characterization help create a sense that the reader can see, hear, and even know a person or character.

Read It

In these sentences from the selections and the Launch Text, the authors use precise, descriptive details to portray characters, settings, and events.

- *The now ghastly pallor of the skin, and the now miraculous luster of the eye, above all things startled and even awed me.* ("The Fall of the House of Usher")

- *[I]t was pleasant to see a pile of tangled wool in her knitting basket fighting a losing battle for a few hours to retain its shape.* ("House Taken Over")

- *As the clouds cleared, a fog rose and filtered the moonlight, casting a bluish hue over the yard.* ("My Introduction to Gothic Literature")

- *The stories helped me see that life can be a mansion full of secrets and dark passages, but also of beauty and light.* ("My Introduction to Gothic Literature")

- *In Poe's descriptions, I could practically smell the dust and mold.* ("My Introduction to Gothic Literature")

Write It

Think about the brief story or anecdote you are going to tell in your essay. Ask yourself, "Which details will make this story come alive for readers *and* support my main point about fear and imagination?" Then, fill in the chart with details. Try to identify details that relate to senses other than sight.

DETAILS ABOUT PEOPLE	DETAILS ABOUT SETTING	DETAILS ABOUT EVENTS

STYLE
Make your descriptions as specific as possible. For example, when writing about a car, instead of "blue car," you might write "light-blue 1960s convertible."

STANDARDS
Writing
• Use precise language and domain-specific vocabulary to manage the complexity of the topic.
• Use precise words and phrases, telling details, and sensory language to convey a vivid picture of the experiences, events, setting, and/or characters.

Revising

Evaluating Your Draft

Use the following checklist to evaluate the effectiveness of your first draft. Then, use your evaluation and the instruction on this page to guide your revision.

FOCUS AND ORGANIZATION	EVIDENCE AND ELABORATION	CONVENTIONS
☐ Provides an introduction that clearly states a central idea about how fear can overcome reason.	☐ Includes specific details and descriptions to create a vivid picture of events and characters.	☐ Attends to the norms and conventions of the discipline, especially using descriptive details and precise language.
☐ Creates a smooth progression of ideas with appropriate transitions.	☐ Includes an anecdote or brief story that supports the central idea of the essay.	
☐ Presents a strong conclusion that follows from and reflects on the ideas and insights in the essay.	☐ Establishes a clear point of view.	

🔗 WORD NETWORK

Include interesting words from your Word Network in your explanatory essay.

▤ STANDARDS

Writing
• Use appropriate and varied transitions to link the major sections of the text, create cohesion, and clarify the relationships among complex ideas and concepts.
• Provide a concluding statement or section that follows from and supports the information or explanation presented.
• Develop and strengthen writing as needed by planning, revising, editing, rewriting, or trying a new approach, focusing on addressing what is most significant for a specific purpose and audience.

Revising for Focus and Organization

Strengthen Your Conclusion Reread your essay, making sure you have set out your central idea in the introduction, developed it thoroughly in the body of your essay, and restated it in your conclusion. If your conclusion seems disconnected from the rest of the essay, consider these revision options:

- Reflect on the insights and ideas you expressed.
- Summarize your insights and ideas.
- Explain why the topic and your insights are important.

Revising for Evidence and Elaboration

Strengthen Transitions Make sure that the transitional words and phrases you use lead your reader logically from one idea to the next, or from an idea to its supporting evidence. Consider this abbreviated list of transitional expressions:

To introduce an example: *for example; to illustrate; in this case*
To introduce a second example: *in addition; furthermore; similarly*
To indicate cause and effect: *as a result; consequently; for this reason*
To indicate emphasis: *above all; in fact; certainly*

There are numerous transitional words, phrases, and expressions in English. Consult a style handbook or other resource to make sure you have chosen the ones that best express your meaning. Add or replace transitions in your essay as needed.

PEER REVIEW

Exchange essays with a classmate. Use the checklist to evaluate your classmate's essay and provide supportive feedback.

1. Does the introduction clearly present the central point of the essay?

☐ yes ☐ no If no, explain what confused you.

2. Are the ideas and evidence, including an anecdote or other narrative, sequenced logically?

☐ yes ☐ no If no, what about the sequence did not work?

3. Does the conclusion flow directly from the writer's insights and reflections about how fear can overcome reason?

☐ yes ☐ no If no, explain what you thought was missing.

4. What is the strongest part of your classmate's essay? Why?

_____

_____

_____

_____

Editing and Proofreading

Edit for Conventions Reread your draft for accuracy and consistency. Correct errors in grammar and word usage. Edit to include a variety of sentence structures so that your essay reads well.

Proofread for Accuracy Read your draft carefully, looking for errors in spelling and punctuation. Quotation marks should surround a speaker's exact words or thoughts.

Publishing and Presenting

Create a final version of your explanatory essay. Share it with a small group so that your classmates can read it and make comments. In turn, review and comment on your classmates' work. Afterward, discuss what your different essays suggest about the ways in which one's imagination may overcome reason. Take turns speaking during the discussion.

Reflecting

Think about what you learned while writing your essay. What did you learn about planning your draft that you would use when writing another essay? What would you work to improve in your next essay? Finally, how did your combining explanation with narrative evidence help you understand imagination and reason better?

▤ STANDARDS
Writing
Develop and strengthen writing as needed by planning, revising, editing, rewriting, or trying a new approach, focusing on addressing what is most significant for a specific purpose and audience.

ESSENTIAL QUESTION:
What is the allure of fear?

In real life, fear is useful because it keeps us from doing dangerous things. However, there are other dimensions to fear that seem less logical. For example, what draws us to go on scary roller coasters? Why do we enjoy literature, movies, and art that let us dabble in our fears? The selections you will read present different answers to these questions. You will work in a group to continue exploring the allure of fear.

Small-Group Learning Strategies

Throughout your life, in school, in your community, and in your career, you will continue to develop strategies when you work in teams.

Review these strategies and the actions you can take to practice them. Add ideas of your own for each step. Get ready to use these strategies during Small-Group Learning.

STRATEGY	ACTION PLAN
Prepare	• Complete your assignments so that you are prepared for group work. • Organize your thinking so you can contribute to your group's discussion. •
Participate fully	• Make eye contact to signal that you are listening and taking in what is being said. • Use text evidence. •
Support others	• Build off ideas from others in your group. • Invite others who have not yet spoken to do so. •
Clarify	• Paraphrase the ideas of others to ensure that your understanding is correct. • Ask follow-up questions. •

SCAN FOR
MULTIMEDIA

CONTENTS

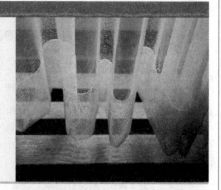

PERFORMANCE TASK

SPEAKING AND LISTENING FOCUS
Deliver an Explanatory Presentation
The Small-Group readings deal with our fears and how we may sometimes invite fear into our lives. After reading, you will produce a presentation on why we sometimes enjoy letting our imaginations get the best of us.

Working as a Team

1. **Choose a topic** In your group, discuss the following question:

    ### Does the emotion of fear make us stronger or weaker?

    As you take turns sharing your responses, be sure to provide details to explain your position. After all group members have shared, discuss some of the circumstances in which fear might make us stronger or weaker.

2. **List Your Rules** As a group, decide on the rules that you will follow as you work together. Samples are provided; add two more of your own. As you work together, you may add or revise the rules based on your experience working together.

    • Everyone should participate in group discussions.

    • People should not interrupt.

    • _____

    _____

    • _____

    _____

3. **Apply the Rules** Share what you have learned about the literature of fear. Make sure each person in the group contributes. Take notes and be prepared to share with the class one thing that you heard from another member of your group.

4. **Name Your Group** Choose a name that reflects the unit topic.

    Our group's name: _____

5. **Create a Communication Plan** Decide how you want to communicate with one another. For example, you might use online collaboration tools, email, or instant messaging.

    Our group's decision: _____

    _____

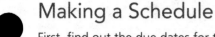

Making a Schedule

First, find out the due dates for the Small-Group activities. Then, preview the texts and activities with your group, and make a schedule for completing the tasks.

SELECTION	ACTIVITIES	DUE DATE
Where Is Here?		
The Dream Collector		
Why Do Some Brains Enjoy Fear?		
beware: do not read this poem The Raven Windigo		

Working on Group Projects

As your group works together, you'll find it more effective if each person has a specific role. Different projects require different roles. Before beginning a project, discuss the necessary roles, and choose one for each group member. Here are some possible roles; add your own ideas.

Project Manager: monitors the schedule and keeps everyone on task

Researcher: organizes research activities

Recorder: takes notes during group meetings

_____

_____

_____

_____

_____

SCAN FOR
MULTIMEDIA

About the Author

Joyce Carol Oates
(b. 1937) began writing novels at age fourteen when she received a typewriter as a gift. In 1960, she graduated first in her class from Syracuse University. Oates, who teaches at Princeton University, is famous for having wide-ranging interests. She has written novels, short stories, poetry, plays, and essays in many different styles and genres. Her writing often combines the small matters of everyday life with violence and horror.

Where Is Here?

Concept Vocabulary

As you perform your first read of "Where Is Here?" you will encounter the following words.

> gregarious   amiably   stoical

Context Clues If these words are unfamiliar to you, try using **context clues**—other words and phrases that appear in the text—to help you determine their meanings. There are various types of context clues that may help you as you read. This box shows three examples.

> **Synonyms:** The recent **dearth** of milk has resulted in a <u>shortage</u> of other dairy products.
>
> **Elaborating Details:** During her campaign, the senator was positively **monomaniacal**, <u>speaking passionately about one issue and one issue only</u>.
>
> **Contrast of Ideas:** The <u>shallowness</u> of the second speech made the **profundity** of the first even more evident.

Apply your knowledge of context clues and other vocabulary strategies to determine the meanings of unfamiliar words you encounter during your first read.

First Read FICTION

Apply these strategies as you conduct your first read. You will have an opportunity to complete a close read after your first read.

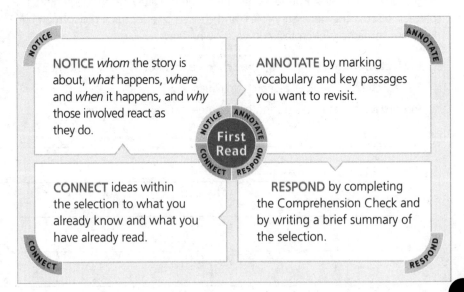

NOTICE *whom* the story is about, *what* happens, *where* and *when* it happens, and *why* those involved react as they do.

ANNOTATE by marking vocabulary and key passages you want to revisit.

CONNECT ideas within the selection to what you already know and what you have already read.

RESPOND by completing the Comprehension Check and by writing a brief summary of the selection.

STANDARDS

Reading Literature
By the end of grade 10, read and comprehend literature, including stories, dramas, and poems at the high end of the grades 9–10 text complexity band independently and proficiently.

Language
• Determine or clarify the meaning of unknown and multiple-meaning words and phrases based on *grades 9–10 reading and content*, choosing flexibly from a range of strategies.

• Use context as a clue to the meaning of a word or phrase.

Where Is Here?
Joyce Carol Oates

BACKGROUND

The novels of Ann Radcliffe, an English writer, and the short stories of Edgar Allan Poe inspired Joyce Carol Oates to write Gothic literature. "Horror is a fact of life," she has said. "As a writer I'm fascinated by all facets of life." In this story, Oates highlights the uncertainty and potential danger that lurk under the surface of everyday events.

SCAN FOR MULTIMEDIA

1   For years they had lived without incident in their house in a quiet residential neighborhood when, one November evening at dusk, the doorbell rang, and the father went to answer it, and there on his doorstep stood a man he had never seen before. The stranger apologized for disturbing him at what was probably the dinner hour and explained that he'd once lived in the house—"I mean, I was a child in this house"—and since he was in the city on business he thought he would drop by. He had not seen the house since January 1949 when he'd been eleven years old and his widowed mother had sold it and moved away but, he said, he thought of it often, dreamt of it often, and never more powerfully than in recent months. The father said, "Would you like to come inside for a few minutes and look around?" The stranger hesitated, then said firmly, "I think I'll just poke around outside for a while, if you don't mind. That might be sufficient." He was in his late forties, the father's approximate age. He wore a dark suit, conservatively cut; he was hatless, with thin silver-tipped neatly combed hair; a plain, sober, intelligent face and frowning eyes. The father, reserved by nature, but genial and even gregarious when taken unaware, said amiably, "Of course we don't mind. But I'm afraid many things have changed since 1949."

2   So, in the chill, damp, deepening dusk, the stranger wandered around the property while the mother set the dining room table and the father peered covertly out the window. The children were upstairs in their rooms. "Where is he now?" the mother asked. "He just went into the garage," the father said. "The garage! What does he want in

NOTES

Mark context clues or indicate another strategy you used that helped you determine meaning.

gregarious (gruh GAIR ee uhs) *adj.*

MEANING:

amiably (AY mee uh blee) *adv.*

MEANING:

there?" the mother said uneasily. "Maybe you'd better go out there with him." "He wouldn't want anyone with him," the father said. He moved stealthily to another window, peering through the curtains. A moment passed in silence. The mother, paused in the act of setting down plates, neatly folded paper napkins, and stainless-steel cutlery, said impatiently, "And where is he now? I don't like this." The father said, "Now he's coming out of the garage," and stepped back hastily from the window. "Is he going now?" the mother asked. "I wish I'd answered the door." The father watched for a moment in silence then said, "He's headed into the backyard." "Doing what?" the mother asked. "Not *doing* anything, just walking," the father said. "He seems to have a slight limp." "Is he an older man?" the mother asked. "I didn't notice," the father confessed. "Isn't that just like you!" the mother said.

3   She went on worriedly, "He could be anyone, after all. Any kind of thief, or mentally disturbed person, or even murderer. Ringing our doorbell like that with no warning and you don't even know what he looks like!"

4   The father had moved to another window and stood quietly watching, his cheek pressed against the glass. "He's gone down to the old swings. I hope he won't sit in one of them, for memory's sake, and try to swing—the posts are rotted almost through." The mother drew breath to speak but sighed instead, as if a powerful current of feeling had surged through her. The father was saying, "Is it possible he remembers those swings from his childhood? I can't believe they're actually that old." The mother said vaguely, "They were old when we bought the house." The father said, "But we're talking about forty years or more, and that's a long time." The mother sighed again, involuntarily. "Poor man!" she murmured. She was standing before her table but no longer seeing it. In her hand were objects—forks, knives, spoons—she could not have named. She said, "We can't bar the door against him. That would be cruel." The father said, "What? No one has barred any door against anyone." "Put yourself in his place," the mother said. "He told me he didn't *want* to come inside," the father said. "Oh—isn't that just like you!" the mother said in exasperation.

5   Without a further word she went to the back door and called out for the stranger to come inside, if he wanted, when he had finished looking around outside.

6   They introduced themselves rather shyly, giving names, and forgetting names, in the confusion of the moment. The stranger's handshake was cool and damp and tentative. He was smiling hard, blinking moisture from his eyes; it was clear that entering his childhood home was enormously exciting yet intimidating to him. Repeatedly he said, "It's so nice of you to invite me in—I truly hate to disturb you—I'm really so grateful, and so—" But the perfect word eluded him. As he spoke his eyes darted about the kitchen almost like eyes out of control. He stood in an odd stiff posture, hands gripping the lapels of his suit as if he meant to crush them. The mother,

meaning to break the awkward silence, spoke warmly of their satisfaction with the house and with the neighborhood, and the father concurred, but the stranger listened only politely, and continued to stare, and stare hard. Finally he said that the kitchen had been so changed—"so modernized"—he almost didn't recognize it. The floor tile, the size of the windows, something about the position of the cupboards—all were different. But the sink was in the same place of course; and the refrigerator and stove; and the door leading down to the basement—"That *is* the door leading down to the basement, isn't it?" He spoke strangely, staring at the door. For a moment it appeared he might ask to be shown the basement but the moment passed, fortunately—this was not a part of their house the father and mother would have been comfortable showing to a stranger.

7   Finally, making an effort to smile, the stranger said, "Your kitchen is so—pleasant." He paused. For a moment it seemed he had nothing further to say. Then, "A—controlled sort of place. My mother— When we lived here—" His words trailed off into a dreamy silence and the mother and father glanced at each other with carefully neutral expressions.

8   On the windowsill above the sink were several lushly blooming African violet plants in ceramic pots and these the stranger made a show of admiring. Impulsively he leaned over to sniff the flowers— "Lovely!"—though African violets have no smell. As if embarrassed, he said, "Mother too had plants on this windowsill but I don't recall them ever blooming."

9   The mother said tactfully, "Oh, they were probably the kind that don't bloom—like ivy."

10   In the next room, the dining room, the stranger appeared to be even more deeply moved. For some time he stood staring, wordless. With fastidious slowness he turned on his heel, blinking, and frowning, and tugging at his lower lip in a rough gesture that must have hurt. Finally, as if remembering the presence of his hosts, and the necessity for some display of civility, the stranger expressed his admiration for the attractiveness of the room, and its coziness. He'd remembered it as cavernous, with a ceiling twice as high. "And dark most of the time," he said wonderingly. "Dark by day, dark by night." The mother turned the lights of the little brass chandelier to their fullest: shadows were dispersed like ragged ghosts and the cut-glass fruit bowl at the center of the table glowed like an exquisite multifaceted jewel. The stranger exclaimed in surprise. He'd extracted a handkerchief from his pocket and was dabbing carefully at his face, where beads of perspiration shone. He said, as if thinking aloud, still wonderingly, "My father was a unique man. Everyone who knew him admired him. He sat *here*," he said, gingerly touching the chair that was in fact the father's chair, at one end of the table. "And Mother sat *there*," he said, merely pointing. "I don't recall my own place or my sister's but I suppose it doesn't matter. . . . I see you have four place settings, Mrs. . . . ? Two children, I suppose?" "A boy

eleven, and a girl thirteen," the mother said. The stranger stared not at her but at the table, smiling. "And so too *we* were—I mean, there were two of us: my sister and me."

11   The mother said, as if not knowing what else to say, "Are you—close?"

12   The stranger shrugged, distractedly rather than rudely, and moved on to the living room.

13   This room, cozily lit as well, was the most carefully furnished room in the house. Deep-piled wall-to-wall carpeting in hunter green, cheerful chintz[1] drapes, a sofa and matching chairs in nubby heather green, framed reproductions of classic works of art, a gleaming gilt-framed mirror over the fireplace: wasn't the living room impressive as a display in a furniture store? But the stranger said nothing at first. Indeed, his eyes narrowed sharply as if he were confronted with a disagreeable spectacle. He whispered, "Here too! Here too!"

14   He went to the fireplace, walking, now, with a decided limp; he drew his fingers with excruciating slowness along the mantel as if testing its materiality. For some time he merely stood, and stared, and listened. He tapped a section of wall with his knuckles—"There used to be a large water stain here, like a shadow."

15   "Was there?" murmured the father out of politeness, and "Was there!" murmured the mother. Of course, neither had ever seen a water stain there.

16   Then, noticing the window seat, the stranger uttered a soft surprised cry, and went to sit in it. He appeared delighted: hugging his knees like a child trying to make himself smaller. "This was one of my happy places! At least when Father wasn't home. I'd hide away here for hours, reading, daydreaming, staring out the window! Sometimes Mother would join me, if she was in the mood, and we'd plot together—oh, all sorts of fantastical things!" The stranger remained sitting in the window seat for so long, tears shining in his eyes, that the father and mother almost feared he'd forgotten them. He was stroking the velvet fabric of the cushioned seat, gropingly touching the leaded windowpanes. Wordlessly, the father and mother exchanged a glance: who was this man, and how could they tactfully get rid of him? The father made a face signaling impatience and the mother shook her head without seeming to move it. For they couldn't be rude to a guest in their house.

17   The stranger was saying in a slow, dazed voice, "It all comes back to me now. How could I have forgotten! Mother used to read to me, and tell me stories, and ask me riddles I couldn't answer. 'What creature walks on four legs in the morning, two legs at midday, three legs in the evening?' 'What is round, and flat, measuring mere inches in one direction, and infinity in the other?' 'Out of what does our life arise? Out of what does our consciousness arise? Why are we here? Where *is* here?'"

---

1. **chintz** *n.* printed cotton fabric used especially for curtains and upholstery.

18   The father and mother were perplexed by these strange words and hardly knew how to respond. The mother said uncertainly, "Our daughter used to like to sit there too, when she was younger. It *is* a lovely place." The father said with surprising passion, "I hate riddles—they're moronic some of the time and obscure the rest of the time." He spoke with such uncharacteristic rudeness, the mother looked at him in surprise.

19   Hurriedly she said, "Is your mother still living, Mr. . . . ?" "Oh no. Not at all," the stranger said, rising abruptly from the window seat, and looking at the mother as if she had said something mildly preposterous. "I'm sorry," the mother said. "Please don't be," the stranger said. "We've all been dead—*they've* all been dead—a long time."

20   The stranger's cheeks were deeply flushed as if with anger and his breath was quickened and audible.

21   The visit might have ended at this point but so clearly did the stranger expect to continue on upstairs, so purposefully, indeed almost defiantly, did he limp his way to the stairs, neither the father nor the mother knew how to dissuade him. It was as if a force of nature, benign at the outset, now uncontrollable, had swept its way into their house! The mother followed after him saying nervously, "I'm not sure what condition the rooms are in, upstairs. The children's rooms especially—" The stranger muttered that he did not care in the slightest about the condition of the household and continued on up without a backward glance.

22   The father, his face burning with resentment and his heart accelerating as if in preparation for combat, had no choice but to follow the stranger and the mother up the stairs. He was flexing and unflexing his fingers as if to rid them of stiffness.

23   On the landing, the stranger halted abruptly to examine a stained-glass fanlight—"My God, I haven't thought of this in years!" He spoke excitedly of how, on tiptoe, he used to stand and peek out through the diamonds of colored glass, red, blue, green, golden yellow: seeing with amazement the world outside so *altered*. "After such a lesson it's hard to take the world on its own terms, isn't it?" he asked. The father asked, annoyed, "On what terms should it be taken, then?" The stranger replied, regarding him levelly, with a just perceptible degree of disdain, "Why, none at all."

24   It was the son's room—by coincidence, the stranger's old room—the stranger most wanted to see. Other rooms on the second floor, the "master" bedroom in particular, he decidedly did not want to see. As he spoke of it, his mouth twitched as if he had been offered something repulsive to eat.

25   The mother hurried on ahead to warn the boy to straighten up his room a bit. No one had expected a visitor this evening! "So you have two children," the stranger murmured, looking at the father with a small quizzical smile. "Why?" The father stared at him as if he hadn't heard correctly. "'Why'?" he asked. "Yes. *Why?*" the stranger repeated. They looked at each other for a long strained moment, then

the stranger said quickly, "But you love them—of course." The father controlled his temper and said, biting off his words, "Of course."

26   "Of course, of course," the stranger murmured, tugging at his necktie and loosening his collar, "otherwise it would all come to an end." The two men were of approximately the same height but the father was heavier in the shoulders and torso; his hair had thinned more severely so that the scalp of the crown was exposed, flushed, damp with perspiration, sullenly alight.

27   With a stiff avuncular[2] formality the stranger shook the son's hand. "So this is your room, now! So you live here, now!" he murmured, as if the fact were an astonishment. Not used to shaking hands, the boy was stricken with shyness and cast his eyes down. The stranger limped past him, staring. "The same!—the same!—walls, ceiling, floor—window—" He drew his fingers slowly along the windowsill; around the frame; rapped the glass, as if, again, testing materiality; stooped to look outside—but it was night, and nothing but his reflection bobbed in the glass, ghostly and insubstantial. He groped against the walls, he opened the closet door before the mother could protest, he sat heavily on the boy's bed, the springs creaking beneath him. He was panting, red-faced, dazed. "And the ceiling overhead,"

---

2. **avuncular** (uh VUHN kyoo luhr) *adj.* having traits considered typical of uncles; jolly, indulgent, stodgy.

he whispered. He nodded slowly and repeatedly, smiling. "And the floor beneath. That is what *is*."

28 He took out his handkerchief again and fastidiously wiped his face. He made a visible effort to compose himself.

29 The father, in the doorway, cleared his throat and said, "I'm afraid it's getting late—it's almost six."

30 The mother said, "Oh yes I'm afraid—I'm afraid it *is* getting late. There's dinner, and the children have their homework—"

31 The stranger got to his feet. At his full height he stood for a precarious moment swaying, as if the blood had drained from his head and he was in danger of fainting. But he steadied himself with a hand against the slanted dormer ceiling. He said, "Oh yes!—I know!—I've disturbed you terribly!—you've been so *kind*." It seemed, surely, as if the stranger *must* leave now, but, as chance had it, he happened to spy, on the boy's desk, an opened mathematics textbook and several smudged sheets of paper, and impulsively offered to show the boy a mathematical riddle—"You can take it to school tomorrow and surprise your teacher!"

32 So, out of dutiful politeness, the son sat down at his desk and the stranger leaned familiarly over him, demonstrating adroitly with a ruler and a pencil how "what we call 'infinity'" can be contained within a small geometrical figure on a sheet of paper. "First you draw a square; then you draw a triangle to fit inside the square; then you draw a second triangle, and a third, and a fourth, each to fit inside the square, but without their points coinciding, and as you continue—here, son, I'll show you—give me your hand, and I'll show you—the border of the triangles' common outline gets more complex and measures larger, and larger, and larger—and soon you'll need a magnifying glass to see the details, and then you'll need a microscope, and so on and so forth, forever, laying triangles neatly down to fit inside the original square *without their points coinciding*—!" The stranger spoke with increasing fervor; spittle gleamed in the corners of his mouth. The son stared at the geometrical shapes rapidly materializing on the sheet of paper before him with no seeming comprehension but with a rapt staring fascination as if he dared not look away.

33 After several minutes of this the father came abruptly forward and dropped his hand on the stranger's shoulder. "The visit is over," he said calmly. It was the first time since they'd shaken hands that the two men had touched, and the touch had a galvanic[3] effect upon the stranger: he dropped ruler and pencil at once, froze in his stooped posture, burst into frightened tears.

34 Now the visit truly was over; the stranger, at last, *was* leaving, having wiped away his tears and made a **stoical** effort to compose himself; but on the doorstep, to the father's astonishment, he made a final, preposterous appeal—he wanted to see the basement. "Just to sit on

Mark context clues or indicate another strategy you used that helped you determine meaning.

stoical (STOH ih kuhl) *adj.*

MEANING:

___

3. **galvanic** (gal VAN ihk) *adj.* startling; stimulating as if by electric current.

the stairs? In the dark? For a few quiet minutes? And you could close the door and forget me, you and your family could have your dinner and—"

35 The stranger was begging but the father was resolute. Without raising his voice he said, "No. *The visit is over.*"

36 He shut the door, and locked it.

37 Locked it! His hands were shaking and his heart beat angrily.

38 He watched the stranger walk away—out to the sidewalk, out to the street, disappearing in the darkness. Had the streetlights gone out?

39 Behind the father the mother stood apologetic and defensive, wringing her hands in a classic stance. "Wasn't that sad! Wasn't that—*sad!* But we had no choice but to let him in, it was the only decent thing to do." The father pushed past her without comment. In the living room he saw that the lights were flickering as if on the brink of going out; the patterned wallpaper seemed drained of color; a shadow lay upon it shaped like a bulbous cloud or growth. Even the robust green of the carpeting looked faded. Or was it an optical illusion? Everywhere the father looked, a pulse beat mute with rage. "*I* wasn't the one who opened the door to that man in the first place," the mother said, coming up behind the father and touching his arm. Without seeming to know what he did the father violently jerked his arm and thrust her away.

40 "Shut up. We'll forget it," he said.

41 "But—"

42 "*We'll forget it.*"

43 The mother entered the kitchen walking slowly as if she'd been struck a blow. In fact, a bruise the size of a pear would materialize on her forearm by morning. When she reached out to steady herself she misjudged the distance of the doorframe—or did the doorframe recede an inch or two—and nearly lost her balance.

44 In the kitchen the lights were dim and an odor of sourish smoke, subtle but unmistakable, made her nostrils pinch.

45 She slammed open the oven door. Grabbed a pair of pot holders with insulated linings. "I wasn't the one, . . ." she cried, panting, "and you know it." ❧

Comprehension Check

Complete the following items after you finish your first read. Review and clarify details with your group.

1. Why has the stranger come to visit the house?

2. What are the initial suspicions that the mother has about the stranger?

3. How does the stranger react when the father tells him, "The visit is over"?

4. How do the rooms of the house seem changed after the stranger's visit?

5. **Notebook** Choose four key events that best capture the plot of the story. Write a summary of the story based on these four events.

- -

RESEARCH

Research to Clarify Choose at least one unfamiliar detail from the text. Briefly research that detail. In what way does the information you learned shed light on an aspect of the story?

Research to Explore This story may spark your curiosity to learn more about the author or the genre. Briefly research a topic that interests you. You may want to share what you learn with your group.

WHERE IS HERE?

Close Read the Text

With your group, revisit sections of the text you marked during your first read. **Annotate** details that you notice. What **questions** do you have? What can you **conclude**?

Analyze the Text

> **CITE TEXTUAL EVIDENCE**
> to support your answers.

Complete the activities.

1. **Review and Clarify** With your group, reread paragraph 25. The stranger discovers the father has two children and asks, "Why?" Do you find that question unsettling? Explain.

2. **Present and Discuss** Now, work with your group to share other key passages from "Where Is Here?" What made you choose these particular passages? Take turns presenting your passages. Discuss what details you noticed, what questions you asked, and what conclusions you reached.

3. **Essential Question: *What is the allure of fear?*** What has this selection taught you about portrayals of fear in literature? Discuss with your group.

LANGUAGE DEVELOPMENT

Concept Vocabulary

gregarious	amiably	stoical

Why These Words? The three concept vocabulary words are related. With your group, determine what the words have in common. How do these word choices enhance the impact of the text?

Practice

🔲 **Notebook** Confirm your understanding of each word by using it in a sentence. Be sure to use context clues that suggest the word's meaning.

Word Study

🔲 **Notebook Adverbs of Manner** An **adverb** is a word that modifies a verb, an adjective, or another adverb. Many adverbs, particularly those describing the manner in which an action verb is performed, are formed by adding the Anglo-Saxon suffix *-ly* to an adjective. Sometimes, the addition of this suffix requires a change in the ending of the adjective. For instance, the father in "Where Is Here?" states something *amiably*—or in an *amiable* manner.

Reread paragraph 2 of the story. Mark the adverbs ending in *-ly*. Then, write the adjectives from which they are formed.

Sidebar

TIP

GROUP DISCUSSION
Keep in mind that there is no "correct" interpretation of certain stories. In these cases, the author deliberately leaves some questions unanswered. As a reader, you should use clues in the text and reasoning to come up with your interpretations or answers to these questions.

⊞ **WORD NETWORK**
Add words related to fear from the text to your Word Network.

▤ **STANDARDS**
Reading Literature
Analyze how an author's choices concerning how to structure a text, order events within it, and manipulate time (e.g., pacing, flashbacks) create such effects.

Language
• Spell correctly.
• Identify and correctly use patterns of word changes that indicate different meanings or parts of speech.

Analyze Craft and Structure

Literary Style Through the use of gloomy settings, suffering characters, supernatural events, and sudden plot twists, traditional Gothic writers such as Edgar Allan Poe constructed stories of imagination, fear, and horror. Today, **modern Gothic** writers still produce stories marked by fear and dread. However, they modify elements to suit modern tastes and ideas.

LITERARY ELEMENT	TRADITIONAL GOTHIC	MODERN GOTHIC
Setting	Remote, exotic settings, such as a gloomy mansion or castle	Ordinary places, which may make strange events more unsettling
Characters	Strange, eccentric people, often of high social standing	Ordinary people, to whom readers can easily relate
Plot Events	Unusual occurrences involving violence or supernatural elements	Situations in which normal life is interrupted in disturbing ways
Endings	Dramatic endings that fully resolve the dark, scary events	Ambiguous endings that leave questions unanswered

The effect of these shifts is to relocate the source of readers' fear. Modern Gothic literature does not allow readers a comfortable distance from dark situations. Instead, the unusual events feel as if they could happen to us.

Practice

CITE TEXTUAL EVIDENCE to support your answers.

Work individually to identify details in "Where Is Here?" that relate to each literary element. Then, discuss your choices with your group. Focus especially on your interpretations of the ambiguous ending.

LITERARY ELEMENTS	DETAILS FROM "WHERE IS HERE?"
Setting	
Characters	
Events	
Ending	

WHERE IS HERE?

Author's Style

Character Development Conversation between characters in a story, or **dialogue,** is one of the tools fiction writers use to make their characters come alive on the page. Authors use dialogue to show readers what characters are like, how they interact with others, how they feel about their situations, and what motivates them. Consider this example from "Where Is Here?":

Example of Dialogue: The stranger hesitated, then said firmly, "I think I'll just poke around outside for a while, if you don't mind. That might be sufficient."

How It Develops Character: Paired with descriptive elements, such as the idea that the stranger "hesitated" but then spoke "firmly," the dialogue reveals that the stranger is polite, well-spoken, and nervous.

Read It

Work individually. Use this chart to analyze the mother in "Where Is Here?" Explain what you learn about her character from each example of dialogue. Then, compare your responses to those of your group.

DIALOGUE	HOW IT DEVELOPS CHARACTER
"Isn't that just like you!" the mother said. *She went on worriedly, "He could be anyone, after all. Any kind of thief, or mentally disturbed person, or even murderer. Ringing our doorbell like that with no warning and you don't even know what he looks like!"*	
The mother sighed again, involuntarily. "Poor man!" she murmured. She was standing before her table but no longer seeing it. In her hand were objects—forks, knives, spoons—she could not have named. She said, "We can't bar the door against him. That would be cruel."	
"I wasn't the one who opened the door to that man in the first place," the mother said, coming up behind the father and touching his arm.	

Write It

📓 **Notebook** Write a paragraph in which you describe an interaction between two people. They may be fictional or real. Use dialogue to make the interaction come alive.

:≡ STANDARDS

Reading Literature
Analyze how complex characters develop over the course of a text, interact with other characters, and advance the plot or develop the theme.

Writing
Write narratives to develop real or imagined experiences or events using effective technique, well-chosen details, and well-structured event sequences.

Writing to Sources

Every work of fiction is set in a particular time and place. In our imaginations, though, the characters exist before and after the story.

Assignment

With your group, write a brief **narrative** that extends the scope of "Where Is Here?" Make sure that your narrative stays true to the characterizations, style, and tone of the story. Choose one of the following topics:

☐ Write a **prequel** that reveals the stranger's past. Who is he, and which details of the story he tells to the family are true? What is the stranger's goal in visiting the house—does he simply want to see his home again, or does he have another, more sinister reason for wanting to return?

☐ Write a **sequel** in which the stranger returns to the house after some time has passed. How has he changed, having seen his childhood home earlier? How is he greeted by the family this time? Are the mother and father more or less suspicious of him and his motives?

☐ Write a **police report** filed after the stranger leaves. Imagine that the mother and father call the police to report the incident. What kinds of questions are the police likely to ask about the stranger? What kinds of answers are they likely to receive?

Project Plan Use this chart to plan your narrative. In the middle column, plan the action. In the right-hand column, explain the goal of each paragraph. Follow the chart to draft the narrative, and then present your narrative to the class. Have different group members read portions of the narrative aloud.

🖉 EVIDENCE LOG

Before moving on to a new selection, go to your Evidence Log and record what you learned from "Where Is Here?"

PARAGRAPH	WHAT HAPPENS	NARRATIVE GOAL
1		
2		
3		
4		

About the Photographer

As a teenager in the Coney Island section of Brooklyn, New York, **Arthur Tress** (b. 1940) liked to photograph the neighborhood's dilapidated amusement parks in various states of disrepair. His style combines improvised elements of everyday life with the theatrical and is referred to as "magical realism." Tress has worked as a photographer for more than 50 years, and he has traveled the world, often photographing people he meets along the way.

from The Dream Collector

Media Vocabulary

The following words will be useful to you as you analyze, discuss, and write about photographs.

Composition: arrangement of the parts of a photograph; the *foreground* is closer to the viewer, whereas the *background* is farther away	• The composition may stress one part of an image more than another. • The composition may show what the photographer thinks is important in the subject.
Perspective or Angle: vantage point from which a photograph is taken	• The camera may be looking down, looking up, or looking head-on at the subject. • The subject may seem very far away, at a middle distance, or very close.
Lighting and Color: use of light, shadow, and color in a photograph	• Some images are full color, whereas others are black and white. • Some parts of an image may be brighter or darker than others.
Subject: primary figure(s), object(s), or other content in a photograph	• The subject may be a person or group of people, often in the foreground. • Alternatively, the subject may be an object, a set of objects, or an entire location.
Location: place or scene in which a photograph is taken	• The location may be indoors, in a particular type of building or context. • Alternatively, the location may be outdoors, and it might be obvious or subtle in its details.

First Review MEDIA: ART AND PHOTOGRAPHY

Apply these strategies as you conduct your first review. You will have an opportunity to complete a close review after your first review.

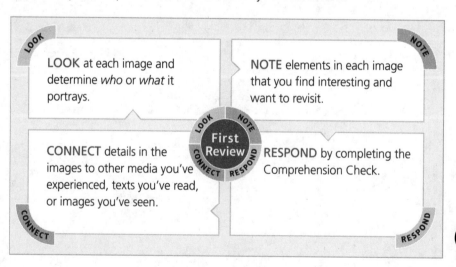

LOOK at each image and determine *who* or *what* it portrays.

NOTE elements in each image that you find interesting and want to revisit.

CONNECT details in the images to other media you've experienced, texts you've read, or images you've seen.

RESPOND by completing the Comprehension Check.

from The Dream Collector

Arthur Tress

BACKGROUND

Photographer Arthur Tress began working on his study of the unconscious mind in the late 1960s by interviewing children about their most memorable dreams. At the time, photography that documented real events was still the dominant form of the medium, and there was some prejudice against staged photography. Tress's photographs from *The Dream Collector* helped elevate the art of photography, and many photographers since have acknowledged their debt to his work.

SCAN FOR MULTIMEDIA

© Copyright Arthur Tress 2015

PHOTO 1: *Flood Dream, Ocean City, New Jersey, 1971*

NOTES

NOTES

PHOTO 3: *Young Boy and Hooded Figure, New York City, 1971*

NOTES

PHOTO 4: *Girl With Dunce Cap, New York City, 1972*

NOTES

PHOTO 5: *Girl With Mask, Rhinebeck, 1972*

NOTES

PHOTO 6: *Boy in Burnt-Out Furniture Store, Newark, 1969*

NOTES

NOTES

Comprehension Check

Use the chart to note details in each of the photographs. Identify people, objects, location, and activities. Review and clarify details with your group.

PHOTO	PEOPLE	OBJECTS	LOCATION	ACTIVITIES
PHOTO 1				
PHOTO 2				
PHOTO 3				
PHOTO 4				
PHOTO 5				
PHOTO 6				
NOTES				

Close Review

With your group, revisit the photographs, your first-review notes, and the Comprehension Check chart. Record any new observations that seem important. What **questions** do you have? What can you **conclude**?

Analyze the Media

Complete the activities.

1. **Present and Discuss** Determine which photograph from the collection seems most closely related to the theme of fear. Prepare to justify your choice with specific details from the photo. Share your analysis with your group.

2. **Review and Synthesize** With your group, look over the photographs. Do they share a common style and theme? Defend or challenge the choice to group them together, citing specific details.

3. 📓 Notebook **Essential Question:** *What is the allure of fear?* What makes something alluring even when it is simultaneously frightening? How can images be particularly effective in getting to the root of this question? Support your responses with evidence from the photographs.

LANGUAGE DEVELOPMENT

Media Vocabulary

composition	lighting and color	location
perspective or angle	subject	

Use the vocabulary in your responses to the following questions.

1. In Photo 2, what is in the foreground? What is in the background? How does the position of the figure in the photo add to its impact?

2. In what ways do the figures shown in Photo 3 present a startling contrast? Explain.

3. In Photo 5, how does the position of the camera in relationship to the subject add to the photo's effect?

4. Which aspects of Photo 6 seem dreamlike, and which seem realistic? Explain.

■ STANDARDS

Speaking and Listening
• Make strategic use of digital media in presentations to enhance understanding of findings, reasoning, and evidence to add interest.
• Adapt speech to a variety of contexts and tasks, demonstrating command of formal English when indicated or appropriate.

Language
Acquire and use accurately general academic and domain-specific words and phrases, sufficient for reading, writing, speaking, and listening at the college and career readiness level; demonstrate independence in gathering vocabulary knowledge when considering a word or phrase important to comprehension or expression.

Speaking and Listening

Assignment

Create a **visual presentation** in which you incorporate both text and images. Choose from the following options.

☐ With your group, review the collection of photographs, and choose one you all prefer. Then, work independently to write a **narrative of a dream** that might accompany the photo you chose. Share your story with your group. Once your group has compiled a set of stories, present them to the class in an organized form.

☐ Working independently, write down a dream that you have had, or a fictional dream. Then, plan and take a **photograph** that you feel represents the dream. As a group, organize your dreams and images into a coherent presentation, and share it with the class.

☐ Imagine that you are responsible for convincing a museum to purchase one of these photos for its permanent collection. As a group, choose the photo you think the museum should purchase. Then, working independently, write a **letter** in which you describe the photo and explain why people should get the chance to see it. Organize your letters into a cohesive presentation, and share it with the class.

Writing From Photographs Working on your own, use the chart to identify elements of the photograph that you will reflect in your narrative, dream, or letter. Consider obvious qualities, such as the setting and large objects. Also, note subtler details—such as facial expressions, clothing, and gestures—that contribute to an effect you will capture in your writing.

IMAGE DESCRIPTION	MAIN ELEMENTS OF PHOTO	IMPORTANT DETAILS IN PHOTO

📝 EVIDENCE LOG

Before moving on to a new selection, go to your Evidence Log and record what you've learned from *The Dream Collector*.

About the Author

Allegra Ringo is a freelance writer and comedian based in Los Angeles, California. Her work includes articles, humorous essays, film reviews, and comedy sketches for the Upright Citizens Brigade Theatre. At California State University, Long Beach, where she completed her undergraduate degree in film, Ringo received the Women in Film Scholarship.

Why Do Some Brains Enjoy Fear?

Technical Vocabulary

As you perform your first read of the interview, you will encounter the following words.

stimulus	dissonance	cognitive

Familiar Word Parts When determining the meaning of an unfamiliar word, look for word parts—base words, roots, prefixes, and suffixes— that you know. Doing so may help you unlock word meanings. Here is an example of applying the strategy.

> **Unfamiliar Word:** *socialization*
>
> **Familiar Base Word:** *social,* meaning "having to do with being part of a group, community, or society."
>
> **Familiar Suffixes:** *-ize,* which forms verbs and means "to make" or "to become"; *-ation,* which forms abstract nouns
>
> **Conclusion:** Combining the meanings of these three familiar word parts, you can determine that the word *socialization* probably means "the process of becoming social, or part of a community."

Apply your knowledge of familiar word parts and other vocabulary strategies to determine the meanings of unfamiliar words you encounter during your first read.

First Read NONFICTION

Apply these strategies as you conduct your first read. You will have an opportunity to complete a close read after your first read.

NOTICE the general ideas of the text. *What* is it about? *Who* is involved?

ANNOTATE by marking vocabulary and key passages you want to revisit.

First Read

CONNECT ideas within the selection to what you already know and what you have already read.

RESPOND by completing the Comprehension Check and by writing a brief summary of the selection.

STANDARDS

Reading Informational Text
By the end of grade 10, read and comprehend literary nonfiction at the high end of the grades 9–10 text complexity band independently and proficiently.

Language
• Determine or clarify the meaning of unknown and multiple-meaning words and phrases based on *grades 9–10 reading and content,* choosing flexibly from a range of strategies.
• Identify and correctly use patterns of word changes that indicate different meanings or parts of speech.

Why Do Some Brains Enjoy Fear?

Allegra Ringo

BACKGROUND

As human beings, we are equipped with a variety of different survival mechanisms. One system detects danger. If we could not recognize dangerous situations, we would not be able to avoid them. For that reason, our brains are hard-wired to feel fear when we encounter a threat. Our fear response releases "fight or flight" chemicals into our bloodstreams, and these help make us stronger, quicker, and more alert. In other words, fear makes us ready to fight or flee.

SCAN FOR
MULTIMEDIA

NOTES

1　This time of year, thrillseekers can enjoy horror movies, haunted houses, and prices so low it's scary. But if fear is a natural survival response to a threat, or danger, why would we seek out that feeling?

2　　Dr. Margee Kerr is the staff sociologist at ScareHouse, a haunted house in Pittsburgh that takes all year to plan. She also teaches at Robert Morris University and Chatham University, and is the only person I've ever heard referred to as a "scare specialist." Dr. Kerr is an expert in the field of fear. I spoke with her about what fear is, and why some of us enjoy it so much.

Why do some people like the feeling of being scared, while others don't?

3　　Not everyone enjoys being afraid, and I don't think it's a stretch to say that no one wants to experience a truly life-threatening situation. But there are those of us (well, a lot of us) who really enjoy the experience. First, the natural high from the fight-or-flight response can feel great. There is strong evidence that this isn't just about personal choice, but our brain chemistry. New research from David Zald shows that people differ in their chemical response to thrilling situations. One of the main hormones released during scary and thrilling activities is dopamine, and it turns out some individuals may get more of a kick from this dopamine response than others do.

Basically, some people's brains lack what Zald describes as "brakes" on the dopamine release and re-uptake[1] in the brain. This means some people are going to really enjoy thrilling, scary, and risky situations while others, not so much.

4   Lots of people also enjoy scary situations because it leaves them with a sense of confidence after it's over. Think about the last time you made it through a scary movie, or through a haunted house. You might have thought, "Yes! I did it! I made it all the way through!" So it can be a real self-esteem boost. But again, self-scaring isn't for everyone, and there are lots of psychological and personal reasons someone may not enjoy scary situations. I've talked to more than a handful of people who will never set foot in a haunted house because they went to a haunt at a young age and were traumatized. I always recommend parents thoroughly check out the content and rating of a haunted attraction before bringing a child. The chemicals that are released during fight-or-flight can work like glue to build strong memories ("flashbulb memories") of scary experiences, and if you're too young to know the monsters are fake, it can be quite traumatic and something you'll never forget, in a bad way.

> To really enjoy a scary situation, we have to know we're in a safe environment.

What happens in our brains when we're scared? Is it different when we're scared "in a fun way" versus being actually afraid?

5   To really enjoy a scary situation, we have to know we're in a safe environment. It's all about triggering the amazing fight-or-flight response to experience the flood of adrenaline, endorphins, and dopamine, but in a completely safe space. Haunted houses are great at this—they deliver a startle scare by triggering one of our senses with different sounds, air blasts, and even smells. These senses are directly tied to our fear response and activate the physical reaction, but our brain has time to process the fact that these are not "real" threats. Our brain is lightning-fast at processing threat. I've seen the process thousands of times from behind the walls in ScareHouse—someone screams and jumps and then immediately starts laughing and smiling. It's amazing to observe. I'm really interested to see where our boundaries are in terms of when and how we really know or feel we're safe.

What qualities do "scary things" share across cultures, or does it vary widely?

6   One of the most interesting things about studying fear is looking at the social constructions of fear, and learned fears versus those fears

---

1. **re-uptake** *n.* reabsorption of a neurotransmitter. This process regulates the levels of a neurotransmitter in the body.

that appear to be more innate, or even genetic. When we look across time and across the world, we find that people truly can become afraid of anything. Through fear conditioning (connecting a neutral **stimulus** with a negative consequence), we can link pretty much anything to a fear response. Baby Albert, of course, is the exemplar case of this. The poor child was made deathly afraid of white rabbits in the 1920's, before researchers were required to be ethical. So we know that we can learn to fear, and this means our socialization and the society in which we are raised is going to have a lot to do with what we find scary.

7   Each culture has its own superhero monsters—the Chupacabra (South America), the Loch Ness Monster, the Yōkai (supernatural monsters from Japanese folklore), Alps (German nightmare creatures)—but they all have a number of characteristics in common. Monsters are defying the general laws of nature in some way. They have either returned from the afterlife (ghosts, demons, spirits) or they are some kind of nonhuman or semihuman creature. This speaks to the fact that things that violate the laws of nature are terrifying. And really anything that doesn't make sense or causes us some sort of **dissonance**, whether it is **cognitive** or aesthetic,[2] is going to be scary (axe-wielding animals, masked faces, contorted bodies).

8   Another shared characteristic of monsters across the globe is their blurred relationship with death and the body. Humans are obsessed with death; we simply have a hard time wrapping our mind around what happens when we die. This contemplation has led to some of the most famous monsters, with each culture creating their own version of the living dead, whether it's zombies, vampires, reanimated and reconstructed corpses, or ghosts. We want to imagine a life that goes on after we die. Or better yet, figure out a way to live forever. Again, though, that would violate the laws of nature and is therefore terrifying. So while the compositions and names of the monsters are different, the motivations and inspirations behind their constructions appear across the globe.

What are some early examples of people scaring themselves on purpose?

9   Humans have been scaring themselves and each other since the birth of the species, through all kinds of methods like storytelling, jumping off cliffs, and popping out to startle each other from the recesses of some dark cave. And we've done this for lots of different reasons—to build group unity, to prepare kids for life in the scary world, and, of course, to control behavior. But it's only really in the last few centuries that scaring ourselves for fun (and profit) has become a highly sought-after experience.

---

2. **aesthetic** (ehs THEHT ihk) *adj.* of or relating to art or beauty.

Mark familiar word parts or indicate another strategy you used that helped you determine meaning.

stimulus (STIHM yuh luhs) *n.*

MEANING:

> Things that violate the laws of nature are terrifying.

dissonance (DIHS uh nuhns) *n.*
MEANING:

cognitive (KOG nuh tihv) *adj.*
MEANING:

10   My favorite example of one of the early discoveries of the joys of self-scaring is actually found in the history of roller coasters. The Russian Ice Slides began, not surprisingly given the name, as extended sleigh rides down a snowy mountain in the mid-17th century. Much like they do today, riders would sit in sleds and speed down the mountain, which sometimes included additional man-made bumps to make it a little more exciting. The Russian Ice Slides became more sophisticated throughout the 18th century, with wooden beams and artificial mountains of ice. Eventually, instead of ice and sleds, tracks and carriages were constructed to carry screaming riders across the "Russian Mountains." Even more exhilarating terror came when innovative creators decided to paint scary scenes on the walls that shocked and thrilled riders as they passed by. These came to be known as "Dark Rides." People were terrified, but they loved it.

11   We haven't just enjoyed physical thrills—ghost stories were told around the campfire long before we had summer camps. The Graveyard Poets of the 18th century, who wrote of spiders, bats, and skulls, paved the road for the Gothic novelists of the 19th century, like Poe and Shelley. These scary stories provided, and continue to deliver, intrigue, exhilaration, and a jolt of excitement to our lives.

12   The 19th century also brought the precursors to the haunted attraction industry. Sideshows or "freak shows," and the museums and houses of "oddities" have existed since the mid-1800s. Perhaps the most notable is Barnum's American Museum, operated by P. T. Barnum, best known for being half of the Ringling Brothers and Barnum and Bailey Circus. His museum contained things like monkey torsos with fish tails attached, and other characters meant to frighten and startle. Much like modern haunts, customers would line up to challenge themselves and their resilience and dare each other to enter the freak shows and face the scary scenes and abnormalities. The haunted attraction industry has come a long way from fish tails and plastic bats—modern haunts incorporate Hollywood-quality sets, and a crazy amount of modern technology all designed to scare us silly.

There's a common belief that if you meet somebody for the first time in a fearful situation, you'll feel more attached or more attracted to that person than you would if you'd met them in a low-stress situation. Is there any truth to that?

13   One of the reasons people love Halloween is because it produces strong emotional responses, and those responses work to build stronger relationships and memories. When we're happy, or afraid, we're releasing powerful hormones, like oxytocin, that are working to make these moments stick in our brain. So we're going to remember the people we're with. If it was a good experience, then we'll remember them fondly and feel close to them, more so than if we

were to meet them during some neutral unexciting event. Shelley Taylor discussed this in her article "Tend and Befriend: Biobehavioral Bases of Affiliation Under Stress." She shows that we do build a special closeness with those we are with when we're in an excited state, and more importantly, that it can be a really good thing. We're social and emotional beings. We need each other in times of stress, so the fact that our bodies have evolved to make sure we feel close to those we are with when afraid makes sense. So yes, take your date to a haunted house or for a ride on a roller coaster; it'll be a night you'll never forget. 🙢

Comprehension Check

Complete the following items after you finish your first read. Review and clarify details with your group.

1. According to Dr. Kerr, how are our bodies affected by things that scare us?

2. According to Dr. Kerr, what critical information do we need to have in order to enjoy a scary situation?

3. What happened to Baby Albert?

4. 📓 **Notebook** Confirm your understanding of the text by writing a summary.

- -

RESEARCH

Research to Clarify Choose at least one unfamiliar detail from the text. Briefly research that detail. In what way does the information you learned shed light on an aspect of the interview?

Research to Explore This interview may spark your curiosity to learn more. Briefly research a topic from the text that interests you. Share what you discover with your group.

WHY DO SOME BRAINS
ENJOY FEAR?

Close Read the Text

With your group, revisit sections of the text you marked during your first read. **Annotate** details that you notice. What **questions** do you have? What can you **conclude**?

Close
Read

Analyze the Text

CITE TEXTUAL EVIDENCE
to support your answers.

📓 Notebook **Complete the activities.**

1. **Review and Clarify** With your group, reread paragraph 6 of the selection. How can fear be both "innate" and "learned"?

2. **Present and Discuss** Work with your group to share the passages from the selection that you found especially relevant. Take turns presenting your passages. Discuss what you noticed in the selection, what questions you asked, and what conclusions you reached.

3. **Essential Question: *What is the allure of fear?*** What has this selection taught you about portrayals of fear? Discuss with your group.

🔗 **WORD NETWORK**

Add words related to fear from the text to your Word Network.

LANGUAGE DEVELOPMENT

Technical Vocabulary

stimulus	dissonance	cognitive

Why These Words? The three technical vocabulary words are related. With your group, discuss the words, and determine the concept they share. How do these words contribute to your understanding of the text?

Practice

📓 Notebook Confirm your understanding of these words by using them in sentences. Include context clues that hint at each word's meaning.

Word Study

Patterns of Word Changes Many Latin roots can combine with both the suffix *-ion*, which forms abstract nouns, and the suffix *-ive*, which forms adjectives—creating a related pair of words. For instance, the abstract noun *cognition* and the related adjective *cognitive* are both formed from the root *-cognit-*, meaning "knowledge" or "thought."

Reread paragraph 10 of the interview. Mark the adjective ending in *-ive*, and write the abstract noun to which it is related.

Analyze Craft and Structure

Speaker's Claims and Evidence An **interview** is a structured conversation between two people that is presented either in written or in broadcast format. Usually, the interviewer is a journalist, and the interviewee is a person with special knowledge. In print, the conversational structure is reflected in the **question-and-answer format,** in which both questions and answers appear in the text.

Interviewees often express **claims,** or assertions of a position or truth. In order to be credible, those claims must be supported with evidence. In interviews that involve personal experiences, evidence may involve impressions and feelings. However, in an interview about a scientific subject, most of the evidence should involve facts rather than feelings. Fact-based evidence includes findings from research studies, data, and other documented information.

Practice

CITE TEXTUAL EVIDENCE to support your answers.

Dr. Margee Kerr is the expert whose claims are expressed in this interview. With your group, complete the chart. Identify the evidence with which Dr. Kerr supports each claim, and consider its credibility.

CLAIM	EVIDENCE	NOTES ON CREDIBILITY
Some people enjoy fear because the natural high of the fight-or-flight response feels great.		
Not everyone enjoys being afraid.		
Being scared is only fun when we recognize it's not "real."		
Much of the appeal of scaring ourselves stems from our fascination with death.		

WHY DO SOME BRAINS
ENJOY FEAR?

STANDARDS

Reading Informational Text
Determine the meaning of words
and phrases as they are used in a
text, including figurative, connotative,
and technical meanings; analyze the
cumulative impact of specific word
choices on meaning and tone.

Writing
Conduct short as well as more
sustained research projects to
answer a question or solve a
problem; narrow or broaden the
inquiry when appropriate; synthesize
multiple sources on the subject,
demonstrating understanding of the
subject under investigation.

Speaking and Listening
Make strategic use of digital
media in presentations to enhance
understanding of findings, reasoning,
and evidence and to add interest.

Author's Style

Scientific and Technical Diction A writer's **diction**, or word choice, reflects his or her purpose, audience, and topic. For example, articles about poetry may include technical literary terms—words such as *meter, scansion,* or *sonnet.* In a similar way, writings about scientific or technical subjects will include **scientific and technical terms**—words and phrases with precise scientific or technical meanings. Consider these two passages based on the interview.

Passage A *It's about triggering a response we have to fear that releases chemicals in our brains.*

Passage B *It's about triggering the amazing fight-or-flight response to experience the flood of adrenaline, endorphins, and dopamine.*

Passage A provides information, but it lacks specificity and leaves questions unanswered: Which response to fear? Which chemicals? In contrast, Passage B uses scientific and technical terms, such as *fight-or-flight, adrenaline,* and *endorphins,* that have exact meanings. Scientific and technical terms allow writers to present information with precision. For this reason, even general-interest articles on scientific topics may include technical language.

Read It

Record sentences containing scientific and technical terms from the interview in this chart. Use context clues to define each term, or to approximate its general meaning. Then, verify definitions using a dictionary. Discuss with your group how each term adds to the reader's understanding of the topic.

SCIENTIFIC/TECHNICAL TERM	SENTENCE	DEFINITION
adrenaline		
dopamine		
endorphins		
sociologist		
fight-or-flight response		
oxytocin		

Write It

📓 **Notebook** Write a paragraph in which you explain how reading this interview gave you insights into why some people seek out scary experiences. Use at least three scientific or technical terms in your paragraph.

Research

Assignment

Research cultural dimensions of the ways in which people experience and express fear. Then, collect your findings and present them in a **digital presentation**. Choose from these options:

☐ Design and conduct a **poll** to determine how people feel about scary but generally safe experiences, such as roller coasters, movies, and even extreme sports. Write a series of at least ten yes/no questions that you will have people answer. Calculate the results, gather visuals, and organize your findings into a presentation to share with the class.

☐ Conduct a **film study** of scary movies from the 1950s or 1960s. Watch two films, or segments of more, and analyze the sources of fear in each one. Draw conclusions about the types of things that scared mid-twentieth-century Americans. Locate images or video clips, and organize your findings and visuals into a report to share with the class. (Clear the movies you will watch with your teacher before proceeding.)

☐ Conduct a **historical study** of comets as objects of fear in ancient societies. Find out how ancient peoples explained what comets were and what they meant, and consider some of the reasons for those perceptions. Locate drawings and other visuals that will help communicate your findings. Then, organize and deliver your presentation.

> **✎ EVIDENCE LOG**
>
> Before moving on to the next selection, go to your Evidence Log and record what you learned from "Why Do Some Brains Enjoy Fear?"

Project Plan List the research, discussion, and writing tasks you will need to accomplish in order to complete your project, and make sure you attend to each one. Consult a variety of reliable research sources to gather accurate information and images. Include citations.

Evaluating Visuals Make sure the visuals you select will enhance your audience's understanding of your information. Use this chart to organize your evaluation and confirm your choices.

DESCRIPTION OF VISUAL	POINT THE VISUAL MAKES	CITATION

beware: do not read this poem

The Raven

Windigo

Concept Vocabulary

As you perform your first read, you will encounter these words.

entreating	implore	beguiling

Familiar Word Parts When determining the meaning of an unfamiliar word, look for word parts—roots and affixes—that you know. Doing so may help you unlock word meanings. Here is an example of applying the strategy.

> **Unfamiliar Word:** *incredulity*
>
> **Familiar Root:** *-cred-*, meaning "believe," as in *credible*
>
> **Familiar Affixes:** the prefix *in-*, which means either "into" or "not"; the suffix *-ity*, which forms abstract nouns
>
> **Conclusion:** You can determine that the word *incredulity* must mean something like "state of not believing."

Apply your knowledge of familiar word parts and other vocabulary strategies to determine the meanings of unfamiliar words you encounter during your first read.

First Read POETRY

Apply these strategies as you conduct your first read. You will have an opportunity to complete a close read after your first read.

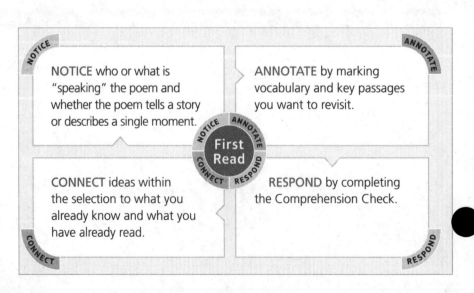

NOTICE who or what is "speaking" the poem and whether the poem tells a story or describes a single moment.

ANNOTATE by marking vocabulary and key passages you want to revisit.

CONNECT ideas within the selection to what you already know and what you have already read.

RESPOND by completing the Comprehension Check.

First Read

NOTICE ANNOTATE CONNECT RESPOND

About the Poets

Ishmael Reed (b. 1938) is a prolific author who has written novels, poems, plays, and essays in a variety of different styles and genres. He was born in Chattanooga, Tennessee, and raised in Buffalo, New York. Reed's works have been translated into many languages and published in a number of notable magazines and newspapers. Reed is the recipient of numerous honors for his work, including a Guggenheim Foundation fellowship, and a MacArthur Foundation "Genius" Award.

Edgar Allan Poe (1809–1849) is internationally recognized as a pioneer of the short story, as well as the horror and detective genres. Poe was born in Boston, Massachusetts, and raised in Richmond, Virginia, by tobacco farmer John Allan. During his lifetime, Poe was only mildly successful as a writer and struggled with poverty and loss. He died somewhat mysteriously at the age of forty. Many of his works, including "The Raven," remain popular today.

Louise Erdrich (b. 1954) is the author of many highly regarded novels and poetry collections. Erdrich was born in Minnesota, grew up on the plains of North Dakota, and was part of the first group of women admitted to Dartmouth College. In her work, Erdrich often explores her Native American heritage through her choices of characters and themes.

Backgrounds

beware: do not read this poem

In the first stanza of the poem, the word *thriller* appears in italic type to indicate it is a reference to a fictional television show. The poem contains abbreviations: *abt* for *about*, *yr* for *your*, and *frm* for *from*.

The Raven

When Poe wrote this poem, he drew from a long tradition that viewed the raven as a bird of ill omen. Yet, in some cultures, the raven enjoys a more positive image. For example, when the Vikings were lost at sea, they would release a raven. The raven would fly toward land, thus directing the lost ship.

Windigo

Windigos are evil, ice-coated, man-eating creatures that appear in many Native American folktales, including those from the poet's Chippewa culture. In Chippewa folklore, it is believed that a person who commits a sin is turned into a Windigo as punishment. The human spirit is said to live inside the creature, but the only escape is death. This poem presents a different perspective on the traditional tale.

beware:
do not read this poem

Ishmael Reed

SCAN FOR
MULTIMEDIA

NOTES

tonite, *thriller* was
abt an ol woman , so vain she
surrounded her self w/
    many mirrors

5 it got so bad that finally she
locked herself indoors & her
whole life became the
    mirrors

one day the villagers broke
10 into her house, but she was too
swift for them. she disappeared
  into a mirror
each tenant who bought the house
after that, lost a loved one to
15   the ol woman in the mirror:
  first a little girl
  then a young woman
  then the young woman/s husband

the hunger of this poem is legendary
20 it has taken in many victims
back off from this poem
it has drawn in yr feet
back off from this poem
it has drawn in yr legs
25 back off from this poem
it is a greedy mirror
you are into this poem. from
 the waist down
nobody can hear you can they?
30 this poem has had you up to here
  belch
this poem aint got no manners
you cant call out frm this poem
relax now & go w/this poem
35 move & roll on to this poem

do not resist this poem
this poem has yr eyes
this poem has his head
this poem has his arms
40 this poem has his fingers
this poem has his fingertips

this poem is the reader & the
reader this poem

statistic: the us bureau of missing persons reports
45   that in 1968 over 100,000 people disappeared
  leaving no solid clues
   nor trace only
a space in the lives of their friends

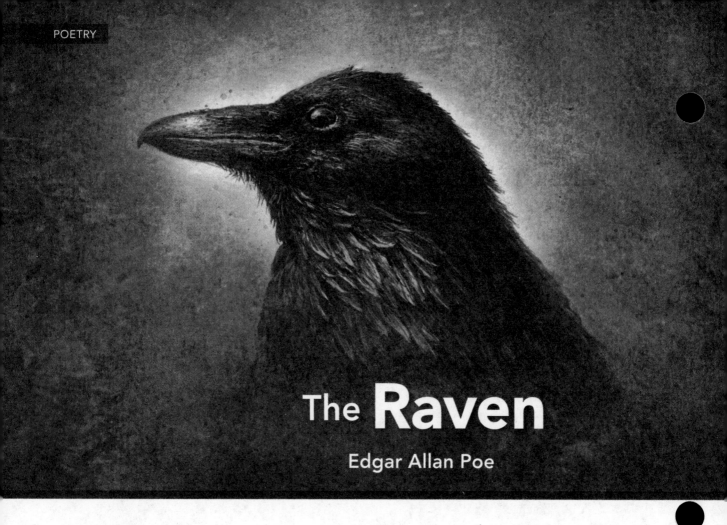

The Raven

Edgar Allan Poe

SCAN FOR
MULTIMEDIA

NOTES

Once upon a midnight dreary, while I pondered, weak and weary,
Over many a quaint and curious volume of forgotten lore—
While I nodded, nearly napping, suddenly there came a tapping,
As of some one gently rapping, rapping at my chamber door.
5 "'Tis some visitor," I muttered, "tapping at my chamber door—
             Only this, and nothing more."

Ah, distinctly I remember it was in the bleak December,
And each separate dying ember wrought its ghost upon the floor.
Eagerly I wished the morrow—vainly I had sought to borrow
10 From my books surcease[1] of sorrow—sorrow for the lost Lenore—
For the rare and radiant maiden whom the angels name Lenore—
             Nameless *here* for evermore.

And the silken, sad, uncertain rustling of each purple curtain
Thrilled me—filled me with fantastic terrors never felt before;
15 So that now, to still the beating of my heart, I stood repeating
"'Tis some visitor entreating entrance at my chamber door—
Some late visitor entreating entrance at my chamber door—
             This it is, and nothing more."

Mark familiar word parts or
indicate another strategy you
used that helped you determine
meaning.

entreating (ehn TREET ihng)
adj.

MEANING:

_____

1. **surcease** *n.* end.

Presently my soul grew stronger; hesitating then no longer,
20 "Sir," said I, "or Madam, truly your forgiveness I **implore**;
But the fact is I was napping, and so gently you came rapping,
And so faintly you came tapping, tapping at my chamber door,
That I scarce was sure I heard you"—here I opened wide the door—
          Darkness there, and nothing more.

25 Deep into that darkness peering, long I stood there wondering, fearing,
Doubting, dreaming dreams no mortal ever dared to dream before;
But the silence was unbroken, and the darkness gave no token,
And the only word there spoken was the whispered word "Lenore?"
This I whispered, and an echo murmured back the word "Lenore!"
30   Merely this, and nothing more.

Back into the chamber turning, all my soul within me burning,
Soon again I heard a tapping somewhat louder than before.
"Surely," said I, "surely that is something at my window lattice;
Let me see, then, what thereat is, and this mystery explore—
35 Let my heart be still a moment and this mystery explore—
          'Tis the wind, and nothing more!"

Open here I flung the shutter, when, with many a flirt and flutter,
In there stepped a stately Raven of the saintly days of yore;
Not the least obeisance² made he; not a minute stopped or stayed he;
40 But, with mien of lord or lady, perched above my chamber door—
Perched upon a bust of Pallas³ just above my chamber door—
          Perched, and sat, and nothing more.

Then this ebony bird **beguiling** my sad fancy into smiling,
By the grave and stern decorum of the countenance⁴ it wore,
45 "Though thy crest be shorn and shaven, thou," I said, "art sure no
          craven,⁵
Ghastly grim and ancient Raven wandering from the Nightly shore—
Tell me what thy lordly name is on the Night's Plutonian⁶ shore!"
          Quoth the Raven, "Nevermore."

Much I marveled this ungainly fowl to hear discourse so plainly,
50 Though its answer little meaning—little relevancy bore;
For we cannot help agreeing that no living human being
Ever yet was blessed with seeing bird above his chamber door—
Bird or beast above the sculptured bust above his chamber door,
          With such name as "Nevermore."

55 But the Raven, sitting lonely on the placid bust, spoke only
That one word, as if his soul in that one word he did outpour.

---

2. **obeisance** (oh BAY suhns) *n.* gesture of respect.
3. **Pallas** *n.* Pallas Athena, Greek goddess of wisdom.
4. **countenance** *n.* facial expression.
5. **craven** *adj.* cowardly.
6. **Plutonian** *adj.* of the underworld; refers to Pluto, Greek god of the underworld.

NOTES

Mark familiar word parts or indicate another strategy you used that helped you determine meaning.

implore (ihm PLAWR) *v.*

MEANING:

Mark familiar word parts or indicate another strategy you used that helped you determine meaning.

beguiling (bih GYL ihng) *adj.*

MEANING:

Nothing further then he uttered—not a feather then he fluttered—
Till I scarcely more than muttered, "Other friends have flown
before—
On the morrow *he* will leave me, as my Hopes have flown before."
60   Quoth the Raven, "Nevermore."

Startled at the stillness broken by reply so aptly spoken,
"Doubtless," said I, "what it utters is its only stock and store,
Caught from some unhappy master whom unmerciful Disaster
Followed fast and followed faster till his songs one burden bore—
65 Till the dirges of his Hope that melancholy burden bore
          Of 'Never—nevermore.'"

But the Raven still beguiling my sad fancy into smiling,
Straight I wheeled a cushioned seat in front of bird, and bust, and
door;
Then, upon the velvet sinking, I betook myself to linking
70 Fancy unto fancy, thinking what this ominous[7] bird of yore—
What this grim, ungainly, ghastly, gaunt, and ominous bird of yore
          Meant in croaking, "Nevermore."

This I sat engaged in guessing, but no syllable expressing
To the fowl whose fiery eyes now burned into my bosom's core;
75 This and more I sat divining, with my head at ease reclining
On the cushion's velvet lining that the lamplight gloated o'er,
But whose velvet violet lining with the lamplight gloating o'er,
          She shall press, ah, nevermore!

Then, methought, the air grew denser, perfumed from an unseen censer
80 Swung by seraphim whose footfalls tinkled on the tufted floor.
"Wretch," I cried, "thy God hath lent thee—by these angels he hath
sent thee
Respite—respite and nepenthe[8] from thy memories of Lenore!
Quaff, oh quaff this kind nepenthe and forget this lost Lenore!"
          Quoth the Raven, "Nevermore."

85 "Prophet!" said I, "thing of evil!—prophet still, if bird or devil!—
Whether Tempter sent, or whether tempest tossed thee here ashore,
Desolate, yet all undaunted, on this desert land enchanted—
On this home by Horror haunted—tell me truly, I implore—
Is there—*is* there balm in Gilead?[9]—tell me—tell me, I implore!"
90   Quoth the Raven, "Nevermore."

"Prophet!" said I, "thing of evil!—prophet still, if bird or devil!

---

7. **ominous** *adj.* threatening or sinister.
8. **nepenthe** (nih PEHN thee) *n.* drug that the ancient Greeks believed could relieve
sorrow.
9. **balm in Gilead** in the Bible, a healing ointment made in Gilead, a region of ancient
Palestine.

By that Heaven that bends above us—by that God we both adore—
Tell this soul with sorrow laden if, within the distant Aidenn,[10]
It shall clasp a sainted maiden whom the angels named Lenore—
95 Clasp a rare and radiant maiden whom the angels named Lenore."
      Quoth the Raven, "Nevermore."

"Be that word our sign of parting, bird or fiend!" I shrieked,
    upstarting—
"Get thee back into the tempest and the Night's Plutonian shore!
Leave no black plume as a token of that lie thy soul hath spoken!
100 Leave my loneliness unbroken!—quit the bust above my door!
Take thy beak from out my heart, and take thy form from off my door!"
      Quoth the Raven, "Nevermore."

And the Raven, never flitting, still is sitting, *still* is sitting
On the pallid bust of Pallas just above my chamber door;
105 And his eyes have all the seeming of a demon's that is dreaming,
And the lamplight o'er him streaming throws his shadow on the floor;
And my soul from out that shadow that lies floating on the floor
      Shall be lifted—nevermore!

_____

10. **Aidenn** *n.* Arabic for Eden or heaven.

Windigo

Louise Erdrich

NOTES

You knew I was coming for you, little one,
when the kettle jumped into the fire.
Towels flapped on the hooks,
and the dog crept off, groaning,
5 to the deepest part of the woods.

In the hackles[1] of dry brush a thin laughter started up.
Mother scolded the food warm and smooth in the pot
and called you to eat.
But I spoke in the cold trees:
10 *New one, I have come for you, child hide and lie still.*

The sumac[2] pushed sour red cones through the air.
Copper burned in the raw wood.
You saw me drag toward you.
Oh touch me, I murmured, and licked the soles of your feet.
15 You dug your hands into my pale, melting fur.

---

1. **hackles** *n.* usually used to mean the hairs on the neck and back of a dog that stiffen when the dog is ready to attack. In this case, the poet is using the word figuratively.
2. **sumac** *n.* bright shrub or small tree with multi-part leaves and fruit clusters.

I stole you off, a huge thing in my bristling armor.
Steam rolled from my wintry arms, each leaf shivered
from the bushes we passed
until they stood, naked, spread like the cleaned spines of fish.

20 Then your warm hands hummed over and shoveled themselves full
of the ice and the snow. I would darken and spill
all night running, until at last morning broke the cold earth
and I carried you home,
a river shaking in the sun.

Comprehension Check

Complete the following items after you finish your first read. Review and clarify details with your group.

BEWARE: DO NOT READ THIS POEM

1. What happened to the vain old woman who surrounded herself with mirrors?

2. After that, what happened to each tenant of the old woman's house?

THE RAVEN

1. At the beginning of the poem, why is the speaker sorrowful?

2. With what word does the Raven respond to all the speaker's questions?

WINDIGO

1. Who is the speaker of the poem?

2. Where does the speaker take the child?

RESEARCH

Research to Clarify Choose at least one unfamiliar detail from one of the poems. Briefly research that detail. In what way does the information you learned shed light on an aspect of the poem?

© Pearson Education, Inc., or its affiliates. All rights reserved.

Poetry Collection **109**

POETRY COLLECTION

Close Read the Text

With your group, revisit sections of the poems you marked during your first read. **Annotate** details that you notice. What **questions** do you have? What can you **conclude**?

Analyze the Text

> **CITE TEXTUAL EVIDENCE**
> to support your answers.

Complete the activities.

1. **Review and Clarify** With your group, reread lines 1–12 of "The Raven." Discuss the ways in which Poe establishes the setting for the poem. How do the time of day and the season match the speaker's state of mind? What overall mood or atmosphere does the poet create?

2. **Present and Discuss** Work with your group to share the passages from the selections that you found especially important. Take turns presenting your passages. Discuss what details you noticed, what questions you asked, and what conclusions you reached.

3. **Essential Question:** *What is the allure of fear?* What have these poems taught you about portrayals of fear in literature?

LANGUAGE DEVELOPMENT

Concept Vocabulary

entreating	implore	beguiling

Why These Words? The three concept vocabulary words are related. With your group, discuss what the words have in common. How do these word choices enhance the impact of the text?

Practice

 Notebook Confirm your understanding of these words by using them in sentences. Include context clues that hint at each word's meaning.

Word Study

Anglo-Saxon Prefix: *be-* The word *beguiling* begins with the Anglo-Saxon prefix *be-*, an ancient suffix with a variety of meanings. Sometimes, it means "to make," as in *becalm*. Other times, it acts as an intensifier meaning "thoroughly" or "completely," as in *bedazzle*.

Identify the base word in each of the following: *becloud, befriend, belittle*. Then, write the meaning of each word. Use a college-level dictionary to verify your definitions.

> **TIP**
>
> **GROUP DISCUSSION**
> Keep in mind that group members will have different interpretations of the poems. These different perspectives enable group members to learn from one another and to clarify their own thoughts. Very often, there is no single interpretation or conclusion.

⊹ WORD NETWORK

Add words related to fear from the texts to your Word Network.

☰ STANDARDS

Reading Literature
Determine a theme or central idea of a text and analyze in detail its development over the course of the text, including how it emerges and is shaped and refined by specific details; provide an objective summary of the text.

Language
• Identify and correctly use patterns of word changes that indicate different meanings or parts of speech.
• Verify the preliminary determination of the meaning of a word or phrase.

Analyze Craft and Structure

Development of Theme A **narrative poem** relates a story in verse. Like a narrator in prose fiction, the **speaker** of a poem is an imaginary voice that "tells" the story. Interpreting a poem often depends on recognizing who the speaker is, whom the speaker is addressing, and what the speaker feels about the subject—his or her **tone.**

A **theme** is a central message or insight expressed in a literary work. Some poems state a theme directly, but most convey their messages indirectly. Readers must look for clues to a poem's theme in its language and details. These details include **imagery,** or sensory language that creates word pictures in readers' minds. Imagery makes a narrative poem more vivid, and also suggests its themes.

Practice

CITE TEXTUAL EVIDENCE to support your answers.

Use the chart to analyze each poem. Consider how the speaker's tone and the poem's imagery reveal the theme.

BEWARE: DO NOT READ THIS POEM	
speaker/speaker's tone	
possible theme	We cannot separate ourselves from the things that we read.
details that develop this theme	

THE RAVEN	
speaker/speaker's tone	
possible theme	Great sorrow may lead to madness.
details that develop this theme	

WINDIGO	
speaker/speaker's tone	
possible theme	Mystery is at the heart of life.
details that develop this theme	

1. Choose one of the poems, and identify another theme it expresses.

2. List details that suggest this theme, and explain your interpretation.

Author's Style

Point of View In narrative literature, whether stories or poems, the point of view is the perspective, or vantage point, from which the story is told. The point of view is very important, since it controls what the reader learns about events and what he or she can logically infer.

In **first-person point of view,** the narrator is a character in the literary work and refers to him- or herself with the first-person pronoun *I* or *me*. Since the narrator participates directly in the action, his or her point of view is *limited*. A first-person narrator can reliably relate only those events he or she witnesses, experiences firsthand, or learns about from others.

In **omniscient third-person point of view,** the narrator is not a character in the story. He or she stands "outside" the story and is, thus, free to be omniscient, or "all-knowing." The omniscient narrator knows what all of the characters are thinking and feeling.

▤ STANDARDS
Reading Literature
Analyze how an author's choices concerning how to structure a text, order events within it, and manipulate time create such effects as mystery, tension, or suspense.

Read It

Work individually. Use this chart to identify the point of view employed in each poem. Then, consider the effects of this choice—what does the point of view allow readers to learn, and what does it keep hidden? When you finish, reconvene as a group to discuss your responses.

BEWARE: DO NOT READ THIS POEM	
Point of view:	Effects:

THE RAVEN	
Point of view:	Effects:

WINDIGO	
Point of view:	Effects:

Write It

🗐 **Notebook** Write two brief versions of the same scene. In one version of the scene, describe events from the first-person point of view. In the other version, describe the same events using the omniscient third-person point of view.

Speaking and Listening

Assignment

Create and deliver a **group presentation**. As you deliver your presentation, pay close attention to such things as eye contact, body language, clear pronunciation, tone, speaking rate, and volume. Choose from the following topics.

☐ Conduct a **mock interview** with one of the poets. Prepare a list of questions you would like to ask the poet about the inspiration behind his or her poem. Each group member should write at least one question and create an answer. Then, one group member should play the poet, while the others pose questions. Present the role-play for the class.

☐ Present a **compare-and-contrast analysis** of two of the poems, focusing on the personalities and tones of the speakers. How do the speakers change over the course of the poems? Cite evidence from the text to support your ideas. Present your analysis to the class.

☐ Present a **retelling** of one of the poems. For example, you might present it as a short story, a hip-hop song, or a play. Present your retelling for the class.

Project Plan Before you begin, make a list of the tasks you will need to accomplish in order to complete the assignment you have chosen. Then, assign individual group members to each task. Use this chart to organize your ideas.

MOCK INTERVIEW	
Tasks:	Additional notes:

COMPARE-AND-CONTRAST ANALYSIS	
Tasks:	Additional notes:

RETELLING	
Tasks:	Additional notes:

📝 EVIDENCE LOG

Before moving on to a new selection, go to your Evidence Log and record what you learned from "beware: do not read this poem," "The Raven," and "Windigo."

▦ STANDARDS

Speaking and Listening
• Initiate and participate effectively in a range of collaborative discussions with diverse partners on *grades 9–10 topics, texts, and issues,* building on others' ideas and expressing their own clearly and persuasively.
• Adapt speech to a variety of contexts and tasks, demonstrating command of formal English, when indicated or appropriate.

Deliver an Explanatory Presentation

Assignment

You have read literature that deals with fear and some of its causes and effects. Work with your group to develop a presentation that addresses this question:

> In literature, how does a sense of uncertainty help to create an atmosphere of fear?

Plan With Your Group

Analyze the Text With your group, discuss the types of situations or dilemmas that different characters face in the selections you have read. Think about whether you as a reader were uncertain about what was happening, as well as whether the characters experienced uncertainty. Use the chart to list your ideas. For each selection, identify how uncertainty relates to an atmosphere of fear. If you choose, you may also draw on experiences in your own life, and discuss whether uncertainty played a role.

TITLE	KEY EXPERIENCES
Where Is Here?	
from The Dream Collector	
Why Do Some Brains Enjoy Fear?	
beware: do not read this poem	
The Raven	
Windigo	
group member's story, if desired	

Gather Evidence and Media Identify specific passages to read from the selections to support your group's ideas. Test your choices by reading the passages to each other, with appropriate inflection and emphasis, to see whether others agree that each one effectively illustrates your ideas about fear and uncertainty. Brainstorm for types of media you can use to enhance the mood and impact of your readings. Consider including images, such as photographs and illustrations. You may also include music and other sound effects.

STANDARDS

Speaking and Listening
- Initiate and participate effectively in a range of collaborative discussions with diverse partners on *grades 9–10 topics, texts, and issues*, building on others' ideas and expressing their own clearly and persuasively.

- Work with peers to set rules for collegial discussions and decision-making, clear goals and deadlines, and individual roles as needed.

- Present information, findings, and supporting evidence clearly, concisely, and logically such that listeners can follow the line of reasoning and the organization, development, substance, and style are appropriate to purpose, audience, and task.

Organize Ideas As a group, organize the script for your presentation. Make decisions about the following content and tasks:

- Who will introduce the group's main findings?
- Who will read the selection passages that illustrate the findings?
- Who will summarize findings and take questions from the audience?
- Who will display and manage visuals?
- Who will play and manage music and sound effects?

Then, plan where in your presentation you will incorporate your media.

Rehearse With Your Group

Practice With Your Group Use this checklist to evaluate the effectiveness of your group's first run-through. Then, use your evaluation and the instruction here to guide your revision.

CONTENT	USE OF MEDIA	PRESENTATION TECHNIQUES
☐ The presentation has a clear introduction and a strong conclusion.	☐ The media are consistent with the mood and tone of the passages from the texts.	☐ Media are visible and audible.
☐ Main ideas are well supported with readings from the texts.	☐ The media add interest to the passages.	☐ Transitions are smooth.
	☐ Media do not distract from the passages or the ideas of the presentation.	☐ Each speaker speaks clearly.

Fine-Tune the Content Make sure you have enough examples that illustrate your main findings about uncertainty and fear. Verify that each passage you choose to read is clear and dramatic, and rehearse the readings for maximum impact. Check with your group to identify key points in your introduction and conclusion that might not be clear to listeners. Find another way to word these ideas.

Improve Your Use of Media Review all visuals, music, and sound effects to make sure they add interest and help create a cohesive presentation. If a visual or sound cue does not capture the right mood, replace it with a more appropriate item.

Brush Up on Your Presentation Techniques Practice delivering your group presentation before you present to the whole class. Make sure that you speak clearly, avoiding slang and informal language, and use appropriate eye contact while you are speaking.

Present and Evaluate

When you present as a group, be sure that each member has taken into account each of the checklist items. As you listen to other groups, evaluate how well they adhere to the checklist.

STANDARDS
Speaking and Listening
• Make strategic use of digital media in presentations to enhance understanding of findings, reasoning, and evidence and to add interest.
• Adapt speech to a variety of contexts and tasks, demonstrating command of formal English when indicated or appropriate.

ESSENTIAL QUESTION:

What is the allure of fear?

Fear is a part of life. It both helps and hurts us, bonds and divides us. In this section, you will complete your study of the literature of fear by exploring an additional selection related to the topic. You'll then share what you learn with classmates. To choose a text, follow these steps.

Look Back Think about the selections you have already studied. What more do you want to know about the topic of fear and its appeal in literature and life?

Look Ahead Preview the selections by reading the descriptions. Which one seems most interesting and appealing to you?

Look Inside Take a few minutes to scan the text you chose. Choose a different one if this text doesn't meet your needs.

Independent Learning Strategies

Throughout your life, in school, in your community, and in your career, you will need to rely on yourself to learn and work on your own. Review these strategies and the actions you can take to practice them during Independent Learning. Add ideas of your own for each category.

STRATEGY	ACTION PLAN
Create a schedule	• Understand your goals and deadlines. • Make a plan for what to do each day. •
Practice what you have learned	• Use first-read and close-read strategies to deepen your understanding. • After reading, evaluate the usefulness of the evidence to help you understand the topic. • Consider the quality and reliability of the source. •
Take notes	• Record important ideas and information. • Review your notes before preparing to share with a group. •

SCAN FOR
MULTIMEDIA

CONTENTS

Choose one selection. Selections are available online only.

PERFORMANCE-BASED ASSESSMENT PREP

Review Evidence for an Explanatory Essay

Complete your Evidence Log for the unit by evaluating what you've learned and synthesizing the information you have recorded.

SCAN FOR MULTIMEDIA

First-Read Guide

Use this page to record your first-read ideas.

🔧 **Tool Kit**
First-Read Guide and
Model Annotation

Selection Title: _____

NOTICE new information or ideas you learn about the unit topic as you first read this text.

ANNOTATE by marking vocabulary and key passages you want to revisit.

First Read

NOTICE · ANNOTATE · CONNECT · RESPOND

CONNECT ideas within the selection to other knowledge and the selections you have read.

RESPOND by writing a brief summary of the selection.

≣ STANDARD
Reading Read and comprehend complex literary and informational texts independently and proficiently.

Close-Read Guide

Use this page to record your close-read ideas.

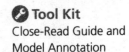 **Tool Kit**
Close-Read Guide and
Model Annotation

Selection Title: _____

Close Read the Text

Revisit sections of the text you marked during your first read. Read these sections closely and **annotate** what you notice. Ask yourself **questions** about the text. What can you **conclude**? Write down your ideas.

Analyze the Text

Think about the author's choices of patterns, structure, techniques, and ideas included in the text. Select one, and record your thoughts about what this choice conveys.

QuickWrite

Pick a paragraph from the text that grabbed your interest. Explain the power of this passage.

_____

_____

_____

_____

_____

_____

_____

_____

_____

▤ STANDARD
Reading Read and comprehend complex literary and informational texts independently and proficiently.

Share Your Independent Learning

Prepare to Share

What is the allure of fear?

Even when you read something independently, your understanding continues to grow when you share what you have learned with others. Reflect on the text you explored independently, and write notes about its connection to the unit. In your notes, consider why this text belongs in this unit.

Learn From Your Classmates

Discuss It Share your ideas about the text you explored on your own. As you talk with others in your class, jot down a few ideas that you learned from them.

Reflect

Review your notes, and mark the most important insight you gained from these writing and discussion activities. Explain how this idea adds to your understanding of the allure of fear in literature.

STANDARDS

Speaking and Listening
• Initiate and participate effectively range of collaborative discussions with diverse partners on *grades 9–10 topics, texts, and issues,* building on others' ideas and expressing their own clearly and persuasively.
• Come to discussions prepared, having read and researched material under study; explicitly draw on that preparation by referring to evidence from texts and other research on the topic or issue to stimulate a thoughtful, well-reasoned exchange of ideas.

Review Evidence for an Explanatory Essay

At the beginning of the unit, you expressed a point about the following question:

> In what ways does transformation play a role in stories meant to scare us?

✐ EVIDENCE LOG

Review your Evidence Log and your QuickWrite from the beginning of the unit. Did you learn anything new?

NOTES

Identify at least three pieces of evidence that interested you about the reasons people enjoy scary literature.

1. _____

2. _____

3. _____

Identify a real-life experience or an example from one of the selections that connects to your new knowledge about the literature of fear.

_____

_____

_____

Develop your thoughts into a topic sentence for an explanatory essay. Complete this sentence starter:

I learned a great deal about literary portrayals of fear when

_____

_____

_____

Evaluate Your Evidence Consider your point of view. How did the texts you read impact your point of view?

☰ STANDARDS

Writing
Introduce a topic; organize complex ideas, concepts, and information to make important connections and distinctions; include formatting, graphics, and multimedia when useful to aiding comprehension.

SOURCES

- WHOLE–CLASS SELECTIONS
- SMALL–GROUP SELECTIONS
- INDEPENDENT–LEARNING SELECTION

PART 1
Writing to Sources: Explanatory Essay

In this unit, you read about various characters whose lives are transformed in scary circumstances. In some cases, the transformations reveal something that was there the whole time but disguised or hidden.

Assignment

Write an **explanatory essay** on the following topic:

> In what ways does transformation play a role in stories meant to scare us?

Use evidence from at least three of the selections you read and researched in this unit to support your perspective. Include a narrative dimension in the form of an anecdote, or brief story from your own experience or that of someone you know. Ensure that your ideas are fully supported, that you use precise words, and that your organization is logical and easy to follow.

Reread the Assignment Review the assignment to be sure you fully understand it. The assignment may reference some of the academic words presented at the beginning of the unit. Be sure you understand each of the words given below in order to complete the assignment correctly.

Academic Vocabulary

dimension	manipulate	psychological
motivate	perspective	

Review the Elements of an Effective Explanatory Text Before you begin writing, read the Explanatory Text Rubric. Once you have completed your first draft, check it against the rubric. If one or more of the elements is missing or not as strong as it could be, revise your essay to add or strengthen that component.

⬒ WORD NETWORK

As you write and revise your explanatory essay, use your Word Network to help vary your word choices.

☰ STANDARDS

Writing
• Write informative/explanatory texts to examine and convey complex ideas, concepts, and information clearly and accurately through the effective selection, organization, and analysis of content.
• Draw evidence from literary or informational texts to support analysis, reflection, and research.
• Write routinely over extended time frames and shorter time frames for a range of tasks, purposes, and audiences.

Explanatory Text Rubric

	Focus and Organization	Evidence and Elaboration	Conventions
4	The introduction engages the reader and states a thesis in a compelling way. The essay includes a clear introduction, body, and conclusion. The essay uses facts and evidence from a variety of reliable, credited sources The conclusion summarizes ideas and offers fresh insight into the thesis.	The essay includes specific reasons, details, facts, narratives, and quotations to support the thesis. If a narrative is used, it is coherent and provides strong support for the thesis. The tone of the essay is appropriately formal and objective for the audience and topic. The language is always precise and appropriate for the audience and purpose.	The essay intentionally uses standard English conventions of usage and mechanics.
3	The introduction engages the reader and sets forth a thesis. The essay includes an introduction, a body, and a conclusion. The essay uses facts and evidence from a variety of credited sources. The conclusion summarizes ideas.	The research includes some specific reasons, details, facts, narratives, and quotations to support the thesis. If a narrative is used, it is coherent and provides some support for the thesis. The tone of the research is mostly appropriate for the audience and topic. The language is generally precise and appropriate for the audience and purpose.	The essay demonstrates general accuracy in standard English conventions of usage and mechanics.
2	The introduction sets forth a thesis. The essay includes an introduction, a body, and a conclusion, but one or more parts are weak. The essay uses facts and evidence from a few credited sources. The conclusion partially summarizes ideas.	The research includes a few reasons, details, facts, narratives, and quotations to support the thesis. If a narrative is used, it provides little support for the thesis. The tone of the research is occasionally appropriate for the audience and topic. The language is somewhat precise and appropriate for the audience and purpose.	The presentation demonstrates some accuracy in standard English conventions of usage and mechanics.
1	The introduction does not state a thesis clearly. The essay does not include an introduction, a body, and a conclusion. The essay does not use a variety of facts, and information and evidence are not credited. The conclusion does not summarize ideas.	Reliable and relevant evidence is not included. If a narrative is used, it provides no support for the thesis. The tone of the essay is not objective or formal. The language used is imprecise and not appropriate for the audience and purpose.	The essay contains mistakes in standard English conventions of usage and mechanics.

PART 2
Speaking and Listening: Informal Talk

Assignment
After completing the final draft of your explanatory essay, use it as the foundation for a three- to five-minute **informal talk.**

Do not read your explanatory essay aloud. Instead, use your knowledge to speak informally but with confidence about your topic. Take the following steps to prepare your talk.

- Go back to your essay, and annotate the most important ideas from your introduction, body paragraphs, and conclusion. Also, note any anecdote or descriptive details you used.
- Use your annotations to make a list of the key points and content you want to share in your informal talk.
- As you speak, refer to your list of ideas to keep your talk focused.

Review the Rubric The criteria by which your informal talk will be evaluated appear in the rubric below. Review these criteria before speaking to ensure that you are prepared.

STANDARDS

Speaking and Listening
Present information, findings, and supporting evidence clearly, concisely, and logically such that listeners can follow the line of reasoning and the organization, development, substance, and style are appropriate to purpose, audience, and task.

	Content	Organization	Presentation
3	The introduction engages and orients the reader by setting out a clear observation or analysis.	The speaker uses time very effectively by spending the right amount of time on each part of the discussion.	The speaker maintains effective eye contact and speaks clearly.
	The talk includes both descriptive details and narrative techniques.	The talk includes a smooth sequence of ideas with clear transitions that listeners can follow.	The speaker varies tone, volume, and emphasis to create an engaging presentation.
	The conclusion follows from and reflects on ideas presented earlier in the talk.		
2	The introduction sets out a problem, situation, or observation.	The speaker uses time effectively by spending adequate time on each part.	The speaker mostly maintains effective eye contact and usually speaks clearly.
	The talk includes some descriptive details and narrative techniques.	The talk includes a smooth sequence of ideas with transitions that listeners can mostly follow.	The speaker sometimes varies tone, volume, and emphasis to create an engaging presentation.
	The conclusion follows from ideas presented earlier in the talk.		
1	The introduction does not set out an observation or analysis.	The speaker does not use time effectively and devotes too much or too little time to each part.	The speaker does not maintain effective eye contact or speak clearly.
	The talk does not include descriptive details or narrative techniques.	The talk does not include a clear sequence of ideas with transitions that listeners can follow.	The speaker does not vary tone, volume, and emphasis to create an engaging presentation.
	The conclusion does not follow from ideas presented earlier in the talk.		

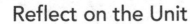
Reflect on the Unit

Now that you've completed the unit, take a few moments to reflect on your learning.

Reflect on the Unit Goals

Look back at the goals at the beginning of the unit. Use a different colored pen to rate yourself again. Think about readings and activities that contributed the most to the growth of your understanding. Record your thoughts.

Reflect on the Learning Strategies

Discuss It Write a reflection on whether you were able to improve your learning based on your Action Plans. Think about what worked, what didn't, and what you might do to keep working on these strategies. Record your ideas before a class discussion.

Reflect on the Text

Choose a selection that you found challenging, and explain what made it difficult.

Explain something that surprised you about a text in the unit.

Which activity taught you the most about the literature of fear? What did you learn?

STANDARDS

Speaking and Listening
• Initiate and participate effectively in a range of collaborative discussions with diverse partners on *grades 9–10 topics, texts, and issues,* building on other's ideas and expressing their own clearly and persuasively.
• Come to discussions prepared, having read and researched material under study; explicitly draw on that preparation by referring to evidence from texts and other research on the topic or issue to stimulate a thoughtful, well-reasoned exchange of ideas.

SCAN FOR
MULTIMEDIA

Outsiders and Outcasts

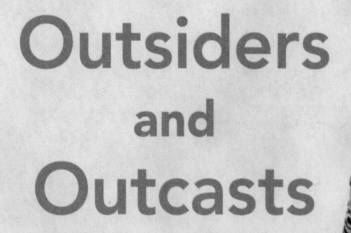

The idea of social isolation is a common thread throughout literature. Is it because being alone is just a natural part of life?

Socrates

💬 **Discuss It** What can happen to great thinkers when their ideas are critical of others?

Write your response before sharing your ideas.

SCAN FOR MULTIMEDIA

UNIT INTRODUCTION

ESSENTIAL QUESTION:

Do people need to belong?

LAUNCH TEXT
ARGUMENT MODEL
Isn't Everyone a Little
Bit Weird?

WHOLE-CLASS LEARNING

ANCHOR TEXT: SHORT STORY

The Metamorphosis
*Franz Kafka,
translated by
Ian Johnston*

MEDIA: VIDEO

**Franz Kafka and
Metamorphosis**
BBC

SMALL-GROUP LEARNING

SHORT STORY

The Doll's House
Katherine Mansfield

POETRY COLLECTION

Sonnet, With Bird
Sherman Alexie

Elliptical
Harryette Mullen

Fences
Pat Mora

ARGUMENT

Revenge of the Geeks
Alexandra Robbins

LECTURE

**Encountering the
Other: The Challenge
for the 21st Century**
Ryszard Kapuscinski

INDEPENDENT LEARNING

MYTH

**The Orphan Boy and
the Elk Dog**
*Blackfoot,
retold by Richard Erdoes
and Alfonso Ortiz*

MEMOIR

By Any Other Name
from **Gifts of Passage**
Santha Rama Rau

NEWSPAPER ARTICLE

**Outsider's Art Is
Saluted at Columbia,
Then Lost Anew**
Vivian Yee

MEDIA: RADIO BROADCAST

**Fleeing to Dismal
Swamp, Slaves and
Outcasts Found
Freedom**
Sandy Hausman

PERFORMANCE TASK

WRITING FOCUS:
Write an Argument

PERFORMANCE TASK

SPEAKING AND LISTENING FOCUS:
Deliver a Multimedia Presentation

PERFORMANCE-BASED ASSESSMENT PREP

Review Evidence for
an Argument

PERFORMANCE-BASED ASSESSMENT

Argument: Essay and Oral Presentation

PROMPT:

Is the experience of being an outsider universal?

Unit Goals

Throughout this unit, you will deepen your perspective of outsiders and outcasts by reading, writing, speaking, presenting, and listening. These goals will help you succeed on the Unit Performance-Based Assessment.

Rate how well you meet these goals right now. You will revisit your ratings later when you reflect on your growth during this unit.

SCALE	1	2	3	4	5
	NOT AT ALL WELL	NOT VERY WELL	SOMEWHAT WELL	VERY WELL	EXTREMELY WELL

READING GOALS	1	2	3	4	5
• Evaluate written arguments by analyzing how authors state and support their claims.	○	○	○	○	○
• Expand your knowledge and use of academic and concept vocabulary.	○	○	○	○	○

WRITING AND RESEARCH GOALS	1	2	3	4	5
• Write an argumentative essay in which you effectively incorporate the key elements of an argument.	○	○	○	○	○
• Conduct research projects of various lengths to explore a topic and clarify meaning.	○	○	○	○	○

LANGUAGE GOAL	1	2	3	4	5
• Correctly use phrases and clauses to convey meaning and add variety and interest to your writing and presentations.	○	○	○	○	○

SPEAKING AND LISTENING GOALS	1	2	3	4	5
• Collaborate with your team to build on the ideas of others, develop consensus, and communicate.	○	○	○	○	○
• Integrate audio, visuals, and text in presentations.	○	○	○	○	○

STANDARDS

Language
Acquire and use accurately general academic and domain-specific words and phrases, sufficient for reading, writing, speaking, and listening at the college and career readiness level; demonstrate independence in gathering vocabulary knowledge when considering a word or phrase important to comprehension or expression.

SCAN FOR MULTIMEDIA

Academic Vocabulary: Argument

Academic terms appear in all subjects and can help you read, write, and discuss with more precision. Here are five academic words that will be useful to you in this unit as you analyze and write arguments.

Complete the chart.

1. Review each word, its base, and the mentor sentences.

2. Use the information and your own knowledge to predict the meaning of each word.

3. For each word, list at least two related words.

4. Refer to a dictionary or other resources if needed.

TIP

FOLLOW THROUGH
Study the words in this chart, and mark them or their forms wherever they appear in the unit.

WORD	MENTOR SENTENCES	PREDICT MEANING	RELATED WORDS
contradict ROOT: **-dict-** "speak"; "talk"	1. Your sister will probably be unhappy if you continue to *contradict* her. 2. The two sources that I used for my research paper *contradict* one another on some important points.		contradiction; contradictory
negate ROOT: **-neg-** "no"; "not"	1. The one time you lie may *negate* all the times you tell the truth. 2. Getting a bad grade on the final exam will *negate* all the hard work I put into this class.		
objection ROOT: **-ject-** "throw"	1. My only *objection* to the plan is that some of the steps seem vague and should be more precise. 2. When you have an *objection* to a proposal, explain your concerns in polite terms.		
verify ROOT: **-ver-** "truth"	1. Maria will *verify* the information before we include it in the presentation. 2. I checked the band's tour schedule to *verify* that the concert is this weekend.		
advocate ROOT: **-voc-** "voice"; "call out"	1. I'm voting for her because she has always been an *advocate* for causes that are important to me. 2. I would *advocate* that we study tonight so that we can go to the movies tomorrow.		

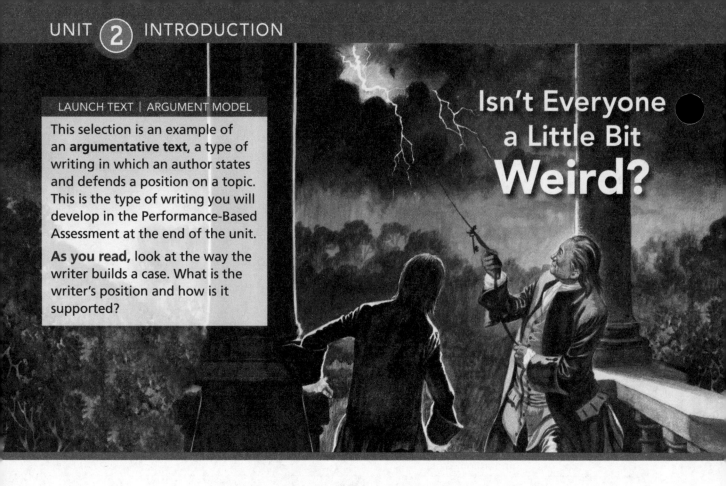

Isn't Everyone a Little Bit Weird?

This selection is an example of an **argumentative text**, a type of writing in which an author states and defends a position on a topic. This is the type of writing you will develop in the Performance-Based Assessment at the end of the unit.

As you read, look at the way the writer builds a case. What is the writer's position and how is it supported?

NOTES

1   Everyone is a little bit weird. That's not a bad thing. It just happens to be true.

2   The common definition of the adjective *weird* is "unusual or strange." The connotation, or implied meaning, of the term is that there is something wrong with a person who is described in this way. While many people might feel the connotation is accurate, I would argue that it's wrong for two reasons. First, the most gifted, successful people are often eccentric. Second, some traits we now think of as being weird were once highly regarded and not weird at all.

3   Consider Benjamin Franklin. One of the framers of the United States Constitution, Franklin (1706–1790) was a leading author, political theorist, politician, scientist, inventor, activist, and businessperson. He invented the lightning rod, bifocal glasses, and the Franklin stove. His discoveries regarding electricity are important to the history of physics. His public push for colonial solidarity was vital to the formation of the Union. He became wealthy as the writer and publisher of *Poor Richard's Almanack*.

4   There's nothing weird in that list of accomplishments. *Brilliant* would better describe Franklin, and yet the man some call "the first American" had certain ways about him you might consider odd. He once pranked a competing publisher by astrologically predicting when the man's life would end. He created his own alphabet, dispensing with the letters *c, j, q, w, x,* and *y,* and adding others he made up to stand in for common sounds. He is said to have favored "air baths," often writing his essays and letters while sitting in a cold room with nothing on.

SCAN FOR MULTIMEDIA

NOTES

5   Some aspects of Franklin's life that people today might see as weird would have been viewed as unremarkable during his lifetime. Take, for example, his appearance. In famous portraits, he wears ruffled shirts, breeches, and tight stockings pulled up to the knee. He wore his hair long well into old age. Today's viewers of those portraits might think him odd, but those were common fashions of his era. Likewise, consider Franklin's education. He quit school at age ten and was apprenticed as a printer at age twelve—a career move that today would be considered both weird and illegal.

6   Perhaps Franklin's oddness actually sparked his genius. He saw things in ways that challenged what other people accepted as fact. Additionally, he had the courage to communicate his insights, act on them, and turn them into achievements. It may have been Franklin's weirdness that made him great.

7   Some might argue that weird people are just plain weird. By most people's standards, an undressed man sitting in a cold room writing with a quill pen is undoubtedly strange. But that view of human nature is too narrow. It doesn't recognize the important idea that many of those who see things differently turn out to be the most creative and ingenious among us.

8   Everyone has eccentricities—slightly odd, perhaps unique ways of thinking or behaving. These might be the first traits you notice in someone, or the last. Being a little bit weird may be one of the things that actually connects us, and makes us uniquely human.

9   Ben Franklin wrote, "Life's tragedy is that we get old too soon and wise too late." It takes wisdom to look past what seems weird in people—what makes them different—to find the offbeat humanity that unites us all.

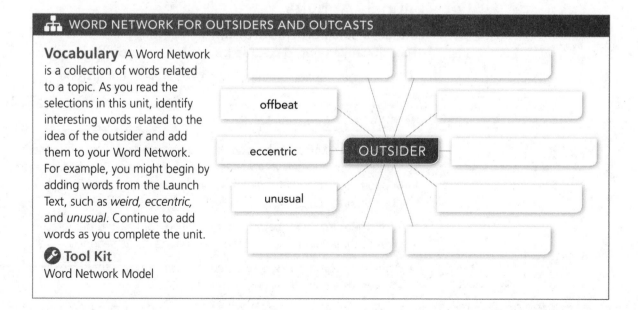

⛓ WORD NETWORK FOR OUTSIDERS AND OUTCASTS

Vocabulary A Word Network is a collection of words related to a topic. As you read the selections in this unit, identify interesting words related to the idea of the outsider and add them to your Word Network. For example, you might begin by adding words from the Launch Text, such as *weird, eccentric,* and *unusual.* Continue to add words as you complete the unit.

🔧 **Tool Kit**
Word Network Model

offbeat

eccentric

unusual

OUTSIDER

Summary

Write a summary of "Isn't Everyone a Little Bit Weird?" A **summary** is a concise, complete, and accurate overview of a text. It should not include a statement of your opinion or an analysis.

Launch Activity

Conduct a Small Group Discussion Consider this question: **Why might exceptionally talented people be considered odd?**

- Record your position on the question and explain your thinking.

- Get together with a small group of students and discuss your responses. Consider similarities in your points of view, and work to clarify differences. Support your ideas with examples from texts you have read or your own observations.

- After your discussion, have a representative from each group present a two- to three-minute summary of the group's conversation.

- After all the groups have presented, discuss as a class the similarities and differences among the views presented.

QuickWrite

Consider class discussions, presentations, the video, and the Launch Text as you think about the prompt. Record your first thoughts here.

PROMPT: **Is the experience of being an outsider universal?**

✎ EVIDENCE LOG FOR OUTSIDERS AND OUTCASTS

Review your QuickWrite, and summarize your initial position in one sentence to record in your Evidence Log. Then, record evidence from "Isn't Everyone a Little Bit Weird?" that supports your position.

After each selection, you will continue to use your Evidence Log to record the evidence you gather and the connections you make.

🔧 **Tool Kit**
Evidence Log Model

Title of Text: _____ Date: _____

CONNECTION TO PROMPT	TEXT EVIDENCE/DETAILS	ADDITIONAL NOTES/IDEAS

How does this text change or add to my thinking?   Date: _____

ESSENTIAL QUESTION:

Do people need to belong?

Do we all feel like outsiders at some point in our lives? Is being an outsider always a negative experience? Can being an outsider offer any advantages? You will work with your whole class to explore the ins and outs of being an outsider.

Whole-Class Learning Strategies

Throughout your life, in school, in your community, and in your career, you will continue to learn and work in large-group environments.

Review these strategies and the actions you can take to practice them as you work with your whole class. Add ideas of your own for each step. Get ready to use these strategies during Whole-Class Learning.

STRATEGY	ACTION PLAN
Listen actively	• Eliminate distractions. For example, put your cell phone away. • Keep your eyes on the speaker. •
Clarify by asking questions	• If you're confused, other people probably are, too. Ask a question to help your whole class. • If you see that you are guessing, ask a question instead. •
Monitor understanding	• Notice what information you already know and be ready to build on it. • Ask for help if you are struggling. •
Interact and share ideas	• Share your ideas and answer questions, even if you are unsure. • Build on the ideas of others by adding details or making a connection. •

SCAN FOR MULTIMEDIA

CONTENTS

About the Author

Franz Kafka (1883–1924) was one of the greatest German-speaking writers of the twentieth century, but he received no support from his family. His mother did not understand his passion for literature. His father, a man obsessed with materialism, would not accept "author" as a legitimate profession. Kafka was also torn between multiple social worlds. His German identity clashed constantly with his Jewish heritage. Themes of domestic pressure and social anxiety recur often in Kafka's fiction.

🔧 **Tool Kit**
First-Read Guide and Model Annotation

📋 STANDARDS

Reading Literature
By the end of grade 10, read and comprehend literature, including stories, dramas, and poems, at the high end of the grades 9-10 text complexity band independently and proficiently.

The Metamorphosis

Concept Vocabulary

You will encounter the following words as you read "The Metamorphosis." Before reading, note how familiar you are with each word. Rank the words in order from most familiar (1) to least familiar (6).

WORD	YOUR RANKING
distress	
amelioration	
aversion	
asphyxiation	
listlessly	
travail	

After completing your first read, come back to the selection vocabulary and review your rankings. Mark changes to your original rankings as needed.

First Read FICTION

Apply these strategies as you conduct your first read. You will have an opportunity to complete the close-read notes after your first read.

NOTICE *whom* the story is about, *what* happens, *where* and *when* it happens, and *why* those involved react as they do.

ANNOTATE by marking vocabulary and key passages you want to revisit.

First Read

CONNECT ideas within the selection to what you already know and what you have already read.

RESPOND by completing the Comprehension Check and by writing a brief summary of the selection.

The Metamorphosis

Franz Kafka

translated by Ian Johnston

BACKGROUND

Many authors produce great writing that moves, challenges, and inspires readers. Only a few, however, make such distinctive contributions that their names become synonymous with specific literary qualities. Such is the case with Kafka. The term *Kafkaesque* describes a nightmarish mood—specifically the feeling that one is trapped in a dangerous, distorted world. This story, which many scholars consider to be one of the greatest literary works of the twentieth century, is a prime example of Kafka's work.

SCAN FOR MULTIMEDIA

~I~

1   One morning, as Gregor Samsa was waking up from anxious dreams, he discovered that in bed he had been changed into a monstrous verminous bug. He lay on his armor-hard back and saw, as he lifted his head up a little, his brown, arched abdomen divided up into rigid bow-like sections. From this height the blanket, just about ready to slide off completely, could hardly stay in place. His numerous legs, pitifully thin in comparison to the rest of his circumference, flickered helplessly before his eyes.

2   "What's happened to me," he thought. It was no dream. His room, a proper room for a human being, only somewhat too small, lay quietly between the four well-known walls. Above the table, on which an unpacked collection of sample cloth goods was spread out (Samsa was a traveling salesman), hung the picture which he had cut out of an illustrated magazine a little while ago and set in a pretty gilt frame. It was a picture of a woman with a fur hat and a fur boa. She sat erect there, lifting up in the direction of the viewer a solid fur muff into which her entire forearm disappeared.

NOTES

CLOSE READ

ANNOTATE: In paragraphs 3–5, mark details that relate to Gregor's physical transformation. Mark other details that show what he is thinking.

QUESTION: Why does Kafka devote so much more space to Gregor's thoughts than to his physical change?

CONCLUDE: What is the effect of this choice?

3   Gregor's glance then turned to the window. The dreary weather (the raindrops were falling audibly down on the metal window ledge) made him quite melancholy. "Why don't I keep sleeping for a little while longer and forget all this foolishness," he thought. But this was entirely impractical, for he was used to sleeping on his right side, and in his present state he couldn't get himself into this position. No matter how hard he threw himself onto his right side, he always rolled again onto his back. He must have tried it a hundred times, closing his eyes, so that he would not have to see the wriggling legs, and gave up only when he began to feel a light, dull pain in his side which he had never felt before.

4   "O God," he thought, "what a demanding job I've chosen! Day in, day out on the road. The stresses of trade are much greater than the work going on at head office, and, in addition to that, I have to deal with the problems of traveling, the worries about train connections, irregular bad food, temporary and constantly changing human relationships, which never come from the heart. To hell with it all!" He felt a slight itching on the top of his abdomen. He slowly pushed himself on his back closer to the bedpost so that he could lift his head more easily, found the itchy part, which was entirely covered with small white spots (he did not know what to make of them), and wanted to feel the place with a leg. But he retracted it immediately, for the contact felt like a cold shower all over him.

5   He slid back again into his earlier position. "This getting up early," he thought, "makes a man quite idiotic. A man must have his sleep. Other traveling salesmen live like harem women. For instance, when I come back to the inn during the course of the morning to write up the necessary orders, these gentlemen are just sitting down to breakfast. If I were to try that with my boss, I'd be thrown out on the spot. Still, who knows whether that mightn't be really good for me. If I didn't hold back for my parents' sake, I would've quit ages ago. I would've gone to the boss and told him just what I think from the bottom of my heart. He would've fallen right off his desk! How weird it is to sit up at the desk and talk down to the employee from way up there. The boss has trouble hearing, so the employee has to step up quite close to him. Anyway, I haven't completely given up that hope yet. Once I've got together the money to pay off the parents' debt to him—that should take another five or six years—I'll do it for sure. Then I'll make the big break. In any case, right now I have to get up. My train leaves at five o'clock."

6   And he looked over at the alarm clock ticking away by the chest of drawers. "Good God," he thought. It was half past six, and the hands were going quietly on. It was past the half hour, already nearly quarter to. Could the alarm have failed to ring? One saw from the bed that it was properly set for four o'clock. Certainly it had rung. Yes, but was it possible to sleep through this noise that made the furniture shake? Now, it's true he'd not slept quietly, but evidently he'd slept all the more deeply. Still, what should he do now? The

next train left at seven o'clock. To catch that one, he would have to go in a mad rush. The sample collection wasn't packed up yet, and he really didn't feel particularly fresh and active. And even if he caught the train, there was no avoiding a blow up with the boss, because the firm's errand boy would've waited for the five o'clock train and reported the news of his absence long ago. He was the boss's minion, without backbone or intelligence. Well then, what if he reported in sick? But that would be extremely embarrassing and suspicious, because during his five years' service Gregor hadn't been sick even once. The boss would certainly come with the doctor from the health insurance company and would reproach his parents for their lazy son and cut short all objections with the insurance doctor's comments; for him everyone was completely healthy but really lazy about work. And besides, would the doctor in this case be totally wrong? Apart from a really excessive drowsiness after the long sleep, Gregor in fact felt quite well and even had a really strong appetite.

7   As he was thinking all this over in the greatest haste, without being able to make the decision to get out of bed (the alarm clock was indicating exactly quarter to seven) there was a cautious knock on the door by the head of the bed.

8   "Gregor," a voice called (it was his mother!), "it's quarter to seven. Don't you want to be on your way?" The soft voice! Gregor was startled when he heard his voice answering. It was clearly and unmistakably his earlier voice, but in it was intermingled, as if from below, an irrepressibly painful squeaking which left the words positively distinct only in the first moment and distorted them in the reverberation, so that one didn't know if one had heard correctly. Gregor wanted to answer in detail and explain everything, but in these circumstances he confined himself to saying, "Yes, yes, thank you, Mother. I'm getting up right away." Because of the wooden door the change in Gregor's voice was not really noticeable outside, so his mother calmed down with this explanation and shuffled off. However, as a result of the short conversation the other family members became aware of the fact that Gregor was unexpectedly still at home, and already his father was knocking on one side door, weakly but with his fist. "Gregor, Gregor," he called out, "what's going on?" And after a short while he urged him on again in a deeper voice. "Gregor! Gregor!" At the other side door, however, his sister knocked lightly. "Gregor? Are you all right? Do you need anything?" Gregor directed answers in both directions, "I'll be ready right away." He made an effort with the most careful articulation and by inserting long pauses between the individual words to remove everything remarkable from his voice. His father turned back to his breakfast. However, his sister whispered, "Gregor, open the door, I beg you." Gregor had no intention of opening the door, but congratulated himself on his precaution, acquired from traveling, of locking all doors during the night, even at home.

© Pearson Education, Inc., or its affiliates. All rights reserved.

9   First he wanted to stand up quietly and undisturbed, get dressed, above all have breakfast, and only then consider further action, for (he noticed this clearly) by thinking things over in bed he would not reach a reasonable conclusion. He remembered that he had already often felt a light pain or other in bed, perhaps the result of an awkward lying position, which later turned out to be purely imaginary when he stood up, and he was eager to see how his present fantasies would gradually dissipate. That the change in his voice was nothing other than the onset of a real chill, an occupational illness of commercial travelers, of that he had not the slightest doubt.

10   It was very easy to throw aside the blanket. He needed only to push himself up a little, and it fell by itself. But to continue was difficult, particularly because he was so unusually wide. He needed arms and hands to push himself upright. Instead of these, however, he had only many small limbs which were incessantly moving with very different motions and which, in addition, he was unable to control. If he wanted to bend one of them, then it was the first to extend itself, and if he finally succeeded doing with this limb what he wanted, in the meantime all the others, as if left free, moved around in an excessively painful agitation. "But I must not stay in bed uselessly," said Gregor to himself.

11   At first he wanted to get out of bed with the lower part of his body, but this lower part (which he incidentally had not yet looked at and which he also couldn't picture clearly) proved itself too difficult to move. The attempt went so slowly. When, having become almost frantic, he finally hurled himself forward with all his force and without thinking, he chose his direction incorrectly, and he hit the lower bedpost hard. The violent pain he felt revealed to him that the lower part of his body was at the moment probably the most sensitive.

12   Thus, he tried to get his upper body out of the bed first and turned his head carefully toward the edge of the bed. He managed to do this easily, and in spite of its width and weight his body mass at last slowly followed the turning of his head. But as he finally raised his head outside the bed in the open air, he became anxious about moving forward any further in this manner, for if he allowed himself eventually to fall by this process, it would take a miracle to prevent his head from getting injured. And at all costs he must not lose consciousness right now. He preferred to remain in bed.

13   However, after a similar effort, while he lay there again sighing as before and once again saw his small limbs fighting one another, if anything worse than before, and didn't see any chance of imposing quiet and order on this arbitrary movement, he told himself again that he couldn't possibly remain in bed and that it might be the most reasonable thing to sacrifice everything if there was even the slightest hope of getting himself out of bed in the process. At the same moment, however, he didn't forget to remind himself from time to time of the fact that calm (indeed the calmest) reflection might

CLOSE READ

ANNOTATE: In paragraph 10, mark words and phrases that describe how Gregor is moving.

QUESTION: What do these details suggest about Gregor's ability to control his new body?

CONCLUDE: What is the effect of this word choice?

be better than the most confused decisions. At such moments, he directed his gaze as precisely as he could toward the window, but unfortunately there was little confident cheer to be had from a glance at the morning mist, which concealed even the other side of the narrow street. "It's already seven o'clock," he told himself at the latest striking of the alarm clock, "already seven o'clock and still such a fog." And for a little while longer he lay quietly with weak breathing, as if perhaps waiting for normal and natural conditions to reemerge out of the complete stillness.

14   But then he said to himself, "Before it strikes a quarter past seven, whatever happens I must be completely out of bed. Besides, by then someone from the office will arrive to inquire about me, because the office will open before seven o'clock." And he made an effort then to rock his entire body length out of the bed with a uniform motion. If he let himself fall out of the bed in this way, his head, which in the course of the fall he intended to lift up sharply, would probably remain uninjured. His back seemed to be hard; nothing would really happen to that as a result of the fall. His greatest reservation was a worry about the loud noise which the fall must create and which presumably would arouse, if not fright, then at least concern on the other side of all the doors. However, it had to be tried.

15   As Gregor was in the process of lifting himself half out of bed (the new method was more of a game than an effort; he needed only to rock with a constant rhythm) it struck him how easy all this would be if someone were to come to his aid. Two strong people (he thought of his father and the servant girl) would have been quite sufficient. They would have only had to push their arms under his arched back to get

distress (dihs TREHS) *n.*
unhappiness or pain

him out of the bed, to bend down with their load, and then merely to exercise patience and care that he completed the flip onto the floor, where his diminutive legs would then, he hoped, acquire a purpose. Now, quite apart from the fact that the doors were locked, should he really call out for help? In spite of all his **distress**, he was unable to suppress a smile at this idea.

16   He had already got to the point where, with a stronger rocking, he maintained his equilibrium with difficulty, and very soon he would finally have to decide, for in five minutes it would be a quarter past seven. Then there was a ring at the door of the apartment. "That's someone from the office," he told himself, and he almost froze while his small limbs only danced around all the faster. For one moment everything remained still. "They aren't opening," Gregor said to himself, caught up in some absurd hope. But of course then, as usual, the servant girl with her firm tread went to the door and opened it. Gregor needed to hear only the visitor's first word of greeting to recognize immediately who it was, the manager himself. Why was Gregor the only one condemned to work in a firm where at the slightest lapse someone immediately attracted the greatest suspicion? Were all the employees then collectively, one and all, scoundrels? Was there then among them no truly devoted person who, if he failed to use just a couple of hours in the morning for office work, would become abnormal from pangs of conscience and really be in no state to get out of bed? Was it really not enough to let an apprentice make inquiries, if such questioning was even necessary? Must the manager himself come, and in the process must it be demonstrated to the entire innocent family that the investigation of this suspicious circumstance could only be entrusted to the intelligence of the manager? And more as a consequence of the excited state in which this idea put Gregor than as a result of an actual decision, he swung himself with all his might out of the bed. There was a loud thud, but not a real crash. The fall was absorbed somewhat by the carpet and, in addition, his back was more elastic than Gregor had thought. For that reason the dull noise was not quite so conspicuous. But he had not held his head up with sufficient care and had hit it. He turned his head, irritated and in pain, and rubbed it on the carpet.

> Then there was a ring at the door of the apartment. "That's someone from the office," he told himself, and he almost froze while his small limbs only danced around all the faster.

17   "Something has fallen in there," said the manager in the next room on the left. Gregor tried to imagine to himself whether anything similar to what was happening to him today could have also happened at some point to the manager. At least one had to concede the possibility of such a thing. However, as if to give a rough answer to this question, the manager now took a few determined steps in the next room, with a squeak of his polished boots. From the neighboring room on the right

his sister was whispering to inform Gregor: "Gregor, the manager is here." "I know," said Gregor to himself. But he did not dare make his voice loud enough so that his sister could hear.

18   "Gregor," his father now said from the neighboring room on the left, "Mr. Manager has come and is asking why you have not left on the early train. We don't know what we should tell him. Besides, he also wants to speak to you personally. So please open the door. He will be good enough to forgive the mess in your room."

19   In the middle of all this, the manager called out in a friendly way, "Good morning, Mr. Samsa." "He is not well," said his mother to the manager, while his father was still talking at the door, "He is not well, believe me, Mr. Manager. Otherwise how would Gregor miss a train! The young man has nothing in his head except business. I'm almost angry that he never goes out at night. Right now he's been in the city eight days, but he's been at home every evening. He sits there with us at the table and reads the newspaper quietly or studies his travel schedules. It's quite a diversion for him if he busies himself with fretwork.[1] For instance, he cut out a small frame over the course of two or three evenings. You'd be amazed how pretty it is. It's hanging right inside the room. You'll see it immediately, as soon as Gregor opens the door. Anyway, I'm happy that you're here, Mr. Manager. By ourselves, we would never have made Gregor open the door. He's so stubborn, and he's certainly not well, although he denied that this morning."

20   "I'm coming right away," said Gregor slowly and deliberately and didn't move, so as not to lose one word of the conversation. "My dear lady, I cannot explain it to myself in any other way," said the manager; "I hope it is nothing serious. On the other hand, I must also say that we businesspeople, luckily or unluckily, however one looks at it, very often simply have to overcome a slight indisposition for business reasons."

21   "So can Mr. Manager come in to see you now?" asked his father impatiently and knocked once again on the door. "No," said Gregor. In the neighboring room on the left a painful stillness descended. In the neighboring room on the right his sister began to sob.

22   Why didn't his sister go to the others? She'd probably just gotten up out of bed now and hadn't even started to get dressed yet. Then why was she crying? Because he wasn't getting up and wasn't letting the manager in; because he was in danger of losing his position, and because then his boss would badger his parents once again with the old demands? Those were probably unnecessary worries right now. Gregor was still here and wasn't thinking at all about abandoning his family. At the moment he was lying right there on the carpet, and no one who knew about his condition would've seriously demanded that he let the manager in. But Gregor wouldn't be casually dismissed right away because of this small discourtesy, for which he would find an easy and suitable excuse later on. It

---

1. **fretwork** (FREHT wurk) *n.* decorative woodworking.

The Metamorphosis   **143**

seemed to Gregor that it might be far more reasonable to leave him in peace at the moment, instead of disturbing him with crying and conversation. But it was the very uncertainty which distressed the others and excused their behavior.

23   "Mr. Samsa," the manager was now shouting, his voice raised, "what's the matter? You are barricading yourself in your room, answer with only a yes and a no, are making serious and unnecessary troubles for your parents, and neglecting (I mention this only incidentally) your commercial duties in a truly unheard-of manner. I am speaking here in the name of your parents and your employer, and I am requesting you in all seriousness for an immediate and clear explanation. I am amazed. I am amazed. I thought I knew you as a calm, reasonable person, and now you appear suddenly to want to start parading around in weird moods. The Chief indicated to me earlier this very day a possible explanation for your neglect— it concerned the collection of cash entrusted to you a short while ago—but in truth I almost gave him my word of honor that this explanation could not be correct. However, now I see here your unimaginable pigheadedness, and I am totally losing any desire to speak up for you in the slightest. And your position is not at all the most secure. Originally I intended to mention all this to you privately, but since you are letting me waste my time here uselessly, I don't know why the matter shouldn't come to the attention of your parents. Your productivity has also been very unsatisfactory recently. Of course, it's not the time of year to conduct exceptional business, we recognize that, but a time of year for conducting no business, there is no such thing at all, Mr. Samsa, and such a thing must never be."

24   "But Mr. Manager," called Gregor, beside himself and in his agitation forgetting everything else, "I'm opening the door immediately, this very moment. A slight indisposition, a dizzy spell, has prevented me from getting up. I'm still lying in bed right now. But now I'm quite refreshed once again. I'm in the midst of getting out of bed. Just have patience for a short moment! Things are not going so well as I thought. But things are all right. How suddenly this can overcome someone! Just yesterday evening everything was fine with me. My parents certainly know that. Actually just yesterday evening I had a small premonition. People must have seen that in me. Why have I not reported that to the office! But people always think that they'll get over sickness without having to stay at home. Mr. Manager! Take it easy on my parents! There is really no basis for the criticisms which you are now making against me, and really nobody has said a word to me about that. Perhaps you have not read the latest orders which I shipped. Besides, now I'm setting out on my trip on the eight o'clock train; the few hours' rest have made me stronger. Mr. Manager, do not stay. I will be at the office in person right away. Please have the goodness to say that and to convey my respects to the Chief."

25   While Gregor was quickly blurting all this out, hardly aware of what he was saying, he had moved close to the chest of drawers without effort, probably as a result of the practice he had already had in bed, and now he was trying to raise himself up on it. Actually, he wanted to open the door; he really wanted to let himself be seen by and to speak with the manager. He was keen to witness what the others now asking after him would say at the sight of him. If they were startled, then Gregor had no more responsibility and could be calm. But if they accepted everything quietly, then he would have no reason to get excited and, if he got a move on, could really be at the station around eight o'clock.

26   At first he slid down a few times from the smooth chest of drawers. But at last he gave himself a final swing and stood upright there. He was no longer at all aware of the pains in his lower body, no matter how they might still sting. Now he let himself fall against the back of a nearby chair, on the edge of which he braced himself with his thin limbs. By doing this he gained control over himself and kept quiet, for he could now hear the manager.

27   "Did you understand a single word?" the manager asked the parents. "Is he playing the fool with us?" "For God's sake," cried the mother already in tears, "perhaps he's very ill and we're upsetting him. Grete! Grete!" she yelled at that point. "Mother?" called the sister from the other side. They were making themselves understood through Gregor's room. "You must go to the doctor right away. Gregor is sick. Hurry to the doctor. Have you heard Gregor speak yet?"

28   "That was an animal's voice," said the manager, remarkably quietly in comparison to the mother's cries.

29   "Anna! Anna!" yelled the father through the hall into the kitchen, clapping his hands, "fetch a locksmith right away!" The two young women were already running through the hall with swishing skirts (how had his sister dressed herself so quickly?) and yanked open the doors of the apartment. One couldn't hear the doors closing at all. They probably had left them open, as is customary in an apartment in which a huge misfortune has taken place.

30   However, Gregor had become much calmer. All right, people did not understand his words any more, although they seemed clear enough to him, clearer than previously, perhaps because his ears had gotten used to them. But at least people now thought that things were not all right with him and were prepared to help him. The confidence and assurance with which the first arrangements had been carried out made him feel good. He felt himself included once again in the circle of humanity and was expecting from both the doctor and the locksmith, without differentiating between them with any real precision, splendid and surprising results. In order to get as clear a voice as possible for the critical conversation which was imminent, he coughed a little, and certainly took the trouble to do this in a really subdued way, since it was possible that even this noise sounded like something different from a human cough. He no longer

trusted himself to decide any more. Meanwhile in the next room it had become really quiet. Perhaps his parents were sitting with the manager at the table and were whispering; perhaps they were all leaning against the door and listening.

31   Gregor pushed himself slowly toward the door, with the help of the easy chair, let go of it there, threw himself against the door, held himself upright against it (the balls of his tiny limbs had a little sticky stuff on them), and rested there momentarily from his exertion. Then he made an effort to turn the key in the lock with his mouth. Unfortunately it seemed that he had no real teeth. How then was he to grab hold of the key? But to make up for that his jaws were naturally very strong; with their help he managed to get the key really moving, and he did not notice that he was obviously inflicting some damage on himself, for a brown fluid came out of his mouth, flowed over the key, and dripped onto the floor.

32   "Just listen for a moment," said the manager in the next room, "he's turning the key." For Gregor that was a great encouragement. But they all should've called out to him, including his father and mother, "Come on, Gregor!" They should've shouted, "Keep going, keep working on the lock!" Imagining that all his efforts were being followed with suspense, he bit down frantically on the key with all the force he could muster. As the key turned more, he danced around the lock. Now he was holding himself upright only with his mouth, and he had to hang onto the key or then press it down again with the whole weight of his body, as necessary. The quite distinct click of the lock as it finally snapped really woke Gregor up. Breathing heavily he

said to himself, "So I didn't need the locksmith," and he set his head against the door handle to open the door completely.

33   Because he had to open the door in this way, it was already open very wide without him yet being really visible. He first had to turn himself slowly around the edge of the door, very carefully, of course, if he did not want to fall awkwardly on his back right at the entrance into the room. He was still preoccupied with this difficult movement and had no time to pay attention to anything else, when he heard the manager exclaim a loud "Oh!" (it sounded like the wind whistling), and now he saw him, nearest to the door, pressing his hand against his open mouth and moving slowly back, as if an invisible constant force was pushing him away. His mother (in spite of the presence of the manager she was standing here with her hair sticking up on end, still a mess from the night) with her hands clasped was looking at his father; she then went two steps toward Gregor and collapsed right in the middle of her skirts spreading out all around her, her face sunk on her breast, completely concealed. His father clenched his fist with a hostile expression, as if he wished to push Gregor back into his room, then looked uncertainly around the living room, covered his eyes with his hands, and cried so that his mighty breast shook.

34   At this point Gregor did not take one step into the room, but leaned his body from the inside against the firmly bolted wing of the door, so that only half his body was visible, as well as his head, tilted sideways, with which he peeped over at the others. Meanwhile it had become much brighter. Standing out clearly from the other side of the street was a part of the endless gray-black house situated opposite (it was a hospital) with its severe regular windows breaking up the facade. The rain was still coming down, but only in large individual drops visibly and firmly thrown down one by one onto the ground. The breakfast dishes were standing piled around on the table, because for his father breakfast was the most important meal time in the day, which he prolonged for hours by reading various newspapers. Directly across on the opposite wall hung a photograph of Gregor from the time of his military service; it was a picture of him as a lieutenant, as he, smiling and worry-free, with his hand on his sword, demanded respect for his bearing and uniform. The door to the hall was ajar, and since the door to the apartment was also open, one saw out into the landing of the apartment and the start of the staircase going down.

35   "Now," said Gregor, well aware that he was the only one who had kept his composure. "I'll get dressed right away, pack up the collection of samples, and set off. You'll allow me to set out on my way, will you not? You see, Mr. Manager, I am not pigheaded, and I am happy to work. Traveling is exhausting, but I couldn't live without it. Where are you going, Mr. Manager? To the office? Really? Will you report everything truthfully? A person can be incapable of work momentarily, but that is precisely the best time to remember the earlier achievements and to consider that later, after

CLOSE READ

ANNOTATE: In paragraph 34, mark details that describe Gregor at a different time in his life.

QUESTION: Why does Kafka include these details?

CONCLUDE: What effect does Kafka achieve by including this description?

the obstacles have been shoved aside, the person will work all the more keenly and intensely. I am really so indebted to Mr. Chief—you know that perfectly well. On the other hand, I am concerned about my parents and my sister. I'm in a fix, but I'll work myself out of it again. Don't make things more difficult for me than they already are. Speak up on my behalf in the office! People don't like traveling salesmen. I know that. People think they earn pots of money and thus lead a fine life. People don't even have any special reason to think through this judgment more clearly. But you, Mr. Manager, you have a better perspective on the interconnections than the other people, even, I tell you in total confidence, a better perspective than Mr. Chairman himself, who in his capacity as the employer may let his judgment make casual mistakes at the expense of an employee. You also know well enough that the traveling salesman who is outside the office almost the entire year can become so easily a victim of gossip, coincidences, and groundless complaints, against which it's impossible for him to defend himself, since for the most part he doesn't hear about them at all and only then when he's exhausted after finishing a trip, and gets to feel in his own body at home the nasty consequences, which can't be thoroughly explored back to their origins. Mr. Manager, don't leave without speaking a word telling me that you'll at least concede that I'm a little in the right!"

36   But at Gregor's first words the manager had already turned away, and now he looked back at Gregor over his twitching shoulders with pursed lips. During Gregor's speech he was not still for a moment, but was moving away toward the door, without taking his eyes off Gregor, but really gradually, as if there was a secret ban on leaving the room. He was already in the hall, and after the sudden movement with which he finally pulled his foot out of the living room, one could have believed that he had just burned the sole of his foot. In the hall, however, he stretched out his right hand away from his body toward the staircase, as if some truly supernatural relief was waiting for him there.

37   Gregor realized that he must not under any circumstances allow the manager to go away in this frame of mind, especially if his position in the firm was not to be placed in the greatest danger. His parents did not understand all this very well. Over the long years, they had developed the conviction that Gregor was set up for life in his firm and, in addition, they had so much to do nowadays with their present troubles that all foresight was foreign to them. But Gregor had this foresight. The manager must be held back, calmed down, convinced, and finally won over. The future of Gregor and his family really depended on it! If only his sister had been there! She was clever. She had already cried while Gregor was still lying quietly on his back. And the manager, this friend of the ladies, would certainly let himself be guided by her. She would have closed the door to the apartment and talked him out of his fright in the hall. But his sister was not even there. Gregor must deal with it himself.

38   Without thinking that as yet he didn't know anything about his present ability to move and without thinking that his speech possibly (indeed probably) had once again not been understood, he left the wing of the door, pushed himself through the opening, and wanted to go over to the manager, who was already holding tight onto the handrail with both hands on the landing in a ridiculous way. But as he looked for something to hold onto, with a small scream Gregor immediately fell down onto his numerous little legs. Scarcely had this happened, when he felt for the first time that morning a general physical well-being. The small limbs had firm floor under them; they obeyed perfectly, as he noticed to his joy, and strove to carry him forward in the direction he wanted. Right away he believed that the final **amelioration** of all his suffering was immediately at hand. But at the very moment when he lay on the floor rocking in a restrained manner quite close and directly across from his mother (apparently totally sunk into herself) she suddenly sprang right up with her arms spread far apart and her fingers extended and cried out, "Help, for God's sake, help!" She held her head bowed down, as if she wanted to view Gregor better, but ran senselessly back, contradicting that gesture, forgetting that behind her stood the table with all the dishes on it. When she reached the table, she sat down heavily on it, as if absentmindedly, and did not appear to notice at all that next to her coffee was pouring out onto the carpet in a full stream from the large overturned container.

amelioration (uh MEEL yuh RAY shuhn) *n.* act of making something better or less painful

39   "Mother, mother," said Gregor quietly, and looked over toward her. The manager momentarily had disappeared completely from his mind; by contrast, at the sight of the flowing coffee he couldn't stop himself snapping his jaws in the air a few times. At that his mother screamed all over again, hurried from the table, and collapsed into the arms of his father, who was rushing toward her. But Gregor had no time right now for his parents: The manager was already on the staircase. His chin level with the banister, the manager looked back for the last time. Gregor took an initial movement to catch up to him if possible. But the manager must have suspected something, because he made a leap down over a few stairs and disappeared, still shouting, "Huh!" The sound echoed throughout the entire stairwell.

> But as he looked for something to hold onto, with a small scream Gregor immediately fell down onto his numerous little legs.

40   Now, unfortunately this flight of the manager also seemed completely to bewilder his father, who earlier had been relatively calm, for instead of running after the manager himself or at least not hindering Gregor from his pursuit, with his right hand he grabbed hold of the manager's cane, which he had left behind with his hat and overcoat on a chair. With his left hand, his father picked up a large newspaper from the table and, stamping his feet on the floor, he set out to drive Gregor back into his room by waving the cane and

the newspaper. No request of Gregor's was of any use; no request would even be understood. No matter how willing he was to turn his head respectfully, his father just stomped all the harder with his feet.

41   Across the room from him his mother had pulled open a window, in spite of the cool weather, and leaning out with her hands on her cheeks, she pushed her face far outside the window. Between the alley and the stairwell a strong draft came up, the curtains on the window flew around, the newspapers on the table swished, and individual sheets fluttered down over the floor. The father relentlessly pressed forward pushing out sibilants, like a wild man. Now, Gregor had no practice at all in going backwards; it was really going very slowly. If Gregor only had been allowed to turn himself around, he would have been in his room right away, but he was afraid to make his father impatient by the time-consuming process of turning around, and each moment he faced the threat of a mortal blow on his back or his head from the cane in his father's hand. Finally Gregor had no other option, for he noticed with horror that he did not understand yet how to maintain his direction going backwards. And so he began, amid constantly anxious sideways glances in his father's direction, to turn himself around as quickly as possible (although in truth this was only very slowly). Perhaps his father noticed his good intentions, for he did not disrupt Gregor

in this motion, but with the tip of the cane from a distance he even directed here and there Gregor's rotating movement.

42   If only there hadn't been his father's unbearable hissing! Because of that Gregor totally lost his head. He was already almost totally turned around, when, always with this hissing in his ear, he just made a mistake and turned himself back a little. But when he finally was successful in getting his head in front of the door opening, it became clear that his body was too wide to go through any further. Naturally his father, in his present mental state, had no idea of opening the other wing of the door a bit to create a suitable passage for Gregor to get through. His single fixed thought was that Gregor must get into his room as quickly as possible. He would never have allowed the elaborate preparations that Gregor required to orient himself and thus perhaps get through the door. On the contrary, as if there were no obstacle and with a peculiar noise, he now drove Gregor forward. Behind Gregor the sound was at this point no longer like the voice of only a single father. Now it was really no longer a joke, and Gregor forced himself, come what might, into the door. One side of his body was lifted up. He lay at an angle in the door opening. His one flank was sore with the scraping. On the white door ugly blotches were left. Soon he was stuck fast and would have not been able to move any more on his own. The tiny legs on one side hung twitching in the air above, the ones on the other side were pushed painfully into the floor. Then his father gave him one really strong liberating push from behind, and he scurried, bleeding severely, far into the interior of his room. The door was slammed shut with the cane, and finally it was quiet.

NOTES

CLOSE READ
ANNOTATE: In paragraphs 41 and 42, mark details that describe the father's voice.

QUESTION: Why does Kafka emphasize what the father sounds like?

CONCLUDE: What effect do these details have?

~‖~

43   Gregor first woke up from his heavy swoon-like sleep in the evening twilight. He would certainly have woken up soon afterwards without any disturbance, for he felt himself sufficiently rested and wide awake, although it appeared to him as if a hurried step and a cautious closing of the door to the hall had aroused him. The shine of the electric streetlights lay pale here and there on the ceiling and on the higher parts of the furniture, but underneath around Gregor it was dark. He pushed himself slowly toward the door, still groping awkwardly with his feelers, which he now learned to value for the first time, to check what was happening there. His left side seemed one single long unpleasantly stretched scar, and he really had to hobble on his two rows of legs. In addition, one small leg had been seriously wounded in the course of the morning incident (it was almost a miracle that only one had been hurt) and dragged lifelessly behind.

44   By the door he first noticed what had really lured him there: It was the smell of something to eat. For there stood a bowl filled with sweetened milk, in which swam tiny pieces of white bread. He

almost laughed with joy, for he now had a much greater hunger than in the morning, and he immediately dipped his head almost up to and over his eyes down into the milk. But he soon drew it back again in disappointment, not just because it was difficult for him to eat on account of his delicate left side (he could eat only if his entire panting body worked in a coordinated way), but also because the milk, which otherwise was his favorite drink and which his sister had certainly placed there for that reason, did not appeal to him at all. He turned away from the bowl almost with **aversion** and crept back into the middle of the room.

45   In the living room, as Gregor saw through the crack in the door, the gas was lit, but where on other occasions at this time of day the father was accustomed to read the afternoon newspaper in a loud voice to his mother and sometimes also to his sister, at the moment not a sound was audible. Now, perhaps this reading aloud, about which his sister had always spoken and written to him, had recently fallen out of their general routine. But it was so still all around, in spite of the fact that the apartment was certainly not empty. "What a quiet life the family leads," said Gregor to himself and, as he stared fixedly out in front of him into the darkness, he felt a great pride that he had been able to provide such a life in a beautiful apartment like this for his parents and his sister. But how would things go if now all tranquility, all prosperity, all contentment should come to a horrible end? In order not to lose himself in such thoughts, Gregor preferred to set himself moving and crawled up and down in his room.

46   Once during the long evening one side door and then the other door was opened just a tiny crack and quickly closed again. Someone presumably needed to come in but had then thought better of it. Gregor immediately took up a position by the living room door, determined to bring in the hesitant visitor somehow or other or at least to find out who it might be. But now the door was not opened any more, and Gregor waited in vain. Earlier, when the door had been barred, they had all wanted to come in to him; now, when he had opened one door and when the others had obviously been opened during the day, no one came any more, and the keys were stuck in the locks on the outside.

47   The light in the living room was turned off only late at night, and now it was easy to establish that his parents and his sister had stayed awake all this time, for one could hear clearly as all three moved away on tiptoe. Now it was certain that no one would come into Gregor any more until the morning. Thus, he had a long time to think undisturbed about how he should reorganize his life from scratch. But the high, open room, in which he was compelled to lie flat on the floor, made him anxious, without his being able to figure out the reason, for he had lived in the room for five years. With a half-unconscious turn and not without a slight shame he scurried under the couch, where, in spite of the fact that his back was a little cramped

aversion (uh VUR zhuhn) *n.* strong dislike

CLOSE READ

ANNOTATE: In paragraph 45, mark details that relate to silence and stillness. Mark other, fewer details that relate to movement.

QUESTION: Why does Kafka include these details?

CONCLUDE: How do these details emphasize Gregor's alienation from his family?

and he could no longer lift up his head, he felt very comfortable and was sorry only that his body was too wide to fit completely under it.

48   There he remained the entire night, which he spent partly in a state of semi-sleep, out of which his hunger constantly woke him with a start, but partly in a state of worry and murky hopes, which all led to the conclusion that for the time being he would have to keep calm and with patience and the greatest consideration for his family tolerate the troubles which in his present condition he was now forced to cause them.

49   Already early in the morning (it was still almost night) Gregor had an opportunity to test the power of the decisions he had just made, for his sister, almost fully dressed, opened the door from the hall into his room and looked eagerly inside. She did not find him immediately, but when she noticed him under the couch (God, he had to be somewhere or other; for he could hardly fly away) she got such a shock that, without being able to control herself, she slammed the door shut once again from the outside. However, as if she was sorry for her behavior, she immediately opened the door again and walked in on her tiptoes, as if she was in the presence of a serious invalid or a total stranger. Gregor had pushed his head forward just to the edge of the couch and was observing her. Would she really notice that he had left the milk standing, not indeed from any lack of hunger, and would she bring in something else to eat more suitable for him? If she did not do it on her own, he would sooner starve to death than call her attention to the fact, although he had a really powerful urge to move beyond the couch, throw himself at his sister's feet, and beg her for something or other good to eat. But his sister noticed right away with astonishment that the bowl was still full, with only a little milk spilled around it. She picked it up immediately (although not with her bare hands but with a rag), and took it out of the room. Gregor was extremely curious what she would bring as a substitute, and he pictured to himself different ideas about that. But he never could have guessed what his sister out of the goodness of her heart in fact did. She brought him, to test his taste, an entire selection, all spread out on an old newspaper. There were old half-rotten vegetables, bones from the evening meal, covered with a white sauce which had almost solidified, some raisins and almonds, cheese, which Gregor had declared inedible two days earlier, a slice of dry bread, a slice of salted bread smeared with butter. In addition to all this, she put down a bowl (probably designated once and for all as Gregor's) into which she had poured some water. And out of her delicacy of feeling, since she knew that Gregor would not eat in front of her, she went away very quickly and even turned the key in the lock, so that Gregor could now observe that he could make himself as comfortable as he wished. Gregor's small limbs buzzed as the time for eating had come. His wounds must, in any case, have already healed completely. He felt no handicap on that score. He was astonished at that and thought about it, how more than a month ago he had cut his finger slightly

with a knife and how this wound had hurt enough even the day before yesterday.

50   "Am I now going to be less sensitive," he thought, already sucking greedily on the cheese, which had strongly attracted him right away, more than all the other foods. Quickly and with his eyes watering with satisfaction, he ate one after the other the cheese, the vegetables, and the sauce; the fresh food, by contrast, didn't taste good to him. He couldn't bear the smell and even carried the things he wanted to eat a little distance away. By the time his sister slowly turned the key as a sign that he should withdraw, he was long finished and now lay lazily in the same spot. The noise immediately startled him, in spite of the fact that he was already almost asleep, and he scurried back again under the couch. But it cost him great self-control to remain under the couch, even for the short time his sister was in the room, because his body had filled out somewhat on account of the rich meal and in the narrow space there he could scarcely breathe. In the midst of minor attacks of **asphyxiation**, he looked at her with somewhat protruding eyes, as his unsuspecting sister swept up with a broom, not just the remnants, but even the foods which Gregor had not touched at all, as if these were also now useless, and as she dumped everything quickly into a bucket, which she closed with a wooden lid, and then carried all of it out of the room. She had hardly turned around before Gregor had already dragged himself out from the couch, stretched out, and let his body expand.

51   In this way Gregor got his food every day, once in the morning, when his parents and the servant girl were still asleep, and a second time after the common noon meal, for his parents were, as before, asleep then for a little while, and the servant girl was sent off by his sister on some errand or other. Certainly they would not have wanted Gregor to starve to death, but perhaps they could not have endured finding out what he ate other than by hearsay. Perhaps his sister wanted to spare them what was possibly only a small grief, for they were really suffering quite enough already.

52   What sorts of excuses people had used on that first morning to get the doctor and the locksmith out of the house Gregor was completely unable to ascertain. Since he was not comprehensible, no one, not even his sister, thought that he might be able to understand others, and thus, when his sister was in her room, he had to be content with listening now and then to her sighs and invocations to the saints. Only later, when she had grown somewhat accustomed to everything (naturally there could never be any talk of her growing completely accustomed to it) Gregor sometimes caught a comment which was intended to be friendly or could be interpreted as such. "Well, today it tasted good to him," she said, if Gregor had really cleaned up what

Certainly they would not have wanted Gregor to starve to death, but perhaps they could not have endured finding out what he ate other than by hearsay.

asphyxiation (uhs fihk see AY shuhn) *n.* state of being unable to breathe

he had to eat; whereas, in the reverse situation, which gradually repeated itself more and more frequently, she used to say sadly, "Now everything has stopped again."

53   But while Gregor could get no new information directly, he did hear a good deal from the room next door, and as soon as he heard voices, he scurried right away to the relevant door and pressed his entire body against it. In the early days especially, there was no conversation which was not concerned with him in some way or other, even if only in secret. For two days at all meal times discussions on that subject could be heard on how people should now behave; but they also talked about the same subject in the times between meals, for there were always at least two family members at home, since no one really wanted to remain in the house alone and people could not under any circumstances leave the apartment completely empty. In addition, on the very first day the servant girl (it was not completely clear what and how much she knew about what had happened) on her knees had begged his mother to let her go immediately, and when she said goodbye about fifteen minutes later, she thanked them for the dismissal with tears in her eyes, as if she was receiving the greatest favor which people had shown her there, and, without anyone demanding it from her, she swore a fearful oath not to betray anyone, not even the slightest bit.

54   Now his sister had to team up with his mother to do the cooking, although that didn't create much trouble because people were eating almost nothing. Again and again Gregor listened as one of them vainly invited another one to eat and received no answer other than "Thank you. I have enough" or something like that. And perhaps they had stopped having anything to drink, too. His sister often asked his father whether he wanted to have a beer and gladly offered to fetch it herself, and when his father was silent, she said, in order to remove any reservations he might have, that she could send the caretaker's wife to get it. But then his father finally said a resounding "No," and nothing more would be spoken about it.

55   Already during the first day his father laid out all the financial circumstances and prospects to his mother and to his sister as well. From time to time he stood up from the table and pulled out of the small lockbox salvaged from his business, which had collapsed five years previously, some document or other or some notebook. The sound was audible as he opened up the complicated lock and, after removing what he was looking for, locked it up again. These explanations by his father were, in part, the first enjoyable thing that Gregor had the chance to listen to since his imprisonment. He had thought that nothing at all was left over for his father from that business; at least his father had told him nothing to contradict that view, and Gregor in any case hadn't asked him about it. At the time Gregor's only concern had been to devote everything he had in order to allow his family to forget as quickly as possible the business misfortune which had brought them all into a state of

CLOSE READ

ANNOTATE: Mark details in paragraph 53 that show how the servant girl behaves when she quits her job.

QUESTION: Why does Kafka describe the servant girl's behavior in such detail?

CONCLUDE: What is the effect of this description?

complete hopelessness. And so at that point he'd started to work with a special intensity and from an assistant had become, almost overnight, a traveling salesman, who naturally had entirely different possibilities for earning money and whose successes at work at once were converted into the form of cash commissions, which could be set out on the table at home in front of his astonished and delighted family. Those had been beautiful days, and they had never come back afterwards, at least not with the same splendor, in spite of the fact that Gregor later earned so much money that he was in a position to bear the expenses of the entire family, expenses which he, in fact, did bear. They had become quite accustomed to it, both the family and Gregor as well. They took the money with thanks, and he happily surrendered it, but the special warmth was no longer present. Only the sister had remained still close to Gregor, and it was his secret plan to send her (in contrast to Gregor she loved music very much and knew how to play the violin charmingly) next year to the conservatory, regardless of the great expense which that must necessitate and which would be made up in other ways. Now and then during Gregor's short stays in the city the conservatory was mentioned in conversations with his sister, but always only as a beautiful dream, whose realization was unimaginable, and their parents never listened to these innocent expectations with pleasure. But Gregor thought about them with scrupulous consideration and intended to explain the matter ceremoniously on Christmas Eve.

56   In his present situation, such futile ideas went through his head, while he pushed himself right up against the door and listened. Sometimes in his general exhaustion he couldn't listen any more and let his head bang **listlessly** against the door, but he immediately pulled himself together, for even the small sound which he made by this motion was heard nearby and silenced everyone. "There he goes on again," said his father after a while, clearly turning toward the door, and only then would the interrupted conversation gradually be resumed again.

57   Gregor found out clearly enough (for his father tended to repeat himself often in his explanations, partly because he had not personally concerned himself with these matters for a long time now, and partly also because his mother did not understand everything right away the first time) that, in spite of all bad luck, a fortune, although a very small one, was available from the old times, on which the interest (which had not been touched) had in the intervening time gradually allowed to increase a little. Furthermore, in addition to this, the money which Gregor had brought home every month (he had kept only a few florins for himself) had not been completely spent and had grown into a small capital amount. Gregor, behind his door, nodded eagerly, rejoicing over this unanticipated foresight and frugality. True, with this excess money, he could have paid off more of his father's debt to his employer and the day on which he could be rid of this position would have been

listlessly (LIHST lihs lee) *adv.* without energy or interest

CLOSE READ

ANNOTATE: In paragraph 57, mark the parts of sentences that are set off in parentheses.

QUESTION: Why does the author separate out this information?

CONCLUDE: What is the effect of setting these sections apart in this way?

a lot closer, but now things were doubtless better the way his father had arranged them.

58   At the moment, however, this money was nowhere near sufficient to permit the family to live on the interest payments. Perhaps it would be enough to maintain the family for one or at most two years, that's all. Thus it came only to an amount which one should not really take out and which must be set aside for an emergency. But the money to live on must be earned. Now, his father was a healthy man, although he was old, who had not worked at all for five years now and thus could not be counted on for very much. He had in these five years, the first holidays of his trouble-filled but unsuccessful life, put on a good deal of fat and thus had become really heavy. And should his old mother now maybe work for money, a woman who suffered from asthma, for whom wandering through the apartment even now was a great strain and who spent every second day on the sofa by the open window laboring for breath? Should his sister earn money, a girl who was still a seventeen-year-old child, whose earlier life style had been so very delightful that it had consisted of dressing herself nicely, sleeping in late, helping around the house, taking part in a few modest enjoyments and, above all, playing the violin? When it came to talking about this need to earn money, at first Gregor went away from the door and threw himself on the cool leather sofa beside the door, for he was quite hot from shame and sorrow.

59   Often he lay there all night long. He didn't sleep a moment and just scratched on the leather for hours at a time. He undertook the very difficult task of shoving a chair over to the window. Then he crept up on the windowsill and, braced in the chair, leaned against the window to look out, obviously with some memory or other of the satisfaction which that used to bring him in earlier times. Actually from day to day he perceived things with less and less clarity, even those a short distance away: The hospital across the street, the all too frequent sight of which he had previously cursed, was not visible at all any more, and if he had not been precisely aware that he lived in the quiet but completely urban Charlotte Street, he could have believed that from his window he was peering out at a featureless wasteland, in which the gray heaven and the gray earth had merged and were indistinguishable. His attentive sister must have observed a couple of times that the chair stood by the window; then, after cleaning up the room, each time she pushed the chair back right against the window and from now on she even left the inner casement open.

60   If Gregor had only been able to speak to his sister and thank her for everything that she had to do for him, he would have tolerated her service more easily. As it was he suffered under it. The sister admittedly sought to cover up the awkwardness of everything as much as possible, and, as time went by, she naturally got more successful at it. But with the passing of time Gregor also came to understand everything more precisely. Even her entrance was terrible for him. As soon as she entered, she ran straight to the window,

without taking the time to shut the door (in spite of the fact that she was otherwise very considerate in sparing anyone the sight of Gregor's room), and yanked the window open with eager hands, as if she was almost suffocating, and remained for a while by the window breathing deeply, even when it was still so cold. With this running and noise she frightened Gregor twice every day. The entire time he trembled under the couch, and yet he knew very well that she would certainly have spared him gladly if it had only been possible to remain with the window closed in a room where Gregor lived.

61   On one occasion (about one month had already gone by since Gregor's transformation, and there was now no particular reason any more for his sister to be startled at Gregor's appearance) she came a little earlier than usual and came upon Gregor as he was still looking out the window, immobile and well positioned to frighten someone. It would not have come as a surprise to Gregor if she had not come in, since his position was preventing her from opening the window immediately. But she not only did not step inside; she even retreated and shut the door. A stranger really could have concluded from this that Gregor had been lying in wait for her and wanted to bite her. Of course, Gregor immediately concealed himself under the couch, but he had to wait until the noon meal before his sister returned, and she seemed much less calm than usual. From this he realized that his appearance was still constantly intolerable to her and must remain intolerable in the future, and that she really had to exert a lot of self-control not to run away from a glimpse of only the small part of his body which stuck out from under the couch. In order to spare her even this sight, one day he dragged the sheet on his back onto the

couch (this task took him four hours) and arranged it in such a way that he was now completely concealed and his sister, even if she bent down, could not see him. If this sheet was not necessary as far as she was concerned, then she could remove it, for it was clear enough that Gregor could not derive any pleasure from isolating himself away so completely. But she left the sheet just as it was, and Gregor believed he even caught a look of gratitude when on one occasion he carefully lifted up the sheet a little with his head to check as his sister took stock of the new arrangement.

62   In the first two weeks his parents could not bring themselves to visit him, and he often heard how they fully acknowledged his sister's present work; whereas, earlier they had often got annoyed at his sister because she had seemed to them a somewhat useless young woman. However, now both his father and his mother often waited in front of Gregor's door while his sister cleaned up inside, and as soon as she came out she had to explain in detail how things looked in the room, what Gregor had eaten, how he had behaved this time, and whether perhaps a slight improvement was perceptible. In any event, his mother comparatively soon wanted to visit Gregor, but his father and his sister restrained her, at first with reasons which Gregor listened to very attentively and which he completely endorsed. Later, however, they had to hold her back forcefully, and when she then cried, "Let me go to Gregor. He's my unlucky son! Don't you understand that I have to go to him?" Gregor then thought that perhaps it would be a good thing if his mother came in, not every day, of course, but maybe once a week. She understood everything much better than his sister, who in spite of all her courage was still a child and, in the last analysis, had perhaps undertaken such a difficult task only out of childish recklessness.

63   Gregor's wish to see his mother was soon realized. While during the day Gregor, out of consideration for his parents, did not want to show himself by the window, he couldn't crawl around very much on the few square meters of the floor. He found it difficult to bear lying quietly during the night, and soon eating no longer gave him the slightest pleasure. So for diversion he acquired the habit of crawling back and forth across the walls and ceiling. He was especially fond of hanging from the ceiling. The experience was quite different from lying on the floor. It was easier to breathe, a slight vibration went through his body, and in the midst of the almost happy amusement which Gregor found up there, it could happen that, to his own surprise, he let go and hit the floor. However, now he naturally controlled his body quite differently, and he did not injure himself in such a great fall. His sister noticed immediately the new amusement which Gregor had found for himself (for as he crept around he left behind here and there traces of his sticky stuff), and so she got the idea of making Gregor's creeping around as easy as possible and thus of removing the furniture which got in the way, especially the chest of drawers and the writing desk.

CLOSE READ

ANNOTATE: In paragraph 63, mark details that describe Gregor's growing comfort in and knowledge of his new body.

QUESTION: Why does the author provide these details?

CONCLUDE: What is the effect of these details?

64   But she was in no position to do this by herself. She did not dare to ask her father to help, and the servant girl would certainly not have assisted her, for although this girl, about sixteen years old, had courageously remained since the dismissal of the previous cook, she had begged for the privilege of being allowed to stay permanently confined to the kitchen and of having to open the door only in answer to a special summons. Thus, his sister had no other choice but to involve his mother while his father was absent. His mother approached Gregor's room with cries of excited joy, but she fell silent at the door. Of course, his sister first checked whether everything in the room was in order. Only then did she let his mother walk in. In great haste Gregor had drawn the sheet down even further and wrinkled it more. The whole thing really looked just like a coverlet thrown carelessly over the couch. On this occasion, Gregor held back from spying out from under the sheet. Thus, he refrained from looking at his mother this time and was just happy that she had come. "Come on; he is not visible," said his sister, and evidently led his mother by the hand. Now Gregor listened as these two weak women shifted the still heavy old chest of drawers from its position, and as his sister constantly took on herself the greatest part of the work, without listening to the warnings of his mother who was afraid that she would strain herself. The work lasted a long time. After about a quarter of an hour had already gone by his mother said that it would be better if they left the chest of drawers where it was, because, in the first place, it was too heavy: they would not be finished before his father's arrival, and with the chest of drawers in the middle of the room it would block all Gregor's pathways, but, in the second place, it might not be certain that Gregor would be pleased with the removal of the furniture. To her the reverse seemed to be true; the sight of the empty walls pierced her right to the heart, and why should Gregor not feel the same, since he had been accustomed to the room furnishings for a long time and in an empty room would thus feel himself abandoned.

65   "And is it not the case," his mother concluded very quietly, almost whispering as if she wished to prevent Gregor, whose exact location she really didn't know, from hearing even the sound of her voice (for she was convinced that he did not understand her words), "and isn't it a fact that by removing the furniture we're showing that we're giving up all hope of an improvement and are leaving him to his own resources without any consideration? I think it would be best if we tried to keep the room exactly in the condition in which it was before, so that, when Gregor returns to us, he finds everything unchanged and can forget the intervening time all the more easily."

66   As he heard his mother's words Gregor realized that the lack of all immediate human contact, together with the monotonous life surrounded by the family over the course of these two months must have confused his understanding, because otherwise he couldn't

explain to himself that he in all seriousness could've been so keen to have his room emptied. Was he really eager to let the warm room, comfortably furnished with pieces he had inherited, be turned into a cavern in which he would, of course, then be able to crawl about in all directions without disturbance, but at the same time with a quick and complete forgetting of his human past as well? Was he then at this point already on the verge of forgetting and was it only the voice of his mother, which he had not heard for a long time, that had aroused him? Nothing was to be removed; everything must remain. In his condition he couldn't function without the beneficial influences of his furniture. And if the furniture prevented him from carrying out his senseless crawling about all over the place, then there was no harm in that, but rather a great benefit.

67   But his sister unfortunately thought otherwise. She had grown accustomed, certainly not without justification, so far as the discussion of matters concerning Gregor was concerned, to act as a special expert with respect to their parents, and so now the mother's advice was for his sister sufficient reason to insist on the removal, not only of the chest of drawers and the writing desk, which were the only items she had thought about at first, but also of all the furniture, with the exception of the indispensable couch. Of course, it was not only childish defiance and her recent very unexpected and hard won self-confidence which led her to this demand. She had also actually observed that Gregor needed a great deal of room to creep about; the furniture, on the other hand, as far as one could see, was not of the slightest use.

68   But perhaps the enthusiastic sensibility of young women of her age also played a role. This feeling sought release at every opportunity, and with it Grete now felt tempted to want to make Gregor's situation even more terrifying, so that then she would be able to do even more for him than now. For surely no one except Grete would ever trust themselves to enter a room in which Gregor ruled the empty walls all by himself. And so she did not let herself be dissuaded from her decision by her mother, who in this room seemed uncertain of herself in her sheer agitation and soon kept quiet, helping his sister with all her energy to get the chest of drawers out of the room. Now, Gregor could still do without the chest of drawers if need be, but the writing desk really had to stay. And scarcely had the women left the room with the chest of drawers, groaning as they pushed it, when Gregor stuck his head out from under the sofa to take a look at how he could intervene cautiously and with as much consideration as possible. But unfortunately it was his mother who came back into the room first, while Grete had her arms wrapped around the chest of drawers in the next room and was rocking it back and forth by herself, without moving it from its position. His mother was not used to the sight of Gregor; he could have made her ill, and so, frightened, Gregor scurried backwards right to the other end of the sofa, but he could no longer prevent the sheet from moving

forward a little. That was enough to catch his mother's attention. She came to a halt, stood still for a moment, and then went back to Grete.

69   Although Gregor kept repeating to himself over and over that really nothing unusual was going on, that only a few pieces of furniture were being rearranged, he soon had to admit to himself that the movements of the women to and fro, their quiet conversations, the scratching of the furniture on the floor affected him like a great swollen commotion on all sides, and, so firmly was he pulling in his head and legs and pressing his body into the floor, he had to tell himself unequivocally that he wouldn't be able to endure all this much longer. They were cleaning out his room, taking away from him everything he cherished; they had already dragged out the chest of drawers in which the fret saw and other tools were kept, and they were now loosening the writing desk which was fixed tight to the floor, the desk on which he, as a business student, a school student, indeed even as an elementary school student, had written out his assignments. At that moment he really didn't have any more time to check the good intentions of the two women, whose existence he had in any case almost forgotten, because in their exhaustion they were working really silently, and the heavy stumbling of their feet was the only sound to be heard.

70   And so he scuttled out (the women were just propping themselves up on the writing desk in the next room in order to take a breather) changing the direction of his path four times. He really didn't know what he should rescue first. Then he saw hanging conspicuously on the wall, which was otherwise already empty, the picture of the woman dressed in nothing but fur. He quickly scurried up over it and pressed himself against the glass that held it in place and which made his hot abdomen feel good. At least this picture, which Gregor at the moment completely concealed, surely no one would now take away. He twisted his head toward the door of the living room to observe the women as they came back in.

71   They had not allowed themselves very much rest and were coming back right away. Grete had placed her arm around her mother and held her tightly. "So what shall we take now?" said Grete and looked around her. Then her glance crossed with Gregor's from the wall. She kept her composure only because her mother was there. She bent her face toward her mother in order to prevent her from looking around, and said, although in a trembling voice and too quickly, "Come, wouldn't it be better to go back to the living room for just another moment?" Grete's purpose was clear to Gregor: she wanted to bring his mother to a safe place and then chase him down from the wall. Well, let her just attempt that! He squatted on his picture and did not hand it over. He would sooner spring into Grete's face.

72   But Grete's words had immediately made the mother very uneasy. She walked to the side, caught sight of the enormous brown splotch on the flowered wallpaper, and, before she became truly aware that what she was looking at was Gregor, screamed out in a high pitched

raw voice "Oh God, oh God" and fell with outstretched arms, as if she was surrendering everything, down onto the couch and lay there motionless. "Gregor, you . . . ," cried out his sister with a raised fist and an urgent glare. Since his transformation those were the first words which she had directed right at him. She ran into the room next door to bring some spirits or other with which she could revive her mother from her fainting spell. Gregor wanted to help as well (there was time enough to save the picture), but he was stuck fast on the glass and had to tear himself loose forcefully. Then he also scurried into the next room, as if he could give his sister some advice, as in earlier times, but then he had to stand there idly behind her, while she rummaged about among various small bottles. Still, she was frightened when she turned around. A bottle fell onto the floor and shattered. A splinter of glass wounded Gregor in the face, some corrosive medicine or other dripped over him. Now, without lingering any longer, Grete took as many small bottles as she could hold and ran with them into her mother. She slammed the door shut with her foot. Gregor was now shut off from his mother, who was perhaps near death, thanks to him. He could not open the door, and he did not want to chase away his sister who had to remain with her mother. At this point he had nothing to do but wait, and overwhelmed with self-reproach and worry, he began to creep and crawl over everything: walls, furniture, and ceiling. Finally, in his despair, as the entire room started to spin around him, he fell onto the middle of the large table.

73   A short time elapsed. Gregor lay there limply. All around was still. Perhaps that was a good sign. Then there was a ring at the door. The servant girl was naturally shut up in her kitchen, and Grete must therefore go to open the door. The father had arrived. "What's happened," were his first words. Grete's appearance had told him everything. Grete replied with a dull voice; evidently she was pressing her face into her father's chest: "Mother fainted, but she's getting better now. Gregor has broken loose."

74   "Yes, I have expected that," said his father. "I always told you that, but you women don't want to listen."

75   It was clear to Gregor that his father had badly misunderstood Grete's short message and was assuming that Gregor had committed some violent crime or other. Thus, Gregor now had to find his father to calm him down, for he had neither the time nor the opportunity to clarify things for him. And so he rushed away to the door of his room and pushed himself against it, so that his father could see right away as he entered from the hall that Gregor fully intended to return at once to his room, that it was not necessary to drive him back, but that one only needed to open the door and he would disappear immediately.

76   But his father was not in the mood to observe such niceties. "Ah," he yelled as soon as he entered, with a tone as if he were all at once angry and pleased. Gregor pulled his head back from the door and

NOTES

CLOSE READ

ANNOTATE: Mark the sentences in paragraph 73 that are five words long or shorter.

QUESTION: How are these sentences different from Kafka's usual sentences?

CONCLUDE: What is the effect of this sentence variation?

raised it in the direction of his father. He had not really pictured his father as he now stood there. Of course, what with his new style of creeping all around, he had in the past while neglected to pay attention to what was going on in the rest of the apartment, as he had done before, and really should have grasped the fact that he would encounter different conditions. Nevertheless, nevertheless, was that still his father? Was that the same man who had lain exhausted and buried in bed in earlier days when Gregor was setting out on a business trip, who had received him on the evenings of his return in a sleeping gown and armchair, totally incapable of standing up, who had only lifted his arm as a sign of happiness, and who in their rare strolls together a few Sundays a year and on the important holidays made his way slowly forward between Gregor and his mother (who themselves moved slowly), always a bit more slowly than them, bundled up in his old coat, all the time setting down his walking stick carefully, and who, when he had wanted to say something, almost always stood still and gathered his entourage around him?

77   But now he was standing up really straight, dressed in a tight fitting blue uniform with gold buttons, like the ones servants wear in a banking company. Above the high stiff collar of his jacket his firm double chin stuck out prominently, beneath his bushy eyebrows the glance of his black eyes was freshly penetrating and alert, his otherwise disheveled white hair was combed down into a carefully exact shining part. He threw his cap, on which a gold monogram (apparently the symbol of the bank) was affixed, in an arc across the entire room onto the sofa and moved, throwing back the edge of the long coat of his uniform, with his hands in his trouser pockets and a grim face, right up to Gregor.

78   He really didn't know what he had in mind, but he raised his foot uncommonly high anyway, and Gregor was astonished at the gigantic size of his sole of his boot. However, he did not linger on that point. For he knew from the first day of his new life that as far as he was concerned his father considered the greatest force the only appropriate response. And so he scurried away from his father, stopped when his father remained standing, and scampered forward again when his father merely stirred. In this way they made their way around the room repeatedly, without anything decisive taking place; indeed because of the slow pace it didn't look like a chase. Gregor remained on the floor for the time being, especially as he was afraid that his father could take a flight up onto the wall or the ceiling as an act of real malice. At any event Gregor had to tell himself that he couldn't keep up this running around for a long time, because whenever his father took a single step, he had to go through an enormous number of movements. Already he was starting to suffer from a shortage of breath, just as in his earlier days his lungs had been quite unreliable. As he now staggered around in this way in order to gather all his energies for running, hardly keeping his eyes open, in his listlessness he had no notion at all of any escape other

CLOSE READ

ANNOTATE: Mark the verbs in paragraph 78 that indicate Gregor's movements. When there is a "not," include that in your annotation.

QUESTION: What kind of movement do these verbs describe?

CONCLUDE: What do these movements indicate about Gregor's feelings toward his father?

than by running and had almost already forgotten that the walls were available to him, although they were obstructed by carefully carved furniture full of sharp points and spikes—at that moment something or other thrown casually flew down close by and rolled in front of him. It was an apple; immediately a second one flew after it. Gregor stood still in fright. Further flight was useless, for his father had decided to bombard him.

79   From the fruit bowl on the sideboard his father had filled his pockets, and now, without for the moment taking accurate aim, was throwing apple after apple. These small red apples rolled as if electrified around on the floor and collided with each other. A weakly thrown apple grazed Gregor's back but skidded off harmlessly. However another thrown immediately after that one drove into Gregor's back really hard. Gregor wanted to drag himself off, as if the unexpected and incredible pain would go away if he changed his position. But he felt as if he was nailed in place and lay stretched out completely confused in all his senses. Only with his final glance did he notice how the door of his room was pulled open and how, right in front of his sister (who was yelling), his mother ran out in her undergarments, for his sister had undressed her in order to give her some freedom to breathe in her fainting spell, and how his mother then ran up to his father, on the way her tied-up skirts one after the other slipped toward the floor, and how, tripping over her skirts, she hurled herself onto his father and, throwing her arms around him, in complete union with him—but at this moment Gregor's powers of sight gave way—as her hands reached to the back of his father's head and she begged him to spare Gregor's life.

~III~

80 Gregor's serious wound, from which he suffered for over a month (since no one ventured to remove the apple, it remained in his flesh as a visible reminder), seemed by itself to have reminded the father that, in spite of his present unhappy and hateful appearance, Gregor was a member of the family, something one should not treat as an enemy, and that it was, on the contrary, a requirement of family duty to suppress one's aversion and to endure—nothing else, just endure. And if through his wound Gregor had now apparently lost for good his ability to move and for the time being needed many, many minutes to crawl across his room, like an aged invalid (so far as creeping up high was concerned, that was unimaginable), nevertheless for this worsening of his condition, in his opinion, he did get completely satisfactory compensation, because every day toward evening the door to the living room, which he was in the habit of keeping a sharp eye on even one or two hours beforehand, was opened, so that he, lying down in the darkness of his room, invisible from the living room, could see the entire family at the illuminated table and listen to their conversation, to a certain extent with their common permission, a situation quite different from what happened before.

81 Of course, it was no longer the animated social interaction of former times, about which Gregor in small hotel rooms had always thought with a certain longing, when, tired out, he had to throw himself in the damp bedclothes. For the most part what went on now was very quiet. After the evening meal the father fell asleep quickly in his armchair; the mother and sister talked guardedly to each other in the stillness. Bent far over, the mother sewed fine undergarments for a fashion shop. The sister, who had taken on a job as a salesgirl, in the evening studied stenography and French, so as perhaps later to obtain a better position. Sometimes the father woke up and, as if he was quite ignorant that he had been asleep, said to the mother, "How long you have been sewing today!" and went right back to sleep, while the mother and the sister smiled tiredly to each other.

82 With a sort of stubbornness the father refused to take off his servant's uniform even at home, and while his sleeping gown hung unused on the coat hook, the father dozed completely dressed in his place, as if he was always ready for his responsibility and even here was waiting for the voice of his superior. As a result, in spite of all the care of the mother and sister, his uniform, which even at the start was not new, grew dirty, and Gregor looked, often for the entire evening, at this clothing, with stains all over it and with its gold buttons always polished, in which the old man, although very uncomfortable, slept peacefully nonetheless.

83 As soon as the clock struck ten, the mother tried encouraging the father gently to wake up and then persuading him to go to bed, on the ground that he couldn't get a proper sleep here and the father,

who had to report for service at six o'clock, really needed a good sleep. But in his stubbornness, which had gripped him since he had become a servant, he insisted always on staying even longer by the table, although he regularly fell asleep and then could only be prevailed upon with the greatest difficulty to trade his chair for the bed. No matter how much the mother and sister might at that point work on him with small admonitions, for a quarter of an hour he would remain shaking his head slowly, his eyes closed, without standing up. The mother would pull him by the sleeve and speak flattering words into his ear; the sister would leave her work to help her mother, but that would not have the desired effect on the father. He would settle himself even more deeply in his armchair. Only when the two women grabbed him under the armpits would he throw his eyes open, look back and forth at the mother and sister, and habitually say, "This is a life. This is the peace and quiet of my old age." And propped up by both women, he would heave himself up, elaborately, as if for him it was the greatest travail, allow himself to be led to the door by the women, wave them away there, and proceed on his own from there, while the mother quickly threw down her sewing implements and the sister her pen in order to run after the father and help him some more.

84   In this overworked and exhausted family who had time to worry any longer about Gregor more than was absolutely necessary? The household was constantly getting smaller. The servant girl was now let go. A huge bony cleaning woman with white hair flapping all over her head came in the morning and the evening to do the heaviest work. The mother took care of everything else in addition to her considerable sewing work. It even happened that various pieces of family jewelry, which previously the mother and sister had been overjoyed to wear on social and festive occasions, were sold, as Gregor found out in the evening from the general discussion of the prices they had fetched. But the greatest complaint was always that they could not leave this apartment, which was too big for their present means, since it was impossible to imagine how Gregor might be moved. But Gregor fully recognized that it was not just consideration for him which was preventing a move (for he could have been transported easily in a suitable box with a few air holes); the main thing holding the family back from a change in living quarters was far more their complete hopelessness and the idea that they had been struck by a misfortune like no one else in their entire circle of relatives and acquaintances.

85   What the world demands of poor people they now carried out to an extreme degree. The father bought breakfast to the petty officials at the bank, the mother sacrificed herself for the undergarments of strangers, the sister behind her desk was at the beck and call of customers, but the family's energies did not extend any further. And the wound in his back began to pain Gregor all over again, when now the mother and sister, after they had escorted the father to bed, came

travail (truh VAYL) *n.* difficult situation or work

back, let their work lie, moved close together, and sat cheek to cheek and when his mother would now say, pointing to Gregor's room, "Close the door, Grete," and when Gregor was again in the darkness, while close by the women mingled their tears or, quite dry-eyed, stared at the table.

86   Gregor spent his nights and days with hardly any sleep. Sometimes he thought that the next time the door opened he would take over the family arrangements just as he had earlier. In his imagination appeared again, after a long time, his employer and supervisor and the apprentices, the excessively gormless custodian, two or three friends from other businesses, a chambermaid from a hotel in the provinces, a loving fleeting memory, a female cashier from a hat shop, whom he had seriously, but too slowly courted— they all appeared mixed in with strangers or people he had already forgotten, but instead of helping him and his family, they were all unapproachable, and he was happy to see them disappear.

87   But then he was in no mood to worry about his family. He was filled with sheer anger over the wretched care he was getting, even though he couldn't imagine anything for which he might have an appetite. Still, he made plans about how he could take from the larder what he at all account deserved, even if he wasn't hungry. Without thinking any more about how one might be able to give Gregor special pleasure, the sister now kicked some food or other very quickly into his room in the morning and at noon, before she ran off to her shop, and in the evening, quite indifferent about whether the food had perhaps only been tasted or, what happened most frequently, remained entirely undisturbed, she whisked it out with one sweep of her broom. The task of cleaning his room, which she now always carried out in the evening, could not be done any more quickly. Streaks of dirt ran along the walls; here and there lay tangles of dust and garbage. At first, when his sister arrived, Gregor positioned himself in a particularly filthy corner in order with this posture to make something of a protest. But he could have well stayed there for weeks without his sister's changing her ways. Indeed, she perceived the dirt as much as he did, but she had decided just to let it stay.

88   In this business, with a touchiness which was quite new to her and which had generally taken over the entire family, she kept watch to see that the cleaning of Gregor's room remained reserved for her. Once his mother had undertaken a major cleaning of Gregor's room, which she had only completed successfully after using a few buckets of water. But the extensive dampness made Gregor sick and he lay supine, embittered and immobile on the couch. However, the mother's punishment was not delayed for long. For in the evening the sister had hardly observed the change in Gregor's room before she ran into the living room mightily offended and, in spite of her mother's hand lifted high in entreaty, broke out in a fit of crying. Her parents (the father had, of course, woken up with a start in

CLOSE READ

ANNOTATE: Mark the nouns in paragraph 86 that name people.

QUESTION: Why does Kafka include these details?

CONCLUDE: What sense of Gregor's past life do these references evoke?

his armchair) at first looked at her astonished and helpless; until they started to get agitated. Turning to his right, the father heaped reproaches on the mother that she was not to take over the cleaning of Gregor's room from the sister and, turning to his left, he shouted at the sister that she would no longer be allowed to clean Gregor's room ever again, while the mother tried to pull the father, beside himself in his excitement, into the bedroom; the sister, shaken by her crying fit, pounded on the table with her tiny fists, and Gregor hissed at all this, angry that no one thought about shutting the door and sparing him the sight of this commotion.

89   But even when the sister, exhausted from her daily work, had grown tired of caring for Gregor as she had before, even then the mother did not have to come at all on her behalf. And Gregor did not have to be neglected. For now the cleaning woman was there. This old widow, who in her long life must have managed to survive the worst with the help of her bony frame, had no real horror of Gregor. Without being in the least curious, she had once by chance opened Gregor's door. At the sight of Gregor, who, totally surprised, began to scamper here and there, although no one was chasing him, she remained standing with her hands folded across her stomach staring at him. Since then she did not fail to open the door furtively a little every morning and evening to look in on Gregor. At first, she also called him to her with words which she presumably thought were friendly, like "Come here for a bit, old dung beetle!" or "Hey, look at the old dung beetle!" Addressed in such a manner, Gregor answered nothing, but remained motionless in his place, as if the door had not been opened at all. If only, instead of allowing this cleaning woman to disturb him uselessly whenever she felt like it, they had instead given her orders to clean up his room every day! One day in the early morning (a hard downpour, perhaps already a sign of the coming spring, struck the window panes) when the cleaning woman started up once again with her usual conversation, Gregor was so bitter that he turned toward her, as if for an attack, although slowly and weakly. But instead of being afraid of him, the cleaning woman merely lifted up a chair standing close by the door and, as she stood there with her mouth wide open, her intention was clear: She would close her mouth only when the chair in her hand had been thrown down on Gregor's back. "This goes no further, all right?" she asked, as Gregor turned himself around again, and she placed the chair calmly back in the corner.

90   Gregor ate hardly anything any more. Only when he chanced to move past the food which had been prepared did he, as a game, take a bit into his mouth, hold it there for hours, and generally spit it out again. At first he thought it might be his sadness over the condition of his room which kept him from eating, but he very soon became reconciled to the alterations in his room. People had grown accustomed to put into storage in his room things which they couldn't put anywhere else, and at this point there were many such

things, now that they had rented one room of the apartment to three lodgers. These solemn gentlemen (all three had full beards, as Gregor once found out through a crack in the door) were meticulously intent on tidiness, not only in their own room but (since they had now rented a room here) in the entire household, and particularly in the kitchen. They simply did not tolerate any useless or shoddy stuff. Moreover, for the most part they had brought with them their own pieces of furniture. Thus, many items had become superfluous, and these were not really things one could sell or things people wanted to throw out. All these items ended up in Gregor's room, even the box of ashes and the garbage pail from the kitchen. The cleaning woman, always in a hurry, simply flung anything that was momentarily useless into Gregor's room. Fortunately Gregor generally saw only the relevant object and the hand which held it. The cleaning woman perhaps was intending, when time and opportunity allowed, to take the stuff out again or to throw everything out all at once, but in fact the things remained lying there, wherever they had ended up at the first throw, unless Gregor squirmed his way through the accumulation of junk and moved it. At first he was forced to do this because otherwise there was no room for him to creep around, but later he did it with a growing pleasure, although after such movements, tired to death and feeling wretched, he didn't budge for hours.

91   Because the lodgers sometimes also took their evening meal at home in the common living room, the door to the living room stayed shut on many evenings. But Gregor had no trouble at all going without the open door. Already on many evenings when it was open he had not availed himself of it, but, without the family noticing, was stretched out in the darkest corner of his room. However, once the cleaning woman had left the door to the living room slightly ajar, and it remained open even when the lodgers came in in the evening and the lights were put on. They sat down at the head of the table, where

in earlier days the mother, the father, and Gregor had eaten, unfolded their serviettes, and picked up their knives and forks. The mother immediately appeared in the door with a dish of meat and right behind her the sister with a dish piled high with potatoes. The food gave off a lot of steam. The gentlemen lodgers bent over the plate set before them, as if they wanted to check it before eating, and in fact the one who sat in the middle (for the other two he seemed to serve as the authority) cut off a piece of meat still on the plate obviously to establish whether it was sufficiently tender and whether or not something should be shipped back to the kitchen. He was satisfied, and the mother and sister, who had looked on in suspense, began to breathe easily and to smile.

92 The family itself ate in the kitchen. In spite of that, before the father went into the kitchen, he came into the room and with a single bow, cap in hand, made a tour of the table. The lodgers rose up collectively and murmured something in their beards. Then, when they were alone, they ate almost in complete silence. It seemed odd to Gregor that out of all the many different sorts of sounds of eating, what was always audible was their chewing teeth, as if by that Gregor should be shown that people needed their teeth to eat and that nothing could be done even with the most handsome toothless jawbone. "I really do have an appetite," Gregor said to himself sorrowfully, "but not for these things. How these lodgers stuff themselves, and I am dying."

93 On this very evening (Gregor didn't remember hearing it all through this period) the violin sounded from the kitchen. The lodgers had already ended their night meal, the middle one had pulled out a newspaper and had given each of the other two a page, and they were now leaning back, reading and smoking. When the violin started playing, they became attentive, got up, and went on tiptoe to the hall door, at which they remained standing pressed up against one another. They must have been audible from the kitchen, because the father called out, "Perhaps the gentlemen don't like the playing? It can be stopped at once."

94 "On the contrary," stated the lodger in the middle, "might the young woman not come in to us and play in the room here, where it is really much more comfortable and cheerful?"

95 "Oh, thank you," cried out the father, as if he were the one playing the violin. The men stepped back into the room and waited. Soon the father came with the music stand, the mother with the sheet music, and the sister with the violin. The sister calmly prepared everything for the recital. The parents, who had never previously rented a room and therefore exaggerated their politeness to the lodgers, dared not sit on their own chairs. The father leaned against the door, his right hand stuck between two buttons of his buttoned up uniform. The mother, however, accepted a chair offered by one lodger. Since she left the chair where the gentleman had chanced to put it, she sat to one side in a corner.

96   The sister began to play. The father and mother followed attentively, one on each side, the movements of her hands. Attracted by the playing, Gregor had ventured to advance a little further forward and his head was already in the living room. He scarcely wondered about the fact that recently he had had so little consideration for the others; earlier this consideration had been something he was proud of. And for that very reason he would've had at this moment more reason to hide away, because as a result of the dust which lay all over his room and flew around with the slightest movement, he was totally covered in dirt. On his back and his sides he carted around with him dust, threads, hair, and remnants of food. His indifference to everything was much too great for him to lie on his back and scour himself on the carpet, as he often had done earlier during the day. In spite of his condition he had no timidity about inching forward a bit on the spotless floor of the living room.

97   In any case, no one paid him any attention. The family was all caught up in the violin playing. The lodgers, by contrast, who for the moment had placed themselves, their hands in their trouser pockets, behind the music stand much too close to the sister, so that they could all see the sheet music, something that must certainly bother the sister, soon drew back to the window conversing in low voices with bowed heads, where they then remained, worriedly observed by the father. It now seemed really clear that, having assumed they were to hear a beautiful or entertaining violin recital, they were disappointed, and were allowing their peace and quiet to be disturbed only out of politeness. The way in which they all blew the smoke from their cigars out of their noses and mouths in particular led one to conclude that they were very irritated. And yet his sister was playing so beautifully. Her face was turned to the side, her gaze followed the score intently and sadly. Gregor crept forward still a little further and kept his head close against the floor in order to be able to catch her gaze if possible. Was he an animal that music so seized him? For him it was as if the way to the unknown nourishment he craved was revealing itself to him. He was determined to press forward right to his sister, to tug at her dress and to indicate to her in this way that she might still come with her violin into his room, because here no one valued the recital as he wanted to value it. He did not wish to let her go from his room any more, at least not as long as he lived. His frightening appearance would for the first time become useful for him. He wanted to be at all the doors of his room simultaneously and snarl back at the attackers. However, his sister should not be compelled but would remain with him voluntarily; she would sit next to him on the sofa, bend down her ear to him, and he would then confide in her that he firmly intended to send her to the conservatory and that, if his misfortune had not arrived in the interim, he would have announced this to everyone last Christmas (had Christmas really already come and gone?) and would have accepted no objections. After this explanation his sister would break

CLOSE READ

ANNOTATE: Beginning with the sentence that starts, "His frightening appearance," mark the auxiliary, or helping, verbs in paragraph 97.

QUESTION: What do those verbs indicate about the scene Gregor describes?

CONCLUDE: How do the verbs contribute to a sense of fantasy or wishing?

out in tears of emotion, and Gregor would lift himself up to her armpit and kiss her throat, which she, from the time she started going to work, had left exposed without a band or a collar.

"Mr. Samsa," called out the middle lodger to the father, and pointed his index finger, without uttering a further word, at Gregor as he was moving slowly forward. The violin fell silent. The middle lodger smiled, first shaking his head once at his friends, and then looked down at Gregor once more. Rather than driving Gregor back again, the father seemed to consider it of prime importance to calm down the lodgers, although they were not at all upset and Gregor seemed to entertain them more than the violin recital. The father hurried over to them and with outstretched arms tried to push them into their own room and simultaneously to block their view of Gregor with his own body. At this point they became really somewhat irritated, although one no longer knew whether that was because of the father's behavior or because of knowledge they had just acquired that they had had, without knowing it, a neighbor like Gregor. They demanded explanations from his father, raised their arms to make their points, tugged agitatedly at their beards, and moved back toward their room quite slowly. In the meantime, the isolation which had suddenly fallen upon his sister after the sudden breaking off of the recital had overwhelmed her. She had held onto the violin and bow in her limp hands for a little while and had continued to look at the sheet music as if she was still playing. All at once she pulled herself together, placed the instrument in her mother's lap (the mother was still sitting in her chair having trouble breathing and with her lungs laboring) and ran into the next room, which the lodgers, pressured by the father, were already approaching more rapidly. One could observe how under the sister's practiced hands the sheets and pillows on the beds were thrown on high and arranged. Even before the lodgers had reached the room, she was finished fixing the beds and was slipping out. The father seemed so gripped once again with his stubbornness that he forgot about the respect which he always owed to his renters. He pressed on and on, until at the door of the room the middle gentleman stamped loudly with his foot and thus brought the father to a standstill. "I hereby declare," the middle lodger said, raising his hand and casting his glance both on the mother and the sister, "that considering the disgraceful conditions prevailing in this apartment and family," with this he spat decisively on the floor, "I immediately cancel my room. I will, of course, pay nothing at all for the days which I have lived here; on the contrary I shall think about whether or not I will initiate some sort of action against you, something which—believe me—will be very easy to establish." He fell silent and looked directly in front of him, as if he was waiting for something. In fact, his two friends immediately joined in with their opinions, "We also give immediate notice." At that he seized the door handle, banged the door shut, and locked it.

99 The father groped his way tottering to his chair and let himself fall in it. It looked as if he was stretching out for his usual evening snooze, but the heavy nodding of his head (which looked as if it was without support) showed that he was not sleeping at all. Gregor had lain motionless the entire time in the spot where the lodgers had caught him. Disappointment with the collapse of his plan and perhaps also his weakness brought on by his severe hunger made it impossible for him to move. He was certainly afraid that a general disaster would break over him at any moment, and he waited. He was not even startled when the violin fell from the mother's lap, out from under her trembling fingers, and gave off a reverberating tone.

100 "My dear parents," said the sister banging her hand on the table by way of an introduction, "things cannot go on any longer in this way. Maybe if you don't understand that, well, I do. I will not utter my brother's name in front of this monster, and thus I say only that we must try to get rid of it. We have tried what is humanly possible to take care of it and to be patient. I believe that no one can criticize us in the slightest."

101 "She is right in a thousand ways," said the father to himself. The mother, who was still incapable of breathing properly, began to cough numbly with her hand held up over her mouth and a manic expression in her eyes.

102 The sister hurried over to her mother and held her forehead. The sister's words seemed to have led the father to certain reflections. He sat upright, played with his uniform hat among the plates, which still lay on the table from the lodgers' evening meal, and looked now and then at the motionless Gregor.

103 "We must try to get rid of it," the sister now said decisively to the father, for the mother, in her coughing fit, wasn't listening to anything. "It is killing you both. I see it coming. When people have to work as hard as we all do, they cannot also tolerate this endless torment at home. I just can't go on any more." And she broke out into such a crying fit that her tears flowed out down onto her mother's face. She wiped them off her mother with mechanical motions of her hands.

104 "Child," said the father sympathetically and with obvious appreciation, "then what should we do?"

105 The sister only shrugged her shoulders as a sign of the perplexity which, in contrast to her previous confidence, had come over her while she was crying.

106 "If only he understood us," said the father in a semi-questioning tone. The sister, in the midst of her sobbing, shook her hand energetically as a sign that there was no point thinking of that.

107 "If he only understood us," repeated the father and by shutting his eyes he absorbed the sister's conviction of the impossibility of this point, "then perhaps some compromise would be possible with him. But as it is . . ."

108 "It must be gotten rid of," cried the sister. "That is the only way, Father. You must try to get rid of the idea that this is Gregor. The fact

that we have believed for so long, that is truly our real misfortune. But how can it be Gregor? If it were Gregor, he would have long ago realized that a communal life among human beings is not possible with such an animal and would have gone away voluntarily. Then we would not have a brother, but we could go on living and honor his memory. But this animal plagues us. It drives away the lodgers, will obviously take over the entire apartment, and leave us to spend the night in the alley. Just look, Father," she suddenly cried out, "he's already starting up again." With a fright which was totally incomprehensible to Gregor, the sister even left the mother, pushed herself away from her chair, as if she would sooner sacrifice her mother than remain in Gregor's vicinity, and rushed behind her father who, excited merely by her behavior, also stood up and half raised his arms in front of the sister as though to protect her.

109   But Gregor did not have any notion of wishing to create problems for anyone and certainly not for his sister. He had just started to turn himself around in order to creep back into his room, quite a startling sight, since, as a result of his suffering condition, he had to guide himself through the difficulty of turning around with his head, in this process lifting and banging it against the floor several times. He paused and looked around. His good intentions seem to have been recognized. The fright had only lasted for a moment. Now they looked at him in silence and sorrow. His mother lay in her chair, with her legs stretched out and pressed together; her eyes were almost shut from weariness. The father and sister sat next to one another. The sister had set her hands around the father's neck.

110   "Now perhaps I can actually turn myself around," thought Gregor and began the task again. He couldn't stop puffing at the effort and had to rest now and then.

111   Besides no one was urging him on. It was all left to him on his own. When he had completed turning around, he immediately began to wander straight back. He was astonished at the great distance which separated him from his room and did not understand in the least how in his weakness he had covered the same distance a short time before, almost without noticing it. Constantly intent only on creeping along quickly, he hardly paid any attention to the fact that no word or cry from his family interrupted him.

112   Only when he was already in the door did he turn his head, not completely, because he felt his neck growing stiff. At any rate he still saw that behind him nothing had changed. Only the sister was standing up. His last glimpse brushed over the mother who was now completely asleep. Hardly was he inside his room when the door was pushed shut very quickly, bolted fast, and barred. Gregor was startled by the sudden commotion behind him, so much so that his little limbs bent double under him. It was his sister who had been in such a hurry. She had stood up right away, had waited, and had then sprung forward nimbly. Gregor had not heard anything of her approach. She cried out, "Finally!" to her parents, as she turned the key in the lock.

113   "What now?" Gregor asked himself and looked around him in the darkness. He soon made the discovery that he could no longer move at all. He was not surprised at that. On the contrary, it struck him as unnatural that he had really been able up to this point to move around with these thin little legs. Besides he felt relatively content. True, he had pains throughout his entire body, but it seemed to him that they were gradually becoming weaker and weaker and would finally go away completely. The rotten apple in his back and the inflamed surrounding area, entirely covered with white dust, he hardly noticed. He remembered his family with deep feeling and love. In this business, his own thought that he had to disappear was, if possible, even more decisive than his sister's. He remained in this state of empty and peaceful reflection until the tower clock struck three o'clock in the morning. From the window he witnessed the beginning of the general dawning outside. Then without willing it, his head sank all the way down, and from his nostrils flowed out weakly his last breath.

114   Early in the morning the cleaning woman came. In her sheer energy and haste she banged all the doors (in precisely the way people had already asked her to avoid), so much so that once she arrived a quiet sleep was no longer possible anywhere in the entire apartment. In her customarily brief visit to Gregor she at first found nothing special. She thought he lay so immobile there intending to play the offended party. She gave him credit for as complete an understanding as possible. Because she happened to hold the long broom in her hand, she tried to tickle Gregor with it from the door. When that was quite unsuccessful, she became irritated and poked Gregor a little, and only when she had shoved him from his place without any resistance did she become attentive. When she quickly realized the true state of affairs, her eyes grew large, she whistled to herself, but didn't restrain herself for long. She pulled open the door of the bedroom and yelled in a loud voice into the darkness, "Come and look. It's kicked the bucket. It's lying there, totally snuffed!"

115   The Samsa married couple sat upright in their marriage bed and had to get over their fright at the cleaning woman before they managed to grasp her message. But then Mr. and Mrs. Samsa climbed very quickly out of bed, one on either side. Mr. Samsa threw the bedspread over his shoulders, Mrs. Samsa came out only in her nightshirt, and like this they stepped into Gregor's room. Meanwhile the door of the living room (in which Grete had slept since the lodgers had arrived on the scene) had also opened. She was fully clothed, as if she had not slept at all; her white face also seemed to indicate that. "Dead?" said Mrs. Samsa and looked questioningly at the cleaning woman, although she could check everything on her own and even understand without a check. "I should say so," said the cleaning woman and, by way of proof, poked Gregor's body with the broom a considerable distance more to the side. Mrs. Samsa made a movement as if she wished to restrain the broom, but didn't

© Pearson Education, Inc., or its affiliates. All rights reserved.

CLOSE READ

ANNOTATE: At the end of paragraph 114 and in paragraph 115, mark details that show how the cleaning woman treats and speaks about Gregor.

QUESTION: Why does Kafka include these details?

CONCLUDE: What is the effect of these details, especially when combined with the family's reaction to Gregor's death?

do it. "Well," said Mr. Samsa, "now we can give thanks to God." He crossed himself, and the three women followed his example.

116   Grete, who did not take her eyes off the corpse, said, "Look how thin he was. He had eaten nothing for such a long time. The meals which came in here came out again exactly the same." In fact, Gregor's body was completely flat and dry. That was apparent really for the first time, now that he was no longer raised on his small limbs and, moreover, now that nothing else distracted one's gaze.

117   "Grete, come into us for a moment," said Mrs. Samsa with a melancholy smile, and Grete went, not without looking back at the corpse, behind her parents into the bedroom. The cleaning woman shut the door and opened the window wide. In spite of the early morning, the fresh air was partly tinged with warmth. It was already the end of March.

118   The three lodgers stepped out of their room and looked around for their breakfast, astonished that they had been forgotten. "Where is the breakfast?" asked the middle one of the gentlemen grumpily to the cleaning woman. However, she laid her finger to her lips and then quickly and silently indicated to the lodgers that they could come into Gregor's room. So they came and stood around Gregor's corpse, their hands in the pockets of their somewhat worn jackets, in the room, which was already quite bright.

119   Then the door of the bedroom opened, and Mr. Samsa appeared in his uniform, with his wife on one arm and his daughter on the other. All were a little tear-stained. Now and then Grete pressed her face onto her father's arm.

120   "Get out of my apartment immediately," said Mr. Samsa and pulled open the door, without letting go of the women. "What do you mean?" said the middle lodger, somewhat dismayed and with a sugary smile. The two others kept their hands behind them and constantly rubbed them against each other, as if in joyful anticipation of a great squabble which must end up in their favor. "I mean exactly what I say," replied Mr. Samsa and went directly with his two female companions up to the lodger. The latter at first stood there motionless and looked at the floor, as if matters were arranging themselves in a new way in his head. "All right, then we'll go," he said and looked up at Mr. Samsa as if, suddenly overcome by humility, he was asking fresh permission for this decision. Mr. Samsa merely nodded to him repeatedly with his eyes open wide.

121   Following that, the lodger actually went immediately with long strides into the hall. His two friends had already been listening for a while with their hands quite still, and now they hopped smartly after him, as if afraid that Mr. Samsa could step into the hall ahead of them and disturb their reunion with their leader. In the hall all three of them took their hats from the coat rack, pulled their canes from the cane holder, bowed silently, and left the apartment. In what turned out to be an entirely groundless mistrust, Mr. Samsa stepped with the two women out onto the landing, leaned against the railing, and

looked down as the three lodgers slowly but steadily made their way down the long staircase, disappeared on each floor in a certain turn of the stairwell and in a few seconds came out again. The deeper they proceeded, the more the Samsa family lost interest in them, and when a butcher with a tray on his head came to meet them and then with a proud bearing ascended the stairs high above them, Mr. Samsa, together with the women, left the banister, and they all returned, as if relieved, back into their apartment.

122   They decided to pass that day resting and going for a stroll. Not only had they earned this break from work, but there was no question that they really needed it. And so they sat down at the table and wrote three letters of apology: Mr. Samsa to his supervisor, Mrs. Samsa to her client, and Grete to her proprietor. During the writing the cleaning woman came in to say that she was going off, for her morning work was finished. The three people writing at first merely nodded, without glancing up. Only when the cleaning woman was still unwilling to depart, did they look up angrily. "Well?" asked Mr. Samsa. The cleaning woman stood smiling in the doorway, as if she had a great stroke of luck to report to the family but would only do it if she was asked directly. The almost upright small ostrich feather in her hat, which had irritated Mr. Samsa during her entire service, swayed lightly in all directions. "All right then, what do you really want?" asked Mrs. Samsa, whom the cleaning lady still usually respected. "Well," answered the cleaning woman (smiling so happily she couldn't go on speaking right away), "about how that rubbish from the next room should be thrown out, you mustn't worry about it. It's all taken care of." Mrs. Samsa and Grete bent down to their letters, as though they wanted to go on writing; Mr. Samsa, who noticed that the cleaning woman wanted to start describing everything in detail, decisively prevented her with an outstretched hand. But since she was not allowed to explain, she remembered the great hurry she was in, and called out, clearly insulted, "Ta ta, everyone," turned around furiously, and left the apartment with a fearful slamming of the door.

123   "This evening she'll be let go," said Mr. Samsa, but he got no answer from either his wife or from his daughter, because the cleaning woman seemed to have upset once again the tranquility they had just attained. They got up, went to the window and remained there, with their arms about each other. Mr. Samsa turned around in his chair in their direction and observed them quietly for a while. Then he called out, "All right, come here then. Let's finally get rid of old things. And have a little consideration for me." The women attended to him at once. They rushed to him, caressed him, and quickly ended their letters.

124   Then all three left the apartment together, something they had not done for months now, and took the electric tram into the open air outside the city. The car in which they were sitting by themselves was totally engulfed by the warm sun. They talked to each other, leaning

back comfortably in their seats, about future prospects, and they discovered that on closer observation these were not at all bad, for all three had employment, about which they had not really questioned each other at all, which was extremely favorable and with especially promising prospects. The greatest improvement in their situation at this moment, of course, had to come from a change of dwelling. Now they wanted to rent an apartment smaller and cheaper but better situated and generally more practical than the present one, which Gregor had found. While they amused themselves in this way, it struck Mr. and Mrs. Samsa almost at the same moment how their daughter, who was getting more animated all the time, had blossomed recently, in spite of all the troubles which had made her cheeks pale, into a beautiful and voluptuous young woman. Growing more silent and almost unconsciously understanding each other in their glances, they thought that the time was now at hand to seek out a good honest man for her. And it was something of a confirmation of their new dreams and good intentions when at the end of their journey the daughter first lifted herself up and stretched her young body. ❧

NOTES

CLOSE READ
ANNOTATE: In paragraph 124, mark words and phrases with positive associations of comfort and health.

QUESTION: Why does Kafka include these details that are so different from those in the rest of the story?

CONCLUDE: What effect does this final paragraph have on the reader?

Comprehension Check

Complete the following items after you finish your first read.

1. Into what kind of creature is Gregor Samsa transformed?

2. How do the family's activities change to accommodate Gregor's new condition?

3. What happens when Grete gives a violin recital for the three lodgers?

4. 📝 **Notebook** Confirm your understanding of the story by writing a summary.

- -

RESEARCH

Research to Clarify Choose at least one unfamiliar detail from the text. Briefly research that detail. In what way does the information you learned shed light on an aspect of the story?

Close Read the Text

1. This model, from paragraph 2 of the story, shows two sample annotations, along with questions and conclusions. Close read the passage, and find another detail to annotate. Then, write a question and your conclusion.

Close Read — ANNOTATE · QUESTION · CONCLUDE

> ANNOTATE: These words suggest something delicate or precious.
>
> QUESTION: What contrast does this description emphasize?
>
> CONCLUDE: The delicacy of the picture emphasizes the awfulness of Gregor's transformation.

> Above the table . . . hung the picture which he had cut out of an illustrated magazine a little while ago and set in a pretty gilt frame. It was a picture of a woman with a fur hat and a fur boa. She sat erect there, lifting up in the direction of the viewer a solid fur muff into which her entire forearm disappeared.

> ANNOTATE: The repetition of *fur* and the use of the word *disappeared* are surprising.
>
> QUESTION: Why does the author use these details?
>
> CONCLUDE: These details reinforce the idea of transformation— like Gregor, the woman seems to be changing into a nonhuman creature.

2. For more practice, go back into the text and complete the close-read notes.

3. Revisit a section of the text you found important during your first read. Read this section closely, and **annotate** what you notice. Ask yourself **questions** such as "Why did the author make this choice?" What can you **conclude**?

🔧 **Tool Kit**
Close-Read Guide and Model Annotation

Analyze the Text

> CITE TEXTUAL EVIDENCE
> to support your answers.

📓 **Notebook** Respond to these questions.

1. (a) **Compare and Contrast** Describe how Gregor's insect-like body changes from the opening of the story to the ending. (b) **Interpret** How do these physical changes reflect Gregor's evolving emotional state?

2. **Make a Judgment** In what ways, if any, are the family members responsible for Gregor's tragic outcome? Consider their actions at the end of the story before you answer.

3. **Hypothesize** Would Gregor's fate have been different if he had been transformed into a different kind of animal? Explain.

4. **Essential Question:** *Do people need to belong?* What have you learned about the condition of being an outsider by reading this story?

📋 **STANDARDS**
Reading Literature
Analyze how an author's choices concerning how to structure a text, order events within it, and manipulate time create such effects as mystery, tension, or surprise.

Analyze Craft and Structure

Literary Movement: Modernism "The Metamorphosis" is one of the landmark works of **Modernism**, an artistic movement that developed during the twentieth century and represented a radical break with the traditions of the past. Modernists such as Kafka responded to dramatic changes in the world, including the rapid rise of industry, the shift from rural to urban society, and the brutal horrors of World War I. Often unsettling and even disturbing, Modernist works present the world as a fractured place in which goodness is not rewarded and evil is not punished. Kafka's story is an example of **Absurdist literature**, a form of Modernist writing that includes these elements:

- **Ambiguity:** The story is open-ended, and key elements are never explained.
- **Fantastic or Dreamlike Elements:** Events blur the boundary between what is real and what is unreal.
- **Themes of Alienation:** Modernist works often feature isolated characters who experience increasing alienation or disconnection.

Practice

CITE TEXTUAL EVIDENCE to support your answers.

🗒 **Notebook** **Respond to these questions.**

1. Use the chart to identify examples from the story that demonstrate each element of Absurdist literature.

AMBIGUITY	FANTASTIC OR DREAMLIKE ELEMENTS	ALIENATION/ISOLATION

2. Toward the end of the story, the family begins to refer to Gregor as "it" rather than "he." How does this pronoun shift relate to the Absurdist emphasis on alienation?

3. Many Modernist works draw attention to the techniques used to create them. In what way is this true of Kafka's tale? Identify passages that remind readers that they are reading a fictional tale.

4. Why do you think Kafka provides no reason for Gregor's transformation?

5. Has Gregor done anything to deserve his fate? Why or why not?

The Metamorphosis **181**

THE METAMORPHOSIS

Concept Vocabulary

distress	aversion	listlessly
amelioration	asphyxiation	travail

Why These Words? These concept words relate to the idea of discomfort, or uneasiness. For example, the narrator describes the *distress* that Gregor feels when he is unable to control his insect body and get out of bed. In response to his difficulties, Gregor shows his frustration by banging his head *listlessly* against the door.

1. How does the concept vocabulary help describe Gregor's alienation?

2. What other words in the selection connect to the concept of discomfort?

Practice

📓 **Notebook** The concept vocabulary words appear in "The Metamorphosis."

1. Use each concept word to complete the paragraph.

The salesperson was horrified by his reassignment to the lunch counter because he had a(n) _____ to fried foods. His _____ only increased when he learned that he was to spend the entire day deep-frying batter-dipped cupcakes. Before the store opened, he stirred the batter _____. He sighed as though he were facing a day's _____ in a coal mine. Though he hoped for a poor turnout, there would be no _____ of his misery, since the new product turned out to be wildly popular. As the greasy steam rose from the hot fat into his face, he was sure _____ would be his fate.

2. Explain the context clues that help you determine the correct words.

Word Study

📓 **Notebook** **Denotation and Connotation** A word's **denotation** is its literal definition, the one you would find in a dictionary. The associations or feelings that a word suggests are its **connotations**. Words with close meanings can express different degrees of an idea. For example, *distress* refers to pain. *Discomfort* and *inconvenience* describe the same idea with less intensity. *Anguish* and *agony* suggest greater intensity.

1. Name synonyms for three of the concept vocabulary words, and tell whether or not their connotations differ in degree of intensity.

2. For each of the three concept words you chose, write three sentences. In the first, use the concept word itself. In the second, use a synonym that has a lower degree of intensity. In the third, use a synonym that has a higher degree of intensity.

WORD NETWORK

Add interesting words related to outsiders from the text to your Word Network.

STANDARDS

Reading Literature
Determine the meaning of words and phrases as they are used in the text, including figurative and connotative meanings; analyze the cumulative impact of specific word choices on meaning and tone.

Language
• Demonstrate command of the conventions of standard English grammar and usage when writing or speaking.
• Use various types of phrases and clauses to convey specific meanings and add variety and interest to writing or presentations.
• Demonstrate understanding of figurative language, word relationships, and nuances in word meanings.
• Analyze nuances in the meaning of words with similar denotations.

Conventions

Types of Phrases Writers use various types of phrases to convey specific meanings. A **verb phrase** consists of a main verb and one or more auxiliary, or helping, verbs. These auxiliary verbs precede the main verb and provide additional information about the verb phrase, such as its tense, its mood, or its voice. Certain forms of the following verbs can be used as auxiliary verbs: *be, do, have, will, shall, can, may,* and *must.*

A verb phrase is often interrupted by one or more other words in a sentence, such as *not, never,* or another adverb. These interrupting words are not considered part of the verb phrase.

Observe how the underlined verb phrases in this sentence from paragraph 25 of "The Metamorphosis" help convey the time relationships of Gregor's various actions.

> While Gregor <u>was</u> quickly <u>blurting</u> all this out, hardly aware of what he <u>was saying</u>, he <u>had moved</u> close to the chest of drawers without effort, probably as a result of the practice he <u>had</u> already <u>had</u> in bed, and now he <u>was trying</u> to raise himself up on it.

Read It

Mark each verb phrase in these sentences from "The Metamorphosis." Remember not to mark any word or words that interrupt the verb phrase.

1. One morning, as Gregor Samsa was waking up from anxious dreams, he discovered that in bed he had been changed into a monstrous verminous bug.

2. He had already got to the point where, with a stronger rocking, he maintained his equilibrium with difficulty, and very soon he would finally have to decide, for in five minutes it would be a quarter past seven.

3. He must have tried it a hundred times, closing his eyes, so that he would not have to see the wriggling legs, and gave up only when he began to feel a light, dull pain in his side which he had never felt before.

Write It

📓 **Notebook** In the example, the sample sentences have been revised to add auxiliary verbs. Rewrite the sentences below to include auxiliary verbs.

> Example
> **Sample:** Gregor gropes awkwardly for many hours.
> **Revision:** Gregor has been groping awkwardly for many hours.
> **Sample:** His family listens at the door.
> **Revision:** His family must have been listening at the door.

1. Gregor climbs the walls and sticks to the ceiling.

2. The lodgers laugh, but soon they storm out of the room.

TIP
CLARIFICATION
Refer to the Grammar Handbook to learn more about verb tense, verb mood, and active and passive voice.

THE METAMORPHOSIS

Writing to Sources

A successful argument presents a careful, well-reasoned analysis of a topic, and draws logical conclusions that are supported with strong evidence. The evidence not only must clearly connect to the topic—it must also appeal to the audience.

Assignment

In a movie pitch, a writer tries to convince a movie studio to make a particular film. Write a **pitch** in which you argue that "The Metamorphosis" should be made into a major Hollywood feature film. In making your pitch, you will need to include a number of selling points.

- the reasons the movie will be entertaining and attractive to a large audience
- specific story details that will capture readers' interest, along with descriptions of how these elements can be adapted for film
- a description of the film's genre and style
- dramatic scenes that will make the film exciting

You might decide to support the visual look of your proposed film by creating a storyboard or flowchart of images to accompany your pitch.

Vocabulary and Conventions Connection Consider including several of the concept vocabulary words in your pitch, and try to use a variety of verb phrases.

distress	aversion	listlessly
amelioration	asphyxiation	travail

Reflect on Your Writing

After you have written your pitch, answer these questions.

1. Which piece of supporting evidence do you think makes your pitch effective?

2. What did you learn about Kafka's story by arguing that it should be adapted for film?

3. **Why These Words?** The words you choose make a difference in your writing. Which words did you specifically choose to add power to your pitch?

STANDARDS

Writing
- Write arguments to support claims in an analysis of substantive topics or texts, using valid reasoning and relevant and sufficient evidence.
- Produce clear and coherent writing in which the development, organization, and style are appropriate to task, purpose, and audience.

Speaking and Listening
- Initiate and participate effectively in a range of collaborative discussions with diverse partners on *grades 9–10 topics, texts, and issues*, building on others' ideas and expressing their own clearly and persuasively.
- Evaluate a speaker's point of view, reasoning, and use of evidence and rhetoric, identifying any fallacious reasoning or exaggerated or distorted evidence.
- Adapt speech to a variety of contexts and tasks, demonstrating command of formal English when indicated or appropriate.

Speaking and Listening

Assignment

Imagine that your school is considering whether to place Kafka's "The Metamorphosis" on its required reading list. Work with a partner to prepare for a **debate** about the question. If you take the "pro" position, you are in favor of placing the story on the list. If you take the "con" position, you are against it. After you have prepared, conduct the debate against an opposing team.

1. **Take a Position** Decide whether you will argue the pro or the con position. Note that you can effectively argue a view you don't personally support.

2. **Organize Ideas and Evidence** With your partner, discuss the arguments in favor of your position. Consider the literary merit of the story, its significance in literary history, and other qualities that you find important. Refer to the text as you work. Use the chart to gather your ideas and evidence.

POINT	SUPPORTING EVIDENCE

3. **Anticipate Counterarguments** In a debate, the opposing team is given the opportunity to present counterarguments in a rebuttal. Discuss with your partner points that the opposing team might make against your position. Prepare to defend your position with reasons and evidence.

4. **Write an Opening Statement** Write a strong opening statement of your position. Practice delivering the statement clearly and with conviction. Continue to speak clearly and forcefully throughout the debate.

📝 EVIDENCE LOG

Before moving on to a new selection, go to your Evidence Log and record what you learned from "The Metamorphosis."

Franz Kafka and Metamorphosis

Media Vocabulary

The following words or concepts will be useful to you as you analyze, discuss, and write about videos.

Stock Footage: film or video that has been shot for one purpose and is available for use in other projects	• Stock footage may be film recycled from past news programs. • It may also be footage from movies, television, or advertising.
Silhouette: dark figure that is seen as a filled-in shape against a light background	• Silhouettes may be created with bright light shining behind a figure. • Silhouettes are a kind of shadow.
Commentators: people who discuss or write about events for film, television, radio, or newspapers	• Documentary films and videos often include commentators who are experts on the topic. • A commentator may share his or her own point of view or present facts.
Background Music: music that is not the focus of a show but is added for effect	• Background music may highlight or contrast with the words and images of a show. • Music may create a mood and influence listeners' feelings about the content of a program.
Editing: taking pieces of film or video and putting them together in a new way	• Film and video editors may work with still photographs and film footage to create many different effects.

First Review MEDIA: VIDEO

Apply these strategies as you conduct your first review.

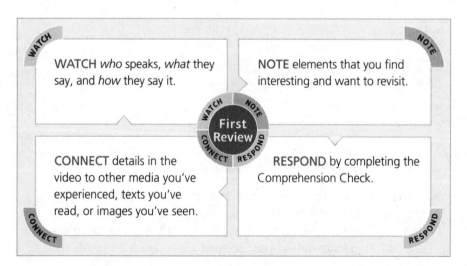

WATCH *who* speaks, *what* they say, and *how* they say it.

NOTE elements that you find interesting and want to revisit.

First Review

CONNECT details in the video to other media you've experienced, texts you've read, or images you've seen.

RESPOND by completing the Comprehension Check.

📓 **Notebook** As you watch, write down your observations and questions, making sure to note time codes so you can easily revisit sections later.

STANDARDS

Reading Informational Text
By the end of grade 10, read and comprehend literary nonfiction at the high end of the grades 9–10 text complexity band independently and proficiently.

Language
Acquire and use accurately general academic and domain-specific words and phrases, sufficient for reading, writing, speaking, and listening at the college and career readiness level; demonstrate independence in gathering vocabulary knowledge when considering a word or phrase important to comprehension or expression.

Franz Kafka and Metamorphosis

BBC

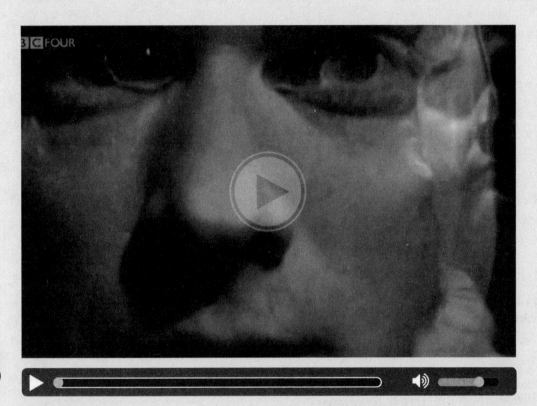

BACKGROUND

Biological transformations are a common occurrence in nature, especially among insects. Such a transformation marks the shift in an organism's development from the juvenile to the adult stage. People, however, transition more slowly from childhood to adulthood. Likewise, we have a sense of continuity in our physical senses of self because we keep most of our physical traits throughout our lives. Perhaps that is one reason the idea of transformation draws both our curiosity and our fear, as this video suggests.

SCAN FOR
MULTIMEDIA

NOTES

Comprehension Check

Complete the following items after you finish your first review.

1. What is this video primarily about?

2. What two works of literature are discussed in the video?

3. According to the second commentator, how do human beings feel about the possibility of change?

4. **Notebook** Confirm your understanding of the video by listing three key ideas it presents.

- -

RESEARCH

Research to Clarify Choose an unfamiliar detail from the video. Briefly research that detail. How does the information you learned clarify an aspect of the video's content?

MEDIA VOCABULARY

Use these words as you discuss and write about the video.

stock footage
silhouette
commentators
background music
editing

WORD NETWORK

Add interesting words related to outsiders from the video to your Word Network.

STANDARDS

Reading Informational Text
Cite strong and thorough textual evidence to support analysis of what the text says explicitly as well as inferences drawn from the text.

Close Review

Watch the video again. Write down any new observations that seem important. What **questions** do you have? What can you **conclude**?

- -

Analyze the Media

Notebook Respond to these questions.

1. (a) What does the first commentator say is bound up with our outer appearance? (b) **Interpret** Why do you think she talks about this with regard to Kafka's "The Metamorphosis"?

2. (a) **Contrast** In what way is Dr. Jekyll's metamorphosis different from Gregor Samsa's? (b) **Interpret** Do you think this difference is important? Explain.

3. (a) According to the video content, in what two ways do human beings transform themselves? (b) **Infer** Based on this evidence, what is the most powerful tool humans have for change?

4. **Essential Question:** *Do people need to belong?* What have you learned about the nature of being an outsider from this video?

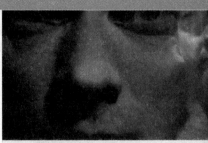

FRANZ KAFKA AND
METAMORPHOSIS

Writing to Sources

Film and video use images to tell stories, set scenes, and create moods. Images often have symbolic meanings. The ability to interpret symbolic images is critical to understanding and writing about film and video.

Assignment

Write a **visual analysis**. Choose one image from the video, such as locusts, smokestacks, or airplanes. In a paragraph, describe the image. In your paragraph, make sure to answer these questions:

- What kind of image is it—a still photograph or a motion picture?
- Does the image include color, or is it in black-and-white?
- Is the background of the image meaningful? Does it emphasize the main subject of the image in some way?
- What emotional quality or mood does the image convey? What elements of the image contribute to that mood?

Then, draw your observations together to write another paragraph in which you answer these questions: Why did the filmmakers use this image as a symbol for metamorphosis? Is that choice effective?

Speaking and Listening

This video comments on Franz Kafka's important short story "The Metamorphosis" and explores the effect change can have on individual identity.

Assignment

With a partner, conduct a **discussion** about the following questions:

- What kinds of metamorphoses, or changes, are discussed or alluded to in the video?
- Are these metamorphoses positive, negative, or both? Explain.
- What insights into the idea of metamorphosis does the video present? Of these insights, which do you think is most surprising or illuminating? Why?

Write a paragraph summarizing your discussion. Then, share your paragraph with the class.

📝 EVIDENCE LOG

Before moving on to a new selection, go to your Evidence Log and record what you learned from "Franz Kafka and Metamorphosis."

☰ STANDARDS

Writing
Write informative/explanatory texts to examine and convey complex ideas, concepts, and information clearly and accurately through the effective selection, organization, and analysis of content.

Speaking and Listening
Present information, findings, and supporting evidence clearly, concisely, and logically such that listeners can follow the line of reasoning and the organization, development, substance, and style are appropriate to purpose, audience, and task.

WRITING TO SOURCES

• THE METAMORPHOSIS

• FRANZ KAFKA AND METAMORPHOSIS

Write an Argument

You have read a short story and viewed a video on the theme of outsiders. In "The Metamorphosis," Franz Kafka tells the story of a man who wakes up one day as some sort of bug-like vermin. The video presents additional insights about both the story and the ideas of transformation and alienation. Now, you will use your knowledge of the story and video to write an argument about people's need to belong.

Assignment

Apply your own experience, your analysis of the short story "The Metamorphosis," and your understanding of the related video to write an **argumentative essay** on this question:

> Are outsiders simply those who are misjudged or misunderstood?

ACADEMIC VOCABULARY

As you craft your essay, consider using some of the academic vocabulary you learned in the beginning of the unit.

contradict

negate

objection

verify

advocate

Elements of an Argument

An **argument** is a logical way of presenting a belief, conclusion, or position. A well-written argumentative essay attempts to convince readers to accept what is written, change their minds, or take a certain action.

An effective argument contains these elements:

- a precise claim, or statement of a position
- consideration of counterclaims, or opposing positions, and a discussion of their strengths and weaknesses
- a logical organization that connects the claim, counterclaim, reasons, and evidence
- valid reasoning and relevant and sufficient evidence
- a concluding statement or section that logically completes the argument
- a formal style and objective tone
- correct grammar, including accurate use of transitions

🔧 **Tool Kit**
Student Model
of an Argument

Model Argument For a model of a well-crafted argumentative essay, see the Launch Text, "Isn't Everyone a Little Bit Weird?"

Challenge yourself to find all of the elements of an effective argument in the text. You will have the opportunity to review these elements as you start to write your own argument.

≡ STANDARDS
Writing
• Write arguments to support claims in an analysis of substantive topics or texts, using valid reasoning and relevant and sufficient evidence.
• Write routinely over extended time frames and shorter time frames for a range of tasks, purposes, and audiences.

Prewriting / Planning

Narrow the Topic The prompt for this assignment—are outsiders simply those who are misjudged or misunderstood?—is a large topic. You will write a more effective essay if you narrow the topic and give it a smaller focus. For example, you might discuss a particular group of people who are misunderstood or a particular cause of misunderstanding. It can help to think about issues with which you have some familiarity. Use this chart to consider ways to narrow the topic.

| Broad Topic |
| Familiar Area |
| Specific Example Within That Area |
| Focused Topic |

Use Varied Types of Evidence There are many different types of evidence you can use in an argument:

- **examples:** specific illustrations of a general idea

- **anecdotes:** brief stories that illustrate a point or insight

- **facts:** data or other information that can be proved true

- **expert opinion:** information or statements from experts

Using a variety of evidence can make your argument stronger. For example, in the Launch Text, the writer uses examples and anecdotes.

> *Take, for example, his appearance. In famous portraits, he wears ruffled shirts, breeches, and tight stockings pulled up to the knee. . . . Today's viewers might think him odd, but those were common fashions of his era. Likewise, consider Franklin's education. He quit school at age ten and was apprenticed as a printer at age twelve—a career move that today would be considered both weird and illegal.*
>
> —"Isn't Everyone a Little Bit Weird?"

Connect Across Texts As you write your argument, you will be using evidence from the selections to support your claims. Incorporate that evidence in different ways. If the precise words are important, use **exact quotations**. To clarify a complex idea, **paraphrase**, or restate it in your own words. Make sure that your paraphrases accurately reflect the original text. Consult an online or print style manual to confirm how to incorporate quotations or paraphrases into your essay correctly.

EVIDENCE LOG

Review your Evidence Log and identify key details you may want to cite in your argument.

STANDARDS

Writing
Develop claim(s) and counterclaims fairly, supplying evidence for each while pointing out the strengths and limitations of both in a manner that anticipates the audience's knowledge level and concerns.

Language
Write and edit work so that it conforms to the guidelines in a style manual appropriate for the discipline and writing type.

Drafting

Organize your ideas in a logical sequence that leads your reader from one part of your argument to the next.

Write an Engaging Introduction Use your introduction to engage your reader. Consider including a compelling statement that will pique readers' interest. For example, the Launch Text begins with a provocative first line: "Everyone is a little bit weird." The writer then explains that sentence just enough to lead the reader to the main claim.

Write your ideas for a compelling introduction:

_____

_____

_____

State a Clear Claim In your introduction, present your main idea, or claim, in clear, uncertain language. Your claim should be a debatable idea—one that can be argued. Your task will be to support your position with the help of strong reasons and evidence.

Order Your Ideas Logically Present supporting reasons for your claim in a logical sequence. Consider using one of these organizational structures:

ORDER OF IMPORTANCE	NESTORIAN ORDER
Present your strongest supporting reasons first, and then your less important reasons.	This is also called "reverse order of importance." It can sometimes be more effective to begin with your weakest reason and build up to your strongest reason.

Anticipate Counterarguments Identify points those who disagree with your position might raise. In this passage, the writer of the Launch Text addresses a counterargument: "Some might argue that weird people are just plain weird." The writer then goes on to state why this counterargument is not convincing.

Write a First Draft Use the organizational ideas you generated to write your first draft. As you write, keep the following points in mind:

- Use a formal, objective **tone,** or attitude.
- Use precise words. Avoid slang, contractions, and other elements of casual language that are inappropriate for academic writing.
- As you draft, new ideas may occur to you. Allow yourself to explore those ideas, but make a note to go back and work them into your logical sequence. Your goal is to carry a consistent set of ideas through from the introduction to the body to the conclusion.

STANDARDS

Writing
- Introduce precise claim(s), distinguish the claim(s) from alternate or opposing claims, and create an organization that establishes clear relationships among claim(s), counterclaims, reasons, and evidence.
- Establish and maintain a formal style and objective tone while attending to the norms and conventions of the discipline in which they are writing.
- Provide a concluding statement or section that follows from and supports the argument presented.

LANGUAGE DEVELOPMENT: AUTHOR'S STYLE

Create Cohesion: Transitions

Transitions and **transitional expressions** are words and phrases that hold your argument together. They show relationships among ideas, and the ways in which one concept leads to another. They help you connect, contrast, and compare ideas. Without accurate transitions, your argument can seem like a random assortment of unrelated information and observations.

Read It

These sentences from the Launch Text use accurate transitions to show how ideas are connected.

- *First, the most gifted, successful people are often eccentric.* (**lists ideas and indicates order of importance**)
- Brilliant *would describe Ben Franklin better, and yet the man some call "the first American" had some ways about him you might consider odd.* (**shows contrast**)
- *Take, for example, his appearance.* (**shows or illustrates idea**)
- *Likewise, consider Franklin's education.* (**shows similarity**)
- *On top of that, he had the courage to communicate his insights, act on them, and turn them into achievements.* (**adds emphasis**)

Write It

As you draft your argument, choose transitions that help readers follow the flow of your ideas from sentence to sentence, paragraph to paragraph, and introduction to conclusion.

Use a chart like this to track your choices of transitions.

If you want to . . .	consider using one of these transitions:
list or add ideas	*first of all, secondly, then, in addition, also*
show similarity	*similarity, equally, likewise*
show contrast	*although, however, yet, on the other hand*
emphasize	*in fact, most importantly, immediately*
show effect	*consequently, as a result, therefore*
illustrate or show	*for example, for instance, specifically*

❚❚ STANDARDS

Writing
Use words, phrases, and clauses to link the major sections of the text, create cohesion, and clarify the relationships between claim(s) and reasons, between reasons and evidence, and between claim(s) and counterclaims.

REVISING

Evaluating Your Draft

Use the following checklist to evaluate the effectiveness of your first draft. Then, use your evaluation and the instruction on this page to guide your revision.

FOCUS AND ORGANIZATION	EVIDENCE AND ELABORATION	CONVENTIONS
☐ Provides an introduction that engages readers and introduces a precise claim.	☐ Develops the claims and opposing claims fairly, supplying evidence for each, while pointing out the strengths and limitations of both.	☐ Attends to the norms and conventions of the discipline, especially the correct use and punctuation of transitions.
☐ Establishes a logical order of supporting reasons and evidence.	☐ Provides adequate examples for each major idea.	
☐ Anticipates and addresses opposing claims.	☐ Uses vocabulary and word choice that is appropriate for the audience and purpose.	
☐ Develops a logical progression from the introduction, through the body, to the conclusion.	☐ Establishes and maintains a formal style and an objective tone.	

Revising for Focus and Organization

Logical Organization Reread your argument, paying special attention to the organization and progression of ideas.

- Jot down the main idea of each paragraph.
- Review these notes to determine whether your ideas flow logically.
- Reorder any paragraphs or sections that do not build in a logical way.
- Add or change transitional words or sentences to help readers understand the connections among ideas.
- Make sure that the ideas in your introduction match the ideas in the conclusion.

Revising for Evidence and Elaboration

Evidence Reread your essay, looking for any points at which the evidence seems weak. Then, find additional details from the text and video in this section to replace or strengthen your evidence.

Style Make sure that you have used an appropriately formal style that includes precise and vivid language, accurate use of academic terms, and transitions that establish clear relationships among your ideas. Reread to ensure that you have used words and phrases that communicate exactly what you mean.

 **WORD NETWORK**

Include interesting words from your Word Network in your argument.

STANDARDS

Writing
- Establish and maintain a formal style and objective tone while attending to the norms and conventions of the discipline in which they are writing.
- Provide a concluding statement or section that follows from and supports the argument presented.

PEER REVIEW

Exchange essays with a classmate. Use the checklist to evaluate your classmate's argumentative essay and provide supportive feedback.

1. Is the claim clear?

☐ yes ☐ no   If no, explain what confused you.

2. Is the counterclaim clear?

☐ yes ☐ no   If no, point out what was unclear.

3. Does the evidence support the argument well?

☐ yes ☐ no   If no, explain how it could be improved.

4. What is the strongest part of your classmate's essay? Why?

Editing and Proofreading

Edit for Conventions Reread your draft for accuracy and consistency. Edit to include a variety of sentence structures so that your essay reads well. If necessary, consult a style manual to clarify sentence types and improve your sentence variety.

Proofread for Accuracy Read your draft carefully, correcting errors in grammar, word usage, spelling, and punctuation.

Publishing and Presenting

Create a final version of your essay. Share it with a small group so that your classmates can read it and make comments. In turn, review and comment on your classmates' work. Afterward, discuss how your arguments answer the question of whether outsiders are simply those who are misjudged or misunderstood. Make sure that everyone takes a turn presenting his or her view, and listen carefully while others speak.

Reflecting

Think about what you learned while writing your argumentative essay. What did you learn about planning your draft that you will use when writing another argument? How did thinking about texts you read and viewed in this section inform your argument? What will you strive to improve in your next argument? For example, you might outline reasons for your claim before writing a first draft.

STANDARDS

Writing
Develop and strengthen writing as needed by planning, revising, editing, rewriting, or trying a new approach, focusing on addressing what is most significant for a specific purpose and audience.

Language
Write and edit work so that it conforms to the guidelines in a style manual appropriate for the discipline and writing type.

ESSENTIAL QUESTION:

Do people need to belong?

Why is it that people often feel like they don't belong? What makes others view certain people as outsiders or as insiders? The selections you will read address these questions and offer a range of differing perspectives. You will work in a group to continue your exploration of outsiders and outcasts.

Small-Group Learning Strategies

Throughout your life, in school, in your community, and in your career, you will continue to learn and work with others.

Review these strategies and the actions you can take to practice them. Add ideas of your own for each step. Use these strategies during Small-Group Learning.

STRATEGY	ACTION PLAN
Prepare	• Complete your assignments so that you are prepared for group work. • Organize your thinking so that you can contribute to your group's discussions. •
Participate fully	• Make eye contact to signal that you are listening and taking in what is being said. • Use text evidence. •
Support others	• Build off ideas from others in your group. • Invite others who have not yet spoken to join the discussion. •
Clarify	• Paraphrase the ideas of others to ensure that your understanding is correct. • Ask follow-up questions. •

SCAN FOR
MULTIMEDIA

CONTENTS

Working as a Team

1. **Choose a topic** In your group, discuss the following question:

   Is the exclusion of others a problem we need to solve, or is the experience of being an outsider simply part of growing up?

   As you take turns sharing your responses, be sure to provide details to explain your position. After all group members have shared, discuss some of the pros and cons of being an outsider.

2. **List Your Rules** As a group, decide on the rules that you will follow as you work together. Samples are provided; add two more of your own. As you work together, you may add or revise rules based on your experience together.

   - Everyone should participate in group discussions.
   - Listen carefully and then contribute your own ideas.

   - _____
     _____

   - _____
     _____

3. **Apply the Rules** Share what you have learned about outsiders and outcasts. Make sure each person in the group contributes. Take notes on and be prepared to share with the class one thing that you heard from another member of your group.

4. **Name Your Group** Choose a name that reflects the unit topic.

   Our group's name: _____

5. **Create a Communication Plan** Decide how you want to communicate with one another. For example, you might use online collaboration tools, email, or instant messaging.

   Our group's decision: _____
   _____

Making a Schedule

First, find out the due dates for the Small-Group activities. Then, preview the texts and activities with your group, and make a schedule for completing the tasks.

SELECTION	ACTIVITIES	DUE DATE
The Doll's House		
Sonnet, With Bird Elliptical Fences		
Revenge of the Geeks		
Encountering the Other: The Challenge for the 21st Century		

Working on Group Projects

As your group works together, you'll find it more effective if each person has a specific role. Different projects require different roles. Before beginning a project, discuss the necessary roles, and choose one for each group member. Some possible roles are listed here. Add your own ideas to the list.

Project Manager: monitors the schedule and keeps everyone on task

Researcher: organizes information-gathering activities

Recorder: takes notes during group meetings

_____

_____

_____

_____

_____

SCAN FOR MULTIMEDIA

About the Author

Katherine Mansfield
(1888–1923) was born in
Wellington, New Zealand,
to an affluent family. She
published her first stories
at age ten and moved
to England in 1903 to
complete her education.
There she married writer
and editor John Middleton
Murry and befriended
Modernist authors Virginia
Woolf and D. H. Lawrence.
Mansfield died tragically
young of tuberculosis. She
is still counted among the
greatest short-story writers
in modern world literature.

The Doll's House

Concept Vocabulary

As you perform your first read of "The Doll's House," you will encounter these words.

> shunned   sneered   spitefully

Context Clues If these words are unfamiliar to you, try using **context clues**—other words and phrases that appear nearby in a text—to help you determine their meanings. There are various types of context clues that may help you as you read.

> **Synonyms:** The mother of the Kelvey girls is a **spry**, energetic little washerwoman.
>
> **Contrast of Ideas:** Normally **docile**, Kezia takes the risk of breaking Aunt Beryl's rules.

Apply your knowledge of context clues and other vocabulary strategies to determine the meanings of unfamiliar words you encounter during your first read. Use a print or online dictionary to verify your definitions.

First Read FICTION

Apply these strategies as you conduct your first read. You will have an opportunity to complete a close read after your first read.

NOTICE *whom* the story is about, *what* happens, *where* and *when* it happens, and *why* those involved react as they do.

ANNOTATE by marking vocabulary and key passages you want to revisit.

First Read

CONNECT ideas within the selection to what you already know and what you have already read.

RESPOND by completing the Comprehension Check and by writing a brief summary of the selection.

STANDARDS

Reading Literature
By the end of grade 10, read and comprehend literature, including stories, dramas, and poems, at the high end of the grades 9–10 text complexity band independently and proficiently.

Language
• Use context as a clue to the meaning of a word or phrase.
• Verify the preliminary determination of the meaning of a word or phrase.

The Doll's House Katherine Mansfield

BACKGROUND

The plot of "The Doll's House" relies on characters' awareness of class—the arrangement of society in order of rank, where the members of each class are considered inherently different from those of other classes. Katherine Mansfield was aware of the divisions in social classes in New Zealand, where she lived as a child, and in England, where she spent her adult life.

SCAN FOR MULTIMEDIA

1   When dear old Mrs. Hay went back to town after staying with the Burnells she sent the children a doll's house. It was so big that the carter and Pat carried it into the courtyard, and there it stayed, propped up on two wooden boxes beside the feed-room door. No harm could come of it; it was summer. And perhaps the smell of paint would have gone off by the time it had to be taken in. For, really, the smell of paint coming from that doll's house ("Sweet of old Mrs. Hay, of course; most sweet and generous!")—but the smell of paint was quite enough to make anyone seriously ill, in Aunt Beryl's opinion. Even before the sacking[1] was taken off. And when it was . . .

2   There stood the doll's house, a dark, oily, spinach green, picked out with bright yellow. Its two solid little chimneys, glued on to the roof, were painted red and white, and the door, gleaming with yellow varnish, was like a little slab of toffee. Four windows, real

NOTES

---

1. **sacking** *n.* coarse fabric.

windows, were divided into panes by a broad streak of green. There was actually a tiny porch, too, painted yellow, with big lumps of congealed paint hanging along the edge.

3 But perfect, perfect little house! Who could possibly mind the smell? It was part of the joy, part of the newness.

4 "Open it quickly, someone!"

5 The hook at the side was stuck fast. Pat pried it open with his penknife, and the whole house front swung back, and—there you were, gazing at one and the same moment into the drawing room and dining room, the kitchen and two bedrooms. That is the way for a house to open! Why don't all houses open like that? How much more exciting than peering through the slit of a door into a mean little hall with a hatstand and two umbrellas! That is—isn't it?—what you long to know about a house when you put your hand on the knocker. Perhaps it is the way God opens houses at the dead of night when He is taking a quiet turn with an angel . . .

6 "Oh-oh!" The Burnell children sounded as though they were in despair. It was too marvelous; it was too much for them. They had never seen anything like it in their lives. All the rooms were papered. There were pictures on the walls, painted on the paper, with gold frames complete. Red carpet covered all the floors except the kitchen; red plush chairs in the drawing room, green in the dining room; tables, beds with real bedclothes, a cradle, a stove, a dresser with tiny plates and one big jug. But what Kezia liked more than anything, what she liked frightfully, was the lamp. It stood in the middle of the dining-room table, an exquisite little amber lamp with a white globe. It was even filled all ready for lighting, though, of course, you couldn't light it. But there was something inside that looked like oil, and moved when you shook it.

7 The father and mother dolls, who sprawled very stiff as though they had fainted in the drawing room, and their two little children asleep upstairs, were really too big for the doll's house. They didn't look as though they belonged. But the lamp was perfect. It seemed to smile at Kezia, to say, "I live here." The lamp was real.

8 The Burnell children could hardly walk to school fast enough the next morning. They burned to tell everybody, to describe, to—well—to boast about their doll's house before the school bell rang.

9 "I'm to tell," said Isabel, "because I'm the eldest. And you two can join in after. But I'm to tell first."

10 There was nothing to answer. Isabel was bossy, but she was always right, and Lottie and Kezia knew too well the powers that went with being eldest. They brushed through the thick buttercups at the road edge and said nothing.

11 "And I'm to choose who's to come and see it first. Mother said I might."

12 For it had been arranged that while the doll's house stood in the courtyard they might ask the girls at school, two at a time, to come

and look. Not to stay to tea, of course, or to come traipsing through the house. But just to stand quietly in the courtyard while Isabel pointed out the beauties, and Lottie and Kezia looked pleased . . .

13   But hurry as they might, by the time they had reached the tarred palings[2] of the boys' playground the bell had begun to jangle. They only just had time to whip off their hats and fall into line before the roll was called. Never mind. Isabel tried to make up for it by looking very important and mysterious and by whispering behind her hand to the girls near her, "Got something to tell you at playtime."

14   Playtime came and Isabel was surrounded. The girls of her class nearly fought to put their arms round her, to walk away with her, to beam flatteringly, to be her special friend. She held quite a court under the huge pine trees at the side of the playground. Nudging, giggling together, the little girls pressed up close. And the only two who stayed outside the ring were the two who were always outside, the little Kelveys. They knew better than to come anywhere near the Burnells.

15   For the fact was, the school the Burnell children went to was not at all the kind of place their parents would have chosen if there had been any choice. But there was none. It was the only school for miles. And the consequence was all the children of the neighborhood, the judge's little girls, the doctor's daughters, the storekeeper's children, the milkman's, were forced to mix together. Not to speak of there being an equal number of rude, rough little boys as well. But the line had to be drawn somewhere. It was drawn at the Kelveys. Many of the children, including the Burnells, were not allowed even to speak to them. They walked past the Kelveys with their heads in the air, and as they set the fashion in all matters of behavior, the Kelveys were **shunned** by everybody. Even the teacher had a special voice for them, and a special smile for the other children when Lil Kelvey came up to her desk with a bunch of dreadfully common-looking flowers.

16   They were the daughters of a spry, hard-working little washerwoman, who went about from house to house by the day. This was awful enough. But where was Mr. Kelvey? Nobody knew for certain. But everybody said he was in prison. So they were the daughters of a washerwoman and a gaolbird.[3] Very nice company for other people's children! And they looked it. Why Mrs. Kelvey made them so conspicuous was hard to understand. The truth was they were dressed in "bits" given to her by the people for whom she worked. Lil, for instance, who was a stout, plain child, with big freckles, came to school in a dress made from a green art-serge[4] tablecloth of the Burnells', with red plush sleeves from the Logans' curtains. Her hat, perched on top of her high forehead, was a grown-up woman's hat, once the property of Miss Lecky, the

NOTES

Mark context clues or indicate another strategy you used that helped you determine meaning.

shunned (shuhnd) *v.*

MEANING:

---

2. **palings** *n.* pieces of wood that form the upright parts of a wooden fence.
3. **gaolbird** (JAYL burd) *n.* British English spelling of *jailbird*, a person who has been in prison often.
4. **serge** (surj) *n.* strong cloth with a pronounced ribbing on the back.

postmistress. It was turned up at the back and trimmed with a large scarlet quill. What a little guy[5] she looked! It was impossible not to laugh. And her little sister, our Else, wore a long white dress, rather like a nightgown, and a pair of little boy's boots. But whatever our Else wore she would have looked strange. She was a tiny wishbone of a child, with cropped hair and enormous solemn eyes—a little white owl. Nobody had ever seen her smile; she scarcely ever spoke. She went through life holding on to Lil, with a piece of Lil's skirt screwed up in her hand. Where Lil went, our Else followed. In the playground, on the road going to and from school, there was Lil marching in front and our Else holding on behind. Only when she wanted anything, or when she was out of breath, our Else gave Lil a tug, a twitch, and Lil stopped and turned round. The Kelveys never failed to understand each other.

17   Now they hovered at the edge; you couldn't stop them listening. When the little girls turned round and **sneered**, Lil, as usual, gave her silly, shamefaced smile, but our Else only looked.

18   And Isabel's voice, so very proud, went on telling. The carpet made a great sensation, but so did the beds with real bedclothes, and the stove with an oven door.

19   When she finished Kezia broke in. "You've forgotten the lamp, Isabel."

20   "Oh, yes," said Isabel, "and there's a teeny little lamp, all made of yellow glass, with a white globe that stands on the dining-room table. You couldn't tell it from a real one."

21   "The lamp's best of all," cried Kezia. She thought Isabel wasn't making half enough of the little lamp. But nobody paid any attention. Isabel was choosing the two who were to come back with them that afternoon and see it. She chose Emmie Cole and Lena Logan. But when the others knew they were all to have a chance, they couldn't be nice enough to Isabel. One by one they put their arms round Isabel's waist and walked her off. They had something to whisper to her, a secret. "Isabel's *my* friend."

22   Only the little Kelveys moved away forgotten; there was nothing more for them to hear.

23 Days passed, and as more children saw the doll's house, the fame of it spread. It became the one subject, the rage. The one question was, "Have you seen Burnells' doll's house? "Oh, ain't it lovely!" "Haven't you seen it? Oh, I say!"

24   Even the dinner hour was given up to talking about it. The little girls sat under the pines eating their thick mutton sandwiches and big slabs of johnnycake[6] spread with butter. While always, as near as they could get, sat the Kelveys, our Else holding on to Lil, listening too, while they chewed their jam sandwiches out of a newspaper soaked with large red blobs.

5. **guy** *n.* British English slang for "person whose appearance is odd."
6. **johnnycake** *n.* bread made with cornmeal.

25   "Mother," said Kezia, "can't I ask the Kelveys just once?"

26   "Certainly not, Kezia."

27   "But why not?"

28   "Run away, Kezia; you know quite well why not."

29   At last everybody had seen it except them. On that day the subject rather flagged. It was the dinner hour. The children stood together under the pine trees, and suddenly, as they looked at the Kelveys eating out of their paper, always by themselves, always listening, they wanted to be horrid to them. Emmie Cole started the whisper.

30   "Lil Kelvey's going to be a servant when she grows up."

31   "O-oh, how awful!" said Isabel Burnell, and she made eyes at Emmie.

32   Emmie swallowed in a very meaning way and nodded to Isabel as she'd seen her mother do on those occasions.

33   "It's true—it's true—it's true," she said.

34   Then Lena Logan's little eyes snapped. "Shall I ask her?" she whispered.

35   "Bet you don't," said Jessie May.

36   "Pooh, I'm not frightened," said Lena. Suddenly she gave a little squeal and danced in front of the other girls. "Watch! Watch me! Watch me now!" said Lena. And sliding, gliding, dragging one foot, giggling behind her hand, Lena went over to the Kelveys.

37   Lil looked up from her dinner. She wrapped the rest quickly away. Our Else stopped chewing. What was coming now?

38   "Is it true you're going to be a servant when you grow up, Lil Kelvey?" shrilled Lena.

39   Dead silence. But instead of answering, Lil only gave her silly, shamefaced smile. She didn't seem to mind the question at all. What a sell for Lena! The girls began to titter.

40   Lena couldn't stand that. She put her hands on her hips; she shot forward. "Yah, yer father's in prison!" she hissed, **spitefully**.

41   This was such a marvelous thing to have said that the little girls rushed away in a body, deeply, deeply excited, wild with joy. Someone found a long rope, and they began skipping. And never did they skip so high, run in and out so fast, or do such daring things as on that morning.

42   In the afternoon Pat called for the Burnell children with the buggy and they drove home. There were visitors. Isabel and Lottie, who liked visitors, went upstairs to change their pinafores.[7] But Kezia thieved out at the back. Nobody was about; she began to swing on the big white gates of the courtyard. Presently, looking along the road, she saw two little dots. They grew bigger, they were coming toward her. Now she could see that one was in front and one close behind. Now she could see that they were the Kelveys. Kezia stopped swinging. She slipped off the gate as if she was going to run away.

NOTES

Mark context clues or indicate another strategy you used that helped you determine meaning.

spitefully (SPYT fuhl ee) *adv.*

MEANING:

---

7. **pinafores** (PIHN uh fawrz) *n.* sleeveless garments fastened in the back and worn as an apron or dress.

Then she hesitated. The Kelveys came nearer, and beside them walked their shadows, very long, stretching right across the road with their heads in the buttercups. Kezia clambered back on the gate; she had made up her mind; she swung out.

43   "Hullo," she said to the passing Kelveys.

44   They were so astounded that they stopped. Lil gave her silly smile. Our Else stared.

45   "You can come and see our doll's house if you want to," said Kezia, and she dragged one toe on the ground. But at that Lil turned red and shook her head quickly.

46   "Why not?" asked Kezia.

47   Lil gasped, then she said, "Your ma told our ma you wasn't to speak to us."

48   "Oh, well," said Kezia. She didn't know what to reply. "It doesn't matter. You can come and see our doll's house all the same. Come on. Nobody's looking."

49   But Lil shook her head still harder.

50   "Don't you want to?" asked Kezia.

51   Suddenly there was a twitch, a tug at Lil's skirt. She turned round. Our Else was looking at her with big, imploring eyes; she was frowning; she wanted to go. For a moment Lil looked at our Else very doubtfully. But then our Else twitched her skirt again. She started forward. Kezia led the way. Like two little stray cats they followed across the courtyard to where the doll's house stood.

52   "There it is," said Kezia.

53   There was a pause. Lil breathed loudly, almost snorted; our Else was still as a stone.

54   "I'll open it for you," said Kezia kindly. She undid the hook and they looked inside.

55   "There's the drawing room and the dining room, and that's the—"

56   "Kezia!"

57   Oh, what a start they gave!

58   "Kezia!"

59   It was Aunt Beryl's voice. They turned round. At the back door stood Aunt Beryl, staring as if she couldn't believe what she saw.

60   "How dare you ask the little Kelveys into the courtyard?" said her cold, furious voice. "You know as well as I do, you're not allowed to talk to them. Run away, children, run away at once. And don't come back again," said Aunt Beryl. And she stepped into the yard and shooed them out as if they were chickens.

61   "Off you go immediately!" she called, cold and proud.

62   They did not need telling twice. Burning with shame, shrinking together, Lil huddling along like her mother, our Else dazed, somehow they crossed the big courtyard and squeezed through the white gate.

63   "Wicked, disobedient little girl!" said Aunt Beryl bitterly to Kezia, and she slammed the doll's house to.

64   The afternoon had been awful. A letter had come from Willie Brent, a terrifying, threatening letter, saying if she did not meet him that evening in Pulman's Bush, he'd come to the front door and ask the reason why! But now that she had frightened those little rats of Kelveys and given Kezia a good scolding, her heart felt lighter. That ghastly pressure was gone. She went back to the house humming.

65   When the Kelveys were well out of sight of Burnells', they sat down to rest on a big red drainpipe by the side of the road. Lil's cheeks were still burning; she took off the hat with the quill and held it on her knee. Dreamily they looked over the hay paddocks, past the creek, to the group of wattles[8] where Logan's cows stood waiting to be milked. What were their thoughts?

66   Presently our Else nudged up close to her sister. But now she had forgotten the cross lady. She put out a finger and stroked her sister's quill; she smiled her rare smile.

67   "I seen the little lamp," she said, softly.

68   Then both were silent once more. 🙚

---

8. **wattles** *n.* walls or other simple structures made of woven reeds or twigs.

Comprehension Check

Complete the following items after you finish your first read. Review and clarify details with your group.

1. What object in the doll's house is Kezia's favorite?

2. How does Lena taunt Lil Kelvey?

3. What does Kezia do that makes Aunt Beryl angry?

4. 🗐 **Notebook** Confirm your understanding of the story by writing a summary.

- -

RESEARCH

Research to Clarify Choose at least one unfamiliar detail from the text. Briefly research that detail. In what way does the information you learned shed light on an aspect of the story?

© Pearson Education, Inc., or its affiliates. All rights reserved.

The Doll's House **207**

THE DOLL'S HOUSE

Close Read the Text

With your group, revisit sections of the text you marked during your first read. **Annotate** details that you notice. What **questions** do you have? What can you **conclude**?

Analyze the Text

CITE TEXTUAL EVIDENCE
to support your answers.

Complete the activities.

1. **Review and Clarify** With your group, reread paragraph 16 of the selection. Discuss the author's description of Lil's and Else's appearances and mannerisms. How does the author succeed in prompting the reader's sympathy for the little girls?

2. **Present and Discuss** Now work with your group to share the passages from the selection that you found especially important. Take turns presenting your passages. Discuss what you notice in the selection, what questions you asked, and what conclusions you reached.

3. **Essential Question:** *Do people need to belong?* What has this story taught you about outsiders and outcasts? Discuss with your group.

LANGUAGE DEVELOPMENT

Concept Vocabulary

shunned	sneered	spitefully

Why These Words? The three concept vocabulary words are related. With your group, discuss the words, and determine what they have in common. How do these word choices enhance the impact of the text?

Practice

📓 **Notebook** Confirm your understanding of these words by using them in sentences. Include context clues that hint at each word's meaning.

Word Study

📓 **Notebook** **Words With Multiple Suffixes** To determine the meaning of a word that ends with multiple suffixes, such as *spitefully*, begin with the meaning of the base word. Then, working from left to right, analyze the effect each suffix has on the word's meaning and part of speech.

Write the meanings of these words: *hopelessness, luminosity, colorization.* Consult a dictionary if needed.

Analyze Craft and Structure

Symbol and Theme In literature, a **symbol** is a character, setting, object, or image that stands both for itself and for something else, often an abstract idea. Traditional literary forms, such as myths or folk tales, often feature universal symbols. For example, water often symbolizes life or rebirth. In modern literature, symbols are often specific to a work rather than universal. In order to understand the deeper meaning of a literary symbol, look at the details used to describe it. Ask questions such as these: *Why is this character, setting, or object important? What do other characters think and say about it? How do they interact with it? What does it look like?*

A **theme** is a central message or insight into life revealed by a literary work. In most works of fiction and poetry, the theme is implicit, or suggested. Readers figure it out by analyzing details and looking for patterns or relationships among them. Symbols are often key elements to the development of a theme.

TIP

GROUP DISCUSSION
Members of your group may state the symbolic meanings and the story's theme in a variety of ways. You should not expect your responses to be identical.

Practice

CITE TEXTUAL EVIDENCE
to support your answers.

Work on your own to complete the chart. Then, share your responses with your group.

SYMBOL	DETAILS IN TEXT	SYMBOLIC MEANING(S)
the lamp	• Kezia is "frightfully" enchanted by it; which suggests it tempts her or challenges her in some way. •	The lamp symbolizes enlightened attitudes, kindness, and acceptance.
the doll's house		
the Kelvey's clothing		

📓 **Notebook** Answer these questions.

1. Why do you think Kezia invites the Kelveys to see the doll's house?

2. What does Else's statement at the end of the story suggest about both the lamp's symbolic meaning and the story's theme?

3. What is a possible theme of the story? Explain.

THE DOLL'S HOUSE

Author's Style

Diction and Syntax In writing and speech, **diction** refers to an author's or speaker's word choice, especially with regard to range of vocabulary, use of slang, and level of formality.

> **Informal Diction:** Are ya gonna drive to the store?
> **Formal Diction:** Who among us will drive to the store?

Syntax refers to the way in which words and phrases are joined together in sentences. A writer's syntax may include short punchy sentences, long complex ones, or a combination of both.

> **Simple Syntax:** We arrived at the theater. There were many cars in the lot.
> **Complex Syntax:** When we arrived at the theater, we saw dozens of cars in the lot and an excited crowd waiting on line.

Diction and syntax are key elements of a writer's style. They also help to reveal a writer's **tone,** or attitude toward the subject. For example, in "The Doll's House," Mansfield often combines informal words and slang with complex sentence structures. The tension between these two aspects of her style hints at the story's conflicts around class and social status.

::: STANDARDS

Reading Literature
Determine the meaning of words and phrases as they are used in the text, including figurative and connotative meanings; analyze the cumulative impact of specific word choices on meaning and tone.

Writing
Write arguments to support claims in an analysis of substantive topics or texts, using valid reasoning and relevant and sufficient evidence.

Read It

Work individually. For each quotation write whether the diction is formal or informal and whether the syntax is simple or complex. Then, write notes about the tone these choices create and the story conflicts they suggest. Discuss your responses with your group.

QUOTATION	DICTION	SYNTAX	NOTES
Not to stay to tea, of course, or to come traipsing through the house. (paragraph 12)			
So they were the daughters of a washerwoman and a gaolbird. Very nice company for other people's children! (paragraph 16)			
"Oh, ain't it lovely!" (paragraph 23)			
Lena couldn't stand that. She put her hands on her hips; she shot forward. "Yah, yer father's in prison!" she hissed, spitefully. (paragraph 40)			

Write It

📝 **Notebook** Write a description of a character and something he or she does. Use informal diction and simple syntax. Then, rewrite the description using elevated diction and complex syntax. Explain the effects of these stylistic choices.

Writing to Sources

Assignment

Write a **response to literature,** a type of argument in which you explain and defend your interpretation of a text. Be sure to state your claim, or main idea, and support it with details and evidence from the story. Choose one of the following topics:

- At the end of the story, the narrator asks about the Kelveys, "What were their thoughts?" In a brief **character analysis** of Lil and Else, use evidence from the story to explain what the Kelveys might have been thinking. Defend your analysis with story details that reveal each girl's character.

- In a **composition** of several paragraphs, compare and contrast social divisions in "The Doll's House" to those in American society today. Cite evidence from the story to support your account of how social divisions are presented in "The Doll's House."

- Write a **critical response** to this statement: In Katherine Mansfield's "The Doll's House," the world of the adults is far crueler than that of the children. Cite evidence from the story to support your response.

Project Plan Work together to discuss the story and gather ideas, but work on your own to draft and revise your response to literature.

Charting Main Ideas Use this chart to record your ideas. Remember to include appropriate citations of evidence.

EVIDENCE LOG

Before moving on to a new selection, go to your Evidence Log and record what you learned from "The Doll's House."

MAIN IDEAS	SUPPORTING DETAILS	EVIDENCE

POETRY COLLECTION

Sonnet, With Bird

Elliptical

Fences

Concept Vocabulary

As you perform your first read of these poems, you will encounter these words.

perspective	entitled	interactions

Base Words If these words are unfamiliar to you, analyze each one to see whether it contains a base word you know. Then, use your knowledge of the "inside" word, along with context, to determine the meaning.

> **Unfamiliar Word:** *extrasensory*
>
> **Familiar Base Word:** *sensory,* which means "of or relating to the senses"
>
> **Context:** *I wrote down the address and took a taxi driven by one of those cabdrivers with **extrasensory** memory.*
>
> **Conclusion:** Cabdrivers are known for their exceptional memories for directions. Perhaps *extrasensory* means "beyond the ordinary perception of the senses."

Apply your knowledge of base words and other vocabulary strategies to determine the meanings of unfamiliar words you encounter during your first read.

First Read POETRY

Apply these strategies as you conduct your first read. You will have the opportunity to complete a close read after your first read.

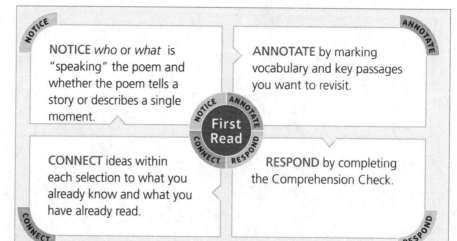

NOTICE who or what is "speaking" the poem and whether the poem tells a story or describes a single moment.

ANNOTATE by marking vocabulary and key passages you want to revisit.

CONNECT ideas within each selection to what you already know and what you have already read.

RESPOND by completing the Comprehension Check.

First Read

STANDARDS

Reading Literature
By the end of grade 10, read and comprehend literature, including stories, dramas, and poems, at the high end of the grades 9–10 text complexity band independently and proficiently.

Language

• Use context as a clue to the meaning of a word or phrase.

• Identify and correctly use patterns of word changes that indicate different meanings or parts of speech.

About the Poets

Sherman Alexie (b. 1966) grew up on the Spokane Indian Reservation in Washington State. As a child, Alexie suffered from seizures and spent much of his time in bed reading. After college, his career as a writer took off. Since then, Alexie has won numerous awards for his novels, stories, screenplays, and poems, including a PEN/Hemingway Award and the National Book Award.

Harryette Mullen (b. 1953) grew up primarily in Texas and now teaches English at the University of California, Los Angeles. Mullen's poetry has been described as "crossing lines" between the political and the personal. Mullen credits much of her success to attending poetry readings in which she realized that poetry is "not just something on the page" but instead something that has to be heard out loud to be fully appreciated.

Pat Mora (b. 1942) grew up in El Paso, Texas, and became a teacher, museum director, and university administrator before turning to writing. Mora writes poetry in both English and Spanish, often including Spanish words and phrases in her English-language poems. Her transcultural style gives a voice to her Mexican American heritage of the Southwest.

Backgrounds

Sonnet, With Bird

The sonnet form is one of the most enduring poetic forms, having survived five centuries essentially unchanged. A sonnet follows a strict fourteen-line arrangement in a specific rhyme scheme. The final two lines of a sonnet resolve or summarize the preceding lines. In this poem, Sherman Alexie reinvents the sonnet, presenting one of our most traditional forms in an entirely new way.

Elliptical

Ellipsis—often represented with punctuation marks known as ellipsis points (. . .)—is the omission, often intentional, of a word or words that would be needed for a thought to be complete. Sometimes, the missing word or words are understood from context. Other times, they are left to the reader's imagination. This poem, whose title means "involving ellipsis," plays with both of these ideas.

Fences

This poem was inspired by Puerto Vallarta, a beach resort city in Mexico. Many places, including Puerto Vallarta, rely on tourism as a major income source. This tourist economy, however, means that many locals must accommodate tourists who enjoy an affluent lifestyle that they themselves cannot afford.

Sonnet, With Bird

Sherman Alexie

SCAN FOR
MULTIMEDIA

NOTES

1. Seventeen months after I moved off the reservation, and on the second plane flight of my life, I traveled to London to promote my first internationally published book. 2. A Native American in England! I imagined the last Indian in England was Maria Tall Chief, the Osage[1] ballerina who was once married to Balanchine.[2] An Indian married to Balanchine! 3. My publishers put me in a quaint little hotel near the Tate Gallery. I didn't go into the Tate. Back then, I was afraid of paintings of and by white men. I think I'm still afraid of paintings of and by white men. 4. This was long before I had a cell phone, so I stopped at payphones to call my wife. I miss the intensity of a conversation measured by a dwindling stack of quarters. 5. No quarters in England, though, and I don't remember what the equivalent British coin was called. 6. As with every other country I've visited, nobody thought I was Indian. This made me lonely. 7. Lonely enough to cry in my hotel bed one night as I kept thinking, "I am the only Indian in this country right now. I'm the only Indian within a five-thousand-mile circle." 8. But I wasn't the only Indian;

1. **Osage** Native American tribe based in the Midwestern United States.
2. **Balanchine** George Balanchine (1904–1983), dance choreographer who founded the New York City Ballet and is considered the father of American ballet.

I wasn't even the only Spokane Indian.[3] 9. On the payphone, my mother told me that a childhood friend from the reservation was working at a London pub. So I wrote down the address and took a taxi driven by one of those cabdrivers with extrasensory memory. 10. When I entered the pub, I sat in a corner, and waited for my friend to discover me. When he saw me, he leapt over the bar and hugged me. "I thought I was the only Indian in England," he said. 11. His name was Aaron and he died of cancer last spring. I'd rushed to see him in his last moments, but he passed before I could reach him. Only minutes gone, his skin was still warm. I held his hand, kissed his forehead, and said, "England." 12. "England," in our tribal language, now means, "Aren't we a miracle?" and "Goodbye." 13. In my strange little hotel near the Tate, I had to wear my suit coat to eat breakfast in the lobby restaurant. Every morning, I ordered eggs and toast. Everywhere in the world, bread is bread, but my eggs were impossibly small. "What bird is this?" I asked the waiter. "That would be quail," he said. On the first morning, I could not eat the quail eggs. On the second morning, I only took a taste. On third day, I ate two and ordered two more. 14. A gathering of quail is called a bevy. A gathering of Indians is called a tribe. When quails speak, they call it a song. When Indians sing, the air is heavy with grief. When quails grieve, they lie down next to their dead. When Indians die, the quail speaks.

3. **Spokane Indian** Native American from the northeastern part of Washington State.

Elliptical

Harryette Mullen

They just can't seem to . . . They should try harder to . . . They ought to be more . . . We all wish they weren't so . . . They never . . . They always . . . Sometimes they . . . Once in a while they . . . However it is obvious that they . . . Their overall tendency has been . . . The consequences of which have been . . . They don't appear to understand that . . . If only they would make an effort to . . . But we know how difficult it is for them to . . . Many of them remain unaware of . . . Some who should know better simply refuse to . . . Of course, their **perspective** has been limited by . . . On the other hand, they obviously feel **entitled** to . . . Certainly we can't forget that they . . . Nor can it be denied that they . . . We know that this has had an enormous impact on their . . . Nevertheless their behavior strikes us as . . . Our **interactions** unfortunately have been . . .

NOTES

Mark base words or indicate another strategy you used that helped you determine meaning.

perspective (puhr SPEHK tihv) *n.*

MEANING:

entitled (ehn TY tuhld) *adj.*

MEANING:

interactions (ihn tuhr AK shuhnz) *n.*

MEANING:

Fences

Pat Mora

SCAN FOR
MULTIMEDIA

NOTES

Mouths full of laughter,
the *turistas* come to the tall hotel
with suitcases full of dollars.

Every morning my brother makes
5 the cool beach new for them.
With a wooden board he smooths
away all footprints.

I peek through the cactus fence
and watch the women rub oil
10 sweeter than honey into their arms and legs
while their children jump waves
or sip drinks from long straws,
coconut white, mango yellow.

Once my little sister
15 ran barefoot across the hot sand
for a taste.

My mother roared like the ocean,
"No. No. It's their beach.
It's their beach."

Comprehension Check

Complete the following items after you finish your first read. Review and clarify details with your group.

SONNET, WITH BIRD

1. Why does the speaker go to London?

2. Whom does the speaker meet in London?

ELLIPTICAL

3. How does each sentence of "Elliptical" end?

4. What pronoun appears in the first nine sentences of the poem?

FENCES

5. What does the speaker's brother do each day?

6. What does the speaker's little sister do that causes the mother to react?

RESEARCH

Research to Clarify Choose at least one unfamiliar detail from one of the poems. Briefly research that detail. In what way does the information you learned shed light on an aspect of the poem.

Close Read the Text

With your group, revisit sections of the text you marked during your first read. **Annotate** details that you notice. What **questions** do you have? What can you **conclude**?

Analyze the Text

CITE TEXTUAL EVIDENCE
to support your answers.

📓 **Notebook** Complete the activities.

1. **Review and Clarify** With your group, reread the lines of "Sonnet, With Bird" numbered 11 and 12. What point does the author make by defining England in two different ways? Explain.

2. **Present and Discuss** Now, work with your group to share other key lines from the poems. What made you choose these particular passages? Take turns presenting your choices. Discuss what you notice in the poem, what questions you asked, and what conclusions you reached.

3. **Essential Question:** *Do people need to belong?* What have these poems taught you about being an outsider? Discuss with your group.

LANGUAGE DEVELOPMENT

Concept Vocabulary

perspective	entitled	interactions

Why These Words? The three concept vocabulary words are related. With your group, identify the concept they have in common. How do these word choices enhance the text?

Practice

📓 **Notebook** Confirm your understanding of these words by using them in sentences. Include context clues that hint at their meanings.

Word Study

📓 **Notebook** **Latin Prefix: en-** The concept vocabulary word *entitled* begins with the Latin prefix *en-*, meaning "in," "into," or "on." Write the meanings of these other words beginning with the prefix *en: enamor, encapsulate, encipher.* Consult a college-level dictionary as needed.

🔗 WORD NETWORK

Add words related to outsiders from the texts to your Word Network.

⧉ STANDARDS

Reading Literature
Analyze how an author's choices concerning how to structure a text, order events within it, and manipulate time create such effects as mystery, tension, or surprise.

Language
• Identify and correctly use patterns of word changes that indicate different meanings or parts of speech.
• Consult general and specialized reference materials, both print and digital, to find the pronunciation of a word or determine or clarify its precise meaning, its part of speech, or its etymology.

Analyze Craft and Structure

Author's Choices: Poetic Form Poems can be written in any number of different poetic forms. A **poetic form** is a set pattern of poetic elements. For example, a poetic form may call for a fixed number of lines, a particular pattern of rhyme or meter, or any combination of those elements. Some poems, however, avoid the use of fixed patterns altogether. For example, **free verse** poems do not follow any set patterns. Instead, they present carefully crafted lines that re-create the rhythms of natural speech or present unexpected combinations of language. To create these effects, free verse poets often play with line breaks, or the ways in which lines end.

- **End-stopped lines** are lines that complete a grammatical unit; they usually end with a punctuation mark, such as a comma or period.
- **Enjambed lines** do not end with a grammatical break and do not make full sense without the line that follows.

The **prose poem** is a poetic form that looks like prose, or a non-poetic work, but sounds like poetry. Prose poems lack the line breaks most often found in poetry, but they may contain other poetic techniques such as repetition or rhyme.

Practice

CITE TEXTUAL EVIDENCE to support your answers.

Work together as a group to answer the following questions.

1. In "Fences," which lines are end-stopped and which are enjambed? Explain how the different types of lines emphasize meaning or affect how a reader hears and understands the poem.

2. (a) What type of poem is "Elliptical"? Explain. (b) In what ways does the choice of form affect how the reader experiences the poem? (c) Rewrite the poem, adding line breaks that make sense to you. Compare with the original. What is lost and what is gained by the poet's choice of form?

3. (a) What poetic techniques does "Sonnet, With Bird" use that make it a poem rather than prose? (b) How does the combination of poetic and prose-like elements affect its meaning?

POETRY COLLECTION

Author's Style

Author's Choices: Poetic Form A traditional, Shakespearean **sonnet** is a fourteen-line poem that contains three four-line stanzas, or **quatrains**, and a final two-line stanza, or **couplet.** It has a regular meter and set pattern of rhyme, or **rhyme scheme.**

Shakespeare's "Sonnet 18" features three quatrains that develop a theme and follow an *abab, cdcd, efef* rhyme pattern. Here is the first quatrain.

> *Shall I compare thee to a summer's day? (a)*
> *Thou art more lovely and more temperate. (b)*
> *Rough winds do shake the darling buds of May, (a)*
> *And summer's lease hath all too short a date. (b)*

The final two lines in the sonnet form a rhyming couplet.

> *So long as men can breathe or eyes can see, (g)*
> *So long lives this and this gives life to thee. (g)*

Traditionally, the rhyming couplet that ends a sonnet dramatically redefines or twists the thematic ideas expressed in the earlier lines.

Read It

In "Sonnet, With Bird," Sherman Alexie uses the sonnet form as a starting point, then changes it drastically. Work individually to reread the poem. Chart how Alexie's poem reimagines the Shakespearean sonnet.

SONNET CHARACTERISTIC	SONNET, WITH BIRD	COMMENT
number of lines		
rhyme scheme		
three quatrains that develop a theme		
final couplet that presents a twist		

Write It

Notebook Write a paragraph in which you explain how Alexie experiments with the Shakespearean sonnet to create a prose poem. Use the information in your chart to cite examples from the poem.

STANDARDS

Reading Literature
• Analyze how an author's choices concerning how to structure a text, order events within it, and manipulate time create such effects as mystery, tension, or surprise.
• Analyze how an author draws on and transforms source material in a specific work.

Speaking and Listening
Present information, findings, and supporting evidence clearly, concisely, and logically such that listeners can follow the line of reasoning and the organization, development, substance, and style are appropriate to purpose, audience, and task.

Speaking and Listening

Assignment

As a group, rewrite one of the poems in this collection, altering a key aspect of its form or content. Then, deliver a **poetry reading** of the revised work. Afterward, take questions from listeners about the decisions you made as you created the revised poem. Choose from the following options:

☐ Complete each sentence in the poem "Elliptical." Work together as a group. Write out the poem in its entirety.

Use questions such as the following to guide your work: *To whom does "they" refer in the original poem? How does completing the sentences change the meaning of the poem? Does the poem have greater impact with completed sentences or without them?*

☐ Change the structure of "Sonnet, With Bird" by rearranging line breaks and phrasing. Note that poets use line breaks and phrasing to group together discrete thoughts, images, and emotions.

Use questions such as the following to guide your work: *Which thoughts, feelings, images, or emotions does the restructuring affect? In what ways? How does the restructuring change the meaning of the poem?*

☐ Rewrite "Fences" as a prose poem. Include the same general information and images as the original, but change the line breaks and modify sentences so that they work as prose. Add more detail if necessary.

Use questions such as the following to guide your work: *How does the change in structure affect the meaning of the poem? Does the poem have a greater impact in its original form or as a prose poem?*

Project Plan Assign each member of the group a portion of the poem to memorize and read aloud as part of the recitation. Before you recite your poem to the class, practice it with your group several times. Provide helpful feedback on the tone, speed, and dramatic qualities of each reading.

Present and Discuss As your present your work to the class, make sure your delivery reflects the structural changes you introduced. Compare the poem your group wrote with those of the other small groups in the class.

✎ EVIDENCE LOG

Before moving on to a new selection, go to your Evidence Log and record what you learned from "Sonnet, With Bird," "Elliptical," and "Fences."

About the Author

Alexandra Robbins
(b. 1976) is a journalist
and bestselling author.
She has written for several
newspapers and magazines,
including the *Los Angeles
Times,* the *Washington Post,*
and the *Atlantic.* Robbins's
journalism is highly regarded;
she was a recipient of the
John Bartlow Martin Award.
Her most recent work, *The
Nurses: A Year of Secrets,
Drama, and Miracles With
the Heroes of the Hospital,*
has been praised for its
investigative merit and
captivating narrative of the
nursing profession.

Revenge of the Geeks

Concept Vocabulary

As you perform your first read of "Revenge of the Geeks," you will
encounter these words.

marginalize	pariah	bigotry

Context Clues If these words are unfamiliar, try using **context clues**—
other words and phrases that appear nearby in the text—to help you
determine their meanings. There are different types of context clues.

Definition: In some cases, **psychologists** and **sociologists** do related
work. The former study individual behavior, whereas the latter study
group behavior.

Elaborating Details: She was once a loner, but is now a media
tycoon and one of the richest women in the world.

Antonym, or Contrast of Ideas: Some members of the group are
sadly **indolent,** but others work extremely hard.

Apply your knowledge of context clues and other vocabulary strategies to
determine the meanings of unfamiliar words you encounter during your
first read. Use a resource such as a dictionary or a thesaurus to verify your
definitions.

First Read NONFICTION

Apply these strategies as you conduct your first read. You will have an
opportunity to complete a close read after your first read.

NOTICE the general ideas of
the text. *What* is it about?
Who is involved?

ANNOTATE by marking
vocabulary and key passages
you want to revisit.

First Read

CONNECT ideas within
the selection to what you
already know and what you
have already read.

RESPOND by completing
the Comprehension Check and
by writing a brief summary of
the selection.

NOTICE   ANNOTATE   CONNECT   RESPOND

STANDARDS

Reading Informational Text
By the end of grade 10, read and
comprehend literary nonfiction at
the high end of the grades 9–10 text
complexity band independently and
proficiently.

Language
• Use context as a clue to the
meaning of a word or phrase.
• Verify the preliminary
determination of the meaning of a
word or phrase.

Revenge of the Geeks

Alexandra Robbins

BACKGROUND

The word *geek* has a long history—one of its earliest appearances was as *gecke* in the works of Shakespeare, as a word for "fool." It became *geek* in the late nineteenth century, and by the middle of the twentieth century it had come to be used as a generic, all-purpose insult. In the 1970s, however, *geek* came to mean, specifically, "an overly eager student," especially one interested in computers.

NOTES

1 Many popular students approach graduation day with bittersweet nostalgia: Excitement for the future is tempered by fear of lost status. But as cap-and-gown season nears, let's also stop to consider the outcasts, students for whom finishing high school feels like liberation from a state-imposed sentence.

2 In seven years of reporting from American middle and high schools, I've seen repeatedly that the differences that cause a student to be excluded in high school are often the same traits or skills that will serve him or her well after graduation.

3 Examples abound: Taylor Swift's classmates left the lunch table as soon as she sat down because they disdained her taste for country music. Last year, the Grammy winner was the nation's top-selling recording artist.

4 Students mocked Tim Gunn's love of making things; now he is a fashion icon with the recognizable catchphrase "Make it work."

5 J. K. Rowling, author of the bestselling "Harry Potter" series, has described herself as a bullied child "who lived mostly in books and daydreams." It's no wonder she went on to write books populated with kids she describes as "outcasts and comfortable with being so."

6 For many, says Sacred Heart University psychology professor Kathryn LaFontana, high school is the "first foray[1] into the adult world where [kids] have to think about their own status." And for

---

1. **foray** *n.* attempt to do something.

teenagers, says LaFontana, who studies adolescent peer relationships and social status, "the worst thing in the world is to be different from other people; that's what makes someone unpopular."

7   In the rabidly conformist school environment, the qualities that make people different make them targets. In adulthood, however, the qualities that make people different make them compelling.

8   Some students are vaguely aware of this reality. An eighth-grade boy in Indiana told me: "I'm always single, so it's tough. Never can get a girl. The smart thing repels girls. I like being smart because I breeze through school. . . . That's the good thing, but the girl thing is killing me."

9   It's hard to know when you're in high school that "the smart thing" is likely to translate into later success, or that "the girl thing" is bound to improve. That's why it's up to adults to convey constantly to teenagers that the characteristics that **marginalize** them can pay off after graduation.

Mark context clues or indicate another strategy you used that helped you determine meaning.

marginalize (MAHR juh nuh lyz) *v.*

MEANING:

10   Geeks profit from their technological knowhow. Emos benefit from being empathetic and unafraid to display emotion. Skaters, punks, and others who pursue their arts with fervor benefit from the creativity they've honed. Gamers have learned both problem-solving skills and the ability to collaborate through collective intelligence.

11   In the adult world, being out is in. "Geek chic" and "nerd merch" are on the rise. Nerdcore hip-hop artists have penetrated mainstream consciousness. And the nerd prom known as Comic Con draws high-profile celebrities and throngs of smitten fans. They're all part of what Jerry Holkins, creator of the Penny Arcade webcomic and video game conference, calls "the social **pariah** outcast aesthetic."

pariah (puh RY uh) *n.*

MEANING:

12   Adults tend to be mature enough to recognize that there would be no progress—cures for diseases, ways to harness new energy sources—without people who are different. Successful scientists think distinctively.

13   So what happens to high school's popular students? Research shows that they are more likely than outsiders to conform, which can also mean they're less likely to innovate. They are more likely to be both targets and instigators of aggression—whether physical or relational, which includes rumors, gossip, and backstabbing. They are more likely to drink and engage in other risky behaviors. Students who are popular and involved in aggression are less likely to do well in school. Psychologists point out that high-status cliques teach the exclusionary behavior that may be the foundation for eventual racism, anti-Semitism, sexism, and other forms of **bigotry**.

bigotry (BIHG uh tree) *n.*

MEANING:

14   That's not to say, of course, that popularity in high school necessarily leads to mediocrity or worse in adulthood. But neither is there necessarily something wrong with a student merely because he is excluded by classmates. We don't view a saxophonist as musically challenged if he can't play the violin. He's just a different kind of musician. A sprinter is still an athlete even if she can't play basketball. She's a different kind of athlete. Similarly, we might acknowledge

that students who don't follow the popular crowd's lead aren't any less socially successful; they're just a different kind of social.

15 The education landscape would be so much more bearable if students could understand this. And if schools found better ways to nurture kids who reject the in-crowd image.

16 The worst aspect of the treatment of student outsiders isn't the name-calling. It isn't the loneliness. It isn't even the demise of attitudes and programs that are important for fostering creativity and independence. The most heartbreaking consequence of this treatment is that tens of thousands of students—imaginative, interesting, impressionable people—think that they have done or felt something wrong.

17 It's not enough to merely tell them that in the real world, "it gets better." They need to know before graduation that being different is not a problem but a strength. ❧

Comprehension Check

Complete the following items after you finish your first read. Review and clarify details with your group.

1. According to the author, why did Taylor Swift's classmates leave the lunch table as soon as Swift sat down?

2. According to psychology professor Kathryn LaFontana, what is the worst thing in the world for teenagers?

3. What does Robbins believe that adults should constantly convey to teenagers?

4. How do successful scientists think, according to Robbins?

5. 🗐 **Notebook** Confirm your understanding by writing a summary of the text.

- -

RESEARCH

Research to Clarify Choose at least one unfamiliar detail from the text. Briefly research that detail. In what way does the information you learned shed light on an aspect of the argument?

REVENGE OF THE GEEKS

Close Read the Text

With your group, revisit sections of the text you marked during your first read. **Annotate** details that you notice. What **questions** do you have? What can you **conclude**?

Analyze the Text

> **CITE TEXTUAL EVIDENCE**
> to support your answers.

📓 **Notebook** Complete the activities.

1. **Review and Clarify** Reread the first five paragraphs of the selection. Where does the author state her claim, or main idea, in this argument? Restate the claim in your own words. What three examples does Robbins cite in this section of the text to support this claim?

2. **Present and Discuss** Now, work with your group to share the passages from the selection that you found especially important. Take turns presenting your passages. Discuss what you notice in the selection, what questions you asked, and what conclusions you reached.

3. **Essential Question:** *Do people need to belong?* What has this text taught you about outsiders and outcasts? Discuss with your group.

LANGUAGE DEVELOPMENT

Concept Vocabulary

| marginalize | pariah | bigotry |

Why These Words? The three concept vocabulary words are related. With your group, determine what the words have in common. How do these word choices enhance the impact of the text?

Practice

📓 **Notebook** Confirm your understanding of these words by using them in sentences. Include context clues that hint at each word's meaning.

Word Study

📓 **Notebook** **Denotation and Connotation** The **denotation** of a word is its literal definition that you would find in a dictionary. A word's **connotations** are its emotional overtones or nuances. For example, the word *pariah* literally means "outcast." Its connotations are overwhelmingly negative. This word came into English from Tamil, an Indian language, where it signified someone from the lowest social caste, or group.

Use a dictionary to research the denotations and connotations of the following words from the selection: *nostalgia, disdain, conformist, smitten, distinctively.* Then, use each word in a sentence that clearly indicates both its denotation and its connotation.

🔗 WORD NETWORK

Add interesting words related to outsiders from the text to your Word Network.

::: STANDARDS

Reading Informational Text
• Delineate and evaluate the argument and specific claims in a text, assessing whether the reasoning is valid and the evidence is relevant and sufficient; identify false statements and fallacious reasoning.

Language
• Determine or clarify the meaning of unknown and multiple-meaning words and phrases based on *grades 9–10 reading and content,* choosing flexibly from a range of strategies.
• Demonstrate understanding of figurative language, word relationships, and nuances in word meanings.
• Analyze nuances in the meaning of words with similar denotations.

Analyze Craft and Structure

Reasoning and Evidence "Revenge of the Geeks" is an **argument,** a type of nonfiction in which a writer states a **claim,** or position on a debatable issue, and then defends that claim with sound reasoning and evidence. **Evidence** includes facts, data, information, explanations, anecdotes, quotations, examples, and any other details that support the writer's reasons or main claim.

When reading an argument, it is important to evaluate both the writer's reasoning and the quality of the evidence he or she uses to support it. Strong reasoning should have clear, logical connections. Strong evidence should have the following qualities:

- **Variety:** A writer should include different types of evidence, such as facts, data, and quotations. It should come from a range of sources.
- **Credibility:** Evidence should be drawn from reliable, authoritative sources. A credible source may present a distinct perspective, but it should not display bias, unfounded judgments, or sweeping generalizations.
- **Relevance:** Evidence should be current and connect logically to the writer's ideas.

Practice

CITE TEXTUAL EVIDENCE to support your answers.

📓 **Notebook** Work on your own to answer the questions. Then, share and discuss your responses with your group.

1. How does Robbins support her claim that the qualities that make students outcasts in high school are those that make them successful in adulthood?
2. How does Robbins develop her argument that being popular in high school may actually work against people when they enter the adult world?
3. Use the chart to identify the types of evidence Robbins uses and to evaluate its credibility and relevance.

CLAIM	EVIDENCE	CREDIBILITY	RELEVANCE

4. Write a paragraph in which you evaluate the validity of Robbins's argument. Cite evidence from your chart as examples.

REVENGE OF THE GEEKS

Author's Style

Parallel Structure Parallelism, or **parallel structure,** is the use of similar grammatical forms or patterns to express ideas of equal significance. Effective use of parallelism creates rhythm and balance and clarifies the relationships among ideas. When writing lacks parallelism, it presents equally significant ideas in an unnecessary mix of grammatical forms. This inconsistency can be awkward, confusing, or distracting for readers.

This chart shows examples of nonparallel and parallel structure.

SENTENCE ELEMENTS	NONPARALLEL	PARALLEL
words	<u>Planning</u>, <u>drafting</u> and **revision** are three steps in the writing process.	<u>Planning</u>, <u>drafting</u>, and **revising** are three steps in the writing process.
phrases	I could not wait <u>to hop on that plane</u> <u>to leave the country</u>, and **for some world exploration**.	I could not wait <u>to hop on that plane</u>, <u>to leave the country</u>, and **to explore the world**.
clauses	Ari likes his new school: <u>The teachers are good</u>, <u>the students are nice</u>, and he **likes the new building**.	Ari likes his new school: <u>The teachers are good</u>, <u>the students are nice</u>, and **the building is new**.

Read It

Mark the parallel sentence elements in each of these passages from "Revenge of the Geeks." Parallel elements may appear in a single sentence or in mutiple sentences.

1. In the rabidly conformist school environment, the qualities that make people different make them targets. In adulthood, however, the qualities that make people different make them compelling.

2. Geeks profit from their technological knowhow. Emos benefit from being empathetic and unafraid to display emotion. Skaters, punks, and others . . . benefit from the skills and the ability to collaborate through collective intelligence.

3. Research shows that they are more likely . . . to conform, which can also mean they're less likely to innovate.

4. Psychologists point out that high-status cliques teach the exclusionary behavior that may be the foundation for eventual racism, anti-Semitism, sexism and other forms of bigotry.

Write It

📝 **Notebook** Write a paragraph about "Revenge of the Geeks." Include at least one example of parallel structure. Mark your examples.

STANDARDS

Language
• Use parallel structure.
• Apply knowledge of language to understand how language functions in different contexts, to make effective choices for meaning or style, and to comprehend more fully when reading or listening.

Speaking and Listening

Assignment

Create a **multimedia presentation** in which you incorporate text and images to explain a subject. Choose from the following options.

☐ Prepare an **informational video** in which you share what you learned from Robbins's argument. Cite evidence from the text that proves your points and supports your opinions.

☐ Design a **social media campaign** with the goal of effecting change in how students who are "different" are treated in school. Explain why change is needed, and cite evidence from Robbins's argument to support your claim. In your presentation, show how your campaign will have a lasting impact.

☐ Choose a side, explaining why you agree or disagree with Robbins. Construct your argument or counterargument using evidence from the text. Create and present a **poster** publicizing your position visually. If members of your group disagree, split into two groups. Have each group complete a poster arguing the side it favors.

Project Plan Before you begin, make a list of the tasks you will need to complete in order to finish your project. Then, assign individual group members to each task. Finally, determine how you will make decisions about choices of images, text, and design elements.

Developing Your Argument Use this chart to collect ideas and images for your presentation. Remember to include appropriate citations for all evidence.

ARGUMENT	EVIDENCE	IMAGE

EVIDENCE LOG

Before moving on to a new selection, go to your Evidence Log and record what you learned from "Revenge of the Geeks."

:: STANDARDS

Speaking and Listening
• Work with peers to set rules for collegial discussions and decision-making, clear goals and deadlines, and individual roles as needed.
• Present information, findings, and supporting evidence clearly, concisely, and logically such that listeners can follow the line of reasoning and the organization, development, substance, and style are appropriate to purpose, audience, and task.
• Make strategic use of digital media in presentations to enhance understanding of findings, reasoning, and evidence and to add interest.

About the Author

Ryszard Kapuscinski

(1932–2007) began his career in journalism by keeping two notepads. In one, he detailed concrete facts for his investigative articles sold to Polish newspapers. The other was filled with personal notes and unique experiences. His first notebook brought him an income, yet his thoughts in the second were the basis for his highly regarded books. Kapuscinski often covered and supported African nations in the fight against colonialism.

Encountering the Other: The Challenge for the 21st Century

Concept Vocabulary

As you perform your first read of "Encountering the Other: The Challenge for the 21st Century," you will encounter the following words.

doctrine	totalitarian	ideologies

Base Words If these words are unfamiliar to you, analyze each one to see whether it contains a base word you know. Then, use your knowledge of the "inside" word, along with context, to determine the meaning of the concept word. Here is an example of how to apply the strategy.

> **Unfamiliar Word:** *dismissively*
>
> **Familiar "Inside" Word:** *dismissive*, meaning "disinterested; scornful"
>
> **Context:** Should they throw themselves in fury on those other people? Or walk past **dismissively** and keep going?
>
> **Conclusion:** The *-ly* ending shows that the word is an adverb that tells the manner in which something is being done. *Dismissively* must mean "behaving in a way that shows disinterest or scorn."

Apply your knowledge of base words and other vocabulary strategies to determine the meanings of unfamiliar words you encounter during your first read.

First Read NONFICTION

Apply these strategies as you conduct your first read. You will have an opportunity to complete a close read after your first read.

NOTICE the general ideas of the text. *What* is it about? *Who* is involved?

ANNOTATE by marking vocabulary and key passages you want to revisit.

CONNECT ideas within the selection to what you already know and what you have already read.

RESPOND by completing the Comprehension Check and by writing a brief summary of the selection.

First Read

:≣ STANDARDS

Reading Informational Text
By the end of grade 10, read and comprehend literary nonfiction at the high end of the grades 9–10 text complexity band independently and proficiently.

Language
• Determine or clarify the meaning of unknown and multiple-meaning words and phrases based on *grades 9–10 reading and content,* choosing flexibly from a range of strategies
• Identify and correctly use patterns of word change that indicate different meanings or parts of speech.

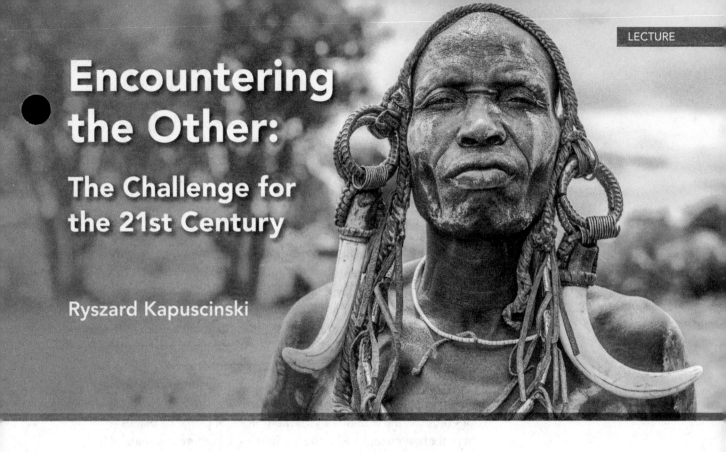

Encountering the Other:
The Challenge for the 21st Century

Ryszard Kapuscinski

BACKGROUND

Globalization is the interaction and integration of people, companies, and governments of different countries. It is one of the most visible trends in modern culture. With increasingly common and efficient intercontinental travel, communication, and trade, regional life has become tied to cultures around the world. The globe is, metaphorically, getting smaller.

SCAN FOR MULTIMEDIA

NOTES

1   The encounter with the Other, with other people, has always been a universal and fundamental experience for our species.

2   Archaeologists tell us that the very earliest human groups were small family-tribes numbering 30 to 50 individuals. Had such a community been larger, it would have had trouble moving around quickly and efficiently. Had it been smaller, it would have found it harder to defend itself effectively and to fight for survival.

3   So here is our little family-tribe going along searching for nourishment, when it suddenly comes across another family-tribe. What a significant movement in the history of the world, what a momentous discovery! The discovery that there are other people in the world! Until then, the members of these primal groups could live in the conviction, as they moved around in the company of 30 to 50 of their kinfolk, that they knew all the people in the world. Then it turned out that they didn't—that other similar beings, other people, also inhabited the world! But how to behave in the face of such a revelation? What to do? What decision to make?

4   Should they throw themselves in fury on those other people? Or walk past dismissively and keep going? Or rather try to get to know and understand them?

5   That same choice that our ancestors faced thousands of years ago faces us today as well, with undiminished intensity—a choice as fundamental and categorical as it was back then. How should we act toward Others? What kind of attitude should we have toward them? It might end up in a duel, a conflict, or a war. Every archive contains evidence of such events, which are also marked by countless battlefields and ruins scattered around the world.

6   All this is proof of man's failure—that he did not know how, or did not want, to reach an understanding with Others. The literature of all countries in all epochs[1] has taken up this situation, this tragedy and weakness, as subject matter of infinite variety and moods.

7   But it might also be the case that, instead of attacking and fighting, this family-tribe that we are watching decides to fence itself off from others, to isolate and separate itself. This attitude leads, over time, to objects like the Great Wall of China, the towers and gates of Babylon, the Roman limes[2] and or the stone walls of the Inca.

8   Fortunately, there is evidence of a different human experience scattered abundantly across our planet. These are the proofs of cooperation—the remains of marketplaces, of ports, of places where there were agoras[3] and sanctuaries, of where the seats of old universities and academies are still visible, and of where there remain vestiges of such trade routes as the Silk Road, the Amber Route, and the Trans-Saharan caravan route.

9   All of these were places where people met to exchange thoughts, ideas, and merchandise, and where they traded and did business, concluded covenants and alliances, and discovered shared goals and values. "The Other" stopped being a synonym of foreignness and hostility, danger and mortal evil. People discovered within themselves a fragment of the Other, and they believed in this and lived confidently.

10   People thus had three choices when they encountered the Other: They could choose war, they could build a wall around themselves, or they could enter into dialogue.

11   Over the expanse of history, mankind has never stopped wavering among these options, and, depending on changing times and cultures, has chosen one or the other; we can see that mankind is fickle here and does not always feel certain, does not always stand on firm ground. War is hard to justify. I think that everyone always loses because war is a disaster for human beings. It exposes their incapacity for understanding, for putting themselves in the shoes of others, for goodness and sense. The encounter with the Other usually ends tragically in such cases, in a catastrophe of blood and death.

12   The idea that led people to build great walls and gaping moats, to surround themselves with them and fence themselves off from

---

1. **epochs** (EHP uks) *n.* periods of historical time.
2. **limes** *n.* walls mortared with quicklime plaster.
3. **agoras** (uh GAWR uhz) *n.* open gathering places.

others, has been given the contemporary name of apartheid.[4] This concept has been erroneously confined to the policies of the now-defunct white regime in South Africa. However, apartheid was already being practiced in the earliest mists of time. In simple terms, proponents of this view proclaim that everyone is free to live as he chooses, as long as it's as far away from me as possible, if he isn't part of my race, religion, or culture. If that were all!

13   In reality, we are looking at a **doctrine** of the structural inequality of the human race. The myths of many tribes and peoples include the conviction that only we are human—the members of our clan, our community—while others, all others, are subhuman or aren't human at all. An ancient Chinese belief expressed it best: A non-Chinese was regarded as the devil's spawn, or at best as a victim of fate who did not manage to be born Chinese. The Other, according to this belief, was presented as a dog, as a rat, as a creeping reptile. Apartheid was and still is a doctrine of hatred, contempt, and revulsion for the Other, the foreigner.

14   How different was the image of the Other in the epoch of anthropomorphic[5] beliefs, the belief that the gods could assume human form and act like people. Back then you could never tell whether the approaching wanderer, traveler, or newcomer was a person or a god in human guise. That uncertainty, that fascinating ambivalence, was one of the roots of the culture of hospitality that mandated showing all kindness to the newcomer, that ultimately unknowable being.

15   Cyprian Norwid writes about this when he ponders, in his introduction to the *Odyssey*, the sources of the hospitality that Odysseus encounters on his journey back to Ithaca. "There, with every beggar and foreign wanderer," Norwid remarks, "the first suspicion was that he might have been sent by God. . . . No one could have been received as a guest if the first question were: 'Who is this newcomer?' But only when the divinity in him was respected did the human questions follow, and that was called hospitality, and for that very reason it was numbered among the pious practices and virtues. There was no 'last among men!' with Homer's Greeks—he was always the first, which means divine."

16   In this Greek understanding of culture, cited by Norwid, things reveal a new significance that is favorable to people. Doors and gates are not only for closing against the Other—they can also open for him and welcome him inside. The road need not serve hostile columns; it can also be a highway along which one of the gods, in pilgrim's garb, comes to us. Thanks to such an interpretation, the world we inhabit

---

4. **apartheid** (uh PAHR tyd) *n.* South African policy of extreme racial segregation under which the native African majority was not allowed to vote and suffered intense repression. Apartheid ended in 1994 with the first free elections. The word is often used to refer to other systems of repressive ethnic segregation.
5. **anthropomorphic** (an thruh poh MAWR fihk) *adj.* described or thought of as having human behaviors or characteristics.

NOTES

Mark base words or indicate another strategy you used that helped you determine meaning.

doctrine (DOK truhn) *n.*

MEANING:

starts being not only richer and more diverse, but also kinder to us, a world in which we ourselves will want to encounter the Other.

17   Emmanuel Levinas calls the encounter with the Other an "event," or even a "fundamental event," the most important experience, reaching to the farthest horizons. Levinas, as we know, was one of the philosophers of dialogue, along with Martin Buber, Ferdinand Ebner, and Gabriel Marcel (a group that later came to include Jozef Tischner), who developed the idea of the Other as a unique and unrepeatable entity, in more or less direct opposition to two phenomena that arose in the 20th century: the birth of the masses that abolished the separateness of the individual, and the expansion of destructive **totalitarian ideologies**.

totalitarian (toh tal uh TAIR ee uhn) *adj.*

MEANING:

18   These philosophers attempted to salvage what they regarded as the paramount value, the human individual—me, you, the Other, the Others—from being obliterated by the actions of the masses and of totalitarianism (which is why these philosophers promoted the concept of "the Other" to emphasize the differences between one individual and another, the differences of non-interchangeable and irreplaceable characteristics).

ideologies (y dee OL uh jeez) *n.*

MEANING:

19   This was an incredibly important movement that rescued and elevated the human being, a movement that rescued and elevated the Other, with whom, as Levinas suggested, one must not only stand face to face and conduct a dialogue, but for whom one must "take responsibility." In terms of relations with the Other and Others, the philosophers of dialogue rejected war because it led to annihilation; they criticized the attitudes of indifference or building walls; instead, they proclaimed the need—or even the ethical obligation—for closeness, openness, and kindness.

20   In the circle of just such ideas and convictions, a similar type of inquiry and reflection, a similar attitude, arises and develops in the great research work of a man who did his undergraduate work and went on to earn a Ph.D. at Jagiellonian University, and who was a member of the Polish Academy of Sciences—Bronislaw Malinowski.

21   Malinowski's problem was how to approach the Other, not as an exclusively hypothetical and abstract entity, but as a concrete person belonging to a different race, with beliefs and values different from ours, and with his own culture and customs.

22   Let us point out that the concept of the Other is usually defined from the white man's—the European's—point of view. But today, when I walk through a village in the mountains of Ethiopia, a crowd of children runs after me, pointing at me in merriment and calling out: "Ferenchi! Ferenchi!"—which means "foreigner, other." This is an example of the dismantling of the hierarchy of the world and its cultures. Others are indeed Others, but for those Others, I am the one who is Other.

23   In this sense, we're all in the same boat. All of us inhabitants of our planet are Other for Others—Me for Them, and Them for Me.

24   In Malinowski's era and in the preceding centuries, the white man, the European, left his continent almost exclusively for gain—to take over new land, capture slaves, trade, or convert. These expeditions, at times, were incredibly bloody—Columbus conquering America, and then the white settlers, the conquest of Africa, Asia, and Australia.

25   Malinowski set out for the Pacific islands with a different goal—to learn about the Other. To learn about his neighbor's customs and language, and to see how he lived. He wanted to see and experience this for himself, personally—to experience it so that he could later tell about it. It might seem like an obvious undertaking, yet it turned out to be revolutionary, and it stood the world on its ear.

26   It laid bare a weakness or perhaps simply a characteristic that appears to a differing degree in all cultures: the fact that cultures have difficulty understanding other cultures, and that people belonging to a given culture—the participants in and carriers of that culture—have this difficulty. Namely, Malinowski stated after arriving at his research site in the Trobriand Islands that the white people who had lived there for years not only knew nothing about the local people and their culture, but also, in fact, held an entirely erroneous image characterized by contempt and arrogance.

NOTES

ˇ A village in the Trobriand Islands

27   He himself, as if to spite all colonial customs, pitched his tent in the middle of a local village and lived among the local people. What he experienced turned out to be no easy experience. In his *A Diary in the Strict Sense of the Term*, he continually mentions problems, bad moods, despair, and depression. You pay a high price for breaking free of your culture. That is why it is so important to have your own distinct identity, and a sense of your own strength, worth, and maturity. Only then can you confidently face a different culture. Otherwise, you will withdraw into your own hiding place and timorously cut yourself off from others.

28   All the more so because the Other is a mirror into which you peer, or in which you are observed, a mirror that unmasks and denudes, which we would prefer to avoid. It is interesting that, while the First World War was under way in Malinowski's native Europe, the young anthropologist was concentrating on research into the culture of exchange, contacts, and common rituals among the inhabitants of the Trobriand Islands, to which he devotes his excellent Argonauts of the Western Pacific, and formulating his important thesis, so seldom observed by others, that "to judge something, you have to be there."

29   Malinowski advanced another thesis, incredibly bold for its time: namely that there is no such thing as a higher or a lower culture— there are only different cultures, with varying ways of meeting the needs and expectations of their participants. For him, a different person, of a different race and culture, is nevertheless a person whose behavior, like ours, is characterized by dignity, respect for acknowledged values, and respect for tradition and customs.

30   While Malinowski began his work at the moment of the birth of the masses, we are living today in the period of transition from that mass society to a new, planetary society. Many factors lie behind this—the electronics revolution, the unprecedented development of all forms of communication, the great advances in transport and movement, and also, in connection with this, the transformation at work in the consciousness of the youngest generation and in culture broadly conceived.

31   How will this alter the relations between us, the people of one culture, and the people of some other culture, or of Other cultures? How will this influence the I-Other relationship within my culture and beyond it? It is very difficult to give an unequivocal final answer, since the process is ongoing and we ourselves, with no chance for the distance that fosters reflection, are immersed in it.

32   Levinas considered the I-Other relation within the bounds of a single, racially and historically homogeneous civilization. Malinowski studied the Melanesian tribes at a time when they were still in their primal state, not yet violated by the influence of Western technology, organization and markets.

33   Today, this is ever less frequently possible. Cultures are becoming increasingly hybridized and heterogeneous. I recently saw something astonishing in Dubai. A girl, surely a Muslim, was walking along the

beach. She was dressed in tight jeans and a close-fitting blouse, but her head, and only her head, was covered so hermetically that not even her eyes were visible.

34 Today there are whole schools of philosophy, anthropology, and literary criticism that devote their major attention to hybridization and linking. This cultural process is under way especially in those regions where the borders of states are the boundaries of different cultures, such as the American-Mexican border, and also in the gigantic megalopolises (like São Paolo, New York, or Singapore) that are home to populations representing the most variegated cultures and races. We say today that the world has become multiethnic and multicultural not because there are more of these communities and cultures than before, but rather because they are speaking out more loudly, with increasing self-sufficiency and forcefulness, demanding acceptance, recognition, and a place at the round table of nations.

35 Yet the true challenge of our time, the encounter with the new Other, derives as well from a broader historical context. Namely, the second half of the 20th century was a time when two-thirds of humanity freed themselves of colonial dependency and became citizens of their own states that, at least nominally, were independent. Gradually, these people are beginning to rediscover their own pasts, myths, and legends, their roots, their feelings of identity and, of course, the pride that flows from this. They are beginning to realize that they are the masters in their own house and the captains of their fate, and they look with abhorrence on any attempts to reduce them to things, to extras, to the victims and passive objects of domination.

36 Today, our planet, inhabited for centuries by a narrow group of free people and broad throngs of the enslaved, is filled with an increasing number of nations and societies that have a growing sense of their own separate value and significance. This process is often occurring amidst enormous difficulties, conflicts, dramas, and losses.

37 We may be moving toward a world so entirely new and changed that our previous historical experience will prove to be insufficient to grasp and move around in it. In any case, the world that we are entering is the Planet of Great Opportunities. Yet these are not unconditional opportunities, but rather opportunities open only to those who take their tasks seriously and thus prove that they take themselves seriously. This is a world that potentially has a lot to offer, but that also demands a lot, and in which taking easy shortcuts is often the road to nowhere.

38 We will constantly be encountering the new Other, who will slowly emerge from the chaos and tumult of the present. It is possible that this new Other will arise from the meeting of two contradictory currents that shape the culture of the contemporary world—the current of the globalization of our reality and the current of the conservation of our diversity, our differences, our uniqueness. The Other may be the offspring and the heir of these two currents.

39   We should seek dialogue and understanding with the new Other. The experience of spending years among remote Others has taught me that kindness toward another being is the only attitude that can strike a chord of humanity in the Other. Who will this new Other be? What will our encounter be like? What will we say? And in what language? Will we be able to listen to each other? To understand each other?

40   Will we both want to appeal, as Joseph Conrad put it, to what "speaks to our capacity for delight and wonder, to the sense of mystery surrounding our lives; to our sense of pity, and beauty, and pain; to the latent feeling of fellowship with all creation—and to the subtle but invincible conviction of solidarity that knits together the loneliness of innumerable hearts: to the solidarity in dreams, in joy, in sorrow, in aspirations, in illusions, in hope, in fear, which binds men to each other, which binds together all humanity—the dead to the living and the living to the unborn." ❧

Comprehension Check

Complete the following items after you finish your first read. Review and clarify details with your group.

1. According to the author, how would an early family-tribe discover that there were other people in the world?

2. What way of treating people began with the idea that any stranger might have been sent by the gods?

3. According to the author, why have Europeans throughout history usually left their own continent to visit others?

4. 📓 **Notebook** Confirm your understanding of the text by writing a summary.

RESEARCH

Research to Clarify Choose at least one unfamiliar detail from the text. Briefly research that detail. In what way does the information you learned shed light on an aspect of the lecture?

Research to Explore Choose something that interested you from the text, and formulate a research question.

ENCOUNTERING THE OTHER:
THE CHALLENGE FOR THE
21ST CENTURY

TIP

GROUP DISCUSSION

Some group members may have very good contributions to make to the discussion but find it difficult to speak up. To make sure that you hear the best ideas, reach out to all group members by asking questions.

WORD NETWORK

Add interesting words related to outsiders from the text to your Word Network.

STANDARDS

Reading Informational Text

• Determine a central idea of a text and analyze its development over the course of the text, including how it emerges and is shaped and refined by specific details; provide an objective summary of the text.

• Analyze in detail how an author's ideas or claims are developed and refined by particular sentences, paragraphs, or larger portions of a text.

Language

• Identify and correctly use patterns of word changes that indicate different meanings or parts of speech.

Close Read the Text

With your group, revisit sections of the text you marked during your first read. **Annotate** details that you notice. What **questions** do you have? What can you **conclude**?

- -

Analyze the Text

> **CITE TEXTUAL EVIDENCE**
> to support your answers.

Complete the activities.

1. **Review and Clarify** With your group, reread paragraph 10 of the selection. Discuss the three choices people can make in dealing with the Other, reminding yourselves of the examples the author gives for each one.

2. **Present and Discuss** Now, share with your group the passages from the selection that you found particularly important. Take turns presenting your passages. Discuss what you noticed in the text, what questions you asked, and what conclusions you reached.

3. **Essential Question:** *Do people need to belong?* What has this lecture taught you about being an outsider and confronting others? Discuss.

LANGUAGE DEVELOPMENT

Concept Vocabulary

doctrine	totalitarian	ideologies

Why These Words? The three concept vocabulary words are related. With your group, discuss the words, and determine what they have in common. Write other words that relate to this concept.

Practice

Notebook Confirm your understanding of these words by using them in sentences. Include context clues that hint at each word's meaning.

Word Study

Greek Root: -log- In "Encountering the Other," the author uses the word *ideologies*. The word *ideologies* is built from two Greek roots: *-ideo-*, which means "idea," and *-log-*, which may mean either "to speak" or "study or theory of." Write the meanings of these words from the selection that contain the root *-log-*: *archaeologists, anthropology, dialogue*. Consult a dictionary as needed.

Analyze Craft and Structure

Literary Nonfiction "Encountering the Other" is a **lecture**—a speech that is given to teach or inform listeners about a topic. The lecturer often uses special techniques to engage listeners and help them understand information. In the **introduction,** or beginning, he or she may use a **rhetorical question.** This is a question that the listener should think about, not answer out loud. In the **discussion**, or body, the lecturer may use **repetition** because hearing information more than once helps listeners remember ideas. In the **conclusion**, or end, the lecturer might summarize ideas or leave the audience with a challenge or lasting thought.

TIP

CLARIFICATION
A lecture often begins and ends with a memorable story, quotation, question, fact, or statement. The intention is to make the listener curious at the beginning and inspired at the end.

Practice

CITE TEXTUAL EVIDENCE to support your answers.

Work independently to gather your notes in the chart. Then, share and discuss your responses with your group.

INTRODUCTION
Which paragraphs make up the introduction?
What story, surprising fact, or rhetorical question appears in the introduction?
What is the main idea statement?

DISCUSSION
Which paragraphs make up the discussion?
Cite statements that develop or explain the main idea.
Cite examples of repetition.

CONCLUSION
Which paragraphs make up the conclusion?
Is there a challenge to listeners? Is there another technique that creates a memorable ending?

ENCOUNTERING THE OTHER:
THE CHALLENGE FOR THE
21ST CENTURY

Conventions

Types of Phrases An **infinitive** is a verb form that generally appears with the word *to* in front of it and acts as a noun, an adjective, or an adverb. An **infinitive phrase** consists of an infinitive and its objects, complements, or modifiers, all acting together as a single part of speech. Like an infinitive, an infinitive phrase acts as a noun, an adjective, or an adverb.

The examples in the chart show uses of infinitives and infinitive phrases.

INFINITIVE	INFINITIVE PHRASE
Used as a Noun *To succeed* requires dedication. (functions as the subject of the sentence)	**Used as a Noun** We chose *to take the old foot path.* (functions as the direct object of the verb *chose*)
Used as an Adjective I wish I had the ability *to fly.* (tells *what kind* of ability)	**Used as an Adjective** Dana's desire *to do well* made Mama proud. (tells *which* desire)
Used as an Adverb When Derrick sat down *to study,* he concentrated. (tells *why* Derrick sat down)	**Used as an Adverb** She called the editor *to voice her opinion.* (tells *why* she called)

Read It

Work individually. Mark the infinitive or infinitive phrase in each sentence from "Encountering the Other," and label it as a noun, an adjective, or an adverb.

1. Had it been smaller, it would have found it harder to defend itself effectively. . . .

2. But it might be the case that . . . this family-tribe that we are watching decides to fence itself off from others. . . .

3. Malinowski set out for the Pacific islands with a different goal—to learn about the Other.

4. This is a world that potentially has a lot to offer, but that also demands a lot. . . .

Write It

:notebook: **Notebook** Write three sentences about this lecture. Use an infinitive or infinitive phrase as a noun in one sentence, an adjective in the second sentence, and an adverb in the third sentence.

:menu: STANDARDS

Writing
• Use technology, including the Internet, to produce, publish, and update individual or shared writing products, taking advantage of technology's capacity to link to other information and to display information flexibly and dynamically.
• Gather relevant information from multiple authoritative print and digital sources, using advanced searches effectively; assess the usefulness of each source in answering the research question; integrate information into the text selectively to maintain the flow of ideas, avoiding plagiarism and following a standard format for citation.

Language
• Demonstrate command of the conventions of standard English grammar and usage when writing or speaking.

Research

Assignment

Research, write, and deliver a **digital presentation** about one of the cultures Kapuscinski mentions in the lecture. Explain how each culture responded to others through combat, isolation, or cooperation. Choose one of the following topics and projects:

☐ Create an **illustrated timeline** showing how the ancient Chinese perceived people from other cultures and responded to outsiders.

☐ Create a **slide show** about the Inca and their architecture.

☐ Create a **video** about the ancient Greek idea of hospitality.

Project Plan Before you begin, make a list of the tasks you will need to accomplish in order to complete your digital presentation, from finding information to researching images to making final choices about design and layout. Decide ahead of time how you will make those final choices. Then, assign group members to each task.

Finding Visuals Use a variety of reliable sources for your images so that they will accurately illustrate your text. Use this chart to keep track of what you want and what you find. Remember to include appropriate citations.

PROCESS

When researching images online, you may start with a search engine. However, you should always go to the page where the image is located to make sure of its accuracy. Collect information to properly credit the source.

✎ EVIDENCE LOG

Before moving on to a new selection, go to your Evidence Log and record what you learned from "Encountering the Other."

Text That Image Illustrates	Description of Image	Source Information for Citation

Deliver a Multimedia Presentation

Assignment

You have read a story, poems, an argument, and a lecture addressing ideas about what it means to belong and what it means to be an outsider. Work with your group to develop a position on the following questions:

Is difference a weakness? Is sameness a strength?

Then, create a **multimedia presentation** in which you use text, audio, and visuals to clearly state and defend your position.

Plan With Your Group

Analyze the Texts With your group, discuss the people—real or fictional—in the selections you have read. For each selection, identify a person or people who are deemed outsiders. Are these people weakened by this label? Are they strengthened by it? Use the chart to gather your ideas and supporting textual evidence. Then, come to a consensus about the questions posed in the prompt.

Title	Ideas About Outsiders	Evidence From Text
The Doll's House		
Sonnet, With Bird		
Elliptical		
Fences		
Revenge of the Geeks		
Encountering the Other: The Challenge for the 21st Century		

Gather Evidence and Media Examples Scan the selections to record specific examples that support your group's position. Then, brainstorm for types of media you can use to illustrate or elaborate on each example. Consider photographs, illustrations, music, charts, graphs, and video clips. Allow each group member to make suggestions.

STANDARDS

Speaking and Listening
Present information, findings, and supporting evidence clearly, concisely, and logically such that listeners can follow the line of reasoning and the organization, development, substance, and style are appropriate to purpose, audience, and task.

Organize Your Ideas Use a graphic organizer like this one to plan the script for your presentation. Decide who will be responsible for each of the various elements. Then, take note of when each section begins, and record what the speaker will say. Also, note where specific media will be used.

MULTIMEDIA PRESENTATION SCRIPT		
	Media Cues	Script
Presenter 1		
Presenter 2		
Presenter 3		

Rehearse With Your Group

Practice With Your Group Use this checklist to evaluate the effectiveness of your group's first run-through. Then, use your evaluation and the instruction here to guide your revision.

CONTENT	USE OF MEDIA	PRESENTATION TECHNIQUES
☐ The presentation presents a clear argument.	☐ The media support the argument.	☐ Media are visible and audible.
☐ Main ideas are supported with evidence from the texts in Small-Group Learning.	☐ The media communicate key ideas.	☐ Transitions are smooth.
	☐ Media are used evenly throughout the presentation.	☐ Each speaker uses eye contact and speaks with adequate volume.
	☐ Equipment functions properly.	

Fine-Tune the Content To make your presentation stronger, you may need to make sure the group has provided adequate evidence to support the argument. Check with your group to identify key points that are not clear to listeners. Find another way to word these ideas.

Improve Your Use of Media Review all visuals, music, and sound effects to make sure they communicate key ideas and help create a cohesive presentation. If a visual or sound cue is not clearly related to the presentation, replace it with a more relevant item.

Brush Up on Your Presentation Techniques Practice your presentation several times before you deliver it. Give one another notes on how to improve speaking skills or how to move smoothly from one segment to another.

Present and Evaluate

When you present as a group, be sure that each member has taken into account each of the checklist items. As you listen to other groups, evaluate how well they meet the checklist.

STANDARDS

Speaking and Listening
• Work with peers to set rules for collegial discussions and decision-making, clear goals and deadlines, and individual roles as needed.
• Make strategic use of digital media in presentations to enhance understanding of findings, reasoning, and evidence and to add interest.

ESSENTIAL QUESTION:

Do people need to belong?

Being an outsider is an experience almost everyone will have at some point in life. In this section, you will complete your study of literature about outsiders by exploring an additional selection related to the topic. You'll then share what you learn with classmates. To choose a text, follow these steps.

Look Back Think about the selections you have already studied. What more do you want to know about the topic of outsiders and outcasts?

Look Ahead Preview the texts by reading the descriptions. Which one seems most interesting and appealing to you?

Look Inside Take a few minutes to scan the text you chose. Choose a different one if this text doesn't meet your needs.

Independent Learning Strategies

Throughout your life, in school, in your community, and in your career, you will need to rely on yourself to learn and work on your own. Review these strategies and the actions you can take to practice them during Independent Learning. Add ideas of your own for each category.

STRATEGY	ACTION PLAN
Create a schedule	• Understand your goals and deadlines. • Make a plan for what to do each day. •
Practice what you've learned	• Use first-read and close-read strategies to deepen your understanding. • After you read, evaluate the usefulness of the evidence to help you understand the topic. • Consider the quality and reliability of the source. •
Take notes	• Record important ideas and information. • Review your notes before preparing to share with a group. • •

SCAN FOR
MULTIMEDIA

Choose one selection. Selections are available online only.

CONTENTS

SCAN FOR MULTIMEDIA

First-Read Guide

Use this page to record your first-read ideas.

Tool Kit
First-Read Guide and
Model Annotation

Selection Title: _____

NOTICE

NOTICE new information or ideas you learn about the unit topic as you first read this text.

ANNOTATE

ANNOTATE by marking vocabulary and key passages you want to revisit.

First Read

NOTICE ANNOTATE CONNECT RESPOND

CONNECT

CONNECT ideas within the selection to other knowledge and the selections you have read.

RESPOND

RESPOND by writing a brief summary of the selection.

STANDARD

Reading Read and comprehend complex literary and informational texts independently and proficiently.

Close-Read Guide

Use this page to record your close-read ideas.

⚙ **Tool Kit**
Close-Read Guide and
Model Annotation

Selection Title: _____

Close Read the Text

Revisit sections of the text you marked during your first read. Read these sections closely and **annotate** what you notice. Ask yourself **questions** about the text. What can you **conclude?** Write down your ideas.

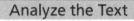

Analyze the Text

Think about the author's choices of patterns, structure, techniques, and ideas included in the text. Select one, and record your thoughts about what this choice conveys.

QuickWrite

Pick a paragraph from the text that grabbed your interest. Explain the power of this passage.

▤ STANDARD

Reading Read and comprehend complex literary and informational texts independently and proficiently.

EVIDENCE LOG

Go to your Evidence Log and record what you learned from the text you read.

Share Your Independent Learning

Prepare to Share

Do people need to belong?

Even when you read something independently, your understanding continues to grow when you share what you have learned with others. Reflect on the text you explored independently and write notes about its connection to the unit. In your notes, consider why this text belongs in this unit.

Learn From Your Classmates

Discuss It Share your ideas about the text you explored on your own. As you talk with your classmates, jot down ideas that you learn from them.

Reflect

Underline the most important insight you gained from these writing and discussion activities. Explain how this idea adds to your understanding of the topic of being an outsider or outcast.

Review Evidence for Argument

At the beginning of this unit, you took a position on the following question:

Is the experience of being an outsider universal?

EVIDENCE LOG

Review your Evidence Log and your QuickWrite from the beginning of the unit. Has your position changed?

☐ YES	☐ NO
Identify at last three pieces of evidence that convinced you to change your mind.	Identify at last three new pieces of evidence that reinforced your initial position.
1.	1.
2.	2.
3.	3.

State your position now: _____

_____

_____

Identify a possible counterclaim: _____

_____

_____

Evaluate the Strength of Your Evidence Consider your argument. Do you have enough evidence to support your claim? Do you have enough evidence to refute a counterclaim? If not, make a plan.

☐ Do more research   ☐ Talk with my classmates

☐ Reread a selection   ☐ Ask an expert

☐ Other:_____

STANDARDS
Writing
Introduce precise claim(s), distinguish the claim(s) from alternate or opposing claims, and create an organization that establishes clear relationships among claim(s), counterclaims, reasons, and evidence.

SOURCES

• WHOLE-CLASS SELECTIONS

• SMALL-GROUP SELECTIONS

• INDEPENDENT-LEARNING SELECTION

PART 1

Writing to Sources: Argument

In this unit, you read about various characters, both real and fictional, who were considered outsiders or outcasts. Some struggled to belong, while others seemed more comfortable with being outside of a group.

Assignment

Write an **argumentative essay** in which you state and defend a claim about the following question:

Is the experience of being an outsider universal?

Use credible evidence from at least three of the selections you read and researched in this unit to support your claim. Try to address possible objections to your argument by presenting and refuting counterclaims. Ensure that your claims are fully supported; that you use a formal, academic tone; and that your organization is logical and easy to follow.

Reread the Assignment Review the assignment to be sure you fully understand it. The task may reference some of the academic words presented at the beginning of the unit. Be sure you understand each of the words given below in order to complete the assignment correctly.

Academic Vocabulary

contradict	negate	objection
advocate	verify	

WORD NETWORK

As you write and revise your argument, use your Word Network to help vary your word choices.

Review the Elements of Effective Argument Before you begin writing, read the Argument Rubric. Once you have completed your first draft, check it against the rubric. If one or more of the elements are missing or not as strong as they could be, revise your essay to add or strengthen those components.

STANDARDS

Writing
• Write arguments to support claims in an analysis of substantive topics or texts, using valid reasoning and relevant and sufficient evidence.
• Draw evidence from literary or informational texts to support analysis, reflection, and research.
• Write routinely over extended time frames and shorter time frames for a range of tasks, purposes, and audiences.

Argument Rubric

	Focus and Organization	Evidence and Elaboration	Conventions
4	The introduction engages the reader and establishes a claim in a compelling way. The argument includes valid reasons and evidence that address and support the claim while clearly acknowledging counterclaims. The ideas progress logically, and transitions make connections among ideas clear. The conclusion offers fresh insight into the claim.	The sources of evidence are comprehensive and specific and contain relevant information. The tone of the argument is always formal and objective. The vocabulary is always appropriate for the audience and purpose.	The argument intentionally uses standard English conventions of usage and mechanics.
3	The introduction engages the reader and establishes the claim. The argument includes reasons and evidence that address and support the claim while acknowledging counterclaims. The ideas progress logically, and some transitions are used to help make connections among ideas clear. The conclusion restates the claim and important information.	The sources of evidence contain relevant information. The tone of the argument is mostly formal and objective. The vocabulary is generally appropriate for the audience and purpose.	The argument demonstrates general accuracy in standard English conventions of usage and mechanics.
2	The introduction establishes a claim. The argument includes some reasons and evidence that address and support the claim while briefly acknowledging counterclaims. The ideas progress somewhat logically. A few sentence transitions are used that connect readers to the argument. The conclusion offers some insight into the claim and restates information.	The sources of evidence contain some relevant information. The tone of the argument is occasionally formal and objective. The vocabulary is somewhat appropriate for the audience and purpose.	The argument demonstrates some accuracy in standard English conventions of usage and mechanics.
1	The introduction does not clearly state the claim. The argument does not include reasons or evidence for the claim. No counterclaims are acknowledged. The ideas do not progress logically. Transitions are not included to connect ideas. The conclusion does not restate any information that is important.	Reliable and relevant evidence is not included. The vocabulary used is limited or ineffective. The tone of the argument is not objective or formal.	The argument contains mistakes in standard English conventions of usage and mechanics.

PART 2
Speaking and Listening: Oral Presentation

Assignment
After completing the final draft of your argument, use it as the foundation for a three- to five-minute **oral presentation.**

Do not simply read your essay aloud. Instead, take the following steps to make your presentation lively and engaging.

- Go back to your essay and annotate the most important claims and supporting details from your introduction, body paragraphs, and conclusion.
- Refer to your annotated text to guide your presentation and keep it focused.
- Deliver your argument with conviction, speaking with adequate volume and maintaining eye contact with your audience.

Review the Oral Presentation Rubric The criteria by which your oral presentation will be evaluated appear in the rubric below. Review these criteria before presenting to ensure that you are prepared.

	Content	Organization	Presentation Technique
3	Introduction is engaging and establishes a claim in a compelling way.	The speaker uses time very effectively by spending the right amount of time on each part.	The speaker maintains effective eye contact.
	Presentation has strong valid reasons and evidence that support the claim while clearly acknowledging counterclaims.	Ideas progress logically, supported by a variety of sentence transitions. Listeners can follow presentation.	The speaker presents with strong conviction and energy.
	Conclusion offers fresh insight into the claim.		
2	Introduction establishes a claim.	The speaker uses time effectively by spending the right amount of time on most parts.	The speaker mostly maintains effective eye contact.
	Presentation includes some valid reasons and evidence that support the claim while acknowledging counterclaims.	Ideas progress logically, supported by some sentence transitions. Listeners are mostly able to follow presentation.	The speaker presents with some level of conviction and energy.
	Conclusion offers some insight into claim and restates important information.		
1	Introduction does not clearly state a claim.	The speaker does not use time effectively; the parts of the presentation are too long or too short.	The speaker does not establish eye contact.
	Presentation does not include reasons or evidence to support a claim or acknowledge counterclaims.	Ideas do not progress logically. Listeners have difficulty following presentation.	The speaker presents without conviction or energy.
	Conclusion does not restate important information about a claim.		

Reflect on the Unit

Now that you've completed the unit, take a few moments to reflect on your learning. Use the questions below to think about where you succeeded, what skills and strategies helped you, and where you can continue to grow in the future.

Reflect on the Unit Goals

Look back at the goals at the beginning of the unit. Use a different colored pen to rate yourself again. Think about readings and activities that contributed the most to the growth of your understanding. Record your thoughts.

Reflect on the Learning Strategies

⊘ **Discuss It** Write a reflection on whether you were able to improve your learning based on your Action Plans. Think about what worked, what didn't, and what you might do to keep working on these strategies. Record your ideas before a class discussion.

Reflect on the Text

Choose a selection that you found challenging and explain what made it difficult.

Explain something that surprised you about a text in the unit.

Which activity taught you the most about whether people need to belong? What did you learn?

⊞ STANDARDS

Speaking and Listening
Present information, findings, and supporting evidence clearly, concisely, and logically such that listeners can follow the line of reasoning and the organization, development, substance, and style are appropriate to purpose, audience, and task.

SCAN FOR MULTIMEDIA

Extending Freedom's Reach

What factors determine who is
free and who remains oppressed?

We Are All Born Free

② Discuss It What are the basic rights and freedoms that
belong to everyone, everywhere?

Write your response before sharing your ideas.

SCAN FOR
MULTIMEDIA

UNIT INTRODUCTION

ESSENTIAL QUESTION:

What is the relationship between power and freedom?

LAUNCH TEXT
INFORMATIVE MODEL
Born Free: Children and the Struggle for Human Rights

WHOLE-CLASS LEARNING

ANCHOR TEXT: SPEECH

from The "Four Freedoms" Speech
Franklin D. Roosevelt

ANCHOR TEXT: SPEECH

Inaugural Address
John F. Kennedy

COMPARE

MEDIA: VIDEO

Inaugural Address
John F. Kennedy

SMALL-GROUP LEARNING

SPEECH

Speech at the United Nations
Malala Yousafzai

MEDIA: INTERVIEW

Diane Sawyer Interviews Malala Yousafzai
ABC News

COMPARE

POETRY COLLECTION

Caged Bird
Maya Angelou

Some Advice To Those Who Will Serve Time in Prison
Nazim Hikmet, translated by Randy Blasing and Mutlu Konuk

SHORT STORY

The Censors
Luisa Valenzuela, translated by David Unger

MEDIA: INFORMATIONAL GRAPHIC

from Freedom of the Press Report 2015
Freedom House

INDEPENDENT LEARNING

MEDIA: INFORMATIONAL TEXT

Law and the Rule of Law: The Role of Federal Courts
Judicial Learning Center

ESSAY

Misrule of Law
Aung San Suu Kyi

SHORT STORY

Harrison Bergeron
Kurt Vonnegut, Jr.

PERSONAL ESSAY

Credo: What I Believe
Neil Gaiman

PERFORMANCE TASK

WRITING FOCUS:
Write an Informative Essay

PERFORMANCE TASK

SPEAKING AND LISTENING FOCUS:
Deliver a Multimedia Presentation

PERFORMANCE-BASED ASSESSMENT PREP

Review Evidence for an Informative Essay

PERFORMANCE-BASED ASSESSMENT

Informative Text: Essay and Multimedia Presentation

PROMPT:

What does it mean to "be free"?

Unit Goals

Throughout the unit, you will deepen your perspective on the literature of freedom by reading, writing, speaking, presenting, and listening. These goals will help you succeed on the Unit Performance-Based Assessment.

Rate how well you meet these goals right now. You will revisit your ratings later when you reflect on your growth during this unit.

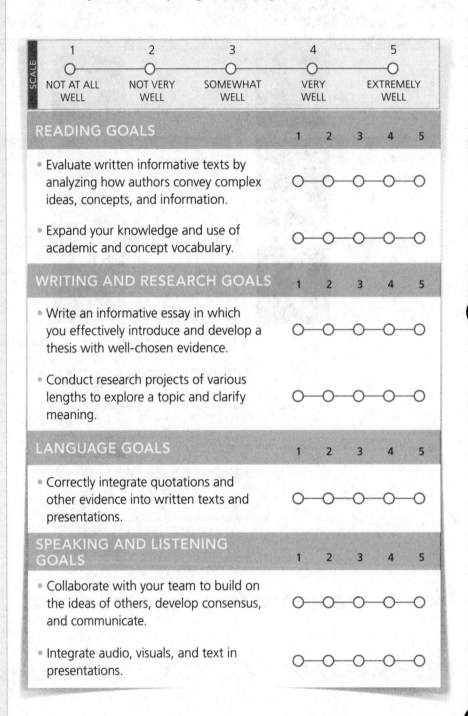

SCALE	1	2	3	4	5
	NOT AT ALL WELL	NOT VERY WELL	SOMEWHAT WELL	VERY WELL	EXTREMELY WELL

READING GOALS   1   2   3   4   5

- Evaluate written informative texts by analyzing how authors convey complex ideas, concepts, and information.

- Expand your knowledge and use of academic and concept vocabulary.

WRITING AND RESEARCH GOALS   1   2   3   4   5

- Write an informative essay in which you effectively introduce and develop a thesis with well-chosen evidence.

- Conduct research projects of various lengths to explore a topic and clarify meaning.

LANGUAGE GOALS   1   2   3   4   5

- Correctly integrate quotations and other evidence into written texts and presentations.

SPEAKING AND LISTENING GOALS   1   2   3   4   5

- Collaborate with your team to build on the ideas of others, develop consensus, and communicate.

- Integrate audio, visuals, and text in presentations.

⏹ STANDARDS

Language
Acquire and use accurately general academic and domain-specific words and phrases, sufficient for reading, writing, speaking, and listening at the college and career readiness level; demonstrate independence in gathering vocabulary knowledge when considering a word or phrase important to comprehension or expression.

SCAN FOR MULTIMEDIA

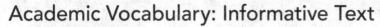

Academic Vocabulary: Informative Text

Academic terms appear in all subjects and can help you read, write, and discuss with more precision. Here are five academic words that will be useful to you in this unit as you analyze and write informative texts.

Complete the chart.

1. Review each word, its root, and the mentor sentences.

2. Use the information and your own knowledge to predict the meaning of each word.

3. For each word, list at least two related words.

4. Refer to a dictionary or other resources if needed.

TIP

FOLLOW THROUGH
Study the words in this chart, and mark them or their forms wherever they appear in the unit.

WORD	MENTOR SENTENCES	PREDICT MEANING	RELATED WORDS
attribute ROOT: **-trib-** "assign"; "give"	1. In the nineteenth century, such an *attribute* was seen as ordinary. 2. They *attribute* their success this season to teamwork and training.		attribution; attributable
hierarchy ROOT: **-hier-** "sacred"; "holy"	1. In high school, freshmen are usually considered to be at the bottom of the social *hierarchy*. 2. Making an outline is a good way to organize a *hierarchy* of ideas.		
demarcate ROOT: **-marc- / -mark-** "separate from"	1. The bold black lines on the map *demarcate* the borders of each country. 2. Our neighbors planted trees to *demarcate* the edge of their property.		
fundamental ROOT: **-fund-** "base"; "bottom"	1. The order of operations is a *fundamental* concept in mathematics. 2. The *fundamental* reason our team lost was because the starting quarterback was injured.		
democracy ROOT: **-demo-** "people"; "populace"	1. In a *democracy*, the people hold the power, and the government represents their interests. 2. When we complained about having a cumulative final exam, our teacher reminded us that her classroom was not a *democracy* and overruled us.		

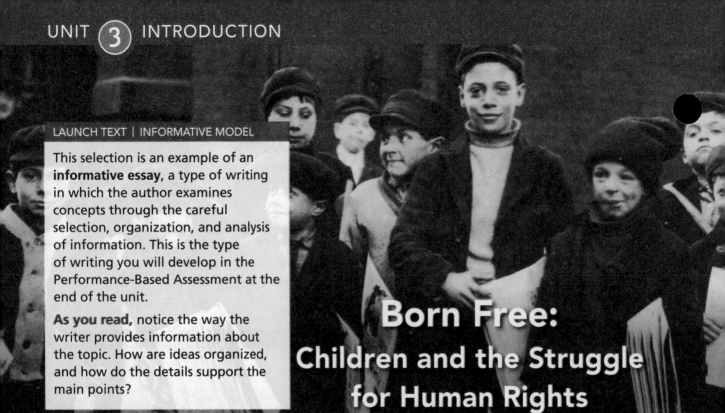

LAUNCH TEXT | INFORMATIVE MODEL

This selection is an example of an **informative essay,** a type of writing in which the author examines concepts through the careful selection, organization, and analysis of information. This is the type of writing you will develop in the Performance-Based Assessment at the end of the unit.

As you read, notice the way the writer provides information about the topic. How are ideas organized, and how do the details support the main points?

Born Free:
Children and the Struggle for Human Rights

NOTES

1   In our national anthem, "The Star-Spangled Banner," we sing of America as "the land of the free and the home of the brave." Throughout much of our history, though, many groups have struggled to share fully in the nation's promise of freedom and justice. Like other groups who have faced unfair or undignified treatment, young people have also realized that in order to be heard, they might have to make some noise.

2   One incident of children raising their voices to advance their rights occurred in New York City during the "newsies" strike of 1899. Newsies were children who sold newspapers on the sidewalks of major cities. In the late 1890s, there were roughly 2,500 newsies in New York City, most between the ages of 6 and 16. The shouts of these children calling, "Extra! Extra! Read all about it!" were part of the soundtrack of urban life. In that long-ago era before computers, smartphones, television, and even radio, newspapers were the main source of news.

3   The newsies suffered a host of problems. While some lived with their families, many others were orphans, homeless, or both. The United States did not institute laws protecting child workers until 1916, and the newsies were victims of unscrupulous business practices. They often worked 10- or 12-hour days. Most gave any money they earned to their families, or used it to pay the costs of food and shelter for a night. Newsies did not go to school.

4   The newsies' circumstances deteriorated even further during the Spanish-American War of 1898. The public's hunger for news of the war led to increased demand for newspapers. Newsies bought the newspapers from publishers and then sold them to the public. During the war, the price newsies paid for a bundle of 100 papers

SCAN FOR MULTIMEDIA

NOTES

rose from 50 to 60 cents. Once the war ended, readership declined. Most newspaper owners responded by returning the price of a bundle to 50 cents, but the two biggest publishers—Joseph Pulitzer of the *New York World* and William Randolph Hearst of the *New York Journal*—refused to lower their prices. In addition, both Pulitzer and Hearst discontinued the practice of buying back unsold papers. Instead, they forced the newsies to absorb the losses.

5   On July 20, 1899, the newsies took on Pulitzer and Hearst by launching a strike. They refused to sell either newspaper and warned off anyone who tried. They brought traffic to a halt by marching through the streets and gathering at the Brooklyn Bridge. They made signs asking the public not to buy Pulitzer and Hearst newspapers, and they chased off men who were attempting to deliver bundles of papers for distribution. The public showed its support, raining coins down on the strikers from the windows of offices and apartments. What began as a localized strike by about 300 newsies near Manhattan's Wall Street soon spread—west to New Jersey, south to Brooklyn, north to the Bronx, and east to Queens.

6   The newspapers that covered the strike found ways to show their disrespect for the newsies. "Dere's t'ree t'ousand of us, and we'll win for sure," is how one newspaper mockingly quoted a newsie's reference to the number of strikers. Another newspaper explained that the newsies were striking for their "rights," using quotation marks to imply that the children had no rights and that it was quaint for them to suggest they did.

7   The strike lasted two weeks. Some newsies were arrested for vandalism. Others were arrested for stealing copies of the Pulitzer or Hearst papers. Although some adults reached out to help the newsies, most of the power stayed where it started. Pulitzer and Hearst did not lower the cost of newspaper bundles to the prewar price, but they did agree to buy back unsold copies from the newsies. It may have been a small victory, but it was more than the newsies would have received had they not raised their voices. ❧

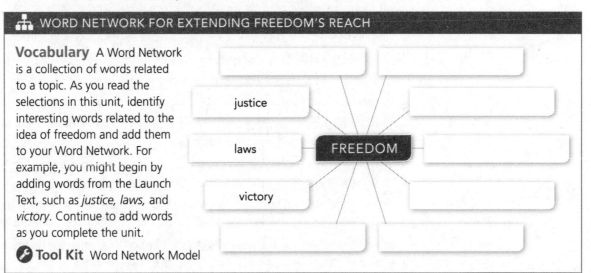

⚏ WORD NETWORK FOR EXTENDING FREEDOM'S REACH

Vocabulary A Word Network is a collection of words related to a topic. As you read the selections in this unit, identify interesting words related to the idea of freedom and add them to your Word Network. For example, you might begin by adding words from the Launch Text, such as *justice, laws,* and *victory.* Continue to add words as you complete the unit.

🔧 **Tool Kit** Word Network Model

justice

laws

victory

FREEDOM

Summary

Write a summary of "Born Free: Children and the Struggle for Human Rights." A **summary** is a concise, complete, and accurate overview of a text. It should not include a statement of your opinion or an analysis.

Launch Activity

Vote Consider this statement: People who stand up for their rights will always win.

- Record your position on the statement, and explain your thinking.

  ☐ Strongly Agree   ☐ Agree   ☐ Disagree   ☐ Strongly Disagree

  _____

  _____

- After everyone has recorded their positions, take a poll of the class to find out how each person voted.

- Count the number of votes in each category, and record those numbers on the board or in another place where everyone can see them.

- Contribute to a discussion about why students took the positions they did. Be sure to provide reasons and examples that support your position.

- At the end of the discussion, take another poll. Has anyone changed his or her mind? If so, why? If not, why not?

QuickWrite

Consider class discussions, the video, and the Launch Text as you think about the prompt. Record your first thoughts here.

PROMPT: **What does it mean to "be free"?**

EVIDENCE LOG FOR EXTENDING FREEDOM'S REACH

Review your QuickWrite, and summarize your initial position in one sentence to record in your Evidence Log. Then, record evidence from "Born Free: Children and the Struggle for Human Rights" that supports your initial position.

Prepare for the Performance-Based Assessment at the end of the unit by completing the Evidence Log after each selection.

🔧 Tool Kit
Evidence Log Model

Title of Text: _____ Date: _____

CONNECTION TO PROMPT	TEXT EVIDENCE/DETAILS	ADDITIONAL NOTES/IDEAS

How does this text change or add to my thinking? Date: _____

 SCAN FOR MULTIMEDIA

ESSENTIAL QUESTION:

What is the relationship between power and freedom?

Can you be free if you don't have power, at least over your own life? Can a government guarantee freedom to its citizens if its leaders fear their own loss of power? The selections you are going to read offer insight into the complex relationship between power and freedom for individuals and for nations.

Whole-Class Learning Strategies

Throughout your life, in school, in your community, and in your career, you will continue to learn and work in large-group environments.

Review these strategies and the actions you can take to practice them as you work with your whole class. Add ideas of your own for each step. Get ready to use these strategies during Whole-Class Learning.

STRATEGY	ACTION PLAN
Listen actively	• Eliminate distractions. For example, put your cellphone away. • Keep your eyes on the speaker. •
Clarify by asking questions	• If you're confused, other people probably are, too. Ask a question to help your whole class. • If you see that you are guessing, ask a question instead. •
Monitor understanding	• Notice what information you already know and be ready to build on it. • Ask for help if you are struggling. •
Interact and share ideas	• Share your ideas and answer questions, even if you are unsure. • Build on the ideas of others by adding details or making a connection. •

SCAN FOR MULTIMEDIA

CONTENTS

from THE "FOUR FREEDOMS" SPEECH

INAUGURAL ADDRESS

Comparing Texts

In this lesson, you will read and compare two famous speeches, Franklin Roosevelt's "Four Freedoms" speech and John F. Kennedy's inaugural address. First, you will complete the first-read and close-read activities for the excerpt from the "Four Freedoms" speech.

About the Speaker

Franklin Delano Roosevelt
(1882–1945) realized his potential as a leader only after falling victim to polio at age thirty-nine. He was twice elected governor of New York; then, in 1932, he defeated President Herbert Hoover to become the nation's thirty-second president. Roosevelt won an unprecedented four terms as president and led the nation through two great challenges: the Great Depression and World War II.

🔧 **Tool Kit**
First-Read Guide and
Model Annotation

≡ STANDARDS

Reading Informational Text
By the end of grade 10, read and comprehend literary nonfiction at the high end of the grades 9–10 text complexity band independently and proficiently.

from The "Four Freedoms" Speech

Concept Vocabulary

You will encounter the following words as you read the excerpt from Roosevelt's "Four Freedoms" speech. Before reading, note how familiar you are with each word. Then, rank the words in order from most familiar (1) to least familiar (6).

WORD	YOUR RANKING
pacification	
tyranny	
propaganda	
disarmament	
appeasement	
treachery	

After completing the first read, come back to the concept vocabulary and review your rankings. Mark changes to your original rankings as needed.

First Read NONFICTION

Apply these strategies as you conduct your first read. You will have an opportunity to complete the close-read notes after your first read.

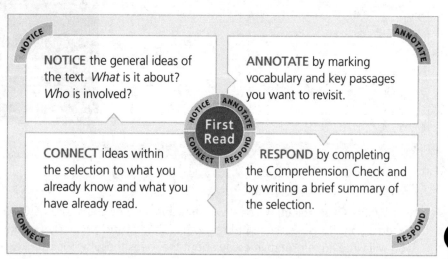

NOTICE the general ideas of the text. *What* is it about? *Who* is involved?

ANNOTATE by marking vocabulary and key passages you want to revisit.

First Read

CONNECT ideas within the selection to what you already know and what you have already read.

RESPOND by completing the Comprehension Check and by writing a brief summary of the selection.

from

The "Four Freedoms" Speech

Franklin Delano Roosevelt

BACKGROUND

Roosevelt gave this speech as a State of the Union address in 1941, following his 1940 election to a third term as president. At the time, much of the world was in turmoil as Nazi Germany, under the leadership of Adolf Hitler, had already invaded Norway, Belgium, the Netherlands, and France, and attacked Great Britain. A significant number of Americans wanted to remain uninvolved in the war, insisting that problems overseas did not affect the United States. However, others felt that German aggression threatened democracy throughout the world and that Hitler must be stopped.

SCAN FOR
MULTIMEDIA

1 *Mr. President, Mr. Speaker, Members of the Seventy-seventh Congress:*

NOTES

2 I address you, the Members of the Seventy-seventh Congress, at a moment unprecedented in the history of the Union. I use the word "unprecedented," because at no previous time has American security been as seriously threatened from without as it is today.

3 Since the permanent formation of our Government under the Constitution, in 1789, most of the periods of crisis in our history have related to our domestic affairs. Fortunately, only one of these—the four-year War Between the States[1]—ever threatened our national

1. **four-year War Between the States** United States Civil War, 1861–1865.

unity. Today, thank God, one hundred thirty million Americans, in forty-eight States, have forgotten points of the compass in our national unity.

4   It is true that prior to 1914 the United States often had been disturbed by events in other continents. We had even engaged in two wars with European nations and in a number of undeclared wars in the West Indies, in the Mediterranean, and in the Pacific for the maintenance of American rights and for the principles of peaceful commerce. But in no case had a serious threat been raised against our national safety or our continued independence.

5   What I seek to convey is the historic truth that the United States as a nation has at all times maintained clear, definite opposition to any attempt to lock us in behind an ancient Chinese wall[2] while the procession of civilization went past. Today, thinking of our children and of their children, we oppose enforced isolation for ourselves or for any other part of the Americas.

6   That determination of ours, extending over all these years, was proved, for example, during the quarter century of wars following the French Revolution.

7   While the Napoleonic struggles did threaten interests of the United States because of the French foothold in the West Indies and in Louisiana, and while we engaged in the War of 1812 to vindicate our right to peaceful trade, it is nevertheless clear that neither France nor Great Britain, nor any other nation, was aiming at domination of the whole world.

8   In like fashion from 1815 to 1914—ninety-nine years—no single war in Europe or in Asia constituted a real threat against our future or against the future of any other American nation.

9   Except in the Maximilian interlude in Mexico,[3] no foreign power sought to establish itself in this hemisphere; and the strength of the British fleet in the Atlantic has been a friendly strength. It is still a friendly strength.

10   Even when the World War broke out in 1914, it seemed to contain only small threat of danger to our own American future. But, as time went on, the American people began to visualize what the downfall of democratic nations might mean to our own democracy.

11   We need not overemphasize imperfections in the Peace of Versailles.[4] We need not harp on failure of the democracies to deal

CLOSE READ

ANNOTATE: Mark words and phrases in paragraph 5 that suggest something that is absolute—unchanging and without compromise.

QUESTION: Why has Roosevelt used words that suggest an unbending point of view?

CONCLUDE: What do these word choices suggest about the quality of leadership Roosevelt is trying to convey?

---

2. **ancient Chinese wall** Great Wall of China, the stone-and-earth wall built as a defense against invaders, starting in the third century B.C.

3. **Maximilian interlude in Mexico** period from 1863 to 1867 during which Maximilian I, Archduke of Austria, ruled as Emperor of Mexico as part of a scheme to remove then-President Benito Juárez.

4. **Peace of Versailles** (vuhr SY) Treaty of Versailles, a treaty signed in 1919 that formally brought an end to World War I (1914–1918).

with problems of world reconstruction. We should remember that the Peace of 1919 was far less unjust than the kind of "pacification" which began even before Munich, and which is being carried on under the new order of tyranny that seeks to spread over every continent today. The American people have unalterably set their faces against that tyranny.

12   Every realist knows that the democratic way of life is at this moment being directly assailed in every part of the world—assailed either by arms or by secret spreading of poisonous propaganda by those who seek to destroy unity and promote discord in nations that are still at peace.

13   During sixteen long months, this assault has blotted out the whole pattern of democratic life in an appalling number of independent nations, great and small. The assailants are still on the march, threatening other nations, great and small.

14   Therefore, as your President, performing my constitutional duty to "give to the Congress information of the state of the Union," I find it, unhappily, necessary to report that the future and the safety of our country and of our democracy are overwhelmingly involved in events far beyond our borders.

15   Armed defense of democratic existence is now being gallantly waged in four continents. If that defense fails, all the population and all the resources of Europe and Asia and Africa and Australasia[5] will be dominated by conquerors. Let us remember that the total of those populations and their resources in those four continents greatly exceeds the sum total of the population and the resources of the whole of the Western Hemisphere—many times over.

16   In times like these it is immature—and, incidentally, untrue—for anybody to brag that an unprepared America, single-handed, and with one hand tied behind its back, can hold off the whole world.

17   No realistic American can expect from a dictator's peace international generosity, or return of true independence, or world disarmament, or freedom of expression, or freedom of religion—or even good business.

18   Such a peace would bring no security for us or for our neighbors. "Those who would give up essential liberty to purchase a little temporary safety deserve neither liberty nor safety."[6]

19   As a nation, we may take pride in the fact that we are softhearted; but we cannot afford to be softheaded.

20   We must always be wary of those who with sounding brass and a tinkling cymbal preach the "ism" of appeasement.

---

5. **Australasia** region consisting of Australia, New Zealand, New Guinea, and the neighboring islands of the Pacific Ocean.
6. **"Those . . . safety"** quotation from a famous letter written by Benjamin Franklin.

NOTES

pacification (pas uh fuh KAY shuhn) *n.* state of peace put in place through diplomacy, or political negotiation; also, use of force to suppress a hostile or resistant population

tyranny (TEER uh nee) *n.* harsh rule over a nation or people

propaganda (prop uh GAN duh) *n.* information, often of a false or misleading nature, used to promote a cause

disarmament (dihs AHR muh muhnt) *n.* limiting or getting rid of weapons

appeasement (uh PEEZ muhnt) *n.* giving in to demands in order to keep peace

21   We must especially beware of that small group of selfish men who would clip the wings of the American eagle in order to feather their own nests.

22   I have recently pointed out how quickly the tempo of modern warfare could bring into our very midst the physical attack which we must eventually expect if the dictator nations win this war.

23   There is much loose talk of our immunity from immediate and direct invasion from across the seas. Obviously, as long as the British Navy retains its power, no such danger exists. Even if there were no British Navy, it is not probable that any enemy would be stupid enough to attack us by landing troops in the United States from across thousands of miles of ocean, until it had acquired strategic bases from which to operate.

24   But we learn much from the lessons of the past years in Europe—particularly the lesson of Norway, whose essential seaports were captured by treachery and surprise built up over a series of years.

treachery (TREHCH uhr ee) *n.* act of betrayal

25   The first phase of the invasion of this hemisphere would not be the landing of regular troops. The necessary strategic points would be occupied by secret agents and by their dupes—and great numbers of them are already here, and in Latin America.

26   As long as the aggressor nations maintain the offensive, they—not we—will choose the time and the place and the method of their attack.

27   That is why the future of all the American republics is today in serious danger.

28   That is why this Annual Message to the Congress is unique in our history.

29   That is why every member of the executive branch of the government and every member of the Congress face great responsibility and great accountability.

CLOSE READ

ANNOTATE: In paragraphs 27–29, mark the group of words that is repeated.

QUESTION: What does the repetition of this particular group of words emphasize?

CONCLUDE: What is the effect of this repetition?

30   The need of the moment is that our actions and our policy should be devoted primarily—almost exclusively—to meeting this foreign peril. For all our domestic problems are now a part of the great emergency.

31   Just as our national policy in internal affairs has been based upon a decent respect for the rights and the dignity of all of our fellow men within our gates, so our national policy in foreign affairs has been based on a decent respect for the rights and the dignity of all nations, large and small. And the justice of morality must and will win in the end.

32   Our national policy is this:

33   First, by an impressive expression of the public will and without regard to partisanship, we are committed to all-inclusive national defense.

34   Second, by an impressive expression of the public will and without regard to partisanship, we are committed to full support of all those resolute peoples, everywhere, who are resisting aggression and are

thereby keeping war away from our hemisphere. By this support, we express our determination that the democratic cause shall prevail, and we strengthen the defense and the security of our own nation.

35 Third, by an impressive expression of the public will and without regard to partisanship, we are committed to the proposition that principles of morality and considerations for our own security will never permit us to acquiesce in a peace dictated by aggressors and sponsored by appeasers. We know that enduring peace cannot be bought at the cost of other people's freedom.

36 In the recent national election, there was no substantial difference between the two great parties in respect to that national policy. No issue was fought out on this line before the American electorate. Today, it is abundantly evident that American citizens everywhere are demanding and supporting speedy and complete action in recognition of obvious danger.

37 Therefore, the immediate need is a swift and driving increase in our armament production. . . .

⌄ Four Freedoms Park, Roosevelt Island, New York

38 Let us say to the democracies: "We Americans are vitally concerned in your defense of freedom. We are putting forth our energies, our resources, and our organizing powers to give you the strength to regain and maintain a free world. We shall send you, in ever-increasing numbers, ships, planes, tanks, guns. This is our purpose and our pledge."

39 In fulfillment of this purpose, we will not be intimidated by the threats of dictators that they will regard as a breach of international law or as an act of war our aid to the democracies which dare to resist their aggression. Such aid is not an act of war, even if a dictator should unilaterally proclaim it so to be.

40 When the dictators—if the dictators—are ready to make war upon us, they will not wait for an act of war on our part. They did not wait for Norway or Belgium or the Netherlands to commit an act of war.

41 Their only interest is in a new one-way international law, which lacks mutuality in its observance and, therefore, becomes an instrument of oppression.

42 The happiness of future generations of Americans may well depend upon how effective and how immediate we can make our aid felt. No one can tell the exact character of the emergency situations that we may be called upon to meet. The nation's hands must not be tied when the nation's life is in danger.

43 We must all prepare to make the sacrifices that the emergency—almost as serious as war itself—demands. Whatever stands in the way of speed and efficiency in defense preparations must give way to the national need.

44 A free nation has the right to expect full cooperation from all groups. A free nation has the right to look to the leaders of business, of labor, and of agriculture to take the lead in stimulating effort, not among other groups but within their own groups.

45 The best way of dealing with the few slackers or troublemakers in our midst is, first, to shame them by patriotic example, and, if that fails, to use the sovereignty of government to save government.

46 As men do not live by bread alone, they do not fight by armaments alone. Those who man our defenses, and those behind them who build our defenses, must have the stamina and the courage which come from unshakable belief in the manner of life which they are defending. The mighty action that we are calling for cannot be based on a disregard of all things worth fighting for.

47 The nation takes great satisfaction and much strength from the things which have been done to make its people conscious of their individual stake in the preservation of democratic life in America. Those things have toughened the fiber of our people, have renewed their faith and strengthened their devotion to the institutions we make ready to protect.

48   Certainly this is no time for any of us to stop thinking about the social and economic problems which are the root cause of the social revolution which is today a supreme factor in the world.

49   For there is nothing mysterious about the foundations of a healthy and strong democracy. The basic things expected by our people of their political and economic systems are simple. They are:

> Equality of opportunity for youth and for others.
>
> Jobs for those who can work.
>
> Security for those who need it.
>
> The ending of special privilege for the few.
>
> The preservation of civil liberties for all.
>
> The enjoyment of the fruits of scientific progress in a wider and constantly rising standard of living.

50   These are the simple, basic things that must never be lost sight of in the turmoil and unbelievable complexity of our modern world. The inner and abiding strength of our economic and political systems is dependent upon the degree to which they fulfill these expectations.

51   Many subjects connected with our social economy call for immediate improvement. As examples:

52   We should bring more citizens under the coverage of old-age pensions and unemployment insurance.

53   We should widen the opportunities for adequate medical care.

54   We should plan a better system by which persons deserving or needing gainful employment may obtain it.

55   I have called for personal sacrifice. I am assured of the willingness of almost all Americans to respond to that call.

56   A part of the sacrifice means the payment of more money in taxes. In my Budget Message, I shall recommend that a greater portion of this great defense program be paid for from taxation than we are paying today. No person should try, or be allowed, to get rich out of this program and the principle of tax payments in accordance with ability to pay should be constantly before our eyes to guide our legislation.

57   If the Congress maintains these principles, the voters, putting patriotism ahead of pocketbooks, will give you their applause.

58   In the future days, which we seek to make secure, we look forward to a world founded upon four essential human freedoms.

59   The first is freedom of speech and expression—everywhere in the world.

60   The second is freedom of every person to worship God in his own way—everywhere in the world.

61   The third is freedom from want—which, translated into world terms, means economic understandings which will secure to every

NOTES

CLOSE READ

ANNOTATE: In paragraph 49, mark changes you see in sentence lengths.

QUESTION: How do the short sentences relate to the long ones?

CONCLUDE: How does this structure help clarify the president's meaning?

nation a healthy peacetime life for its inhabitants—everywhere in the world.

62   The fourth is freedom from fear—which, translated into world terms, means a worldwide reduction of armaments to such a point and in such a thorough fashion that no nation will be in a position to commit an act of physical aggression against any neighbor—anywhere in the world.

63   That is no vision of a distant millennium. It is a definite basis for a kind of world attainable in our own time and generation. That kind of world is the very antithesis of the so-called new order of tyranny which the dictators seek to create with the crash of a bomb.

64   To that new order we oppose the greater conception—the moral order. A good society is able to face schemes of world domination and foreign revolutions alike without fear.

65   Since the beginning of our American history, we have been engaged in change—in a perpetual peaceful revolution—a revolution which goes on steadily, quietly adjusting itself to changing conditions—without the concentration camp or the quicklime in the ditch. The world order which we seek is the cooperation of free countries, working together in a friendly, civilized society.

66   This nation has placed its destiny in the hands and heads and hearts of its millions of free men and women, and its faith in freedom under the guidance of God. Freedom means the supremacy of human rights everywhere. Our support goes to those who struggle to gain those rights or keep them. Our strength is our unity of purpose. To that high concept there can be no end save victory. ❧

Comprehension Check

Complete the following items after you finish your first read.

1. According to Roosevelt, with what nations and events is the future of the United States intertwined?

2. What does Roosevelt say about attempts to isolate the United States from the rest of the world?

3. What does Roosevelt say is happening at that present moment to the democratic way of life around the world?

4. According to Roosevelt, what are the four freedoms to which everyone in the world is entitled?

5. 📓 **Notebook** Write a summary of this excerpt from the "Four Freedoms" speech.

- -

RESEARCH

Research to Clarify Choose at least one unfamiliar detail from the text. Briefly research that detail. In what way does the information you learned shed light on an aspect of the speech?

Research to Explore Choose a topic from the speech that sparked your interest. Then, formulate a research question about that topic.

from THE "FOUR FREEDOMS" SPEECH

Close Read the Text

1. This model, from paragraph 36 of the text, shows sample annotations, with questions and conclusions. Close read the passage, and find another detail to annotate. Then, write a question and your conclusion.

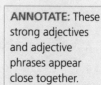

> **ANNOTATE:** Roosevelt restates information about election results and American voters.
>
> **QUESTION:** What is his purpose in restating this information?
>
> **CONCLUDE:** He wants to convince his listeners that Americans are unified in their views.

In the recent national election, there was no substantial difference between the two great parties in respect to that national policy. No issue was fought out on this line before the American electorate. Today, it is abundantly evident that American citizens everywhere are demanding and supporting speedy and complete action in recognition of obvious danger.

> **ANNOTATE:** These strong adjectives and adjective phrases appear close together.
>
> **QUESTION:** Why does Roosevelt use all these powerful words and phrases in sequence?
>
> **CONCLUDE:** Roosevelt wants to emphasize the urgency of the moment and his certainty about the best way forward.

2. For more practice, go back into the text, and complete the close-read notes.

3. Revisit a section of the text you found important during your first read. Read this section closely, and **annotate** what you notice. Ask yourself **questions** such as "Why did the author make this choice?" What can you **conclude**?

Analyze the Text

CITE TEXTUAL EVIDENCE to support your answers.

 Notebook Respond to these questions.

1. (a) **Connect** How does Roosevelt link his assertion that this speech occurs at an unprecedented moment to his later claim that this speech "is unique in our history"? (b) **Analyze** What language does Roosevelt use to emphasize the unique circumstances surrounding the speech?

2. **Evaluate** How effectively does Roosevelt's discussion of domestic issues help him build his case for helping other countries? Use examples from the speech to support your evaluation.

3. **Essential Question:** *What is the relationship between power and freedom?* What has this speech taught you about power and freedom?

 Tool Kit

Close-Read Guide and Model Annotation

STANDARDS

Reading Informational Text
• Determine a central idea of a text and analyze its development over the course of the text, including how it emerges and is shaped and refined by specific details; provide an objective summary of the text.
• Determine an author's point of view or purpose in a text and analyze how an author uses rhetoric to advance that point of view or purpose.
• Delineate and evaluate the argument and specific claims in a text, assessing whether the reasoning is valid and the evidence is relevant and sufficient; identify false statements and fallacious reasoning.
• Analyze seminal U.S. documents of historical and literary significance, including how they address related themes and concepts.

Speaking and Listening
• Evaluate a speaker's point of view, reasoning, and use of evidence and rhetoric, identifying any fallacious reasoning or exaggerated or distorted evidence.

Analyze Craft and Structure

Seminal Documents: Persuasive Appeals This speech by President Roosevelt is a seminal document that helped shape history. Knowing that his **central idea**—his main claim or position—will not be popular with all of his listeners, the president uses persuasion to present a convincing case. Roosevelt employs three kinds of **persuasive appeals:**

- **Appeals to logic** ask the audience to follow a line of reasoning. Roosevelt uses verifiable evidence to support his interpretation of the world's crisis and the validity of his plan.
- **Appeals to emotion** evoke listeners' feelings, including sympathy for others. These types of appeals often use words that have strong positive or negative connotations. They may also refer to moral, religious, or patriotic feelings.
- **Appeals to authority** encourage the audience to trust the speaker's credibility. In some cases, such an appeal can be a **logical fallacy,** or an argument that does not have a true foundation. However, by invoking his power and the privileged knowledge he has as president, Roosevelt attempts to strengthen his argument.

Practice

CITE TEXTUAL EVIDENCE to support your answers.

📝 **Notebook** Respond to these questions.

1. **(a)** Review paragraphs 2–10, and identify closely related words and phrases that Roosevelt repeats. **(b)** Does this use of repetition represent an appeal to logic, to emotions, to his own authority, or to a combination of these? Explain.
2. **(a)** Why does Roosevelt refer to a "realist" in paragraph 12 and to a "realistic American" in paragraph 17? **(b)** How do these references relate to paragraph 19? Explain.
3. Use the chart to link Roosevelt's reasoning to his central idea. First, identify the central idea of the speech. Then, give three examples of appeals to logic in the speech, and note how each example shapes or refines the central idea.

Central Idea: _____

EXAMPLE OF APPEAL TO LOGIC	HOW IT SHAPES OR REFINES THE CENTRAL IDEA

4. Read the paragraphs that follow Roosevelt's list of four freedoms (paragraphs 63–66). **(a)** What persuasive appeals does Roosevelt use in these paragraphs? **(b)** What is his purpose for using these particular appeals?

from THE "FOUR FREEDOMS" SPEECH

Concept Vocabulary

pacification	propaganda	appeasement
tyranny	disarmament	treachery

Why These Words? The concept vocabulary words all relate to conflicts between or among nations or other political groups. For example, *pacification* is the attempt to achieve, maintain, or force an end to hostilities. People might try to do this by promoting policies of *appeasement* or *disarmament*.

1. As expressed in this speech, what is Roosevelt's opinion of each concept these words represent?

2. Identify another word in the selection that relates to pacification and another word in the selection that relates to tyranny. Define each word.

Practice

📓 **Notebook** The concept words appear in the "Four Freedoms" speech.

1. Use pairs of concept words in sentences that demonstrate their meanings. Write three sentences, each with two of the concept words.

2. Rewrite the sentences you just wrote using an antonym for each concept word. Consult a thesaurus as needed. How do your replacements change the impact each sentence would have on a reader?

Word Study

Latin Root: *-pac-* The word *pacification* contains the Latin root *-pac-,* which comes from the Latin word *pax,* meaning "peace." The words in the chart all share this same root. Using your knowledge of suffixes, write the meaning of each word. Use a college-level dictionary to verify your definitions.

WORD	MEANING
pacifier	
pacific	
pacifist	
pacify	

🖧 WORD NETWORK

Add words related to power and freedom from the text to your Word Network.

▤ STANDARDS

Language
• Demonstrate command of the conventions of standard English grammar and usage when writing or speaking.
• Use various types of phrases and clauses to convey specific meanings and add variety and interest to writing or presentations.
• Identify and correctly use patterns of word changes that indicate different meanings or parts of speech.
• Verify the preliminary determination of the meaning of a word or phrase.

Conventions

Types of Phrases Writers and speakers, such as President Roosevelt, use various types of phrases, such as noun phrases, to convey specific meanings. A **noun phrase** consists of a noun, called the head noun, and one or more modifiers that tell *which one* or *what kind*. Modifiers may consist of adjectives, adjective phrases, prepositional phrases, participles, articles, or other grammatical elements. They can appear before the noun, after the noun, or in both locations. This chart shows some examples of noun phrases.

NOUN	NOUN PHRASES
people	those **people**; those **people** in huts; those **people** in huts and villages
threat	the small **threat**; the small, but real, **threat**; the small, but real, **threat** of danger
member	every **member**; every former **member**; every former **member** of Congress

Read It

1. Mark the noun phrases and head nouns in these sentences based on President Roosevelt's "Four Freedoms" speech. Each sentence may contain more than one noun phrase, and one noun phrase may form part of another.

   a. That is why the future of the American Republics is today in serious danger.

   b. The first phase of the invasion would not be the landing of regular troops.

   c. Our national policy in foreign affairs has been based on a decent respect for all nations, large and small.

2. Choose a sentence from paragraph 63 of the "Four Freedoms" speech. Mark the head nouns and modifiers in its noun phrases.

CLARIFICATION
One noun phrase may form part of another. For example, read this sentence: "He sat in the rocking chair on the porch." The short noun phrase "the porch" forms part of the longer noun phrase "the rocking chair on the porch."

Write It

📓 **Notebook** In the example, the original sentence has been revised to include another noun phrase. Following the example, rewrite each sentence below by adding a noun phrase. Mark the noun phrase you added, as well as its head noun.

> EXAMPLE
>
> **ORIGINAL:** The United States still had not declared war.
>
> **REVISION:** The United States still had not declared war against <u>the other Axis powers.</u>

1. Roosevelt's program calls for jobs.

2. The program increases insurance coverage.

Comparing Texts

You will now read Kennedy's inaugural address. First, complete the first-read and close-read activities. Then, compare the ways in which Roosevelt and Kennedy use persuasive appeals.

from THE "FOUR FREEDOMS" SPEECH

INAUGURAL ADDRESS

About the Speaker

John F. Kennedy
(1917–1963) graduated from Harvard University and served with distinction in the United States Navy during World War II. After his service, Kennedy won election to the House of Representatives in 1946, and was elected Senator from Massachusetts in 1952. In 1960, at the age of forty-three, Kennedy became the youngest person ever to be elected to the office of the presidency. Tragically, Kennedy was assassinated on November 22, 1963, in Dallas, Texas.

🔧 **Tool Kit**
First-Read Guide and Model Annotation

Inaugural Address

Concept Vocabulary

You will encounter the following words as you read John F. Kennedy's inaugural address. Before reading, note how familiar you are with each word. Then, rank the words in order from most familiar (1) to least familiar (6).

WORD	YOUR RANKING
revolution	
asunder	
invective	
belaboring	
invoke	
beachhead	

After completing the first read, come back to the concept vocabulary and review your rankings. Mark changes to your original rankings as needed.

First Read NONFICTION

Apply these strategies as you conduct your first read, You will have an opportunity to complete the close-read notes after your first read.

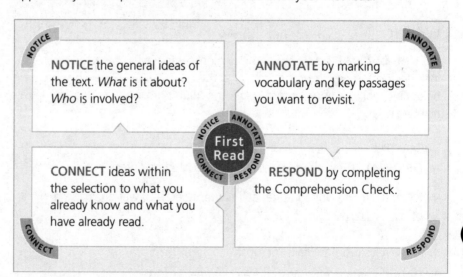

NOTICE the general ideas of the text. *What* is it about? *Who* is involved?

ANNOTATE by marking vocabulary and key passages you want to revisit.

CONNECT ideas within the selection to what you already know and what you have already read.

RESPOND by completing the Comprehension Check.

First Read

STANDARDS
Reading Informational Text
By the end of grade 10, read and comprehend literary nonfiction at the high end of the grades 9–10 text complexity band independently and proficiently.

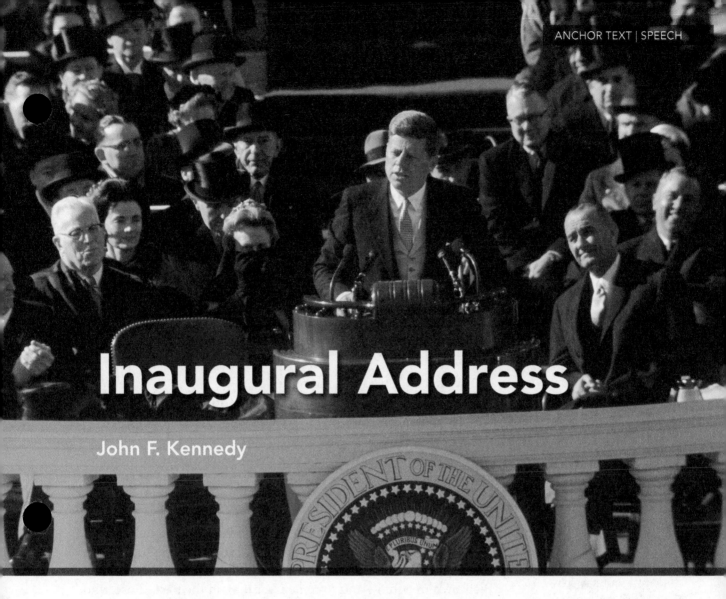

Inaugural Address

John F. Kennedy

BACKGROUND

When John F. Kennedy took office in 1961, the United States was locked in a potentially explosive stalemate with the Soviet Union and its allies. Fierce adversaries in the Cold War, the United States and the Soviet Union were stockpiling nuclear weapons, creating the possibility of a disastrous war that could destroy the earth.

SCAN FOR MULTIMEDIA

1 *Vice President Johnson, Mr. Speaker, Mr. Chief Justice, President Eisenhower, Vice President Nixon, President Truman,[1] Reverend Clergy, fellow citizens:*

2 We observe today not a victory of party but a celebration of freedom—symbolizing an end as well as a beginning—signifying renewal as well as change. For I have sworn before you and Almighty God the same solemn oath our forbears prescribed nearly a century and three quarters ago.

3 The world is very different now. For man holds in his mortal hands the power to abolish all forms of human poverty and all forms of

NOTES

---

1. **Vice President . . . Truman** present at Kennedy's inauguration were Lyndon B. Johnson, Kennedy's vice president; Dwight D. Eisenhower, 34th president; Richard M. Nixon, Eisenhower's vice president; and Harry S. Truman, 33rd president.

revolution (rehv uh LOO shuhn) *n.* overthrow of a government that is replaced by a new system

asunder (uh SUHN duhr) *adv.* divided; torn into separate pieces

CLOSE READ

ANNOTATE: In paragraphs 5–12, mark references to specific nations or groups the president is addressing in this speech.

QUESTION: Why does Kennedy acknowledge all these groups?

CONCLUDE: What is the effect of these references?

human life. And yet the same revolutionary beliefs for which our forebears fought are still at issue around the globe—the belief that the rights of man come not from the generosity of the state but from the hand of God.

4   We dare not forget today that we are the heirs of that first **revolution**. Let the word go forth from this time and place, to friend and foe alike, that the torch has been passed to a new generation of Americans—born in this century, tempered by war, disciplined by a hard and bitter peace, proud of our ancient heritage—and unwilling to witness or permit the slow undoing of those human rights to which this nation has always been committed, and to which we are committed today at home and around the world.

5   Let every nation know, whether it wishes us well or ill, that we shall pay any price, bear any burden, meet any hardship, support any friend, oppose any foe to assure the survival and the success of liberty.

6   This much we pledge—and more.

7   To those old allies whose cultural and spiritual origins we share, we pledge the loyalty of faithful friends. United there is little we cannot do in a host of cooperative ventures. Divided there is little we can do—for we dare not meet a powerful challenge at odds and split **asunder.**[2]

8   To those new states whom we welcome to the ranks of the free, we pledge our word that one form of colonial control shall not have passed away merely to be replaced by a far more iron tyranny. We shall not always expect to find them supporting our view. But we shall always hope to find them strongly supporting their own freedom—and to remember that, in the past, those who foolishly sought power by riding the back of the tiger ended up inside.

9   To those people in the huts and villages of half the globe struggling to break the bonds of mass misery, we pledge our best efforts to help them help themselves, for whatever period is required—not because the communists[3] may be doing it, not because we seek their votes, but because it is right. If a free society cannot help the many who are poor, it cannot save the few who are rich.

10   To our sister republics south of our border, we offer a special pledge—to convert our good words into good deeds—in a new alliance for progress—to assist free men and free governments in casting off the chains of poverty. But this peaceful revolution of hope cannot become the prey of hostile powers. Let all our neighbors know that we shall join with them to oppose aggression or subversion anywhere in the Americas. And let every other

---

2. **United . . . Divided . . . split asunder** Kennedy echoes the famous lines from Abraham Lincoln's second inaugural address: "United we stand . . . divided we fall."
3. **communists** *n.* refers to members or allies of the Soviet Union, a state whose government was based on the principles of communism, such as total government ownership of land and factories, laid out by Karl Marx (1818–1883).

power know that this hemisphere intends to remain the master of its own house.

11 To that world assembly of sovereign states, the United Nations, our last best hope in an age where the instruments of war have far outpaced the instruments of peace, we renew our pledge of support—to prevent it from becoming merely a forum for **invective**—to strengthen its shield of the new and the weak—and to enlarge the area in which its writ may run.

12 Finally, to those nations who would make themselves our adversary, we offer not a pledge but a request: that both sides begin anew the quest for peace, before the dark powers of destruction unleashed by science[4] engulf all humanity in planned or accidental self-destruction.

13 We dare not tempt them with weakness. For only when our arms are sufficient beyond doubt can we be certain beyond doubt that they will never be employed.

14 But neither can two great and powerful groups of nations take comfort from our present course—both sides overburdened by the cost of modern weapons, both rightly alarmed by the steady spread of the deadly atom, yet both racing to alter that uncertain balance of terror that stays the hand of mankind's final war.

15 So let us begin anew—remembering on both sides that civility is not a sign of weakness, and sincerity is always subject to proof. Let us never negotiate out of fear. But let us never fear to negotiate.

16 Let both sides explore what problems unite us instead of **belaboring** those problems which divide us.

17 Let both sides, for the first time, formulate serious and precise proposals for the inspection and control of arms—and bring the absolute power to destroy other nations under the absolute control of all nations.

18 Let both sides seek to **invoke** the wonders of science instead of its terrors. Together let us explore the stars, conquer the deserts, eradicate disease, tap the ocean depths, and encourage the arts and commerce.

19 Let both sides unite to heed in all corners of the earth the command of Isaiah—to "undo the heavy burdens . . . [and] let the oppressed go free."[5]

20 And if a **beachhead** of cooperation may push back the jungle of suspicion, let both sides join in creating a new endeavor, not a new balance of power, but a new world of law, where the strong are just and the weak secure and the peace preserved.

21 All this will not be finished in the first one hundred days. Nor will it be finished in the first one thousand days, nor in the life of this administration, nor even perhaps in our lifetime on this planet. But let us begin.

---

4. **dark powers of destruction unleashed by science** nuclear war.
5. **"Isaiah . . . free"** refers to a Biblical passage, Isaiah 58:6.

NOTES

invective (ihn VEHK tihv)
n. negative, aggressive language that seeks to harm

CLOSE READ
ANNOTATE: In paragraph 11, mark the verbs that follow the word *we.*

QUESTION: What do these words have in common?

CONCLUDE: What does this set of verbs show about Kennedy's attitude toward the United Nations?

belaboring (bih LAY buhr ihng)
n. focusing on something too much

invoke (ihn VOHK) *v.* call on

beachhead (BEECH hehd)
n. secure starting point; foothold

22   In your hands, my fellow citizens, more than mine, will rest the final success or failure of our course. Since this country was founded, each generation of Americans has been summoned to give testimony to its national loyalty. The graves of young Americans who answered the call to service surround the globe.

23   Now the trumpet summons us again—not as a call to bear arms, though arms we need—not as a call to battle, though embattled we are—but as a call to bear the burden of a long twilight struggle, year in and year out, "rejoicing in hope, patient in tribulation"[6]—a struggle against the common enemies of man: tyranny, poverty, disease, and war itself.

24   Can we forge against these enemies a grand and global alliance, North and South, East and West, that can assure a more fruitful life for all mankind? Will you join in that historic effort?

25   In the long history of the world, only a few generations have been granted the role of defending freedom in its hour of maximum danger. I do not shrink from this responsibility—I welcome it. I do not believe that any of us would exchange places with any other people or any other generation. The energy, the faith, the devotion which we bring to this endeavor will light our country and all who serve it—and the glow from that fire can truly light the world.

26   And so, my fellow Americans: Ask not what your country can do for you—ask what you can do for your country.

27   My fellow citizens of the world: Ask not what America will do for you—but what together we can do for the freedom of man.

28   Finally, whether you are citizens of America or citizens of the world, ask of us here the same high standards of strength and sacrifice which we ask of you. With a good conscience our only sure reward, with history the final judge of our deeds, let us go forth to lead the land we love, asking His blessing and His help, but knowing that here on earth God's work must truly be our own. ❧

---

6. **"rejoicing . . . tribulation"** refers to a Biblical passage, Romans 12:12. In Paul's letter to the Romans, he calls people to work together in love and mutual respect.

Comprehension Check

Complete the following items after you finish your first read.

1. According to Kennedy, inauguration day is not a celebration of the victory of a party. Of what is it a celebration?

2. How far does Kennedy say the United States is willing to go to assure liberty for all nations?

3. Kennedy singles out one group of countries that the United States will defend against any attacker. What countries are they?

4. At the end of the speech, what does Kennedy urge his fellow Americans to do?

RESEARCH

Research to Clarify Choose at least one unfamiliar detail from the text. Briefly research that detail. How does the information you learned shed light on an aspect of the speech?

INAUGURAL ADDRESS

Close Read the Text

This model, from paragraph 25 of the text, shows two sample annotations, along with questions and conclusions. Close read the passage, and find another detail to annotate. Then, write a question and your conclusion.

ANNOTATE QUESTION
Close Read
ANNOTATE CONCLUDE

ANNOTATE: These nouns in sequence are very powerful.

QUESTION: Why does Kennedy use these emotionally charged words?

CONCLUDE: These words emphasize Kennedy's conviction that America is a force for good in the world.

ANNOTATE: Kennedy connects the abstract idea of defending freedom to the concrete idea of fire.

QUESTION: Why does the president use this comparison?

CONCLUDE: Fire represents light, warmth, and safety. Kennedy's comparison creates a vision of a world that is a safe haven for all.

> The energy, the faith, the devotion, which we bring to this endeavor will light our country and all who serve it—and the glow from that fire can truly light the world.

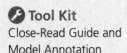
Tool Kit
Close-Read Guide and
Model Annotation

2. For more practice, go back into the text, and complete the close-read notes.

3. Revisit a section of the text you found important during your first read. Read this section closely, and **annotate** what you notice. Ask yourself **questions** such as "Why did the author make this choice?" What can you **conclude**?

STANDARDS
Reading Informational Text
• Cite strong and thorough textual evidence to support analysis of what the text says explicitly as well as inferences drawn from the text.

• Determine a central idea of a text and analyze its development over the course of the text, including how it emerges and is shaped and refined by specific details; provide an objective summary of the text.

• Determine an author's point of view or purpose in a text and analyze how an author uses rhetoric to advance that point of view or purpose.

• Analyze seminal U.S. documents of historical and literary significance, including how they address related themes and concepts.

Analyze the Text

CITE TEXTUAL EVIDENCE
to support your answers.

Notebook **Respond to these questions.**

1. (a) **Compare and Contrast** What similarities and differences does Kennedy see between the world now and the world as it was during the American Revolution? (b) **Interpret** How does he think these similarities and differences affect the American commitment to human rights?

2. **Infer** Why does Kennedy repeatedly refer to "both sides" in the middle of the speech? What effect might this repetition have on listeners, including those from the other "side"?

3. **Synthesize** Kennedy chooses language meant to remind people of wartime experiences and quotes religious literature. How do these choices reflect the purpose and occasion of the speech?

4. **Essential Question:** *What is the relationship between power and freedom?* What have you learned about power and freedom from reading this speech?

Analyze Craft and Structure

Seminal Documents: Emotional Appeals Kennedy's inaugural address is an example of **persuasion**, a type of writing in which an author or speaker attempts to influence an audience to think a certain way or take a particular action. The rhetorical techniques Kennedy uses in the speech, including charged language and restatement, appeal to listeners' emotions, thus making listeners more receptive to the ideas he expresses.

- **Charged Language:** words and phrases that have strong positive or negative connotations—Charged language encourages listeners to connect with a speaker's message through emotion rather than logic. Kennedy's listeners would have been stirred by his description of Americans as "tempered by war, disciplined by a hard and bitter peace." The words *tempered, disciplined,* and *bitter* are emotionally charged. They suggest toughness and self-control in the face of hardship.

- **Restatement:** the expression of similar ideas in different words— Speakers use restatement to clarify and emphasize ideas and to add urgency. For example, in paragraph 5, Kennedy says, "we shall pay any price, bear any burden, meet any hardship." The restatements emphasize the idea of America's commitment to freedom, while adding a sense of urgency and rhythmic intensity.

Practice

CITE TEXTUAL EVIDENCE to support your answers.

📓 **Notebook** Respond to these questions.

1. Reread paragraphs 9 and 10 of Kennedy's inaugural address. **(a)** Which words and phrases have negative connotations, and what do they describe? **(b)** What do these examples of charged language reveal about Kennedy's purpose in the speech?

2. Reread paragraphs 21 and 22. What idea does Kennedy reinforce through restatement?

3. Use this chart to further analyze Kennedy's speech. Find at least three ways Kennedy uses restatement to emphasize his message of working together. Then, find at least three instances of charged language with which Kennedy describes atomic weapons. Finally, describe how his use of rhetoric supports Kennedy's purpose in this speech.

RESTATEMENT	CHARGED LANGUAGE

How rhetoric supports purpose:

INAUGURAL ADDRESS

Concept Vocabulary

| revolution | invective | invoke |
| asunder | belaboring | beachhead |

Why These Words? These concept words all relate to instances of physical or verbal confrontation. *Revolution* and *beachhead* call up images of military conflict. *Asunder* emphasizes the division of something that was once united. Speakers *invoke* powerful aid as they appeal for help. An abusive speaker uses *invective,* whereas a *belaboring* speaker deflects attention from significant issues by focusing too much on one topic.

1. Read paragraphs 11 and 16, and consider the context in which Kennedy uses the concept words *invective* and *belaboring*. What do the paragraphs have in common? How does Kennedy's word choice connect the paragraphs?

2. Find other words in the speech that refer to physical confrontation. Which ones does Kennedy use to suggest that people are in danger? Which ones does he use to inspire people to stand up for what they believe?

WORD NETWORK

Add words related to freedom and power from the text to your Word Network.

Practice

📓 **Notebook** The concept words appear in Kennedy's inaugural address.

1. Use each concept word in a sentence about a current event that demonstrates your understanding of the word's meaning.

2. For each sentence you just wrote, write a companion sentence about a historical event that uses the same concept word.

Word Study

Latin Root: *-vol-* In his inaugural address, Kennedy uses the concept vocabulary word *revolution* twice—once when referring to the American Revolutionary War and once when describing a new "peaceful revolution of hope." *Revolution* is formed from the Latin root *-vol-*, meaning "to roll" or "to turn." The words in the chart all share this same root. Use a print or online dictionary to look up each word, and write its meaning.

STANDARDS

Reading Informational Text
Determine an author's point of view or purpose in a text and analyze how an author uses rhetoric to advance that point of view or purpose.

Language
• Use parallel structure.
• Identify and correctly use patterns of word changes that indicate different meanings or parts of speech.
• Consult general and specialized reference materials, both print and digital, to find the pronunciation of a word or determine or clarify its precise meaning, its part of speech, or its etymology.

WORD	MEANING
voluble	
convolution	
involve	
revolve	
evolve	

Author's Style

Author's Choices: Use of Language Rhetorical devices are special patterns of words and ideas that create emphasis and stir emotion, especially in speeches or other oratory. In his inaugural address, Kennedy uses three closely related rhetorical devices: repetition, parallelism, and antithesis.

- **Repetition** is the use multiple times of the same word or phrase to emphasize key concepts.

  Example: "Let freedom ring from every hill and molehill of Mississippi. From every mountainside, let freedom ring."—from the "I Have a Dream" speech, Martin Luther King, Jr.

- **Parallelism** is the repetition of related ideas in the same grammatical structure. There are many kinds of parallelism, all of which establish a rhythm that makes ideas memorable. One kind is **anaphora**, in which a word or group of words repeats at the beginnings of phrases, clauses, or sentences that appear in close succession.

  Example: "This blessed plot, this earth, this realm, this England . . ." —from *Richard III*, William Shakespeare

- In **antithesis**, two strongly contrasting ideas, expressed using parallel structure, are placed side-by-side.

  Example: "To err is human; to forgive divine." —from "An Essay on Criticism," Alexander Pope

Read It

1. Identify the rhetorical device in each passage as either simple parallelism or antithesis. Then, explain your choice.

   a. We shall not always expect to find them supporting our view. But we shall always hope to find them strongly supporting their own freedom. . . .

   b. Let every nation know . . . that we shall pay any price, bear any burden, meet any hardship, support any friend, oppose any foe to assure the survival and the success of liberty.

2. Find at least one example each of parallelism, anaphora, and antithesis in paragraphs 16–20 of Kennedy's inaugural address. For each passage you chose, identify the type of rhetorical device being used. Then, explain why the passage is a good example of that device.

Write It

🗐 **Notebook** Rewrite the following sentences to create one sentence that uses parallelism.

> We walked through the forest quietly. Loudly over a stream we splashed. We happily climbed up a mountain.

INAUGURAL ADDRESS

from THE "FOUR
FREEDOMS" SPEECH

Writing to Compare

You have studied two seminal American texts—Roosevelt's "Four Freedoms" speech, delivered in 1941, and Kennedy's inaugural address, delivered in 1961. Now, deepen your understanding of the two speeches by comparing and writing about them.

Assignment

Both of these speeches were given at critical moments in American history. They reflect the concerns of the era, and define each president's vision for the country and its role in the world. Write a **comparison-and-contrast essay** in which you explain what each leader means when he talks about "freedom." Include the following elements in your essay:

- a summary of the historical context of each speech—The **historical context** involves the state of the country and the world at these two moments in history.

- an explanation of each speaker's purpose—the call to action each leader issues

- an explanation of the role each president thinks America should play in the world

Prewriting

Notebook Make sure you are clear about the historical context of each speech. Answer these questions to clarify your understanding.

1. **(a)** As Roosevelt delivers his speech, what conflict is growing around the world? **(b)** How does Roosevelt want America to respond to that conflict?
2. **(a)** What concerns about the Cold War does Kennedy express in his speech? **(b)** What does Kennedy want the opposing side in that conflict to consider?

Analyze the Texts Reread each speech, and identify passages related to the concept of freedom, particularly in regard to America's responsibilities in the world.

PASSAGES RELATED TO FREEDOM	
"FOUR FREEDOMS" SPEECH	INAUGURAL ADDRESS

≣ STANDARDS

Reading Informational Text
Analyze seminal U.S. documents of historical and literary significance, including how they address related themes and concepts.

Writing
- Write informative/explanatory texts to examine and convey complex ideas, concepts, and information clearly and accurately through the effective selection, organization, and analysis of content.
- Apply *grades 9–10 Reading standards* to literary nonfiction.

Drafting

Write a Thesis Statement In a comparison-and-contrast essay about literary nonfiction, the thesis statement should indicate the major similarities and differences between the two works being compared. Draft a thesis statement consisting of two or three sentences. State how the "Four Freedoms" speech and the inaugural address are similar, as well as how they are different. Use comparison-and-contrast key words, such as those underlined in this thesis frame:

> **Thesis Frame:**
> Both Roosevelt's "Four Freedoms" speech and Kennedy's inaugural address _____,
> However, Roosevelt's speech _____,
> whereas Kennedy's speech _____.

Choose a Structure Decide how best to organize your essay. Point-by-point organization and block organization are two commonly used structures for essays of comparison.

- **Block Format:** Discuss the historical context, purpose, and meaning of freedom in one speech. Then, discuss the historical context, purpose, and meaning of freedom in the other speech.

- **Point-by-Point Format:** First, discuss the historical context and purpose of each speech. Next, discuss the meaning of freedom presented in each speech.

Make sure to include a section in which you explain the vision of America and its role in the world that the two presidents put forward.

Use Varied Evidence Include supporting evidence in a variety of ways.

- **Direct Quotations:** use of exact language from the text

  Avoid misrepresenting a speaker's meaning. For example, if one part of a quotation supports your ideas, but another part does not, explain the discrepancy—don't use only the part that fits your analysis.

- **Summaries:** brief retellings of parts of the text

  Summarize complex sequences of events or ideas so that readers have the information they need to understand your analysis. The use of summaries can help you give readers necessary knowledge without unnecessary detail.

- **Paraphrases:** restatements of a text in your own words

  Use paraphrases when the speaker's exact words are not that distinctive, or when you wish to clarify someone else's ideas or demonstrate your knowledge of a text.

Review, Revise, and Edit

When you have finished drafting, reread your essay. Mark ideas that need more support, and then return to your Prewriting notes or the texts themselves to find additional evidence. Check for logical, clear transitions between paragraphs. Edit your work for grammar, sentence structure, and word choice. Finally, proofread your essay to eliminate spelling and punctuation errors.

✎ EVIDENCE LOG

Before moving on to a new selection, go to your Evidence Log and record what you learned from Roosevelt's "Four Freedoms" speech and Kennedy's inaugural address.

About the Speaker

John F. Kennedy (1917–1963) came from a family with extensive political connections and ambitions, but it was Joseph, his older brother, who was expected to run for high office. Joseph, however, died in World War II, and John became the family's political hope. As a United States senator, he advocated for foreign aid to developing nations in Africa and Asia, and for France to grant Algerian independence. A concern with foreign affairs would become a major element of his presidency.

Inaugural Address

Media Vocabulary

The following words or concepts will be useful to you as you analyze, discuss, and write about videos.

tone: sound of a voice with respect to pitch, volume, and overall quality	• Pitch refers to how high or low in frequency a voice sounds. • Overall quality refers to such traits as squeakiness, depth, resonance, or thinness.
inflection: changes to pitch or volume within a single word or between words	• Inflection can go up or down or be loud or soft. • Speakers use inflection to emphasize certain words, to modify rhythm, or to add drama.
gesture: movement of the body that conveys meaning	• Gestures are a form of nonverbal communication that help emphasize meaning. • Some gestures, such as a thumbs-up sign, have meanings that are essentially the same in any situation. Other gestures, such as a wave of the hands, reflect a speaker's emotions and meaning in a specific situation.
enunciation: manner in which a speaker pronounces words	• A speaker with good enunciation speaks clearly and avoids slurring words, omitting syllables, or dropping word endings. • Enunciation is sometimes referred to as "diction."

First Review MEDIA: VIDEO

Apply these strategies as you conduct your first review. You will have an opportunity to complete a close review after your first review.

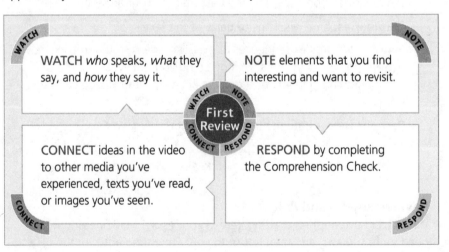

WATCH *who* speaks, *what* they say, and *how* they say it.

NOTE elements that you find interesting and want to revisit.

CONNECT ideas in the video to other media you've experienced, texts you've read, or images you've seen.

RESPOND by completing the Comprehension Check.

▥ STANDARDS

Reading Informational Text
By the end of grade 10, read and comprehend literary nonfiction at the high end of the grades 9–10 text complexity band independently and proficiently.

Language
Acquire and use accurately general academic and domain-specific words and phrases, sufficient for reading, writing, speaking, and listening at the college and career readiness level; demonstrate independence in gathering vocabulary knowledge when considering a word or phrase important to comprehension or expression.

Inaugural Address

John F. Kennedy

BACKGROUND

Harry S. Truman was the first United States president to deliver a televised inaugural address. Kennedy, in turn, was the first to deliver a televised inaugural address on color TV. Furthermore, Kennedy used the newly global mass media of television to speak to both the American people and the entire world, addressing the country's allies and adversaries, the United Nations, and other international audiences.

SCAN FOR MULTIMEDIA

NOTES

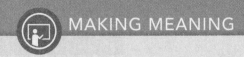

Comprehension Check

Complete the following items after you finish your first review.

1. Describe the setting in which Kennedy delivers the speech.

2. What are some phrases Kennedy emphasizes with voice and gestures?

3. Which parts of the speech does the audience respond to most enthusiastically?

RESEARCH

Research to Explore Choose an element of the speech that sparked your interest. Then, formulate a research question about that topic.

MEDIA VOCABULARY

Use these words as you discuss and write about the video.

tone
inflection
gesture
enunciation

WORD NETWORK

Add words related to freedom and power from the text to your Word Network.

Close Review

Watch and listen to the speech again. Write any new observations that seem important. What **questions** do you have? What can you **conclude**?

Analyze the Media

CITE TEXTUAL EVIDENCE to support your answers.

Notebook Respond to these questions.

1. **(a) Interpret** Rewatch the part of the speech that starts at the 8:12 mark—beginning with "we dare not tempt them with weakness"—and ends at 9:19. What international issue is Kennedy addressing?
(b) Connect What do Kennedy's references to "both sides" suggest about the issue?

2. **(a) Interpret** Listen for the word *pledge* in the speech. For whom is Kennedy speaking when he uses this word? **(b) Evaluate** How credible are the promises he makes in these statements? Explain.

3. **Connect** To date, John F. Kennedy is the youngest elected United States president. Listen for the word *generation* as you review the speech. What connections does Kennedy make between his generation and his vision for the future? Explain.

4. **Essential Question:** *What is the relationship between power and freedom?* What have you learned about power and freedom from listening to this speech?

STANDARDS

Speaking and Listening
• Evaluate a speaker's point of view, reasoning, and use of evidence and rhetoric, identifying any fallacious reasoning or exaggerated or distorted evidence.
• Adapt speech to a variety of contexts and tasks, demonstrating command of formal English when indicated or appropriate.

Writing to Sources

INAUGURAL ADDRESS (video)

Assignment

Imagine you are a television journalist in 1961 covering the Kennedy inauguration. Write the text for a **news report** about the event.

- **Write an introduction.** Find the answers to questions such as these: *What were the major issues in the 1960 election? Against whom did Kennedy run? How close was the election?*

- **Describe the scene.** Answer questions such as these: *What is the weather like? How many people seem to be in attendance? What is the mood of the crowd? Who is assembled on the steps of the Capitol building?*

- **Describe Kennedy's delivery.** Answer questions such as these: *How does Kennedy look? What is the tone of his speech? How do his gestures and body language affect his message? What can you say about his rhetoric?*

- **Review the content of the speech.** State Kennedy's central idea, and describe the crowd's reception of that idea. Report what Kennedy says about the country's rich and poor, its allies and enemies. Also, identify what you consider to be the high points of the address. What challenge does Kennedy issue to the American public?

Speaking and Listening

Assignment

Adapt the text of the news report you wrote, and deliver it as a **newscast**. You may either present it live or record it and share it digitally.

- **Integrate visuals.** Review your news report, and find visuals or audio that will enhance its transition into a newscast. Plan how to integrate the visuals into your presentation.

- **Consider your speaking style.** Choose a speaking style that suits your audience and purpose. Your style might be informal, but still highly informational. Alternatively, you might choose a formal approach in acknowledgment of the importance of the event.

- **Vary your pitch and volume.** Avoid speaking in a monotone. Instead, vary the pitch and volume of your voice. Likewise, find a middle ground between speaking too slowly and too quickly. Make sure you clearly enunciate so that listeners fully understand what you are saying.

- **Rehearse your delivery.** Practice your newscast either in front of a mirror if you plan to perform live, or in an audio recording if you plan to share a digital version. Look for ways in which you can strengthen your delivery through gestures, tone, or enunciation.

📝 EVIDENCE LOG

Before moving on to a new selection, go to your Evidence Log and record what you learned from listening to and watching Kennedy's inaugural address.

WRITING TO SOURCES

• *from* THE "FOUR FREEDOMS" SPEECH

• INAUGURAL ADDRESS

• INAUGURAL ADDRESS (video)

🔧 **Tool Kit**
Student Model of an Informative Essay

ACADEMIC VOCABULARY

As you craft your informative essay, consider using some of the academic vocabulary you learned in the beginning of the unit.

attribute
hierarchy
demarcate
fundamental
democracy

☰ **STANDARDS**

Writing
• Write informative/explanatory texts to examine and convey complex ideas, concepts, and information clearly and accurately through the effective selection, organization, and analysis of content.
• Conduct short as well as more sustained research projects to answer a question or solve a problem; narrow or broaden the inquiry when appropriate; synthesize multiple sources on the subject, demonstrating understanding of the subject under investigation.
• Write routinely over extended time frames and shorter time frames for a range of tasks, purposes, and audiences.

Write an Informative Essay

You have read two speeches that shed light on the relationship between power and freedom. In his "Four Freedoms" speech, Franklin D. Roosevelt speaks of the need for the United States to protect itself during a time of danger, and of universal freedoms that deserve protection throughout the world. In his inaugural address, John F. Kennedy argues that Americans must appreciate their own freedom while understanding the country's importance in the world.

> **Assignment**
> Use the knowledge you have gained from reading Roosevelt's "Four Freedoms" speech and from reading and listening to Kennedy's inaugural address to write about the power of the individual. Write a brief **informative essay** in which you focus on answering this question:
>
> **What can one person do to defend the human rights of all people?**

Elements of an Informative Essay

An **informative essay** develops a thesis, or main idea, about a topic through the effective selection, organization, and analysis of content. An effective informative essay includes these elements:

- an engaging introduction to its topic
- the writer's main idea about the topic, supported by facts, definitions, details, examples, quotations, and other information from credible sources
- an organization that helps readers make connections and distinctions among ideas
- clear transitions that clarify relationships among ideas
- a conclusion that restates the thesis and follows from the information presented
- correct grammar, a formal style, and an objective tone

Model Informative Essay For a model of a well-crafted informative essay, see the Launch Text, "Born Free: Children and the Struggle for Human Rights."

Challenge yourself to find all of the elements of effective informative writing in the text. You will have the opportunity to review these elements as you start to write your own informative essay.

Prewriting / Planning

Develop a Working Thesis Reread the assignment and rephrase it to state your topic. Then, compose an answer to the question. This is your initial thesis, or main idea. You may return to it and change it as you gather more information and work through the writing process.

Topic: _____

Thesis: _____

_____

Review the texts and media that you have studied in this unit so far. Take note of details that support your main idea. Then, decide whether outside research will help you develop your ideas more fully.

Focus Research If a short research project is in order, plan to use several sources. Focus your efforts by developing a research question, such as "Who are three individuals known for their defense of human rights?" or "What opportunities exist in my hometown for a person to defend human rights?" You can find primary and secondary sources in print or online. You can conduct original research as well, through surveys or personal interviews.

Research Question: _____

_____

Possible Sources:

1. _____

2. _____

3. _____

Gather Evidence Be sure that your sources are reliable. Ask your librarian about the best sources to use. This excerpt from the Launch Text shows that the writer used newspapers as a source of information.

> *"Dere's t'ree t'ousand of us, and we'll win for sure," is how one newspaper mockingly quoted a newsie's reference to the number of strikers.*
>
> —from "Born Free: Children and the Struggle for Human Rights"

Take notes as you find and connect relevant information from multiple sources, and keep a reference list of every source you use. Create a notecard that includes each source's author, title, publisher, city, and date of publication, along with the fact or idea you discovered. For Internet sources, record the name and Web address of the site, as well as the date you accessed the information. For print sources, note the page numbers on which you found useful information.

Connect Across Texts As you write your informative essay, you will be combining facts, examples, and details from multiple sources. Remember to identify the source of every exact quotation. Cite President Roosevelt, President Kennedy, and any other authority who helps you formulate and support your main idea. As you compile evidence from various texts, note any information that may help you revise or refine your main idea.

✐ EVIDENCE LOG

Review your Evidence Log and identify key details you may want to cite in your informative essay.

≣ STANDARDS

Writing
• Introduce a topic; organize complex ideas, concepts, and information to make important connections and distinctions; include formatting, graphics, and multimedia when useful to aiding comprehension.
• Develop the topic with well-chosen, relevant, and sufficient facts, extended definitions, concrete details, quotations, or other information and examples appropriate to the audience's knowledge of the topic.

Drafting

Organize Your Essay Consider your topic statement, your main idea, and the supporting information you have gathered, and then choose an organizational structure. Make sure your choice will help you sequence information so that it flows logically from your introduction, through your body paragraphs, to your conclusion. There are a variety of useful structures, including the ones described here. Place a check in the box of the one you plan to use.

☐ **Problem-Solution Order:** Present a problem, such as a specific example of a human rights violation, and offer information about possible solutions. In your conclusion, identify the solution that most strongly supports your main idea.

☐ **Order of Importance:** State your thesis in your introduction. Then, present your supporting reasons and evidence in order of importance, from most important to least.

☐ **Nestorian Order, or Reverse Order of Importance:** State your thesis in your introduction. Then, offer supporting reasons and evidence starting with weaker or less dramatic ideas and building to stronger or more dramatic ones. This can be an effective way to lead readers to a powerful conclusion.

☐ **Cause-Effect Order:** Present a person's actions as a cause that has the effect of defending human rights, or present defending human rights as a cause that has the effect of inspiring individual actions.

☐ **Steps in a Process:** Present the stages through which an individual progresses in his or her defense of human rights. In your conclusion, link this process to your main idea.

Notice how the Launch Text is organized. The first paragraph states, "young people have also realized that in order to be heard, they might have to make some noise." The body paragraphs report causes and effects in chronological order. The concluding paragraph revisits the main idea: "It may have been a small victory, but it was more than the newsies would have received had they not raised their voices."

Write a First Draft Use your chosen organization to write a first draft. As you write, your style should be formal, and your tone should be objective. Avoid revealing your own personal biases, and do not use slang or expressions that sound overly conversational. Instead, choose words that convey your ideas precisely, and define or explain terms that may be unfamiliar to your audience. Make sure to include transitional words and phrases that clarify the relationships among your ideas.

▤ STANDARDS

Writing
• Introduce a topic; organize complex ideas, concepts, and information to make important connections and distinctions; include formatting, graphics, and multimedia when useful to aiding comprehension.
• Develop the topic with well-chosen, relevant, and sufficient facts, extended definitions, concrete details, quotations, or other information and examples appropriate to the audience's knowledge of the topic.
• Use appropriate and varied transitions to link the major sections of the text, create cohesion, and clarify the relationships among complex ideas and concepts.
• Use precise language and domain-specific vocabulary to manage the complexity of the topic.
• Establish and maintain a formal style and objective tone while attending to the norms and conventions of the discipline in which they are writing.
• Provide a concluding statement or section that follows from and supports the information or explanation presented.

LANGUAGE DEVELOPMENT: STYLE

Create Cohesion: Integrate Information in Different Ways

As you write your draft, use the following methods to present the ideas, facts, examples, and quotations you use to support your thesis. In each case, you must credit the source.

- **Direct Quotations:** Use the writer's exact words when they provide the strongest support for an idea. Indicate omitted material with ellipses.
- **Paraphrase:** Restate a writer's specific ideas in your own words, accurately reflecting the original meaning.
- **Summary:** To provide background or general information, condense complex material into a briefer statement in your own words.

NOTE: If you find a fact in only one source, include documentation. If you find identical facts in multiple sources, you need not provide documentation.

Read It

These sentences from the Launch Text show different methods of incorporating information.

- *In our national anthem, "The Star-Spangled Banner," we sing of America as "the land of the free and the home of the brave."* (direct quotation)
- *Another newspaper explained that newsies were striking for their "rights," using quotation marks to suggest that the children had no rights and that it was quaint for them to suggest they did.* (direct quotation combined with paraphrase)
- *The newsies' circumstances deteriorated even further during the Spanish-American War of 1898.* (summary)

Write It

As you draft your essay, keep track of your sources, and include appropriate citations to avoid plagiarism, or the presentation of another's work as your own. You may use a chart like this to track your information.

Source title	
Author	
Publisher or site	
Date of publication or update	
Date you accessed (for online sources)	
Website URL (for online sources)	
Direct quotation	
Summary or paraphrase	

TIP

PUNCTUATION
Make sure to enclose direct quotations in quotation marks. Do not use quotation marks for paraphrased remarks.

≡ STANDARDS

Writing
Gather relevant information from multiple authoritative print and digital sources, using advanced searches effectively; assess the usefulness of each source in answering the research question; integrate information into the text selectively to maintain the flow of ideas, avoiding plagiarism and following a standard format for citation.

Revising

Evaluating Your Draft

Use the following checklist to evaluate the effectiveness of your first draft. Then, use your evaluation and the instruction on this page to guide your revision.

FOCUS AND ORGANIZATION	EVIDENCE AND ELABORATION	CONVENTIONS
☐ The introduction clearly states the topic.	☐ Specific reasons, details, facts, and quotations support the main idea.	☐ Attends to the norms and conventions of the discipline, especially regarding the proper crediting of sources.
☐ The introduction presents a specific thesis.	☐ The main idea is developed with relevant information from multiple credible sources.	☐ Uses precise language appropriate for the audience and purpose.
☐ The organization is logical, allowing for effective development of ideas.		
☐ The conclusion clearly connects back to the introduction.	☐ Accurate credit is provided to sources of information.	☐ Establishes an objective tone and formal style.

⊹ WORD NETWORK

Include interesting words from your Word Network in your informative essay.

Revising for Focus and Organization

Internal Logic Reread your essay, making sure the ideas you set up in the introduction are clearly developed in the body and echoed in the conclusion. Rearrange paragraphs or sections that do not build in a logical way. Consider adding or revising transitional words and phrases to clarify the connections you want to emphasize.

Revising for Evidence and Elaboration

Correct Citations Consider how you have used and cited researched information in your essay. Have you accurately identified the sources of all the evidence you use to support your main idea? If not, review your notes to find and add the proper citations.

Language Clear, strong language will help make your ideas memorable. Consider these options:

- **Comparatives and Superlatives:** Comparative adjectives, such as *sharper* and *bolder*, clarify ideas. Avoid overuse of predictable or subjective superlatives, such as *best, strongest,* or *bravest*.
- **Action Verbs:** Whenever possible, replace weaker linking verbs with stronger action verbs.

▤ STANDARDS

Writing
Gather relevant information from multiple authoritative print and digital sources, using advanced searches effectively; assess the usefulness of each source in answering the research question; integrate information into the text selectively to maintain the flow of ideas, avoiding plagiarism and following a standard format for citation.

> EXAMPLE
> **LINKING VERB:** The policy *is* unfair.
>
> **ACTION VERB:** The policy *cheats* us all.

Review your essay, looking for any ineffective uses of language. Replace weaker word choices with stronger alternatives.

PEER REVIEW

Exchange essays with a classmate. Use the checklist to evaluate your classmate's informative essay and provide supportive feedback.

1. Is the thesis, or main idea, clear?

☐ yes   ☐ no   If no, explain what confused you.

2. Is the text organized logically?

☐ yes   ☐ no   If no, what aspect of organization does not work?

3. Does the essay fully address the assignment?

☐ yes   ☐ no   If no, write a brief note explaining what you thought was missing.

4. What is the strongest part of your classmate's essay? Why?

_____

_____

_____

_____

Editing and Proofreading

Edit for Conventions Reread your draft for accuracy and consistency. Correct errors in grammar and word usage. Use a style guide if you need help crediting your sources correctly.

Proofread for Accuracy Read your draft carefully, looking for errors in spelling and punctuation. Double-check that you have used quotation marks correctly and that there is an ending quotation mark for every beginning quotation mark.

Publishing and Presenting

Create a final version of your essay and share it with your classmates. Together, determine what your different essays convey about the values Roosevelt and Kennedy promote in their speeches.

Reflecting

Think about what you learned while writing your essay. What techniques did you learn that you could use when writing another informative essay? How could you improve the process? For example, you might choose to spend more time examining primary sources.

::: STANDARDS

Writing
Develop and strengthen writing as needed by planning, revising, editing, rewriting, or trying a new approach, focusing on addressing what is most significant for a specific purpose and audience.

Language
• Demonstrate command of the conventions of standard English grammar and usage when writing or speaking.
• Demonstrate command of the conventions of standard English capitalization, punctuation, and spelling when writing.
• Spell correctly.

ESSENTIAL QUESTION:

What is the relationship between power and freedom?

What does it mean to have your freedom to learn, read, or think what you want threatened? Is freedom of thought and expression something we treasure only when we might lose it? The selections you will read present various perspectives on these questions. You will work in a group to continue your exploration of the relationship between power and freedom.

Small-Group Learning Strategies

Throughout your life, in school, in your community, and in your career, you will continue to develop strategies when you work in teams.

Review these strategies and the actions you can take to practice them. Add ideas of your own for each step. Get ready to use these strategies during Small-Group Learning.

STRATEGY	ACTION PLAN
Prepare	• Complete your assignments so that you are prepared for group work. • Organize your thinking so you can contribute to your group's discussions. •
Participate fully	• Make eye contact to signal that you are listening and taking in what is being said. • Use text evidence when making a point. •
Support others	• Build off ideas from others in your group. • Invite others who have not yet spoken to do so. •
Clarify	• Paraphrase the ideas of others to ensure that your understanding is correct. • Ask follow-up questions. •

SCAN FOR
MULTIMEDIA

CONTENTS

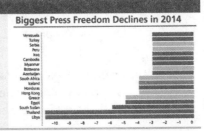

Biggest Press Freedom Declines in 2014

PERFORMANCE TASK

SPEAKING AND LISTENING FOCUS
Deliver a Multimedia Presentation
The Small-Group readings explore the conflicts that arise when governments try to
control the freedom to create and share knowledge and information. After reading,
your group will create a multimedia presentation about these concepts.

Working as a Team

1. **Take a Position** With your group, discuss the following question:

   > In what ways do laws both protect and limit our personal freedom?

   As you take turns sharing your ideas, be sure to provide supporting reasons and examples. After all group members have shared, discuss which aspect of the law you think is more important—the power to protect or the power to restrict.

2. **List Your Rules** As a group, decide on the rules that you will follow as you work together. Samples are provided; add two more of your own. As you work together, you may add or revise rules based on your experience together.

   - Everyone should participate in group discussions.
   - People should not interrupt.

   - _____

     _____

   - _____

     _____

3. **Apply the Rules** Practice working as a group. Share what you have learned about personal freedom and the law. Make sure each person in the group contributes. Take notes on and be prepared to share with the class one thing that you heard from another member of your group.

4. **Name Your Group** Choose a name that reflects the unit topic.

   Our group's name: _____

5. **Create a Communication Plan** Decide how you want to communicate with one another. For example, you might use online collaboration tools, email, or instant messaging.

   Our group's decision: _____

   _____

Making a Schedule

First, find out the due dates for the small-group activities. Then, preview the texts and activities with your group, and make a schedule for completing the tasks.

SELECTION	ACTIVITIES	DUE DATE
Speech at the United Nations		
Diane Sawyer Interviews Malala Yousafzai		
Caged Bird Some Advice To Those Who Will Serve Time in Prison		
The Censors		
from Freedom of the Press Report 2015		

Working on Group Projects

As your group works together, you'll find it more effective if each person has a specific role. Different projects require different roles. Before beginning a project, discuss the necessary roles, and choose one for each group member. Here are some possible roles; add your own ideas.

Project Manager: monitors the schedule and keeps everyone on task

Researcher: organizes research activities

Recorder: takes notes during group meetings

SCAN FOR
MULTIMEDIA

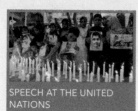

SPEECH AT THE UNITED
NATIONS

Comparing Texts

In this lesson, you will compare the speech that
Malala Yousafzai delivered at the United Nations
with an interview of Yousafzai by journalist Diane
Sawyer. First, complete the first-read and close-
read activities for Yousafzai's speech.

DIANE SAWYER INTERVIEWS
MALALA YOUSAFZAI

About the Speaker

Malala Yousafzai (b. 1997)
was born and raised in the
Swat Valley of Pakistan. In
2007, the area was invaded
by the Taliban, a radical
Islamist group. When the
Taliban outlawed education
for girls, Yousafzai spoke
out, becoming a highly
visible advocate. For this
reason, when she was just
15 years old, a member of
the Taliban shot her in the
head. Miraculously, she
recovered. Since then, she
has spoken publicly about
universal education and
gender equality. In 2014, she
became the youngest person
ever awarded the Nobel
Peace Prize.

Speech at the United Nations

Concept Vocabulary

As you perform your first read, you will encounter these words.

> beneficent   envoy   initiative

Familiar Word Parts Separating a word into its parts can often help you
identify its meaning. Those parts might include base words, roots, or affixes.

> **Unfamiliar Word:** *unidirectional*
>
> **Familiar Base Word:** *direction*, meaning "point toward which
> something faces or moves"
>
> **Familiar Affixes:** the prefix *uni-*, meaning "one"; the suffix *-al*,
> which forms adjectives
>
> **Conclusion:** *Unidirectional* may mean "moving in only one
> direction, or toward only one point."

Apply your knowledge of familiar word parts and other vocabulary strategies
to determine the meanings of unfamiliar words you encounter during your
first read.

First Read NONFICTION

Apply these strategies as you conduct your first read. You will have an
opportunity to complete a close read after your first read.

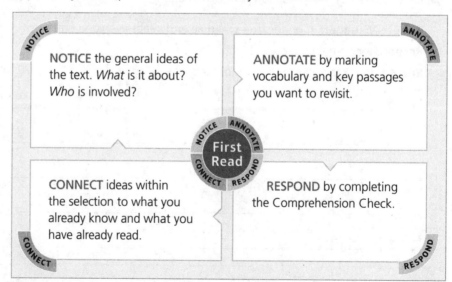

NOTICE the general ideas of
the text. *What* is it about?
Who is involved?

ANNOTATE by marking
vocabulary and key passages
you want to revisit.

CONNECT ideas within
the selection to what you
already know and what you
have already read.

RESPOND by completing
the Comprehension Check.

First
Read

☰ STANDARDS

Reading
By the end of grade 10, read and
comprehend literary nonfiction at
the high end of the grades 9–10 text
complexity band independently and
proficiently.

Language
Identify and correctly use patterns of
word changes that indicate different
meanings or parts of speech.

Speech at the United Nations

Malala Yousafzai

BACKGROUND

The Taliban emerged following the defeat and withdrawal of Russian forces from Afghanistan in the early 1990s. The Taliban's mission is to restore its interpretation of strict Sharia, or Islamic, law, which calls for such things as banning music, covering the faces of women, and forbidding school for girls. By the time Malala Yousafzai was growing up in northern Pakistan, the Taliban were a major force in her area.

1   In the name of God, The Most **Beneficent**, The Most Merciful.

2   Honorable UN Secretary-General Mr. Ban Ki-moon,

3   Respected President of the General Assembly Vuk Jeremic,

4   Honorable UN **envoy** for Global education Mr. Gordon Brown,

5   Respected elders and my dear brothers and sisters;

6   Today, it is an honor for me to be speaking again after a long time. Being here with such honorable people is a great moment in my life.

SCAN FOR
MULTIMEDIA

NOTES

Mark familiar word parts or indicate another strategy you used that helped you determine meaning.

beneficent (buh NEHF uh suhnt) *adj.*

MEANING:

envoy (EHN voy) *n.*

MEANING:

7   I don't know where to begin my speech. I don't know what people would be expecting me to say. But first of all, thank you to God, for whom we all are equal, and thank you to every person who has prayed for my fast recovery and a new life. I cannot believe how much love people have shown me. I have received thousands of good-wish cards and gifts from all over the world. Thank you to all of them. Thank you to the children, whose innocent words encouraged me. Thank you to my elders, whose prayers strengthened me.

8   I would like to thank my nurses, doctors, and the staff of the hospitals in Pakistan and the UK, and the UAE government, who have helped me get better and recover my strength. I fully support Mr. Ban Ki-moon, the Secretary-General, in his Global Education First **Initiative**; and the work of the UN Special Envoy, Mr. Gordon Brown. And I thank them both for the leadership they continue to give. They continue to inspire all of us to action.

9   Dear brothers and sisters, do remember one thing: Malala Day is not my day. Today is the day of every woman, every boy, and every girl who have raised their voice for their rights. There are hundreds of human-rights activists and social workers who are not only speaking for their rights, but who are struggling to achieve their goals of peace, education, and equality. Thousands of people have been killed by the terrorists, and millions have been injured. I am just one of them.

10   So here I stand . . . one girl among many.

11   I speak—not for myself, but for all girls and boys.

12   I raise up my voice—not so that I can shout, but so that those without a voice can be heard.

13   Those who have fought for their rights:

Their right to live in peace.
Their right to be treated with dignity.
Their right to equality of opportunity.
Their right to be educated.

14   Dear friends, on the ninth of October 2012, the Taliban shot me on the left side of my forehead. They shot my friends, too. They thought that the bullets would silence us. But they failed. And then, out of that silence came thousands of voices. The terrorists thought that they would change my aims and stop my ambitions, but nothing changed in my life except this: Weakness, fear, and hopelessness died. Strength, power, and courage were born. I am the same Malala. My ambitions are the same. My hopes are the same. My dreams are the same.

15   Dear sisters and brothers, I am not against anyone. Neither am I here to speak in terms of personal revenge against the Taliban or any other terrorist group. I am here to speak up for the right of education of every child. I want education for the sons and daughters of the Taliban and all terrorists and extremists.

16   I do not even hate the Talib[1] who shot me. Even if there is a gun in my hand and he stands in front of me, I would not shoot him. This is the compassion that I have learned from Muhammad—the prophet of mercy—Jesus Christ, and Lord Buddha. This is the legacy of change that I have inherited from Martin Luther King, Nelson Mandela, and Muhammad Ali Jinnah.[2] This is the philosophy of nonviolence that I have learned from Gandhi Jee,[3] Bacha Khan,[4] and Mother Teresa.[5] And

---

1. **Talib** member of the Taliban.
2. **Muhammad Ali Jinnah** politician who fought for a Muslim state separate from India during the early twentieth century. He became the founder of this state, now known as Pakistan.
3. **Gandhi Jee** Mohandas "Mahatma" Gandhi, a religious leader who fought for India's independence from Great Britain during the early twentieth century.
4. **Bacha Khan** twentieth century leader of the Pashtuns, an ethnic group in Afghanistan and Pakistan, and a close friend and follower of Gandhi.
5. **Mother Teresa** Catholic nun who received the Nobel Peace Prize in 1979 for her work helping poor and sick people in India.

this is the forgiveness that I have learned from my father and mother. This is what my soul is telling me: Be peaceful, and love everyone.

17   Dear sisters and brothers, we realize the importance of light when we see darkness. We realize the importance of our voice when we are silenced. In the same way, when we were in Swat, the north of Pakistan, we realized the importance of pens and books when we saw the guns.

18   The wise saying "The pen is mightier than the sword" was true. The extremists were, and they are, afraid of books and pens. The power of education frightens them. They are afraid of women. The power of the voice of women frightens them. And that is why they killed 14 innocent students in the recent attack in Quetta.[6] And that is why they killed female teachers and polio workers in Khyber Pukhtoon Khwa[7] and FATA.[8] That is why they are blasting schools every day. Because they were, and they are, afraid of change, afraid of the equality, that we will bring into our society.

19   I remember that there was a boy in our school who was asked by a journalist, "Why are the Taliban against education?" He answered very simply. By pointing to his book, he said, "A Talib doesn't know what is written inside this book." They think that God is a tiny, little conservative being who would send girls to hell just because of going to school. The terrorists are misusing the name of Islam and Pashtun society for their own personal benefits. Pakistan is a peace-loving, democratic country. Pashtuns want education for their daughters and sons. And Islam is a religion of peace, humanity, and brotherhood. Islam says that it is not only each child's right to get education; rather, it is their duty and responsibility.

20   Honorable Secretary-General, peace is necessary for education. In many parts of the world, especially Pakistan and Afghanistan, terrorism, wars, and conflicts stop children to go to their schools. We are really tired of these wars. Women and children are suffering in many ways in many parts of the world. In India, innocent and poor children are victims of child labor. Many schools have been destroyed in Nigeria. People in Afghanistan have been affected by the hurdles of extremism for decades. Young girls have to do domestic child labor and are forced to get married at early age. Poverty, ignorance, injustice, racism, and the deprivation of basic rights are the main problems faced by both men and women.

21   Dear fellows, today I am focusing on women's rights and girls' education because they are suffering the most. There was a time

---

6. **Quetta** (KWEHT uh) city in Pakistan.
7. **Khyber Pukhtoon Khwa** (KY buhr PUHK toon KWAH) northernmost province in Pakistan.
8. **FATA** *abbr.* Federally Administered Tribal Areas, a semi-independent area of Pakistan.

when women social activists asked men to stand up for their rights. But this time, we will do it by ourselves. I am not telling men to step away from speaking for women's rights; rather, I am focusing on women to be independent to fight for themselves.

22   Dear sisters and brothers, now it's time to speak up.

23   So today, we call upon the world leaders to change their strategic policies in favor of peace and prosperity.

24   We call upon the world leaders that all the peace deals must protect women and children's rights. A deal that goes against the rights of women is unacceptable.

25   We call upon all governments to ensure free compulsory education all over the world for every child.

26   We call upon all governments to fight against terrorism and violence; to protect children from brutality and harm.

27   We call upon the developed nations to support the expansion of educational opportunities for girls in the developing world.

28   We call upon all communities to be tolerant; to reject prejudice based on caste, creed, sect, color, religion, or gender; to ensure freedom and equality for women so that they can flourish. We cannot all succeed when half of us are held back.

29   We call upon our sisters around the world to be brave; to embrace the strength within themselves and realize their full potential.

30   Dear brothers and sisters, we want schools and education for every child's bright future. We will continue our journey to our destination of peace and education. No one can stop us. We will speak up for our rights, and we will bring change through our voice. We believe in the power and the strength of our words. Our words can change the whole world.

31   Because we are all together, united for the cause of education. And if we want to achieve our goal, then let us empower ourselves with the weapon of knowledge, and let us shield ourselves with unity and togetherness.

32   Dear brothers and sisters, we must not forget that millions of people are suffering from poverty, injustice, and ignorance. We must not forget that millions of children are out of schools. We must not forget that our sisters and brothers are waiting for a bright peaceful future.

33   So let us wage a global struggle against illiteracy, poverty, and terrorism. Let us pick up our books and pens. They are our most powerful weapons.

34   One child, one teacher, one book, and one pen can change the world.

35   Education is the only solution. Education First.

36   Thank you. ❧

Comprehension Check

Complete the following items after you finish your first read. Review and clarify details with your group.

1. According to Yousafzai, whom does Malala Day honor?

2. What does Yousafzai believe the terrorists hope to accomplish through violence?

3. Cite three people Yousafzai names as role models.

4. According to Yousafzai, what basic condition is necessary for education?

5. 📓 **Notebook** Confirm your understanding of the speech by stating at least two actions Yousafzai urges world leaders to take.

- -

RESEARCH

Research to Clarify Choose at least one unfamiliar detail from the text. Briefly research that detail. In what way does the information you learned shed light on an aspect of the speech?

Research to Explore Choose something that interested you from the text, and formulate a research question.

Close Read the Text

With your group, revisit sections of the text you marked during your first read. **Annotate** what you notice. What **questions** do you have? What can you **conclude**?

ANNOTATE · QUESTION · CONCLUDE
Close Read

Analyze the Text

CITE TEXTUAL EVIDENCE
to support your answers.

📓 **Notebook** Complete the activities.

1. **Review and Clarify** With your group, reread paragraph 15 of the speech. Why do you think Yousafzai wants the sons and daughters of extremists to receive an education? Why might their education be particularly important? What does this idea suggest about the importance of education?

2. **Present and Discuss** Now, work with your group to share the passages from the text that you found especially important. Take turns presenting your passages. Discuss what you notice in the text, what questions you asked, and what conclusions you reached.

3. **Essential Question:** *What is the relationship between power and freedom?* What has this speech taught you about power and freedom? Discuss with your group.

Concept Vocabulary

beneficent	envoy	initiative

Why These Words? The three concept vocabulary words are related. With your group, determine what the words have in common. Write your ideas, and add another word that fits the category.

Practice

With your group, conduct an informal discussion on an issue of your choice. During the conversation, challenge yourselves to include the concept vocabulary as normally as possible. Be sure you are using the words correctly.

Word Study

Latin Prefix: *bene-* The concept vocabulary word *beneficent* includes the Latin prefix *bene-*, meaning "well." Reread paragraph 19 of Yousafzai's speech. Mark the word that contains the prefix *bene-*, and write the word's meaning. With your group, identify other words that contain this prefix, and discuss their meanings.

🔗 WORD NETWORK

Add words related to power and freedom from the text to your Word Network.

▤ STANDARDS
Language
Identify and correctly use patterns of word changes that indicate different meanings or parts of speech.

SPEECH AT THE UNITED NATIONS

Analyze Craft and Structure

Author's Purpose: Rhetorical Devices An **author's purpose** is his or her reason for speaking or writing. General purposes are *to inform, to entertain,* and *to persuade.* Speakers also have specific purposes that vary with the topic and audience. Most speeches delivered in the public arena, including this one by Yousafzai, are primarily persuasive. They may also provide information or entertain, but the speaker's main agenda is to convince listeners to think or do something specific. In order to advance that purpose, persuasive speakers employ a variety of different types of **evidence,** or supporting content. In this speech, Yousafzai uses anecdotes, proverbs, and examples.

- **Anecdote:** a brief story that illustrates a point
- **Proverb:** a pithy, clever saying that offers wisdom about life or communicates a belief or value
- **Example: a** specific instance of a general issue or idea

Speakers include different types of evidence to achieve particular effects. They may clarify a point, add emotional intensity, or serve another function.

Practice

CITE TEXTUAL EVIDENCE
to support your answers.

Work independently to complete the chart. Identify at least one example from Yousafzai's speech of each type of evidence noted. Explain how each example develops her key ideas, adds emotional intensity, or has another effect. Then, share and discuss your responses with your group.

TYPE OF EVIDENCE	PASSAGE(S) FROM THE SPEECH	EFFECT
Anecdote		
Proverb		
Example		

Conventions

Types of Clauses Writers and speakers, such as Yousafzai, use various types of clauses to clarify the relationships among ideas and to add variety to sentences. An **adverbial clause** is a type of clause that begins with a subordinating conjunction and functions as an adverb in a sentence. It tells *when*, *where*, *why*, *to what extent*, *in what way*, or *under what condition*. This box shows twenty common **subordinating conjunctions** that may begin adverbial clauses.

after	because	so that	when
although	before	than	whenever
as	even though	though	where
as if	if	unless	wherever
as long as	since	until	while

These sentences from Yousafzai's speech at the United Nations show examples of adverbial clauses and their functions.

SENTENCE	FUNCTION
I raise up my voice . . . <u>so that</u> <u>those without a voice can be heard</u>. (paragraph 12)	tells *why* she is raising up her voice
Dear sisters and brothers, we realize the importance of light <u>when we see darkness</u>. (paragraph 17)	tells *when* or *under what condition* we realize the importance of light

Read It

Working individually, read each of these sentences from Yousafzai's speech at the United Nations. Mark the adverbial clause in each sentence, identify the subordinating conjunction, and describe the clause's function in the sentence. Discuss your answers with your group.

1. In the same way, when we were in Swat, the north of Pakistan, we realized the importance of pens and books. . . .

2. Dear fellows, today I am focusing on women's rights and girls' education because they are suffering the most.

3. And if we want to achieve our goal, then let us empower ourselves with the weapon of knowledge. . . .

Write It

Notebook Using what you've learned from Yousafzai's speech, write a paragraph that explains when a person should speak up for his or her rights and why doing so is important. Use at least three adverbial clauses in your paragraph.

TIP

CLARIFICATION
Recall that a **subordinate clause** is a group of words that includes a subject and a verb but cannot stand on its own as a complete sentence. Refer to the Grammar Handbook to learn more about this and other terms.

EVIDENCE LOG

Before moving on to a new selection, go to your Evidence Log and record what you learned from "Speech at the United Nations."

STANDARDS
Language
Use various types of phrases and clauses to convey specific meanings and add variety and interest to writing or presentations.

Comparing Text to Media

In this part of the lesson, you will view Diane Sawyer's interview with Malala Yousafzai. As you watch the interview, think back to Yousafzai's United Nations speech. Consider ways in which the two texts connect with one another.

DIANE SAWYER INTERVIEWS MALALA YOUSAFZAI

About the Journalist

Diane Sawyer (b. 1945) began her career as a TV journalist on a local station in Kentucky. From there, Sawyer went on to the Nixon White House where she worked in the press office. In 1984, she joined CBS News and became the first woman correspondent for the highly acclaimed *60 Minutes*. Since then, Sawyer has assumed lead roles in a number of high-profile newscasts and special reports. Sawyer conducted her interview of Malala Yousafzai as the anchor for *ABC WorldNews*.

Diane Sawyer Interviews Malala Yousafzai

Media Vocabulary

The following words or concepts will be useful to you as you analyze, discuss, and write about newscasts.

Lead-In: in a newscast, the short preliminary section that is used to set up the main story or interview	• The purpose of the lead-in is to spark interest in the story that follows. • The lead-in usually provides important background information.
Close-Up Shot: close-range view of the subject	• Close-ups typically focus on a single face. • Close-ups are often used to show increasing emotion. • Close-ups may also focus on objects, such as the fine print on a sign.
Slant: attitude or opinion that a reporter takes toward a story	• A slant can be positive or negative, objective or subjective, critical or noncritical. • Typical slants a reporter may take: an analytical slant, a humorous slant, a skeptical slant.

First Review MEDIA: VIDEO

Apply these strategies as you conduct your first review. You will have an opportunity to complete a close review after your first review.

WATCH who speaks, *what* they say, and *how* they say it.

NOTE elements that you find interesting and want to revisit.

First Review

CONNECT ideas in the video to other media you've experienced, texts you've read, or images you've seen.

RESPOND by completing the Comprehension Check and by writing a brief summary of the selection.

▦ STANDARDS

Reading Informational Text
By the end of grade 10, read and comprehend literary nonfiction at the high end of the grades 9–10 text complexity band independently and proficiently.

Language
Acquire and use accurately general academic and domain-specific words and phrases, sufficient for reading, writing, speaking, and listening at the college and career readiness level; demonstrate independence in gathering vocabulary knowledge when considering a word or phrase important to comprehension or expression.

Diane Sawyer Interviews
Malala Yousafzai

ABC News

BACKGROUND

After the United States invaded Afghanistan in 2001, the country of Pakistan allied itself with the United States in the battle against terrorism. The Pakistani government had denounced the Taliban, a terrorist group operating both within Pakistan and elsewhere. However, the Taliban continued to maintain control of a few Pakistani regions and provinces, including Malala Yousafzai's home of Swat Province. There, they imposed a strict interpretation of religious ideology, fought the Pakistani army, and planned attacks against Western nations.

SCAN FOR
MULTIMEDIA

NOTES

Comprehension Check

Complete the following items after you finish your first review. Review and clarify details with your group.

1. What publication coincides with the airing of this interview?

2. As a young child, how did Yousafzai begin to publicize her ideas for a larger audience?

3. According to Yousafzai, what is more powerful than guns?

4. Before her attack, how did Yousafzai imagine she might speak to an attacker?

5. 📝 **Notebook** Confirm your understanding of the interview by writing a summary of it.

- -

RESEARCH

Research to Clarify Choose at least one unfamiliar detail from the interview. Briefly research that detail. In what way does the information you learned shed light on an aspect of Yousafzai's story?

Research to Explore Choose something that interested you from the interview, and formulate a research question.

Close Review

Watch the interview again. Write any new observations that seem important. What **questions** do you have? What can you **conclude**?

DIANE SAWYER INTERVIEWS
MALALA YOUSAFZAI

Analyze the Media

Complete the activities.

1. **Present and Discuss** Identify the comment from Yousafzai you found most powerful. Share your choice with your group, and explain why you chose it. Explain why you found the comment powerful, and share any questions it raised for you. Discuss the conclusions you reached about it.

2. **Review and Synthesize** With your group, listen again to the retelling of Yousafzai's shooting. Note details Yousafzai provides, as well as those Diane Sawyer adds. How would you describe Yousafzai's character, based on her actions that day? Discuss.

3. 🗐 **Notebook Essential Question:** *What is the relationship between power and freedom?* What does Yousafzai's experience suggest about an individual's power to secure freedom for herself and others? Support your response with evidence from the interview.

Media Vocabulary

lead-in	close-up	slant

Use the vocabulary words in your responses to the questions.

1. How does the introduction to the interview engage viewers' attention?

2. What camera techniques help viewers understand the mood on the day of Yousafzai's shooting? Explain.

3. How would you describe Sawyer's approach to the interview? Explain.

⛓ WORD NETWORK

Add words related to power and freedom from the text to your Word Network.

≣ STANDARDS

Reading Informational Text
Cite strong and thorough textual evidence to support analysis of what the text says explicitly as well as inferences drawn from the text.

Language
Acquire and use accurately general academic and domain-specific words and phrases, sufficient for reading, writing, speaking, and listening at the college and career readiness level; demonstrate independence in gathering vocabulary knowledge when considering a word or phrase important to comprehension or expression.

SPEECH AT THE UNITED NATIONS

DIANE SAWYER INTERVIEWS
MALALA YOUSAFZAI

Writing to Compare

You have read Malala Yousafzai's speech at the United Nations and watched her interview with Diane Sawyer. Both texts recount the young woman's experience and convey her undaunted passion for education.

Assignment

Write an **explanatory essay** in which you discuss why Yousafzai has been able to attract supporters from all over the world. What makes her message and her story so compelling? Consider which details are emphasized in the speech and the interview, as well as the effect these details have on your understanding of Yousafzai, her experience, and her activism. Cite evidence from both texts in your essay.

Planning and Prewriting

Analyze the Texts Reread the speech, and—with your group—watch the interview again. Look for mirror details, or those that are very similar in the speech and the interview. Consider how these details are presented in the two texts. Also, look for details that appear in only one text or the other. Collect your observations in the chart.

BOTH TEXTS	JUST THE INTERVIEW	JUST THE SPEECH

📓 **Notebook** Answer these questions.

1. How do both texts depict Yousafzai's character, the conditions under which she lived in Pakistan, and her development as an activist?

2. **(a)** Which facts or other information appear in both the speech and the interview but are presented differently? **(b)** How do you account for those differences? Consider the medium of each text—one a written text, and one a work of broadcast journalism.

≣ STANDARDS

Reading Informational Text
Analyze various accounts of a subject told in different mediums, determining which details are emphasized in each account.

Writing
• Write informative/explanatory texts to examine and convey complex ideas, concepts, and information clearly and accurately through the effective selection, organization, and analysis of content.
• Apply *grades 9–10 Reading standards* to literary nonfiction.

Drafting

Write a Thesis Work on your own to plan and write your essay. First, review the notes you took with your group. Organize observations into logical categories. For example, you might group one set of details related to facts, another set related to emotional impact, and another set related to the way information can be presented in a written text versus a broadcast. Then, use the sentence starter to write a working thesis.

> **Working Thesis:** As both her speech at the United Nations and her interview with Diane Sawyer demonstrate, Malala Yousafzai is a compelling figure because _____
> _____
> _____.

Provide Varied Details Include supporting evidence for every point you make. Try to use different types of evidence to make your essay more interesting.

- **Exact quotations** can illustrate a speaker's attitude.
- **Examples** can help readers visualize a reporter's actions or an interviewee's responses.
- **Paraphrases,** or restatements using your own words, can help clarify others' ideas.

Establish a Structure Follow this guide to plan the order in which you will present your ideas and evidence.

Introduction	Body	Conclusion
• Grab readers' attention • Briefly summarize Yousafzai's story • State thesis	• Present supporting ideas • Use a new paragraph for each idea • Use supporting details	• End in a strong, memorable way • Restate thesis

Review, Revise, and Edit

Share your writing with your group, and review one another's work. Ask for feedback about the clarity of your organization and the strength of your supporting details. Use the feedback to improve any elements that are unclear or ineffective. Then, check your essay for spelling or grammatical errors, and make any necessary fixes.

EVIDENCE LOG

Before moving on to a new selection, go to the Evidence Log and record what you've learned from Malala Yousafzai's speech at the United Nations and "Diane Sawyer Interviews Malala Yousafzai."

POETRY COLLECTION

Caged Bird
Some Advice to Those Who Will Serve Time in Prison

Concept Vocabulary

As you perform your first read of these poems, you will encounter the following words.

current	trill	flurry

Context Clues If these words are unfamiliar, try using **context clues**— other words and phrases that appear nearby in the text—to help you determine their meanings. There are various types of context clues that you may find useful as you read.

> **Synonyms:** Sadly, Tim concluded that his laptop computer was **obsolete**, rendered <u>outdated</u> by new advances in technology.
>
> **Restatement of Ideas:** Sara's facial expression was **enigmatic**, so <u>no one could tell for sure what she was thinking</u>.
>
> **Contrast of Ideas:** <u>Though</u> usually quite **prudent**, they <u>threw caution to the wind</u> and jumped into the pounding surf.

Apply your knowledge of context clues and other vocabulary strategies to determine the meanings of unfamiliar words you encounter during your first read.

First Read POETRY

Apply these strategies as you conduct your first read. You will have an opportunity to complete a close read after your first read.

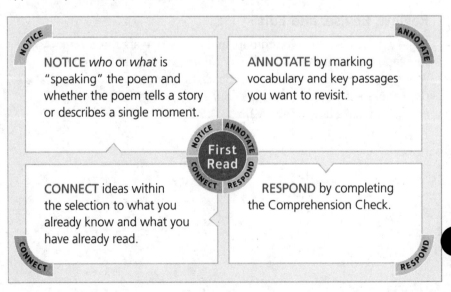

NOTICE *who* or *what* is "speaking" the poem and whether the poem tells a story or describes a single moment.

ANNOTATE by marking vocabulary and key passages you want to revisit.

CONNECT ideas within the selection to what you already know and what you have already read.

RESPOND by completing the Comprehension Check.

STANDARDS

Reading Literature
• By the end of grade 10, read and comprehend literature, including stories, dramas, and poems, at the high end of the grades 9–10 text complexity band independently and proficiently.

Language
• Determine or clarify the meaning of unknown and multiple-meaning words and phrases based on *grades 9–10 reading and content*, choosing flexibly from a range of strategies.
• Use context as a clue to the meaning of a word or phrase.

About the Poets

Maya Angelou (1928–2014) was born in St. Louis, Missouri, and raised in a rural, segregated section of Arkansas. Growing up, she faced racial discrimination, but she also learned strong values. As a single mother, she worked a wide array of jobs to support her family before discovering her talent as a writer. Angelou raised her voice during the Civil Rights movement, speaking out for racial and gender equality. She received numerous awards for her work, including more than fifty honorary doctorates and the 2011 Presidential Medal of Freedom.

Nazim Hikmet (1902–1963) was raised in Istanbul, Turkey, but attended university in Moscow, Russia. He returned to Turkey after completing his studies and was jailed by the anti-Communist government, which objected to Hikmet's writing in support of leftist causes. Although Hikmet resisted, the regime's harshness forced him to eventually leave Turkey forever. Hikmet's writing was censored during his lifetime, but his poetry and other writings became widely available after his death. Today, Hikmet is regarded as one of the greatest international poets of the twentieth century.

Backgrounds

Caged Bird

This poem joins a number of others by important African American poets in which a caged or injured bird is a central image. For example, in Paul Laurence Dunbar's poem "Sympathy," the speaker says, "I know what the caged bird feels," and "I know why the caged bird sings." Likewise, in Langston Hughes's poem "Dreams," life becomes a "broken-winged bird / that cannot fly."

Some Advice to Those Who Will Serve Time in Prison

This poem is informed by Nazim Hikmet's personal experiences. Repeatedly arrested for his political beliefs and writings, Hikmet spent most of his life either in prison or in exile from Turkey, his home country.

Caged Bird

Maya Angelou

A free bird leaps
on the back of the wind
and floats downstream
till the **current** ends
5 and dips his wing
in the orange sun rays
and dares to claim the sky.

But a bird that stalks
down his narrow cage
10 can seldom see through
his bars of rage
his wings are clipped and
his feet are tied
so he opens his throat to sing.

15 The caged bird sings
with a fearful **trill**
of things unknown
but longed for still
and his tune is heard
20 on the distant hill
for the caged bird
sings of freedom.

The free bird thinks of another breeze
and the trade winds soft through the sighing trees
25 and the fat worms waiting on a dawn bright lawn
and he names the sky his own

But a caged bird stands on the grave of dreams
his shadow shouts on a nightmare scream
his wings are clipped and his feet are tied
30 so he opens his throat to sing.

The caged bird sings
with a fearful trill
of things unknown
but longed for still
35 and his tune is heard
on the distant hill
for the caged bird
sings of freedom.

NOTES

Mark context clues or indicate another strategy you used that helped you determine meaning.

current (KUR uhnt) *n.*
MEANING:

trill (trihl) *n.*
MEANING:

Some Advice
to Those Who Will
Serve Time in Prison

Nazim Hikmet

translated by
Randy Blasing and Mutlu Konuk

SCAN FOR
MULTIMEDIA

NOTES

If instead of being hanged by the neck
    you're thrown inside
    for not giving up hope
in the world, your country, and people,
5   if you do ten or fifteen years
    apart from the time you have left,
you won't say,
        "Better I had swung from the end of a rope
            like a flag"—

10 you'll put your foot down and live.
It may not be a pleasure exactly,
but it's your solemn duty
　　to live one more day
　　　　to spite the enemy.
15 Part of you may live alone inside,
　　　　like a stone at the bottom of a well.
But the other part
　　must be so caught up
　　in the **flurry** of the world
20 　　　that you shiver there inside
　when outside, at forty days' distance, a leaf moves.
To wait for letters inside,
to sing sad songs,
or to lie awake all night staring at the ceiling
25 　　　　　is sweet but dangerous.
Look at your face from shave to shave,
forget your age,
watch out for lice
　　　　and for spring nights,
30 　　and always remember
　　　　to eat every last piece of bread—
also, don't forget to laugh heartily.
And who knows,
the woman you love may stop loving you.
35 Don't say it's no big thing:
it's like the snapping of a green branch
　　　　　　　to the man inside.

To think of roses and gardens inside is bad,
to think of seas and mountains is good.
40 Read and write without rest,
and I also advise weaving
and making mirrors.
I mean, it's not that you can't pass
　　ten or fifteen years inside
45 　　　　　and more—
　　you can,
　　as long as the jewel
　　on the left side of your chest doesn't lose its luster!

Comprehension Check

Complete the following items after you finish your first read. Review and clarify details with your group.

CAGED BIRD

1. According to the speaker, what are three things the free bird does?

2. What has been done to the caged bird's wings and feet?

3. What is the subject of the caged bird's song?

4. How does the free bird regard the sky?

5. Where is the caged bird's song heard?

1. According to the speaker, for what reasons might someone be imprisoned, or "thrown inside"?

2. According to the speaker, what is the prisoner's "solemn duty"?

3. How does the speaker say the prisoner should be affected by the movement of a leaf at forty days' distance?

4. According to the speaker, what kinds of scenes are "bad" and what kinds are "good" for prisoners to imagine?

5. According to the speaker, of what must the prisoner make sure in order to "pass ten or fifteen years inside"?

RESEARCH

Research to Clarify Choose at least one unfamiliar detail from one of the poems. Briefly research that detail. In what way does the information you learned shed light on an aspect of the poem?

Research to Explore Locate another poem by one of the poets, or research his or her life in greater detail. Share what you find with your group.

Close Read the Text

With your group, revisit sections of the poems you marked during your first read. **Annotate** details that you notice. What **questions** do you have? What can you **conclude**?

Analyze the Text

CITE TEXTUAL EVIDENCE
to support your answers.

 Notebook Complete the activities.

1. **Review and Clarify** Reread the second stanza of "Caged Bird." What feelings does the caged bird experience? What does this suggest about the song the caged bird sings?

2. **Present and Discuss** Now, work with your group to share the passages from the texts that you found especially important. Take turns presenting your passages. Discuss what you noticed in the texts, what questions you asked, and what conclusions you reached.

3. **Essential Question:** *What is the relationship between power and freedom?* What have these poems taught you about the connection between power and freedom? Discuss with your group.

TIP

GROUP DISCUSSION
There are many different kinds of cages or prisons—physical ones, emotional ones, intellectual ones. As you discuss the poems with your group, consider whether their meanings change when you view them in the context of various types of cages or prisons.

WORD NETWORK

Add words related to power and freedom from the texts to your Word Network.

STANDARDS

Reading Literature
• Cite strong and thorough textual evidence to support analysis of what the text says explicitly as well as inferences drawn from the text.

• Determine the meaning of words and phrases as they are used in the text, including figurative and connotative meanings; analyze the cumulative impact of specific word choices on meaning and tone.

• Analyze a particular point of view or cultural experience reflected in a work of literature from outside the United States, drawing on a wide reading of world literature.

Language
Determine or clarify the meaning of unknown and multiple-meaning words and phrases based on *grades 9–10 reading and content*, choosing flexibly from a range of strategies.

LANGUAGE DEVELOPMENT

Concept Vocabulary

current	trill	flurry

Why These Words? The three concept vocabulary words are related. With your group, determine what the words have in common. Write your ideas, and add another word that fits the category.

Practice

 Notebook Confirm your understanding of the concept words by using them in sentences. Include context clues that hint at each word's meaning.

Word Study

 Notebook Multiple-Meaning Words Many English words have multiple meanings, or more than one distinct definition. For instance, the concept vocabulary word *current* can be a noun, as it is in "Caged Bird," but it can also be an adjective meaning "up-to-date."

Identify two meanings for each of the following words: *grave, well, weaving, care, chain.* First, determine the word's meaning in either "Caged Bird" or "Some Advice to Those Who Will Serve Time in Prison." Then, determine another meaning of the word, consulting a dictionary as needed. Record both meanings for each word.

Analyze Craft and Structure

Author's Choices: Figurative Language Language that is used imaginatively rather than literally is referred to as **figurative language**. Poets rely on figurative language because it helps them express ideas in vivid ways and invest even small details with meaning. Simile, metaphor, and extended metaphor are three commonly used types of figurative language.

- A **simile** is a direct comparison, using the words *like* or *as,* that shows similarities between two seemingly unlike things: "life is too much like a pathless wood" (from "Birches," by Robert Frost).

- A **metaphor** is a comparison of two seemingly unlike things that does not use an explicit comparison word: "The sun and the moon are eternal voyagers" (from "Narrow Road of the Interior," by Bashō).

- An **extended metaphor** involves a metaphorical comparison that does not end after a single line or image, but continues for several lines or throughout an entire work.

Practice

CITE TEXTUAL EVIDENCE to support your answers.

1. Working individually, use this chart to identify and analyze three similes and one metaphor that appear in Nazim Hikmet's poem. Compare and discuss your responses with your group.

EXAMPLE	THINGS COMPARED	MEANING AND EFFECT
Simile:		
Simile:		
Simile:		
Metaphor:		

2. **Notebook** Explain how Maya Angelou's "Caged Bird" can be read as an extended metaphor. What implied comparison is the poet making between the free bird, the caged bird, and people or ideas in the real world?

Author's Style

Specific Details An **image** is a word or phrase that appeals to one or more of the senses—sight, hearing, touch, taste, or smell. We often refer to multiple images or patterns of images as **imagery**. Poets use images to create word pictures in readers' minds. Imagery enriches meaning, suggests emotions, and adds vividness to a text.

> **Image appealing to taste and touch:** "sweet, slippery mango slices"
> **Image appealing to sight and hearing:** "glaring lights and wailing sirens"

Read It

Work individually. Use this chart to identify images in each poem. Then, explain how each image helps create meaning. Discuss your responses with your group.

CAGED BIRD	SOME ADVICE TO THOSE WHO WILL SERVE TIME IN PRISON
Images:	Images:
Meaning:	Meaning:

Write It

🗒 **Notebook** Write a paragraph that includes at least three images.

STANDARDS

Reading Literature
Determine the meaning of words and phrases as they are used in the text, including figurative and connotative meanings; analyze the cumulative impact of specific word choices on meaning and tone.

Writing
• Write narratives to develop real or imagined experiences or events using effective techniques, well-chosen details, and well-structured event sequences.
• Use precise words and phrases, telling details, and sensory language to convey a vivid picture of the experiences, events, setting, and/or characters.

Writing to Sources

Assignment

Working individually, write an original **poem** based on one of the poems in this collection. Choose from the following prompts:

- [ ] Using "Caged Bird" as a model, write a poem on the theme of freedom/imprisonment that develops a different extended metaphor.

- [ ] Imagine that the speaker of "Some Advice to Those Who Will Serve Time in Prison" is set free after many years of unjust imprisonment. Using the poem as a model, write another poem of advice from the speaker's point of view about a first day of freedom.

- [ ] Choose an image in one of the poems that you thought was particularly powerful. Use this image as a starting point for your own poem about freedom, imprisonment, or both.

Project Plan As a group, decide whether you will all work on the same prompt or will each choose the one you prefer. Then, work together to help one another brainstorm for ideas or clarify your thoughts.

Identifying Models As you plan your poem, go back to the poem you chose as inspiration, and identify elements you like or find effective. For example, notice how the poet uses repetition or rhyme, and think about how you can incorporate those elements into your work. Use this chart to record examples of elements you would like to use and how you might do so.

EVIDENCE LOG

Before moving on to a new selection, go to your Evidence Log and record what you learned from "Caged Bird" and "Some Advice to Those Who Will Serve Time in Prison."

ELEMENT TO INCLUDE IN POEM	EXAMPLE FROM TEXT	NOTES

About the Author

Luisa Valenzuela (b. 1938) was born in Buenos Aires, Argentina. She first pursued a career as a painter, but she soon discovered her true calling as a writer. Like many contemporary Latin American writers, Valenzuela takes an experimental approach to literary style and language. She believes that writers derive their power and influence from the way they use and define words. Influenced by the political turmoil in Argentina, Valenzuela examines the repression of speech and identity in much of her fiction.

The Censors

Concept Vocabulary

As you perform your first read of "The Censors," you will encounter the following words.

sabotage	intercept	subversive

Context Clues If these words are unfamiliar, try using **context clues**— other words and phrases that appear nearby in the text—to help you determine their meanings. There are various types of context clues that you may find useful as you read.

Synonyms: The newspaper editor **incited** the rebellion, stirring up the government's opponents.

Restatement of Ideas: Periodically, Sam grew **nostalgic**, as he yearned to see his homeland once more.

Contrast of Ideas: Abandoning her customary **nonchalance**, Sofia felt anxious and tense that afternoon.

Apply your knowledge of context clues and other vocabulary strategies to determine the meanings of unfamiliar words you encounter during your first read. Use a resource such as a dictionary or a thesaurus to verify the meanings you identify.

First Read FICTION

Apply these strategies as you conduct your first read. You will have an opportunity to complete a close read after your first read.

NOTICE *whom* the story is about, *what* happens, *where* and *when* it happens, and *why* those involved react as they do.

ANNOTATE by marking vocabulary and key passages you want to revisit.

First Read

CONNECT ideas within the selection to what you know and what you have already read.

RESPOND by completing the Comprehension Check and by writing a brief summary of the selection.

☷ STANDARDS

Reading Literature
By the end of grade 10, read and comprehend literature, including stories, dramas, and poems, at the high end of the grades 9–10 text complexity band independently and proficiently.

Language
• Use context as a clue to the meaning of a word or phrase.
• Verify the preliminary determination of the meaning of a word or phrase.

The Censors

Luisa Valenzuela
translated by David Unger

BACKGROUND

Like many other Latin American writers, Luisa Valenzuela often addresses political issues in her fiction. Her native country, Argentina, now a democracy, has had a troubled history of censorship and extreme human-rights violations. In the 1970s, a military regime took power, brutally hunted down suspected political foes, and censored news and mail. In "The Censors," Valenzuela explores the absurd aspects of life under such oppression.

SCAN FOR
MULTIMEDIA

NOTES

1   Poor Juan! One day they caught him with his guard down before he could even realize that what he had taken as a stroke of luck was really one of fate's dirty tricks. These things happen the minute you're careless, as one often is. Juancito let happiness—a feeling you can't trust—get the better of him when he received from a confidential source Mariana's new address in Paris and knew that she hadn't forgotten him. Without thinking twice, he sat down at his table and wrote her a letter. *The* letter that now keeps his mind off his job during the day and won't let him sleep at night (what had he scrawled, what had he put on that sheet of paper he sent to Mariana?).

2   Juan knows there won't be a problem with the letter's contents, that it's irreproachable, harmless. But what about the rest? He knows that they examine, sniff, feel, and read between the lines of each and every letter, and check its tiniest comma and most accidental stain. He knows that all letters pass from hand to hand and go through all sorts of tests in the huge censorship offices and that, in the end, very few continue on their way. Usually it takes months, even years, if there aren't any snags; all this time the freedom, maybe even the life, of both sender and receiver is in jeopardy. And that's why Juan's so troubled: thinking that something might happen to Mariana because of his letters. Of all people, Mariana, who must finally feel safe there where she always dreamt she'd live. But he knows that the *Censor's Secret Command* operates all over the world and cashes in on the discount in airfares; there's nothing to stop them from going as far as

that hidden Paris neighborhood, kidnapping Mariana, and returning to their cozy homes, certain of having fulfilled their noble mission.

3 Well, you've got to beat them to the punch, do what everyone tries to do: **sabotage** the machinery, throw sand in its gears, get to the bottom of the problem so as to stop it.

4 This was Juan's sound plan when he, like many others, applied for a censor's job—not because he had a calling or needed a job: no, he applied simply to **intercept** his own letter, a consoling albeit unoriginal idea. He was hired immediately, for each day more and more censors are needed and no one would bother to check on his references.

5 Ulterior motives couldn't be overlooked by the *Censorship Division*, but they needn't be too strict with those who applied. They knew how hard it would be for the poor guys to find the letter they wanted and even if they did, what's a letter or two when the new censor would snap up so many others? That's how Juan managed to join the *Post Office's Censorship Division*, with a certain goal in mind.

6 The building had a festive air on the outside that contrasted with its inner staidness. Little by little, Juan was absorbed by his job, and he felt at peace since he was doing everything he could to get his letter for Mariana. He didn't even worry when, in his first month, he was sent to *Section K* where envelopes are very carefully screened for explosives.

7 It's true that on the third day, a fellow worker had his right hand blown off by a letter, but the division chief claimed it was sheer negligence on the victim's part. Juan and the other employees were allowed to go back to their work, though feeling less secure. After work, one of them tried to organize a strike to demand higher wages for unhealthy work, but Juan didn't join in; after thinking it over, he reported the man to his superiors and thus got promoted.

8 You don't form a habit by doing something once, he told himself as he left his boss's office. And when he was transferred to *Section F*, where letters are carefully checked for poison dust, he felt he had climbed a rung in the ladder.

9 By working hard, he quickly reached *Section E* where the job became more interesting, for he could now read and analyze the letters' contents. Here he could even hope to get hold of his letter, which, judging by the time that had elapsed, had gone through the other sections and was probably floating around in this one.

10 Soon his work became so absorbing that his noble mission blurred in his mind. Day after day he crossed out whole paragraphs in red ink, pitilessly chucking many letters into the censored basket. These were horrible days when he was shocked by the subtle and conniving ways employed by people to pass on **subversive** messages; his instincts were so sharp that he found behind a simple "the weather's unsettled" or "prices continue to soar" the wavering hand of someone secretly scheming to overthrow the Government.

11 His zeal brought him swift promotion. We don't know if this made him happy. Very few letters reached him in *Section B*—only a handful passed the other hurdles—so he read them over and over again,

passed them under a magnifying glass, searched for microprint with an electronic microscope, and tuned his sense of smell so that he was beat by the time he made it home. He'd barely manage to warm up his soup, eat some fruit, and fall into bed, satisfied with having done his duty. Only his darling mother worried, but she couldn't get him back on the right track. She'd say, though it wasn't always true: Lola called, she's at the bar with the girls, they miss you, they're waiting for you. Or else she'd leave a bottle of red wine on the table. But Juan wouldn't overdo it: any distraction could make him lose his edge and the perfect censor had to be alert, keen, attentive, and sharp to nab cheats. He had a truly patriotic task, both self-denying and uplifting.

12   His basket for censored letters became the best fed as well as the most cunning basket in the whole *Censorship Division*. He was about to congratulate himself for having finally discovered his true mission, when his letter to Mariana reached his hands. Naturally, he censored it without regret. And just as naturally, he couldn't stop them from executing him the following morning, another victim of his devotion to his work. 🐾

Comprehension Check

Complete the following items after you finish your first read. Review and clarify details with your group.

1. Why does Juan take a job as a censor?

2. Why is the Censorship Division not particularly careful about whom it hires?

3. What is the result of Juan's enthusiasm on the job?

4. What does Juan do when he finds his letter to Mariana?

5. 🗐 **Notebook** Confirm your understanding of the story by writing a summary.

- -

RESEARCH

Research to Clarify Choose at least one unfamiliar detail from the text. Briefly research that detail. In what way does the information you learned shed light on an aspect of the story?

THE CENSORS

Close Read the Text

With your group, revisit sections of the text you marked during your first read. **Annotate** what you notice. What **questions** do you have? What can you **conclude**?

Close Read

Analyze the Text

CITE TEXTUAL EVIDENCE
to support your answers.

Notebook Complete the activities.

1. **Review and Clarify** Reread the first two paragraphs of "The Censors" carefully. What emotion leads Juan to write and send Mariana a letter? How does he feel after he has sent the letter? Why do his feelings change? What does this communicate about the society in which he lives?

2. **Present and Discuss** Now, work with your group to share the passages from the text that you found especially important. Take turns presenting your passages. Discuss what you notice in the text, what questions you asked, and what conclusions you reached.

3. **Essential Question:** *What is the relationship between power and freedom?* What has this story taught you about the nature of freedom and power in an oppressive society? Discuss with your group.

LANGUAGE DEVELOPMENT

Concept Vocabulary

sabotage	intercept	subversive

Why These Words? The three concept vocabulary words are related. With your group, determine what the words have in common. Write your ideas, and add another word that fits the category.

Practice

Notebook Confirm your understanding of these words by using them in sentences. Include context clues that hint at each word's meaning.

Word Study

Notebook **Latin Prefix: sub-** The concept vocabulary word *subversive* begins with the Latin prefix *sub-*, meaning "under," "below," or "from beneath."

Use your understanding of the prefix *sub-* to determine the meaning of each of the following words: *submissive, subculture, subterranean*. After you have recorded a meaning for each word, use a dictionary to confirm or correct your definitions.

TIP

GROUP DISCUSSION
Keep in mind that the narrator plays an important role in this short story. Consider how the narration affects your understanding of the story as you analyze and discuss the text.

WORD NETWORK

Add words related to power and freedom from the text to your Word Network.

STANDARDS

Reading Literature
• Determine the meaning of words and phrases as they are used in the text, including figurative and connotative meanings; analyze the cumulative impact of specific word choices on meaning and tone.
• Analyze a particular point of view or cultural experience reflected in a work of literature from outside the United States, drawing on a wide reading of world literature.

Language
• Identify and correctly use patterns of word changes that indicate different meanings or parts of speech.
• Verify the preliminary determination of the meaning of a word or phrase.

Analyze Craft and Structure

Author's Choices: Satire A **satire** is a work that ridicules individuals, ideas, institutions, social conventions, or humanity in general. While satire may be funny, its purpose is serious—to improve society by exposing absurdity, corruption, or other social ills. Because of this serious purpose, satire is a vehicle for **social commentary,** or writing that criticizes institutions or behaviors.

Satiric writings vary in **tone,** or attitude toward the subject and reader. Some satire is bitter and cynical, whereas other satire is gentle and funny. A writer establishes tone through word choice, details, and even grammatical structures.

Practice

CITE TEXTUAL EVIDENCE
to support your answers.

Work independently to complete the following items. Then, share your responses with your group, and discuss any differences in your ideas.

1. What tone is created by the narrator's use of expressions such as "beat them to the punch" and "throw sand in its gears"? Explain.

2. Use the chart to identify three other examples of diction (or word choice) that contribute to the narrator's tone. Explain the tone each example helps create.

PASSAGE	TONE IT CREATES

3. Briefly describe the social ills that are the target of the satire in this story.

4. 📓 **Notebook** **(a)** How does the tone of this story contrast with the seriousness of its subject? Explain. **(b)** In what ways does the tone of the story add to the satire? Explain.

THE CENSORS

Author's Style

Word Choice Many satiric works use the literary devices of hyperbole and understatement to add humor. These devices also help emphasize specific qualities in the target of the satire.

- **Hyperbole** is a deliberate exaggeration or overstatement, often to emphasize emotion or to create a comic effect. For example, calling the discovery of a missing sock a "joyous reunion" is an example of hyperbole.

- **Understatement** is the opposite of hyperbole. It is the deliberate minimizing of the seriousness or gravity of an event or idea. Mark Twain is famous for this understated comment: "The reports of my death are greatly exaggerated."

Read It

Work individually. Use the chart to record examples of hyperbole and understatement in "The Censors." Then, explain how these elements help create humor and add to the satire of the story. Discuss your responses with your group.

HYPERBOLE	UNDERSTATEMENT
Examples:	Examples:
Effects:	Effects:

STANDARDS

Reading Literature
Determine the meaning of words and phrases as they are used in the text, including figurative and connotative meanings; analyze the cumulative impact of specific word choices on meaning and tone.

Speaking and Listening
Initiate and participate effectively in a range of collaborative discussions with diverse partners on *grades 9–10 topics, texts, and issues*, building on others' ideas and expressing their own clearly and persuasively.

Language
Interpret figures of speech in context and analyze their role in the text.

Write It

Notebook Write a brief, humorous invitation to an event such as a birthday party or a school dance. Include at least one example of hyperbole and one example of understatement.

Speaking and Listening

Assignment

Conduct a **small-group discussion** about one of the following topics. Then, summarize the main points of the discussion, and share your ideas with the class.

☐ How would your life be different if mail and other forms of communication—such as text messages and emails—were censored? Connect your sense of privacy to Juan's experiences in the story.

☐ How might various characters in the story describe Juan? Consider what Mariana, Juan's mother, and his coworkers at the Censorship Bureau might say about him.

☐ Discuss the evolution of Juan's work ethic and his feelings about his job at the Censorship Bureau. Why does he become so dedicated to his job?

Discussing Juan's Character If your group chooses to discuss how other characters view Juan, use the chart to record your notes.

CHARACTER	VIEW OF JUAN
Mariana	
Juan's Mother	
Juan's Coworkers	

📝 EVIDENCE LOG

Before moving on to a new selection, go to your Evidence Log and record what you learned from "The Censors."

About the Organization

Freedom House is an independent, nonprofit organization dedicated to the expansion of freedom around the world. The organization was established in 1941 in response to the Nazi threat then growing throughout Europe. In the decades following the war, Freedom House has sought to fight oppressive ideologies through the spread of democracy, the strengthening of human rights, and the expansion of civil liberties for all. The organization publishes a number of significant documents each year, including the *Freedom of the Press* report.

from Freedom of the Press Report 2015

Media Vocabulary

The following words or concepts will be useful to you as you analyze, discuss, and write about informational graphics.

Infographic: display that combines text with visual elements and design to represent data	• The word *infographic* is short for *informational graphic*. • An infographic allows the user to see trends and make comparisons at a glance.
Bar Graph: representation of data points using rectangular bars	• Bar graphs can be organized vertically or horizontally. • Bar graphs can compare two or more data points in the same segment by clustering bars of different colors.
Line Graph: representation of data points using a line that connects points	• Line graphs are especially useful for showing how data changes over time. • Line graphs can compare two (or more) sets of data with two (or more) lines.
Pie Chart: representation of data points using a circle cut into segments	• Pie charts are especially useful for showing how the size of each data point compares to the total size of all the data. • Typically, each segment is a different color.

First Read

Apply these strategies as you conduct your first read. You will have an opportunity to complete a close read after your first read.

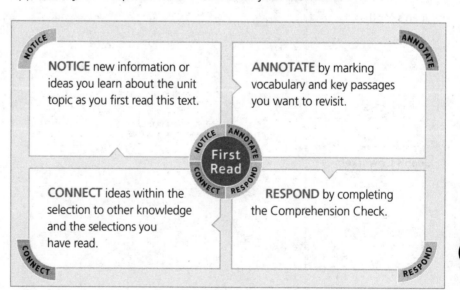

NOTICE new information or ideas you learn about the unit topic as you first read this text.

ANNOTATE by marking vocabulary and key passages you want to revisit.

CONNECT ideas within the selection to other knowledge and the selections you have read.

RESPOND by completing the Comprehension Check.

First Read

▤ STANDARDS

Reading Informational Text
By the end of grade 10, read and comprehend literary nonfiction at the high end of the grades 9–10 text complexity band independently and proficiently.

Language
Acquire and use accurately general academic and domain-specific words and phrases, sufficient for reading, writing, speaking, and listening at the college and career readiness level; demonstrate independence in gathering vocabulary knowledge when considering a word or phrase important to comprehension or expression.

from Freedom of the Press Report 2015

Freedom House

BACKGROUND

From the introduction to the *Freedom of the Press Report* 2015: "Conditions for the media deteriorated sharply in 2014 as journalists around the world faced mounting restrictions on the free flow of news and information—including grave threats to their own lives. Governments employed tactics including arrests and censorship to silence criticism. Terrorists and other nonstate forces kidnapped and murdered journalists attempting to cover armed conflicts and organized crime. . . . The share of the world's population that enjoys a free press stood at 14 percent, meaning only one in seven people live in countries where coverage of political news is robust, the safety of journalists is guaranteed, state intrusion in media affairs is minimal, and the press is not subject to onerous legal or economic pressures."

SCAN FOR MULTIMEDIA

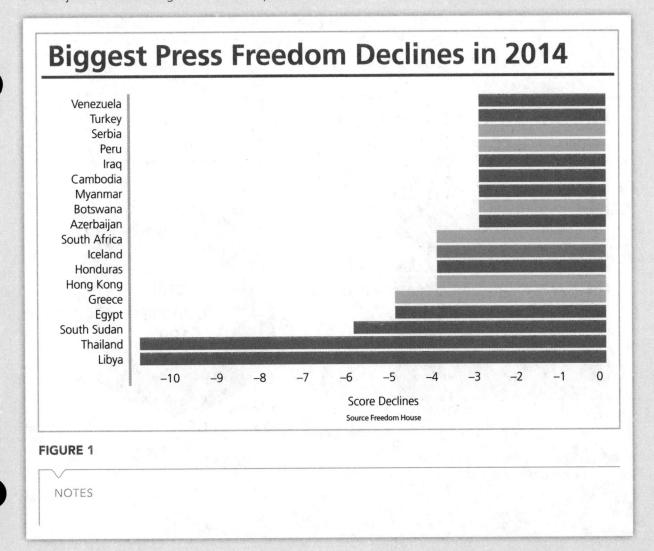

FIGURE 1

NOTES

The Global Average Press Freedom Score Has Declined Sharply Since 2004

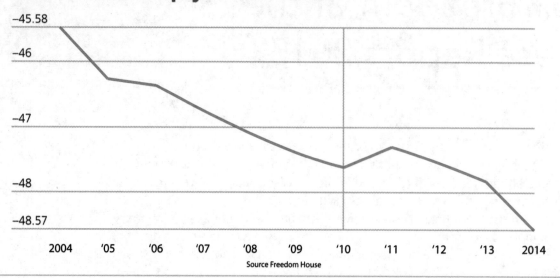

Source Freedom House

FIGURE 2

Global Status for Press Freedom

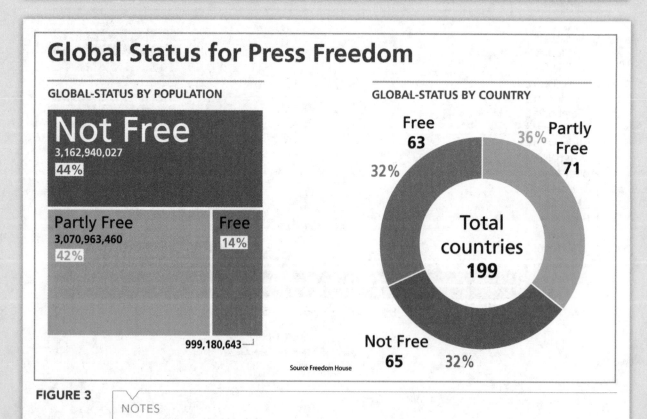

GLOBAL-STATUS BY POPULATION

Not Free
3,162,940,027
44%

Partly Free
3,070,963,460
42%

Free
14%

999,180,643

GLOBAL-STATUS BY COUNTRY

Free
63
32%

Partly
Free
71
36%

Not Free
65
32%

Total
countries
199

Source Freedom House

FIGURE 3

Comprehension Check

Complete the following items after you finish your first read. Review and clarify details with your group.

1. What two countries showed the greatest decline in press freedom in 2014?

2. What has happened to global average press freedom since 2004?

3. In which year between 2004 and 2014 did global average press freedom increase?

4. By what two different measures is press freedom measured in Figure 3?

5. Which category was greater in 2014: the number of nations with free press or the number of nations without free press?

RESEARCH

Research to Clarify Choose at least one unfamiliar detail from the infographics. Briefly research that detail. In what way does the information you learned shed light on an aspect of the infographics?

from FREEDOM OF THE
PRESS REPORT 2015

Close Read

With your group, look at the infographic again. **Annotate** details that you notice. What **questions** do you have? What can you **conclude**?

Analyze the Media

Complete the activities.

1. **Review and Clarify** With your group, review Figures 2 and 3. How is it possible that 32 percent of the countries in the world have a free press, but only 14 percent of the world's people have access to a free press? Discuss.

2. **Present and Discuss** Now, work with your group to share other important data from the infographics. Take turns presenting your data. Discuss what you noticed in the data, what questions you asked, and what conclusions you reached.

3. **Essential Question:** *What is the relationship between power and freedom?* What have the data in this infographic taught you about power and freedom? Discuss with your group.

TIP

GROUP DISCUSSION
Consider what it means for the press to truly operate freely and independently. What conditions would have to be met? Keep this in mind as you analyze and discuss the data in the graphs.

LANGUAGE DEVELOPMENT

Media Vocabulary

| infographic | bar graph | line graph | pie chart |

Use the vocabulary words in your responses to these questions.

1. In Figure 1, how does the presentation of the data enable readers to make comparisons?

2. In Figure 2, how does the type of graph help illustrate a trend in the change of global average press freedom over time?

3. In what way are the images in Figure 3 similar to pie charts?

STANDARDS

Language
Acquire and use accurately general academic and domain-specific words and phrases, sufficient for reading, writing, speaking, and listening at the college and career readiness level; demonstrate independence in gathering vocabulary knowledge when considering a word or phrase important to comprehension or expression.

Research

Assignment

Research the issue of freedom of the press in at least two countries, and then create an **infographic** that captures your findings. Your research can begin with the information provided in the informational graphics from *Freedom of the Press Report* 2015.

Use the following questions as a starting point for your research:

- Who owns or controls the major media outlets in each country? The government? Private owners?
- What are the consequences of violating a regulation or publishing unpopular information in each country?
- In each country, how free are journalists to pursue stories?
- Are foreign journalists allowed to report in each country?

Add more questions of your own as you gather information.

Plan Your Research As a group, decide which countries you will research. Then, consider how to collect the kinds of information and data you need. Use the space here to record your decisions. Then, split the work among your team members, and gather information.

Country 1: _____

Country 2: _____

Types of Information and Data: _____

_____

_____

_____

_____

Assess Your Data Meet regularly to evaluate the data you have collected, and to consider any elements that are missing or need more work. Once you have all the information and data you need, consider how best to organize it. Will one infographic be sufficient, or do you need two or more to present information clearly and effectively?

Create and Deliver the Presentation Write an introduction to your findings. Explain which countries you chose and why, as well as how you conducted your research. Also, explain how you chose to organize the data. If possible, share your presentation digitally by posting it online or using a computer and projector to display it. Alternatively, print your presentation and distribute it to the class.

🖉 EVIDENCE LOG

Before moving on to a new selection, go to your Evidence Log and record what you learned from *Freedom of the Press Report* 2015.

☰ STANDARDS

Writing
Use technology, including the internet, to produce, publish, and update individual or shared writing products, taking advantage of technology's capacity to link to other information and to display information flexibly and dynamically.

Speaking and Listening
• Work with peers to set rules for collegial discussions and decision-making, clear goals and deadlines, and individual roles as needed.
• Present information, findings, and supporting evidence clearly, concisely, and logically such that listeners can follow the line of reasoning and the organization, development, substance, and style are appropriate to purpose, audience, and task.
• Make strategic use of digital media in presentations to enhance understanding of findings, reasoning, and evidence and to add interest.

Deliver a Multimedia Presentation

Assignment

You have read many selections and watched an interview that deal with issues of power and freedom. Work with your group to develop, refine, and deliver a **multimedia presentation** that addresses this question:

> When, if ever, are limits on freedom necessary?

Plan With Your Group

Analyze the Texts With your group, discuss the purposes and messages of the selections you have read and viewed in this section. As you conduct your discussion, consider the idea that freedom offers both privileges and obligations. Talk about what those privileges and obligations might be, and how limits on freedom may or may not be necessary. Use the chart to list your ideas. Then, come to a consensus about which ideas you want to include in your presentation.

TITLE	PRIVILEGES AND OBLIGATIONS OF FREEDOM
Speech at the United Nations	
Diane Sawyer Interviews Malala Yousafzai	
Caged Bird	
Some Advice to Those Who Will Serve Time in Prison	
The Censors	
from Freedom of the Press Report 2015	

Gather Evidence and Media Examples Identify specific details from the selections that support your group's ideas. Number the details in order of relevance to your position—from most to least relevant. Use this analysis to choose the details you will include in your presentation. Then, brainstorm for types of media you can use to elaborate on each detail. Consider photographs, illustrations, charts, graphs, music, and audio and video clips. Allow each group member to make suggestions.

STANDARDS

Speaking and Listening
• Come to discussions prepared, having read and researched material under study; explicitly draw on that preparation by referring to evidence from texts and other research on the topic or issue to stimulate a thoughtful, well-reasoned exchange of ideas.
• Present information, findings, and supporting evidence clearly, concisely, and logically such that listeners can follow the line of reasoning and the organization, development, substance, and style are appropriate to purpose, audience, and task.

Organize Your Ideas Decide who will perform which task in each part of the presentation. Use a chart like the one shown to note when each section begins, and what each speaker will say. Also note where images, music, and audio and video clips will be used.

MULTIMEDIA PRESENTATION SCRIPT		
	Media Cues	Script
Presenter 1		
Presenter 2		
Presenter 3		

Rehearse With Your Group

Practice With Your Group Use this checklist to evaluate the effectiveness of your group's first run-through. Then, use your evaluation and the instruction here to guide your revision.

CONTENT	USE OF MEDIA	PRESENTATION TECHNIQUES
☐ The presentation conveys main ideas clearly.	☐ Appropriate types of media are used to convey main ideas.	☐ Media are visible and audible.
☐ Main ideas are supported with relevant evidence from the texts in Small-Group Learning.	☐ Media are distributed evenly throughout the presentation.	☐ Transitions between media segments are smooth.
	☐ Equipment functions properly.	☐ Each presenter makes eye contact and speaks at an appropriate volume and pace.

Fine-Tune the Content Strengthen your presentation by ensuring that ideas are conveyed clearly. With your group, identify any points of confusion or vagueness. Revise the content to clarify these elements, adding supporting material as needed.

Improve Your Use of Media Review all multimedia elements to ensure that they add interest and help create a cohesive presentation. If an element is not clearly related to the presentation, replace it with a more relevant item or omit it.

Brush Up on Your Presentation Techniques Practice your presentation before you deliver it to the class. During the presentation, speak clearly and with both liveliness and conviction.

Present and Evaluate

When you deliver your presentation, be sure that each member has taken into account all of the checklist items. As you listen to other groups' presentations, evaluate how well they meet the checklist requirements.

STANDARDS

Speaking and Listening
• Work with peers to set rules for collegial discussions and decision-making, clear goals and deadlines, and individual roles as needed.
• Make strategic use of digital media in presentations to enhance understanding of findings, reasoning, and evidence and to add interest.
• Adapt speech to a variety of contexts and tasks, demonstrating command of formal English when indicated or appropriate.

ESSENTIAL QUESTION:

What is the relationship between power and freedom?

The struggle for human rights around the world is an ongoing battle. In this section, you will complete your study of the literature of freedom by exploring an additional selection related to the topic. You'll then share what you learn with classmates. To choose a text, follow these steps.

Look Back Think about the selections you have already studied. What more do you want to know about the topic of power and freedom?

Look Ahead Preview the texts by reading the descriptions. Which one seems most interesting and appealing to you?

Look Inside Take a few minutes to scan the text you chose. Choose a different one if this text doesn't meet your needs.

Independent Learning Strategies

Throughout your life, in school, in your community, and in your career, you will need to rely on yourself to learn and work on your own. Review these strategies and the actions you can take to practice them during Independent Learning. Add ideas of your own for each category.

STRATEGY	ACTION PLAN
Create a schedule	• Understand your goals and deadlines. • Make a plan for what to do each day. •
Practice what you've learned	• Use first-read and close-read strategies to deepen your understanding. • After you read, evaluate the usefulness of the evidence to help you understand the topic. • Consider the quality and reliability of the source. •
Take notes	• Record important ideas and information. • Review your notes before preparing to share with a group. • •

SCAN FOR MULTIMEDIA

Choose one selection. Selections are available online only.

CONTENTS

SCAN FOR MULTIMEDIA

First-Read Guide

Use this page to record your first-read ideas.

Selection Title: _____

🔧 **Tool Kit**
First-Read Guide and
Model Annotation

NOTICE new information or ideas you learn about the unit topic as you first read this text.

NOTICE

ANNOTATE by marking vocabulary and key passages you want to revisit.

ANNOTATE

First Read

NOTICE • ANNOTATE • CONNECT • RESPOND

CONNECT ideas within the selection to other knowledge and the selections you have read.

CONNECT

RESPOND by writing a brief summary of the selection.

RESPOND

☰ STANDARD

Reading Read and comprehend complex literary and informational texts independently and proficiently.

Close-Read Guide

Use this page to record your close-read ideas.

Selection Title: _____

Close Read the Text

Revisit sections of the text you marked during your first read. Read these sections closely and **annotate** what you notice. Ask yourself **questions** about the text. What can you **conclude?** Write down your ideas.

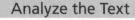

Analyze the Text

Think about the author's choices of patterns, structure, techniques, and ideas included in the text. Select one, and record your thoughts about what this choice conveys.

QuickWrite

Pick a paragraph from the text that grabbed your interest. Explain the power of this passage.

≣ STANDARD
Reading Read and comprehend complex literary and informational texts independently and proficiently.

Share Your Independent Learning

Prepare to Share

What is the relationship between power and freedom?

Even when you read or learn something independently, you can continue to grow by sharing what you have learned with others. Reflect on the text you explored independently, and write notes about its connection to the unit. In your notes, consider why this text belongs in this unit.

Learn From Your Classmates

💬 **Discuss It** Share your ideas about the text you explored on your own. As you talk with your classmates, jot down ideas that you learn from them.

Reflect

Mark the most important insight you gained from these writing and discussion activities. Explain how this idea adds to your understanding of the topics of power and freedom.

Review Evidence for an Informative Essay

At the beginning of the unit, you responded to the following question:

> What does it mean to "be free"?

✐ EVIDENCE LOG

Review your Evidence Log and your QuickWrite from the beginning of the unit. Have your ideas changed?

☐ YES	☐ NO
Identify at least three pieces of evidence that influenced your ideas.	Identify at least three pieces of evidence that reinforced your initial ideas.
1.	1.
2.	2.
3.	3.

State your ideas now: _____
_____
_____

Identify a possible addition: _____
_____
_____

Evaluate the Strength of Your Evidence Do you have enough evidence to support your ideas? If not, make a plan.

☐ Do more research   ☐ Talk with my classmates

☐ Reread a selection   ☐ Ask an expert

☐ Other:_____

STANDARDS

Writing
Introduce a topic; organize complex ideas, concepts, and information to make important connections and distinctions; include formatting, graphics and multimedia when useful to aiding comprehension.

⧉ WORD NETWORK

As you write and revise your informative essay, use your Word Network to help vary your word choices.

PART 1
Writing to Sources: Informative Essay

In this unit, you read about various people, both real and fictional, who have struggled to extend freedom's reach. Their efforts focused on both people in their own countries and their fellows around the world.

Assignment

Write an **informative essay** in which you gather and present information to respond to the following question:

What does it mean to "be free"?

Introduce the topic by defining freedom and explaining what it means to be free. Then, develop the topic with facts, details, quotations, examples, and other evidence from at least three of the selections you read. Select the most relevant ideas about fundamental human freedoms and democracy from the texts, and organize these ideas logically using appropriate and varied transitions. Conclude by clearly restating the main idea. Use a formal style and an objective tone, and follow the conventions of standard English.

Reread the Assignment Review the assignment to be sure you fully understand it. The assignment may reference some of the academic words presented at the beginning of the unit. Be sure you understand each of the words given here in order to complete the assignment correctly.

Academic Vocabulary

attribute	demarcate	democracy
hierarchy	fundamental	

Review the Elements of Informative Text Before you begin writing, read the Informative Text Rubric. Once you have completed your first draft, check it against the rubric. If one or more of the elements is missing or not as strong as it could be, revise your essay to add or strengthen that component.

⊞ STANDARDS

Writing
- Write informative/explanatory texts to examine and convey complex ideas, concepts, and information clearly and accurately through the effective selection, organization, and analysis of content.
- Draw evidence from literary or informational texts to support analysis, reflection, and research.
- Write routinely over extended time frames and shorter time frames for a range of tasks, purposes, and audiences.

Informative Text Rubric

	Focus and Organization	Evidence and Elaboration	Language Conventions
4	The introduction is very engaging and features a clear and complete explanation of the topic. All ideas are organized logically using appropriate and varied transitions. The conclusion clearly restates the main idea and connects it to the supporting information.	The topic is developed fully with well-chosen evidence from three or more texts. The most relevant text evidence is used to support and elaborate on the topic.	A formal style and an objective tone are maintained throughout the entire essay. The conventions of standard English are maintained throughout the entire essay.
3	The introduction is somewhat engaging and features an adequate explanation of the topic. Most ideas are organized logically using appropriate and varied transitions. The conclusion provides a clear restatement of the main idea but the connection to supporting information is unclear.	The topic is developed adequately with sufficient evidence from at least three texts. Relevant text evidence is used to support and elaborate on the topic.	A formal style and an objective tone are maintained throughout most of the essay. The conventions of standard English are maintained throughout most of the essay.
2	The introduction is unclear or contains only a partial explanation of the topic. Some ideas are organized logically using transitions; some transitions may be incorrect or overused. The conclusion is unclear or provides only a partial restatement of the main idea.	The topic is only partially developed with evidence from three texts or includes evidence from fewer than three texts. Tangential or less relevant text evidence is used to support and elaborate on the topic.	An informal style and a nonobjective tone are sometimes used in the essay. The conventions of standard English are sometimes used in the essay.
1	The introduction is missing or does not contain an adequate explanation of the topic. Ideas are not organized logically using transitions, or transitions are mostly absent or used incorrectly. The conclusion is missing or does not provide an adequate restatement of the main idea.	The topic is not adequately developed with text evidence. Irrelevant text evidence is used to support and elaborate on the topic, or text evidence is mostly or completely absent.	An informal style and a nonobjective tone appear throughout the essay. The conventions of standard English are rarely or never used in the essay.

PART 2
Speaking and Listening: Multimedia Presentation

Assignment

After completing the final draft of your informative essay, use it as the foundation for a five- to ten-minute **multimedia presentation.**

Follow these steps to create an informative, engaging presentation.

- Annotate the most important ideas and supporting details in your essay. Consider which ideas and details could best be enhanced by digital media.

- Choose various digital media (e.g, audio and video clips, images, interactive elements) to include in your presentation.

- Mark your essay to note when to present each multimedia element. Use these annotations to keep your presentation on track.

- As you deliver your presentation, speak clearly and at an adequate volume and rate. Maintain eye contact with your audience.

Review the Multimedia Presentation Rubric The criteria by which your multimedia presentation will be evaluated appear in this rubric. Review these criteria before presenting to ensure that you are prepared.

⊞ STANDARDS

Speaking and Listening
- Present information, findings, and supporting evidence clearly, concisely, and logically such that listeners can follow the line of reasoning and the organization, development, substance, and style are appropriate to purpose, audience, and task.
- Make strategic use of digital media in presentations to enhance understanding of findings, reasoning, and evidence and to add interest.
- Adapt speech to a variety of contexts and tasks, demonstrating command of formal English when indicated or appropriate.

	Content	Use of Media	Presentation Technique
3	The presentation conveys main ideas clearly and thoroughly. Main ideas are strongly supported with relevant evidence from texts.	Well-chosen media are used to support all or most main ideas. Media are distributed evenly throughout the presentation.	Media are sufficiently visible and audible. Transitions between media segments are consistently smooth. Each presenter maintains appropriate eye contact, volume, and pacing throughout the presentation.
2	The presentation conveys main ideas somewhat clearly and thoroughly. Main ideas are partially supported with evidence from the texts.	Somewhat well-chosen media are used to support some main ideas. Media are distributed somewhat evenly throughout the presentation.	Media are somewhat visible and audible. Transitions between media segments are somewhat smooth. Each presenter uses eye contact and speaks at an appropriate volume and pace at times during the presentation.
1	The presentation does not convey main ideas clearly or thoroughly. Main ideas are not supported with evidence from the texts.	Poorly chosen media are used and do not support main ideas. Media are not used or are distributed very unevenly throughout the presentation.	Media are insufficiently visible and audible. Transitions between media segments are very disjointed or are absent. Each presenter does not use eye contact or speak at an appropriate volume or pace throughout the presentation.

Reflect on the Unit

Now that you've completed the unit, take a few moments to reflect on your learning. Use the questions below to think about where you succeeded, what skills and strategies helped you, and where you can continue to grow in the future.

Reflect on the Unit Goals

Look back at the goals at the beginning of the unit. Use a different colored pen to rate yourself again. Think about readings and activities that contributed the most to the growth of your understanding. Record your thoughts.

Reflect on the Learning Strategies

Discuss It Write a reflection on whether you were able to improve your learning based on your Action Plans. Think about what worked, what didn't, and what you might do to keep working on these strategies. Record your ideas before a class discussion.

Reflect on the Text

Choose a selection that you found challenging, and explain what made it difficult.

Explain something that surprised you about a text in the unit.

Which activity taught you the most about the relationship between power and freedom? What did you learn?

STANDARDS

Speaking and Listening
• Initiate and participate effectively in a range of collaborative discussions with diverse partners on *grades 9–10 topics, texts, and issues*, building on others' ideas and expressing their own clearly and persuasively.
• Come to discussions prepared, having read and researched material under study; explicitly draw on that preparation by referring to evidence from texts and other research on the topic or issue to stimulate a thoughtful, well-reasoned exchange of ideas..

SCAN FOR MULTIMEDIA

RESOURCES

CONTENTS

Marking the Text: Strategies and Tips for Annotation

When you close read a text, you read for comprehension and then reread to unlock layers of meaning and to analyze a writer's style and techniques. Marking a text as you read it enables you to participate more fully in the close-reading process.

Following are some strategies for text mark-ups, along with samples of how the strategies can be applied. These mark-ups are suggestions; you and your teacher may want to use other mark-up strategies.

✱	Key Idea
!	I love it!
?	I have questions
◯	Unfamiliar or important word
----	Context Clues

Suggested Mark-Up Notations

WHAT I NOTICE	HOW TO MARK UP	QUESTIONS TO ASK
Key Ideas and Details	• Highlight key ideas or claims. • Underline supporting details or evidence.	• What does the text say? What does it leave unsaid? • What inferences do you need to make? • What details lead you to make your inferences?
Word Choice	• Circle unfamiliar words. • Put a dotted line under context clues, if any exist. • Put an exclamation point beside especially rich or poetic passages.	• What inferences about word meaning can you make? • What tone and mood are created by word choice? • What alternate word choices might the author have made?
Text Structure	• Highlight passages that show key details supporting the main idea. • Use arrows to indicate how sentences and paragraphs work together to build ideas. • Use a right-facing arrow to indicate foreshadowing. • Use a left-facing arrow to indicate flashback.	• Is the text logically structured? • What emotional impact do the structural choices create?
Author's Craft	• Circle or highlight instances of repetition, either of words, phrases, consonants, or vowel sounds. • Mark rhythmic beats in poetry using checkmarks and slashes. • Underline instances of symbolism or figurative language.	• Does the author's style enrich or detract from the reading experience? • What levels of meaning are created by the author's techniques?

TOOL KIT: CLOSE READING

First Read

NOTICE · ANNOTATE · RESPOND · CONNECT

In a first read, work to get a sense of the main idea of a text. Look for key details and ideas that help you understand what the author conveys to you. Mark passages which prompt a strong response from you.

Here is how one reader marked up this text.

* **Key Idea**
! **I love it!**
? **I have questions**
◯ **Unfamiliar or important word**
---- **Context Clues**

TOOL KIT: CLOSE READING

NOTES

MODEL

INFORMATIONAL TEXT

from Classifying the Stars

Cecilia H. Payne

*

1   Sunlight and starlight are composed of waves of various lengths, which the eye, even aided by a telescope, is unable to separate. We must use more than a telescope. In order to sort out the component colors, the light must be dispersed by a prism, or split up by some other means. For instance, sunbeams passing through rain drops, are transformed into the ◯myriad◯ tinted rainbow. The familiar rainbow spanning the sky is Nature's most glorious demonstration that light is composed of many colors.

*

2   The very beginning of our knowledge of the nature of a star dates back to 1672, when Isaac Newton gave to the world the results of his experiments on passing sunlight through a prism. To describe the beautiful band of rainbow tints, produced when sunlight was dispersed by his three-cornered piece of glass, he took from the Latin the word *spectrum*, meaning an appearance. The rainbow is the ◯spectrum◯ of the Sun. . . .

*

3   In 1814, more than a century after Newton, the spectrum of the Sun was obtained in such purity that an amazing detail was seen and studied by the German optician, Fraunhofer. He saw that the multiple spectral tints, ranging from delicate violet to deep red, were crossed by hundreds of fine dark lines. In other words, there were narrow gaps in the spectrum where certain shades were wholly blotted out. We must remember that the word spectrum is applied not only to sunlight, but also to the light of any glowing substance when its rays are sorted out by a prism or a ◯grating.◯

First-Read Guide

Use this page to record your first-read ideas.

You may want to use a guide like this to organize your thoughts after you read. Here is how a reader completed a First-Read Guide.

Selection Title: _Classifying the Stars_

NOTICE

NOTICE new information or ideas you learned about the unit topic as you first read this text.

Light = different waves of colors. (Spectrum)

Newton - the first person to observe these waves using a prism.

Faunhofer saw gaps in the spectrum.

ANNOTATE

ANNOTATE by marking vocabulary and key passages you want to revisit.

Vocabulary
  myriad
  grating
  component colors

Different light types = different lengths

Isaac Newton also worked theories of gravity.

<u>Multiple spectral tints?</u> "colors of various appearance"

Key Passage:
Paragraph 3 shows that Fraunhofer discovered more about the nature of light spectrums: he saw the spaces in between the tints.

First Read

CONNECT

CONNECT ideas within the selection to other knowledge and the selections you have read.

I remember learning about prisms in science class.

Double rainbows! My favorite. How are they made?

RESPOND

RESPOND by writing a brief summary of the selection.

Science allows us to see things not visible to the naked eye. What we see as sunlight is really a spectrum of colors. By using tools, such as prisms, we can see the components of sunlight and other light. They appear as single colors or as multiple colors separated by gaps of no color. White light contains a rainbow of colors.

TOOL KIT: CLOSE READING

ANNOTATE · QUESTION · Close Read · CONCLUDE

* **Key Idea**

! **I love it!**

? **I have questions**

◯ **Unfamiliar or important word**

---- **Context Clues**

In a close read, go back into the text to study it in greater detail. Take the time to analyze not only the author's ideas but the way that those ideas are conveyed. Consider the genre of the text, the author's word choice, the writer's unique style, and the message of the text.

Here is how one reader close read this text.

NOTES

MODEL

INFORMATIONAL TEXT

from **Classifying the Stars**

Cecilia H. Payne

explanation of sunlight and starlight

What is light and where do the colors come from?

*

1 Sunlight and starlight are composed of waves of various lengths, which the eye, even aided by a telescope, is unable to separate. We must use more than a telescope. In order to sort out the component colors, the light must be dispersed by a prism, or split up by some other means. For instance, sunbeams passing through rain drops, are transformed into the (myriad)-tinted rainbow. The familiar rainbow spanning the sky is Nature's most glorious demonstration that light is composed of many colors.

?

!

This paragraph is about Newton and the prism.

What discoveries helped us understand light?

*

2 The very beginning of our knowledge of the nature of a star dates back to 1672, when Isaac Newton gave to the world the results of his experiments on passing sunlight through a prism. To describe the beautiful band of rainbow tints, produced when sunlight was dispersed by his three-cornered piece of glass, he took from the Latin the word *spectrum*, meaning an appearance. The rainbow is the (spectrum) of the Sun. . . .

*

Fraunhofer and gaps in spectrum

3 In 1814, more than a century after Newton, the spectrum of the Sun was obtained in such purity that an amazing detail was seen and studied by the German optician, Fraunhofer. He saw that the multiple spectral tints, ranging from delicate violet to deep red, were crossed by hundreds of fine dark lines. In other words, there were narrow gaps in the spectrum where certain shades were wholly blotted out. We must remember that the word spectrum is applied not only to sunlight, but also to the light of any glowing substance when its rays are sorted out by a prism or a (grating).

Close-Read Guide

Use this page to record your close-read ideas.

Selection Title: Classifying the Stars

You can use the Close-Read Guide to help you dig deeper into the text. Here is how a reader completed a Close-Read Guide.

Close Read the Text

Revisit sections of the text you marked during your first read. Read these sections closely and **annotate** what you notice. Ask yourself **questions** about the text. What can you **conclude?** Write down your ideas.

Paragraph 3: Light is composed of waves of various lengths. Prisms let us see different colors in light. This is called the spectrum. Fraunhofer proved that there are gaps in the spectrum, where certain shades are blotted out.

More than one researcher studied this and each built off the ideas that were already discovered.

Analyze the Text

Think about the author's choices of patterns, structure, techniques, and ideas included in the text. Select one, and record your thoughts about what this choice conveys.

The author showed the development of human knowledge of the spectrum chronologically. Helped me see how ideas were built upon earlier understandings. Used dates and "more than a century after Newton" to show time.

QuickWrite

Pick a paragraph from the text that grabbed your interest. Explain the power of this passage.

The first paragraph grabbed my attention, specifically the sentence "The familiar rainbow spanning the sky is Nature's most glorious demonstration that light is composed of many colors." The paragraph began as a straightforward scientific explanation. When I read the word "glorious," I had to stop and deeply consider what was being said. It is a word loaded with personal feelings. With that one word, the author let the reader know what was important to her.

TOOL KIT: CLOSE READING

Argument

When you think of the word *argument*, you might think of a disagreement between two people, but an argument is more than that. An argument is a logical way of presenting a belief, conclusion, or stance. A good argument is supported with reasoning and evidence.

Argument writing can be used for many purposes, such as to change a reader's point of view or opinion or to bring about an action or a response from a reader.

Elements of an Argumentative Text

An **argument** is a logical way of presenting a viewpoint, belief, or stand on an issue. A well-written argument may convince the reader, change the reader's mind, or motivate the reader to take a certain action.

An effective argument contains these elements:

- a precise claim
- consideration of counterclaims, or opposing positions, and a discussion of their strengths and weaknesses
- logical organization that makes clear connections among claim, counterclaim, reasons, and evidence
- valid reasoning and evidence
- a concluding statement or section that logically completes the argument
- formal and objective language and tone
- error-free grammar, including accurate use of transitions

ARGUMENT: SCORE 1

Selfies, Photoshop, and You: Superficial Image Culture is Hurtful for Teens

Selfies are kind of cool, also kind of annoying, and some say they might be bad for you if you take too many. Selfies of celebrities and ordinary people are everywhere. People always try to smile and look good, and they take a lot of selfies when they are somewhere special, like at the zoo or at a fair. Some people spend so much time taking selfies they forget to just go ahead and have fun.

TV and other media are full of beautiful people. Looking at all those model's and celebrities can make kids feel bad about their one bodies, even when they are actually totally normal and fine and beautiful they way they are. Kids start to think they should look like the folks on TV which is mostly impossible. It's also a cheat because lots of the photos we see of celebrities and model's have been edited so they look even better.

Selfies make people feel even worse about the way they look. They're always comparing themselves and feeling that maybe they aren't as good as they should be. Selfies can make teens feel bad about their faces and bodies, and the stuff they are doing every day.

Regular people edit and change things before they post their pictures. That means, the pictures are kind of fake and it's impossible to compete with something that is fake. It's sad to think that teens can start to hate themselves and feel depressed just because they don't and can't look like a faked photo of a movie star.

Kids and teens post selfies to hear what others think about them, to show off, and to see how they compare with others. It can be kind of full of pressure always having to look great and smile. Even if you get positive comments about a selfie that you post, and everyone says you look beautiful, that feeling only lasts for a few minutes. After all, what you look like is just something on the outside. What's more important is what you are on the inside and what you do.

It's great for those few minutes, but then what? If you keep posting, people will not want to keep writing nice comments. Kids and teens should take a break from posting selfies all the time. It's better to go out and have fun rather than always keeping on posting selfies.

The writer does not clearly state the claim in the introduction.

The argument contains mistakes in standard English conventions of usage and mechanics.

The tone of the argument is informal, and the vocabulary is limited or ineffective.

The writer does not address counterclaims.

The conclusion does not restate any information that is important.

TOOL KIT: WRITING

MODEL

ARGUMENT: SCORE 2

Selfies and You: Superficial Image Culture is Hurtful for Teens

Selfies are bad for teens and everyone else. Selfies of celebrities and ordinary people are everywhere. It seems like taking and posting selfies is not such a big deal and not harmful, but that's not really true. Actually, taking too many selfies can be really bad.

TV and other media are full of beautiful people. Looking at all those models and celebrities can make kids feel bad about their own bodies. Kids start to think they should look like the folks on TV which is mostly impossible. It's also a cheat because lots of the photos we see of celebrities and model's have been edited so they look even better.

Regular people use image editing software as well. They edit and change things before they post their pictures. That means, the pictures are kind of fake and it's impossible to compete with something that is fake.

Selfies make people feel even worse about the way they look. They're always comparing themselves and feeling that maybe they aren't as good as they should be. Selfies can make teens feel bad about their faces and bodies.

But maybe selfies are just a fun way to stay in touch, but that's not really how people use selfies, I don't think. Kids and teens post selfies show off. It can be full of pressure always having to look great and smile.

Sometimes posting a selfie can make you feel good if it gets lots of 'likes' and positive comments. But you can never tell. Someone also might say something mean. Also, even if you get positive comments and everyone says you look beautiful, that feeling only lasts for a few minutes. It's great for those few minutes, but then what? If you keep posting and posting, people will not want to keep writing nice comments.

The selfie culture today is just too much. Kids and teens can't be happy when they are always comparing themselves and worrying about what they look like. It's better to go out and have fun rather than always keeping on posting selfies.

> The introduction establishes the writer's claim.

> The tone of the argument is occasionally formal and objective.

> The writer briefly acknowledges one counterclaim.

> The conclusion offers some insight into the claim and restates information.

ARGUMENT: SCORE 3

Selfies and You: Superficial Image Culture is Hurtful for Teens

Selfies are everywhere. Check out any social media site and you'll see an endless parade of perfect smiles on both celebrities and ordinary people. It may seem as if this flood of seflies is harmless, but sadly that is not true. Selfies promote a superficial image culture that is harmful and dangerous for teens.

The problem starts with the unrealistic: idealized images teens are exposed to in the media. Most models and celebrities are impossibly beautiful and thin. Even young children can feel that there is something wrong with they way they look. According to one research group, more than half of girls and one third of boys ages 6-8 feel their ideal body is thinner than their current body weight. Negative body image can result in serious physical and mental health problems.

When teens look at selfies they automatically make comparisons with the idealized images they have in their minds. This can make them feel inadequate and sad about themselves, their bodies, and their lives. And with social media sites accessible 24/7, it's difficult to get a break from the constant comparisons, competition, and judgment.

Image editing software plays a role too. A recent study carried out by the Renfrew Center Foundation said that about 50% of people edit pictures of themselves before posting. They take away blemishes, change skin tone, maybe even make themselves look thinner. And why not? Even the photos of models and celebrities are heavily edited. Teens can start to hate themselves and feel depressed just because they don't and can't look like a faked photo of a movie star.

Some say that posting a selfie is like sending a postcard to your friends and family, but that's not how selfies are used: teens post selfies to get feedback, to compare themselves with others, and to present a false image to the world. There is a lot of pressure to look great and appear happy.

It's true that sometimes a selfie posted on social media gets 'likes' and positive comments that can make a person feel pretty. However, the boost you get from feeling pretty for five minutes doesn't last.

A million selfies are posted every day—and that's way too many. Selfies promote a superficial image culture that is harmful to teens. In the end, the selfie life is not a healthy way to have fun. Let's hope the fad will fade.

The argument's claim is clearly stated.

The tone of the argument is mostly formal and objective.

The writer includes reasons and evidence that address and support claims.

The ideas progress logically, and the writer includes sentence transitions that connect the reader to the argument.

The conclusion restates important information.

TOOL KIT: WRITING

MODEL

ARGUMENT: SCORE 4

Selfies and You: Superficial Image Culture Is Hurtful for Teens

Smile, Snap, Edit, Post—Repeat! That's the selfie life, and it's everywhere. A million selfies are posted every day. But this **tsunami** of self-portraits is not as harmless as it appears. Selfies promote a superficial image culture that is hurtful and dangerous for teens.

It all starts with the unrealistic: When teens look at selfies they automatically make comparisons with the idealized images they have in their minds. This can cause them to feel inadequate and sad about themselves, their bodies, and their lives. According to Common Sense Media, more than half of girls and one third of boys ages 6-8 feel their ideal body is thinner than their current body weight. Negative body image can result in serious physical and mental health problems such as anorexia and other eating disorders.

To make matter worse, many or even most selfies have been edited. A recent study carried out by the Renfrew Center Foundation concluded that about 50% of people edit their own images before posting. They use image-editing software to take away blemishes, change skin tone, maybe even make themselves look thinner. And why not? Even the photos of models and celebrities are heavily edited.

Some say that selfies are a harmless and enjoyable way to communicate: posting a selfie is like sending a postcard to your friends and family, inviting them to share in your fun. But that is not how selfies are used: teens post selfies to get feedback, to compare themselves with others, and to present an (often false) image to the world.

It's true that posting a selfie on social media can generate 'likes' and positive comments that can make a person feel good.

However, the boost one gets from feeling pretty for five minutes is like junk food: it tastes good but it is not nourishing.

The selfie culture that is the norm today is out of control. The superficial image culture promoted by selfies is probably behind the recent 20 percent increase in plastic surgery—something with its own dangers and drawbacks. Let's hope the fad will fade, and look forward to a future where people are too busy enjoying life to spend so much time taking, editing, and posting pictures of themselves.

The introduction is engaging, and the writer's claim is clearly stated at the end of the paragraph.

The writer has included a variety of sentence transitions such as "To make matters worse…" "Some say…" "Another claim…" "It is true that…"

The sources of evidence are specific and contain relevant information.

The writer clearly acknowledges counterclaims.

The conclusion offers fresh insights into the claim.

Argument Rubric

	Focus and Organization	Evidence and Elaboration	Conventions
4	The introduction engages the reader and establishes a claim in a compelling way. The argument includes valid reasons and evidence that address and support the claim while clearly acknowledging counterclaims. The ideas progress logically, and transitions make connections among ideas clear. The conclusion offers fresh insight into the claim.	The sources of evidence are comprehensive and specific and contain relevant information. The tone of the argument is always formal and objective. The vocabulary is always appropriate for the audience and purpose.	The argument intentionally uses standard English conventions of usage and mechanics.
3	The introduction engages the reader and establishes the claim. The argument includes reasons and evidence that address and support my claim while acknowledging counterclaims. The ideas progress logically, and some transitions are used to help make connections among ideas clear. The conclusion restates the claim and important information.	The sources of evidence contain relevant information. The tone of the argument is mostly formal and objective. The vocabulary is generally appropriate for the audience and purpose.	The argument demonstrates general accuracy in standard English conventions of usage and mechanics.
2	The introduction establishes a claim. The argument includes some reasons and evidence that address and support the claim while briefly acknowledging counterclaims. The ideas progress somewhat logically. A few sentence transitions are used that connect readers to the argument. The conclusion offers some insight into the claim and restates information.	The sources of evidence contain some relevant information. The tone of the argument is occasionally formal and objective. The vocabulary is somewhat appropriate for the audience and purpose.	The argument demonstrates some accuracy in standard English conventions of usage and mechanics.
1	The introduction does not clearly state the claim. The argument does not include reasons or evidence for the claim. No counterclaims are acknowledged. The ideas do not progress logically. Transitions are not included to connect ideas. The conclusion does not restate any information that is important.	Reliable and relevant evidence is not included. The vocabulary used is limited or ineffective. The tone of the argument is not objective or formal.	The argument contains mistakes in standard English conventions of usage and mechanics.

Informative/Explanatory Texts

Informative and explanatory writing should rely on facts to inform or explain. Informative writing serves several purposes: to increase readers' knowledge of a subject, to help readers better understand a procedure or process, or to provide readers with an enhanced comprehension of a concept. It should also feature a clear introduction, body, and conclusion.

Elements of Informative/Explanatory Texts

Informative/explanatory texts present facts, details, data, and other kinds of evidence to give information about a topic. Readers turn to informational and explanatory texts when they wish to learn about a specific idea, concept, or subject area, or if they want to learn how to do something.

An effective informative/explanatory text contains these elements:

- a topic sentence or thesis statement that introduces the concept or subject
- relevant facts, examples, and details that expand upon a topic
- definitions, quotations, and/or graphics that support the information given
- headings (if desired) to separate sections of the essay
- a structure that presents information in a direct, clear manner
- clear transitions that link sections of the essay
- precise words and technical vocabulary where appropriate
- formal and object language and tone
- a conclusion that supports the information given and provides fresh insights

INFORMATIVE/EXPLANATORY: SCORE 1

Moai: The Giant Statues of Easter Island

Easter Island is a tiny Island. It's far out in the middle of the pacific ocean, 2200 miles off the coast. The closest country is Chile, in south america. The nearest island where people live is called Pitcairn, and that's about 1,300 miles away, and only about 60 people live so their most of the time. Easter island is much bigger than Pitcairn, and lots more people live there now—about 5,000-6,000. Although in the past there were times when only about 111 people lived there.

Even if you don't really know what it is, you've probably seen pictures of the easter island Statues. You'd recognize one if you saw it, with big heads and no smiles. Their lots of them on the island. Almost 900 of them. But some were never finished They're called *moai*. They are all different sizes. All the sizes together average out to about 13 feet tall and 14 tons of heavy.

Scientists know that Polynesians settled Easter Island (it's also called Rapa Nui, and the people are called the Rapanui people). Polynesians were very good at boats. And they went big distances across the Pacific. When these Polynesians arrived was probably 300, but it was probably 900 or 1200.

The island was covered with forests. They can tell by looking at pollin in lakes. The Rapanui people cut trees, to build houses. They didn't know that they wood run out of wood). They also carved *moai*.

The *moai* were made for important chiefs. They were made with only stone tools. They have large heads and narrow bodies. No 2 are the same. Although they look the same as far as their faces are concerned. They are very big and impressive and special.

Over the years, many of the statues were tipped over and broken. But some years ago scientists began to fix some of them and stand them up again. They look more better like that. The ones that have been fixed up are probably the ones you remember seeing in photographs.

The essay does not include a thesis statement.

The writer includes many details that are not relevant to the topic of the essay.

The essay has many errors in grammar, spelling, capitalization, punctuation. The errors detract from the fluency and effectiveness of the essay.

The sentences are often not purposeful, varied, or well-controlled.

The essay ends abruptly and lacks a conclusion.

TOOL KIT: WRITING

MODEL

INFORMATIVE/EXPLANATORY: SCORE 2

Moai: The Giant Statues of Easter Island

Easter Island is a tiny Island. It's far out in the middle of the pacific ocean, 2200 miles off the coast. The closest South American country is Chile. The nearest island where people live is called Pitcairn, and that's almost 1,300 miles away. Even if don't know much about it, you've probably seen pictures of the Easter Island statues. You'd recognize one if you saw it. They're almost 900 of them. They're called *moai.* The average one is about 13 feet high (that's tall) and weighs a lot— almost 14 tons.

Scientists know that Polynesians settled Easter Island (it's also called Rapa Nui, and the people are called the Rapanui). Polynesians were very good sailers. And they traveled big distances across the Pacific. Even so, nobody really can say exactly *when* these Polynesians arrived and settled on the Island. Some say 300 A.D., while others say maybe as late as 900 or even 1200 A.D.

Scientists can tell that when the settlers first arrived, the island was covered with forests of palm and hardwood. They can tell by looking at pollin deposits in lakes on the island. The Rapanui people cut trees, built houses, planted crops, and a thriving culture. They didn't know that cutting so many trees would cause problems later on (like running out of wood). They also began to carve *moai.*

The *moai* were built to honor important Rapanui ancestors or chiefs. The statutes all have large heads and narrow bodies, but no too are exactly the same. There faces are all similar. Some have places where eyes could be inserted.

Why did the Rapanui stopped making *moai*? Part of it might have been because there were no more trees and no more of the wood needed to transport them. Part of it was maybe because the people were busy fighting each other because food and other necessary things were running out. In any case, they stopped making moai and started tipping over and breaking the ones that were there already. Later on, archeologists began to try to restore some of the statues and set them up again. But even now that some have been set up again, we still don't know a lot about them. I guess some things just have to remain a mystery!

The writer does not include a thesis statement.

Some of the ideas are reasonably well developed.

The essay has many errors in grammar, spelling, capitalization, punctuation. The errors decrease the effectiveness of the essay.

The writer's word choice shows that he is not fully aware of the essay's purpose and tone.

The writer does not include a clear conclusion.

Moai: The Giant Statues of Easter Island

Easter Island is a tiny place, far out in the middle of the Pacific Ocean, 2200 miles off the coast of South America. Another name for the island is Rapa Nui. Even if you don't know much about it, you would probably recognize the colossal head-and-torso carvings known as *moai*. Even after years of research by scientists, many questions about these extraordinary statues remain unanswered.

Scientists now agree that it was Polynesians who settled Easter Island. Earlier some argued South American voyagers were the first. But the Polynesians were expert sailors and navigators known to have traveled huge distances across the Pacific Ocean. However, scientists do not agree about *when* the settlers arrived. Some say A.D. 300, while others suggest as late as between A.D. 900 and 1200.

Scientists say that when the settlers first arrived on Rapa Nui, the island was covered with forests of palm and hardwood. They can tell by looking at the layers of pollen deposited over the years in the lakes on the island. The Rapa Nui began to carve *moai*. They developed a unique artistic and architectural tradition all of their own.

Archeologists agree that the *moai* were created to honor ancestor's or chief's. Most *moai* are made from a soft rock called *tuff* that's formed from hardened volcanic ash. The statues all have large heads on top of narrow bodies, but no two are exactly the same. Some have indented eye sockets where eyes could be inserted.

At some point, the Rapanui stopped making *moai*. Why? Was it because there were no more trees and no longer enough wood needed to transport them? Was it because the people were too busy fighting each other over resources which had begun to run out? No one can say for sure. Rival groups began toppling their enemys' *moai* and breaking them. By the 19th century, most of the statues were tipped over, and many were destroyed. It wasn't until many years later that archeologists began to restore some of the statues.

The *moai* of Easter Island are one of the most awe-inspiring human achievements ever. Thanks to scientific studies, we know much more about the *moai*, *ahu*, and Rapanui people than we ever did in the past. But some questions remain unanswered. At least for now, the *moai* are keeping their mouths shut, doing a good job of guarding their secrets.

The thesis statement is clearly stated.

The essay has many interesting details, but some do not relate directly to the topic.

There are very few errors in grammar, usage, and punctuation. These errors do not interrupt the fluency and effectiveness of the essay.

The writer's conclusion sums up the main points of the essay and supports the thesis statement.

TOOL KIT: WRITING

WRITING

INFORMATIVE/EXPLANATORY: SCORE 4

Moai: The Giant Statues of Easter Island

Easter Island, 2200 miles off the coast of South America, is "the most remote inhabited island on the planet." Few have visited this speck in the middle of the vast Pacific Ocean, but we all recognize the colossal statues that bring this tiny island its fame: the head-and-torso carvings known as *moai*. Yet even after years of research by scientists, many questions about the *moai* remain unanswered.

Scientists now agree that it was Polynesians, not South Americans, who settled Easter Island (also known as Rapa Nui). Polynesians were expert sailors and navigators known to have traveled huge distances across the Pacific Ocean. Even so, there is little agreement about *when* the settlers arrived. Some say A.D. 300, while others suggest as late as between A.D. 900 and 1200.

Most archeologists agree that the *moai* were created to honor ancestors, chiefs, or other important people. Most *moai* are made from a soft rock called *tuff* that's formed from hardened volcanic ash. The statues have large heads atop narrow torsos, with eyes wide open and lips tightly closed. While the moai share these basic characteristics, no two are exactly the same: while all are huge, some are bigger than others. Some are decorated with carvings. Some have indented eye sockets where white coral eyes could be inserted. It's possible that the eyes were only put in for special occasions.

In the late 1600s, the Rapanui stopped carving *moai*. Was it because the forests had been depleted and there was no longer enough wood needed to transport them? Was it because they were too busy fighting each other over dwindling resources? No one can say for sure. What is known is that rival groups began toppling their enemies' *moai* and breaking them. By the 19th century, most of the statues were tipped over, and many were destroyed. It wasn't until many years later that archeologists began restoration efforts.

The *moai* of Easter Island are one of humanity's most awe-inspiring cultural and artistic achievements. Part of Rapa Nui was designated as a World Heritage Site in 1995 to recognize and protect these extraordinary creations. Thanks to scientific studies, we know much more about the *moai* than we ever did in the past. But some questions remain unanswered, some mysteries unsolved. Don't bother asking the *moai*: their lips are sealed.

The thesis statement of is clearly stated in an engaging manner.

The ideas in the essay relate to the thesis statement and focus on the topic.

The writer includes many specific and well-chosen details that add substance to the essay.

The fluency of the writing and effectiveness of the essay are unaffected by errors.

The conclusion relates to the thesis statement and is creative and memorable.

TOOL KIT: WRITING

Informative/Explanatory Rubric

	Focus and Organization	Evidence and Elaboration	Conventions
4	The introduction engages the reader and states a thesis in a compelling way. The essay includes a clear introduction, body, and conclusion. The conclusion summarizes ideas and offers fresh insight into the thesis.	The essay includes specific reasons, details, facts, and quotations from selections and outside resources to support the thesis. The tone of the essay is always formal and objective. The language is always precise and appropriate for the audience and purpose.	The essay uses standard English conventions of usage and mechanics. The essay contains no spelling errors.
3	The introduction engages the reader and sets forth the thesis. The essay includes an introduction, body, and conclusion. The conclusion summarizes ideas and supports the thesis.	The essay includes some specific reasons, details, facts, and quotations from selections and outside resources to support the thesis. The tone of the essay is mostly formal and objective. The language is generally precise and appropriate for the audience and purpose.	The essay demonstrates general accuracy in standard English conventions of usage and mechanics. The essay contains few spelling errors.
2	The introduction sets forth the thesis. The essay includes an introduction, body, and conclusion, but one or more parts are weak. The conclusion partially summarizes ideas but may not provide strong support of the thesis.	The essay includes a few reasons, details, facts, and quotations from selections and outside resources to support the thesis. The tone of the essay is occasionally formal and objective. The language is somewhat precise and appropriate for the audience and purpose.	The essay demonstrates some accuracy in standard English conventions of usage and mechanics. The essay contains some spelling errors.
1	The introduction does not state the thesis clearly. The essay does not include an introduction, body, and conclusion. The conclusion does not summarize ideas and may not relate to the thesis.	Reliable and relevant evidence is not included. The tone of the essay is not objective or formal. The language used is imprecise and not appropriate for the audience and purpose.	The essay contains mistakes in standard English conventions of usage and mechanics. The essay contains many spelling errors.

Narration

Narrative writing conveys experience, either real or imaginary, and uses time to provide structure. It can be used to inform, instruct, persuade, or entertain. Whenever writers tell a story, they are using narrative writing. Most types of narrative writing share certain elements, such as characters, setting, a sequence of events, and, often, a theme.

Elements of a Narrative Text

A **narrative** is any type of writing that tells a story, whether it is fiction, nonfiction, poetry, or drama.

An effective nonfiction narrative usually contains these elements:

- an engaging beginning in which characters and setting are established
- characters who participate in the story events
- a well-structured, logical sequence of events
- details that show time and place
- effective story elements such as dialogue, description, and reflection
- the narrator's thoughts, feelings, or views about the significance of events
- use of language that brings the characters and setting to life

An effective fictional narrative usually contains these elements:

- an engaging beginning in which characters, setting, or a main conflict is introduced
- a main character and supporting characters who participate in the story events
- a narrator who relates the events of the plot from a particular point of view
- details that show time and place
- conflict that is resolved in the course of the narrative
- narrative techniques such as dialogue, description, and suspense
- use of language that vividly brings to life characters and events

NARRATIVE: SCORE 1

The Remark-a-Ball

Eddie decided to invent a Remark-a-Ball. Eddie thought Barnaby should be able to speak to him.

That's when he invited the Remark-a-Ball.

Barnaby had a rubber ball. It could make a bunchs of sounds that made Barnaby bark. It had always seemed that Barnaby was using his squeaky toy to talk, almost.

This was before Barnaby got hit by a car and died. This was a big deal. He took his chemistry set and worked real hard to created a thing that would make the toy ball talk for Barnaby, his dog.

Eddie made a Remark-a-Ball that worked a little too well, tho. Barnaby could say anything he wanted too. And now he said complaints—his bed didn't feel good, he wanted to be walks, he wanted to eat food.

Barnaby became bossy to Eddy to take him on walks or wake up. It was like he became his boss. Like my dad's boss. Eddy didn't like having a mean boss for a dog.

Eddy wished he hadn't invented the Remark-a-Ball.

The story's beginning is choppy and vague.

The sequence of events is unclear and hard to follow.

The narrative lacks descriptive details and sensory language.

The narrative contains many errors in standard English conventions of usage and mechanics.

The conclusion is abrupt and unsatisfying.

MODEL

NARRATIVE: SCORE 2

The Remark-a-Ball

Eddie couldn't understand what his dog was barking about, so he decided to invent a Remark-a-Ball. Eddie thought Barnaby should be able to speak to him.

That's when he invented the Remark-a-Ball.

Barnaby had a rubber ball the size of an orange. It could make a bunch of sounds that made Barnaby bark. It had always seemed to Eddie that Barnaby was almost talking with his squeaky toy.

This was a big deal. Eddy would be the first human ever to talk to a dog, which was a big deal! He took his chemistry set and worked real hard to created a thing that would make the toy ball talk for Barnaby, his dog.

Eddie made a Remark-a-Ball that worked a little too well, tho. Barnaby could say anything he wanted now. And now he mostly said complaints—his bed didn't feel good, he wanted to be walked all the time, he wanted to eat people food.

Barnaby became bossy to Eddy to take him on walks or wake him up. It was like he became his boss. His really mean boss, like my dad's boss. Eddy didn't like having a mean boss for a dog.

Eddy started to ignore his best friend, which used to be his dog named Barnaby. He started tot think maybe dogs shouldn't be able to talk.

Things were much better when Barnaby went back to barking

The story's beginning provides few details to establish the situation.

Narrative techniques such as dialogue, pacing, and description are used sparingly.

The narrative contains some errors in standard English conventions of usage and mechanics.

The conclusion comes abruptly and provides little insight about the story's meaning.

NARRATIVE: SCORE 3

The Remark-a-Ball

Any bark could mean anything: *I'm hungry*, *Take me outside*, or *There's that dog again*. Eddie thought Barnaby should be able to speak to him.

And that's how the Remark-a-Ball was born.

Barnaby had a rubber ball the size of an orange. It could make a wide range of sounds that made Barnaby howl. It had always seemed to Eddie that Barnaby was almost communicating with his squeaky toy.

This was big. This was epic. He would be the first human ever to bridge the communication gap between species! He dusted off his old chemistry set and, through trial and error, created a liquid bath that would greatly increase the toy's flexibility, resilience, and mouth-feel.

Eddie had a prototype that worked—perhaps too well. Barnaby was ready to speak his mind. This unleashed a torrent of complaints—his bed was lumpy, he couldn't *possibly* exist on just three walks a day, he wanted table food like the poodle next door.

Barnaby made increasingly specific demands to Eddie to take him on walks or wake him up. This kind of conversation did not bring them closer, as Eddie had thought, but instead it drove them apart.

Eddie started to avoid his former best friend, and he came to the realization that there is a good reason different species don't have a common language.

So Eddie quit letting Barnaby use the toy.

"Hey, Barn, want to go outside?" Eddie would say, and the dog, as if a switch was turned on, would shake, wag, pant, run in circles, and bark—just like he used to.

The story's beginning establishes the situation and the narrator's point of view but leaves some details unclear.

The narrative consistently uses standard English conventions of usage and mechanics.

Narrative techniques such as dialogue and description are used occasionally.

The conclusion resolves the situation or problem, but does not clearly convey the significance of the events in the story.

TOOL KIT: WRITING

MODEL

NARRATIVE: SCORE 4

The Remark-a-Ball

Barnaby, for no apparent reason, leapt up and began to bark like a maniac. "Why are you barking?" asked Eddie, holding the leash tight. But Barnaby, being a dog, couldn't say. It could have been anything—a dead bird, a half-eaten sandwich, the Taj Mahal.

This was one of those times Eddie wished that Barnaby could talk. Any bark could mean anything: *I'm hungry, Take me outside,* or *There's that dog again.* Eddie thought, as buddies, they should be able to understand each other.

And that's how the Remark-a-Ball was born.

Barnaby had a squeaky toy—a rubber ball the size of an orange. It could emit a wide range of sounds. It made Barnaby howl even as he was squeaking it. And it had always seemed to Eddie that through this process Barnaby was almost communicating.

This was big. This was epic. He, Edward C. Reyes III, would be the first human ever to bridge the communication gap between species! He dusted off his old chemistry set and, through trial and error, created a liquid bath that would greatly increase the toy's flexibility, resilience, and mouth-feel.

By the end of the week Eddie had a prototype that worked— perhaps too well. Barnaby was ready to speak his mind. This unleashed a torrent of complaints—his bed was lumpy, he couldn't *possibly* exist on just three walks a day, he wanted table food like the poodle next door.

Barnaby made increasingly specific demands, such as "Wake me in ten minutes," and "I want filtered water." This kind of conversation did not bring them closer, as Eddie had thought, but instead it drove them apart.

Eddie started to avoid his former best friend, and he came to the realization that there is a good reason different species don't have a common language. It didn't take long for the invention to be relegated to the very bottom of Barnaby's toy chest, too far down for him to get.

There followed a period of transition, after which Eddie and Barnaby returned to their former mode of communication, which worked out just fine.

"Hey, Barn, want to go outside?" Eddie would say, and the dog, as if a switch was turned on, would shake, wag, pant, run in circles, and bark—just like he used to.

"You're a good boy, Barnaby," Eddie would say, scratching him behind the ears.

The story's beginning is engaging, sets up a point of view, and establishes characters and tone.

The narrative uses standard English conventions of usage and mechanics, except where language is manipulated for effect.

Events are presented in a logical sequence, and the progression from one even to another is smooth.

Narrative techniques are used effectively to develop characters and events.

The conclusion resolves the situation or problem and clearly conveys the significance of the events in the story.

Narrative Rubric

	Focus and Organization	Development of Ideas/Elaboration	Conventions
4	The introduction establishes a clear context and point of view. Events are presented in a clear sequence, building to a climax, then moving toward the conclusion. The conclusion follows from and reflects on the events and experiences in the narrative.	Narrative techniques such as dialogue, pacing, and description are used effectively to develop characters, events, and setting. Descriptive details, sensory language, and precise words and phrases are used to convey the experiences in the narrative and to help the reader imagine the characters and setting. Voice is established through word choice, sentence structure, and tone.	The narrative uses standard English conventions of usage and mechanics. Deviations from standard English are intentional and serve the purpose of the narrative. Rules of spelling and punctuation are followed.
3	The introduction gives the reader some context and sets the point of view. Events are presented logically, though there are some jumps in time. The conclusion logically ends the story, but provides only some reflection on the experiences related in the story.	Narrative techniques such as dialogue, pacing, and description are used occasionally. Descriptive details, sensory language, and precise words and phrases are used occasionally. Voice is established through word choice, sentence structure, and tone occasionally, though not evenly.	The narrative mostly uses standard English conventions of usage and mechanics, though there are some errors. There are few errors in spelling and punctuation.
2	The introduction provides some description of a place. The point of view can be unclear at times. Transitions between events are occasionally unclear. The conclusion comes abruptly and provides only a small amount of reflection on the experiences related in the narrative.	Narrative techniques such as dialogue, pacing, and description are used sparingly. The story contains few examples of descriptive details and sensory language. Voice is not established for characters, so that it becomes difficult to determine who is speaking.	The narrative contains some errors in standard English conventions of usage and mechanics. There are many errors in spelling and punctuation.
1	The introduction fails to set a scene or is omitted altogether. The point of view is not always clear. The events are not in a clear sequence, and events that would clarify the narrative may not appear. The conclusion does not follow from the narrative or is omitted altogether.	Narrative techniques such as dialogue, pacing, and description are not used. Descriptive details are vague or missing. No sensory language is included. Voice has not been developed.	The text contains mistakes in standard English conventions of usage and mechanics. Rules of spelling and punctuation have not been followed.

Conducting Research

We are lucky to live in an age when information is accessible and plentiful. However, not all information is equally useful, or even accurate. Strong research skills will help you locate and evaluate information.

Narrowing or Broadening a Topic

The first step of any research project is determining your topic. Consider the scope of your project and choose a topic that is narrow enough to address completely and effectively. If you can name your topic in just one or two words, it is probably too broad. Topics such as Shakespeare, jazz, or science fiction are too broad to cover in a single report. Narrow a broad topic into smaller subcategories.

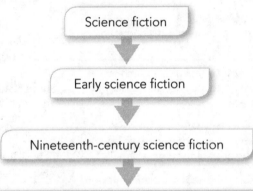

Science fiction

↓

Early science fiction

↓

Nineteenth-century science fiction

↓

Nineteenth-century science fiction that predicted the future accurately

When you begin to research a topic, pay attention to the amount of information available. If you feel overwhelmed by the number of relevant sources, you may need to narrow your topic further.

If there isn't enough information available as your research, you might need to broaden your topic. A topic is too narrow when it can be thoroughly presented in less space than the required size of your assignment. It might also be too narrow if you can find little or no information in library and media sources, so consider broadening your topic to include other related ideas.

Generating Research Questions

Use research questions to focus your research. Specific questions can help you avoid time-wasting digressions. For example, instead of simply hunting for information about Mark Twain, you might ask, "What jobs did Mark Twain have, other than being a writer?" or "Which of Twain's books was most popular during his lifetime?"

In a research report, your research question often becomes your thesis statement, or may lead up to it. The question will also help you focus your research into a comprehensive but flexible search plan, as well as prevent you from gathering unnecessary details. As your research teaches you more about your topic, you may find it necessary to refocus your original question.

Consulting Print and Digital Sources

Effective research combines information from several sources, and does not rely too heavily on a single source. The creativity and originality of your research depends on how you combine ideas from multiple sources. Plan to consult a variety of resources, such as the following:

- **Primary and Secondary Sources:** To get a thorough view of your topic, use primary sources (firsthand or original accounts, such as interview transcripts, eyewitness reports, and newspaper articles) and secondary sources (accounts, created after an event occurred, such as encyclopedia entries).

- **Print and Digital Resources:** The Internet allows fast access to data, but print resources are often edited more carefully. Use both print and digital resources in order to guarantee the accuracy of your findings.

- **Media Resources:** You can find valuable information in media resources such as documentaries, television programs, podcasts, and museum exhibitions. Consider attending public lectures given by experts to gain an even more in-depth view of your topic.

- **Original Research:** Depending on your topic, you may wish to conduct original research to include among your sources. For example, you might interview experts or eyewitnesses, or conduct a survey of people in your community.

Evaluating Sources It is important to evaluate the credibility, validity, and accuracy of any information you find, as well as its appropriateness for your purpose and audience. You may find the information you need to answer your research question in specialized and authoritative sources, such as almanacs (for social, cultural, and natural statistics), government publications (for law, government programs, and subjects such as agriculture), and information services. Also, consider consumer, workplace, and public documents.

Ask yourself questions such as these to evaluate these additional sources:

- **Authority:** Is the author well known? What are the author's credentials? Does the source include references to other reliable sources? Does the author's tone win your confidence? Why or why not?

- **Bias:** Does the author have any obvious biases? What is the author's purpose for writing? Who is the target audience?

- **Currency:** When was the work created? Has it been revised? Is there more current information available?

Using Online Encyclopedias

Online encyclopedias are often written by anonymous contributors who are not required to fact-check information. These sites can be very useful as a launching point for research, but should not be considered accurate. Look for footnotes, endnotes, or hyperlinks that support facts with reliable sources that have been carefully checked by editors.

TOOL KIT: RESEARCH

RESEARCH

Using Search Terms

Finding information on the Internet can be both easy and challenging. Type a word or phrase into a general search engine and you will probably get hundreds—or thousands—of results. However, those results are not guaranteed to be relevant or accurate.

These strategies can help you find information from the Internet:

- Create a list of keywords that apply to your topic before you begin using a search engine. Consult a thesaurus to expand your list.
- Enter six to eight keywords.
- Choose precise nouns. Most search engines ignore articles and prepositions. Verbs may be used in multiple contexts, leading to sources that are not relevant. Use modifiers, such as adjectives, when necessary to specify a category.
- Use quotation marks to focus a search. Place a phrase in quotation marks to find pages that include exactly that phrase. Add several phrases in quotation marks to narrow your results.
- Spell carefully. Many search engines autocorrect spelling, but they cannot produce accurate results for all spelling errors.
- Scan search results before you click them. The first result isn't always the most relevant. Read the text and consider the domain before make a choice.
- Utilize more than one search engine.

Evaluating Internet Domains

Not everything you read on the Internet is true, so you have to evaluate sources carefully. The last three letters of an Internet URL identify the Website's domain, which can help you evaluate the information of the site.

- **.gov**—Government sites are sponsored by a branch of the United States federal government, such as the Census Bureau, Supreme Court, or Congress. These sites are considered reliable.
- **.edu**—Education domains include schools from kindergartens to universities. Information from an educational research center or department is likely to be carefully checked. However, education domains can also include student pages that are not edited or monitored.
- **.org**—Organizations are nonprofit groups and usually maintain a high level of credibility. Keep in mind that some organizations may express strong biases.
- **.com** and **.net**—Commercial sites exist to make a profit. Information may be biased to show a product or service in a good light. The company may be providing information to encourage sales or promote a positive image.

Taking Notes

Take notes as you locate and connect useful information from multiple sources, and keep a reference list of every source you use. This will help you make distinctions between the relative value and significance of specific data, facts, and ideas.

For long-term research projects, create source cards and notecards to keep track of information gathered from multiple resources.

Source Cards
Create a card that identifies each source.

- For print materials, list the author, title, publisher, date of publication, and relevant page numbers.
- For Internet sources, record the name and Web address of the site, and the date you accessed the information.
- For media sources, list the title, person, or group credited with creating the media, and the year of production.

Notecards
Create a separate notecard for each item of information.

- Include the fact or idea, the letter of the related source card, and the specific page(s) on which the fact or idea appears.
- Use quotation marks around words and phrases taken directly from print or media resources.
- Mark particularly useful or relevant details using your own annotation method, such as stars, underlining, or colored highlighting.

Source Card   [A]

Marsh, Peter. *Eye to Eye: How People Interact.* Salem House Publishers, 1988.

Notecard

Gestures vary from culture to culture. The American "OK" symbol (thumb and forefinger) is considered insulting in Greece and Turkey.

Source Card: A, p. 54.

Quote Accurately Responsible research begins with the first note you take. Be sure to quote and paraphrase your sources accurately so you can identify these sources later. In your notes, circle all quotations and paraphrases to distinguish them from your own comments. When photocopying from a source, include the copyright information. When printing out information from an online source, include the Web address.

Reviewing Research Findings

While conducting research, you will need to review your findings, checking that you have collected enough accurate and appropriate information.

Considering Audience and Purpose

Always keep your audience in mind as you gather information, since different audiences may have very different needs. For example, if you are writing an in-depth analysis of a text that your entire class has read together and you are writing for your audience, you will not need to gather background information that has been thoroughly discussed in class. However, if you are writing the same analysis for a national student magazine, you cannot assume that all of your readers have the same background information. You will need to provide facts from reliable sources to help orient these readers to your subject. When considering whether or not your research will satisfy your audience, ask yourself:

- Who am I writing for?
- Have I collected enough information to explain my topic to this audience?
- Are there details in my research that I can omit because they are already familiar to my audience?

Your purpose for writing will also influence your review of research. If you are researching a question to satisfy your own curiosity, you can stop researching when you feel you understand the answer completely. If you are writing a research report that will be graded, you need to consider the criteria of the assignment. When considering whether or not you have enough information, ask yourself:

- What is my purpose for writing?
- Will the information I have gathered be enough to achieve my purpose?
- If I need more information, where might I find it?

Synthesizing Sources

Effective research writing does not merely present facts and details; it synthesizes—gathers, orders, and interprets—them. These strategies will help you synthesize information effectively:

- Review your notes and look for connections and patterns among the details you have collected.
- Arrange notes or notecards in different ways to help you decide how to best combine related details and present them in a logical way.
- Pay close attention to details that support one other, emphasizing the same main idea.
- Also look for details that challenge each other, highlighting ideas about which there is no single, or consensus, opinion. You might decide to conduct additional research to help you decide which side of the issue has more support.

Types of Evidence

When reviewing your research, also consider the kinds of evidence you have collected. The strongest writing contains a variety of evidence effectively. This chart describes three of the most common types of evidence: statistical, testimonial, and anecdotal.

TYPE OF EVIDENCE	DESCRIPTION	EXAMPLE
Statistical evidence includes facts and other numerical data used to support a claim or explain a topic.	Examples of statistical evidence include historical dates and information, quantitative analyses, poll results, and quantitative descriptions.	"Although it went on to become a hugely popular novel, the first edition of William Goldman's book sold fewer than 3,000 copies."
Testimonial evidence includes any ideas or opinions presented by others, especially experts in a field.	Firsthand testimonies present ideas from eyewitnesses to events or subjects being discussed.	"The ground rose and fell like an ocean at ebb tide." —Fred J. Hewitt, eyewitness to the 1906 San Francisco earthquake
	Secondary testimonies include commentaries on events by people who were not involved. You might quote a well-known literary critic when discussing a writer's most famous novel, or a prominent historian when discussing the effects of an important event	Gladys Hansen insists that "there was plenty of water in hydrants throughout [San Francisco] . . . The problem was this fire got away."
Anecdotal evidence presents one person's view of the world, often by describing specific events or incidents.	Compelling research should not rely solely on this form of evidence, but it can be very useful for adding personal insights and refuting inaccurate generalizations. An individual's experience can be used with other forms of evidence to present complete and persuasive support.	Although many critics claim the novel is universally beloved, at least one reader "threw the book against a wall because it made me so angry."

TOOL KIT: RESEARCH

RESEARCH

Incorporating Research Into Writing

Avoiding Plagiarism

Plagiarism is the unethical presentation of someone else's ideas as your own. You must cite sources for direct quotations, paraphrased information, or facts that are specific to a single source. When you are drafting and revising, circle any words or ideas that are not your own. Follow the instructions on pages R32 and R33 to correctly cite those passages.

Review for Plagiarism Always take time to review your writing for unintentional plagiarism. Read what you have written and take note of any phrases or sentences that do not have your personal writing voice. Compare those passages with your resource materials. You might have copied them without remembering the exact source. Add a correct citation to give credit to the original author. If you cannot find the questionable phrase in your notes, revise it to ensure that your final report reflects your own thinking and not someone else's work.

Quoting and Paraphrasing

When including ideas from research into your writing, you will decide to quote directly or paraphrase.

Direct Quotation Use the author's exact words when they are interesting or persuasive. You might decide to include direct quotations for these reasons:

- to share an especially clear and relevant statement
- to reference a historically significant passage
- to show that an expert agrees with your position
- to present an argument that you will counter in your writing.

Include complete quotations, without deleting or changing words. If you need to omit words for space or clarity, use ellipsis points to indicate the omission. Enclose direct quotations in quotation marks and indicate the author's name.

Paraphrase A paraphrase restates an author's ideas in your own words. Be careful to paraphrase accurately. Beware of making sweeping generalizations in a paraphrase that were not made by the original author. You may use some words from the original source, but a legitimate paraphrase does more than simply rearrange an author's phrases, or replace a few words with synonyms.

Original Text	"*The Tempest* was written as a farewell to art and the artist's life, just before the completion of his forty-ninth year, and everything in the play bespeaks the touch of autumn." Brandes, Georg. "Analogies Between *The Tempest* and *A Midsummer Night's Dream*." *The Tempest*, by William Shakespeare, William Heinemann, 1904, p. 668.
Patchwork Plagiarism phrases from the original are rearranged, but too closely follows the original text.	A farewell to art, Shakespeare's play, *The Tempest*, was finished just before the completion of his forty-ninth year. The artist's life was to end within three years. The touch of autumn is apparent in nearly everything in the play.
Good Paraphrase	Images of autumn occur throughout *The Tempest*, which Shakespeare wrote as a way of saying goodbye to both his craft and his own life.

Maintaining the Flow of Ideas

Effective research writing is much more that just a list of facts. Be sure to maintain the flow of ideas by connecting research information to your own ideas. Instead of simply stating a piece of evidence, use transition words and phrases to explain the connection between information you found from outside resources and your own ideas and purpose for writing. The following transitions can be used to introduce, compare, contrast, and clarify.

Useful Transitions

When providing examples:

for example   for instance   to illustrate   in [name of resource], [author]

When comparing and contrasting ideas or information:

in the same way   similarly   however   on the other hand

When clarifying ideas or opinions:

in other words   that is   to explain   to put it another way

Choosing an effective organizational structure for your writing will help you create a logical flow of ideas. Once you have established a clear organizational structure, insert facts and details from your research in appropriate places to provide evidence and support for your writing.

ORGANIZATIONAL STRUCTURE	USES
Chronological order presents information in the sequence in which it happens.	historical topics; science experiments; analysis of narratives
Part-to-whole order examines how several categories affect a larger subject.	analysis of social issues; historical topics
Order of importance presents information in order of increasing or decreasing importance.	persuasive arguments; supporting a bold or challenging thesis
Comparison-and-contrast organization outlines the similarities and differences of a given topic.	addressing two or more subjects

TOOL KIT: RESEARCH

Formats for Citing Sources

In research writing, cite your sources. In the body of your paper, provide a footnote, an endnote, or a parenthetical citation, identifying the sources of facts, opinions, or quotations. At the end of your paper, provide a bibliography or a Works Cited list, a list of all the sources referred to in your research. Follow an established format, such as Modern Language Association (MLA) style.

Parenthetical Citations (MLA Style)

A parenthetical citation briefly identifies the source from which you have taken a specific quotation, factual claim, or opinion. It refers readers to one of the entries on your Works Cited list. A parenthetical citation has the following features:

- It appears in parentheses.
- It identifies the source by the last name of the author, editor, or translator, or by the title (for a lengthy title, list the first word only).
- It provides a page reference, the page(s) of the source on which the information cited can be found.

A parenthetical citation generally falls outside a closing quotation mark but within the final punctuation of a clause or sentence. For a long quotation set off from the rest of your text, place the citation at the end of the excerpt without any punctuation following.

Sample Parenthetical Citations

It makes sense that baleen whales such as the blue whale, the bowhead whale, the humpback whale, and the sei whale (to name just a few) grow to immense sizes (Carwardine et al. 19–21). The blue whale has grooves running from under its chin to partway along the length of its underbelly. As in some other whales, these grooves expand and allow even more food and water to be taken in (Ellis 18–21).

Authors' last names

Page numbers where information can be found

Works Cited List (MLA Style)

A Works Cited list must contain accurate information to enable a reader to locate each source you cite. The basic components of an entry are as follows:

- name of the author, editor, translator, and/or group responsible for the work
- title of the work
- publisher
- date of publication

For print materials, the information for a citation generally appears on the copyright and title pages. For the format of a Works Cited list, consult the examples on this page and in the MLA Style for Listing Sources chart.

Sample Works Cited List (MLA 8th Edition)

Carwardine, Mark, et al. *The Nature Company Guides: Whales, Dolphins, and Porpoises.* Time-Life, 1998.

"Discovering Whales." *Whales on the Net.* Whales in Danger, 1998, www.whales.org.au/discover/index.html. Accessed 11 Apr. 2017.

Neruda, Pablo. "Ode to Spring." *Odes to Opposites,* translated by Ken Krabbenhoft, edited and illustrated by Ferris Cook, Little, 1995, p. 16.

The Saga of the Volsungs. Translated by Jesse L. Byock, Penguin, 1990.

List an anonymous work by title.

List both the title of the work and the collection in which it is found.

Works Cited List or Bibliography?

A Works Cited list includes only those sources you paraphrased or quoted directly in your research paper. By contrast, a bibliography lists all the sources you consulted during research—even those you did not cite.

MLA (8th Edition) Style for Listing Sources

Book with one author	Pyles, Thomas. *The Origins and Development of the English Language.* 2nd ed., Harcourt Brace Jovanovich, 1971. [Indicate the edition or version number when relevant.]
Book with two authors	Pyles, Thomas, and John Algeo. *The Origins and Development of the English Language.* 5th ed., Cengage Learning, 2004.
Book with three or more authors	Donald, Robert B., et al. *Writing Clear Essays.* Prentice Hall, 1983.
Book with an editor	Truth, Sojourner. *Narrative of Sojourner Truth.* Edited by Margaret Washington, Vintage Books, 1993.
Introduction to a work in a published edition	Washington, Margaret. Introduction. *Narrative of Sojourner Truth,* by Sojourner Truth, edited by Washington, Vintage Books, 1993, pp. v–xi.
Single work in an anthology	Hawthorne, Nathaniel. "Young Goodman Brown." *Literature: An Introduction to Reading and Writing,* edited by Edgar V. Roberts and Henry E. Jacobs, 5th ed., Prentice Hall, 1998, pp. 376–385. [Indicate pages for the entire selection.]
Signed article from an encyclopedia	Askeland, Donald R. "Welding." *World Book Encyclopedia,* vol. 21, World Book, 1991, p. 58.
Signed article in a weekly magazine	Wallace, Charles. "A Vodacious Deal." *Time,* 14 Feb. 2000, p. 63.
Signed article in a monthly magazine	Gustaitis, Joseph. "The Sticky History of Chewing Gum." *American History,* Oct. 1998, pp. 30–38.
Newspaper article	Thurow, Roger. "South Africans Who Fought for Sanctions Now Scrap for Investors." *Wall Street Journal,* 11 Feb. 2000, pp. A1+. [For a multipage article that does not appear on consecutive pages, write only the first page number on which it appears, followed by the plus sign.]
Unsigned editorial or story	"Selective Silence." Editorial. *Wall Street Journal,* 11 Feb. 2000, p. A14. [If the editorial or story is signed, begin with the author's name.]
Signed pamphlet or brochure	[Treat the pamphlet as though it were a book.]
Work from a library subscription service	Ertman, Earl L. "Nefertiti's Eyes." *Archaeology,* Mar.–Apr. 2008, pp. 28–32. *Kids Search,* EBSCO, New York Public Library. Accessed 7 Jan. 2017. [Indicating the date you accessed the information is optional but recommended.]
Filmstrips, slide programs, videocassettes, DVDs, and other audiovisual media	*The Diary of Anne Frank.* 1959. Directed by George Stevens, performances by Millie Perkins, Shelley Winters, Joseph Schildkraut, Lou Jacobi, and Richard Beymer, Twentieth Century Fox, 2004. [Indicating the original release date after the title is optional but recommended.]
CD-ROM (with multiple publishers)	Simms, James, editor. *Romeo and Juliet.* By William Shakespeare, Attica Cybernetics / BBC Education / Harper, 1995.
Radio or television program transcript	"Washington's Crossing of the Delaware." *Weekend Edition Sunday,* National Public Radio, 23 Dec. 2013. Transcript.
Web page	"Fun Facts About Gum." ICGA, 2005–2017, www.gumassociation.org/index.cfm/facts-figures/fun-facts-about-gum. Accessed 19 Feb. 2017. [Indicating the date you accessed the information is optional but recommended.]
Personal interview	Smith, Jane. Personal interview, 10 Feb. 2017.

All examples follow the style given in the MLA Handbook, 8th edition, published in 2016.

MODEL

Evidence Log

Unit Title: __Discovery__

Perfomance-Based Assessment Prompt:
Do all discoveries benefit humanity?

My initial thoughts:
Yes - all knowledge moves us forward.

As you read multiple texts about a topic, your thinking may change. Use an Evidence Log like this one to record your thoughts, to track details you might use in later writing or discussion, and to make further connections.

Here is a sample to show how one reader's ideas deepened as she read two texts.

Title of Text: __Classifying the Stars__   Date: __Sept. 17__

CONNECTION TO THE PROMPT	TEXT EVIDENCE/DETAILS	ADDITIONAL NOTES/IDEAS
Newton shared his discoveries and then other scientists built on his discoveries.	Paragraph 2: "Isaac Newton gave to the world the results of his experiments on passing sunlight through a prism." Paragraph 3: "In 1814 . . . the German optician, Fraunhofer . . . saw that the multiple spectral tints . . . were crossed by hundreds of fine dark lines."	It's not always clear how a discovery might benefit humanity in the future.

How does this text change or add to my thinking? This confirms what I think.   Date: __Sept. 20__

Title of Text: __Cell Phone Mania__   Date: __Sept. 21__

CONNECTION TO THE PROMPT	TEXT EVIDENCE/DETAILS	ADDITIONAL NOTES/IDEAS
Cell phones have made some forms of communication easier, but people don't talk to each other as much as they did in the past.	Paragraph 7: "Over 80% of young adults state that texting is their primary method of communicating with friends. This contrasts with older adults who state that they prefer a phone call."	Is it good that we don't talk to each other as much? Look for article about social media to learn more about this question.

How does this text change or add to my thinking?   Date: __Sept. 25__
Maybe there are some downsides to discoveries. I still think that knowledge moves us forward, but there are sometimes unintended negative effects.

Word Network

A word network is a collection of words related to a topic. As you read the selections in a unit, identify interesting theme-related words and build your vocabulary by adding them to your Word Network.

Use your Word Network as a resource for your discussions and writings. Here is an example:

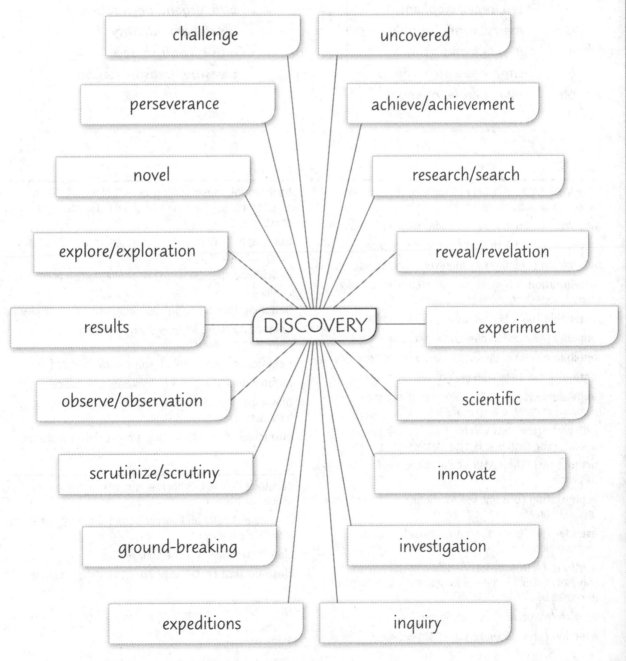

challenge

uncovered

perseverance

achieve/achievement

novel

research/search

explore/exploration

reveal/revelation

results

DISCOVERY

experiment

observe/observation

scientific

scrutinize/scrutiny

innovate

ground-breaking

investigation

expeditions

inquiry

ACADEMIC / CONCEPT VOCABULARY

Academic vocabulary appears in **blue type**.

Pronunciation Key

Symbol	Sample Words	Symbol	Sample Words
a	_at, catapult, Alabama_	oo	_boot, soup, crucial_
ah	_father, charms, argue_	ow	_now, stout, flounder_
ai	_care, various, hair_	oy	_boy, toil, oyster_
aw	_law, maraud, caution_	s	_say, nice, press_
awr	_pour, organism, forewarn_	sh	_she, abolition, motion_
ay	_ape, sails, implication_	u	_full, put, book_
ee	_even, teeth, really_	uh	_ago, focus, contemplation_
eh	_ten, repel, elephant_	ur	_bird, urgent. perforation_
ehr	_merry, verify, terribly_	y	_by, delight, identify_
ih	_it, pin, hymn_	yoo	_music, confuse, few_
o	_shot, hopscotch, condo_	zh	_pleasure, treasure, vision_
oh	_own, parole, rowboat_		

A

advocate (AD vuh kiht) _n._ supporter; (AD vuh kayt) _v._ represent or support publicly

allocate (AL uh kayt) _v._ set aside; assign or portion

allusion (uh LOO zhuhn) _n._ indirect reference

altercation (awl tuhr KAY shuhn) _n._ angry dispute; quarrel

amelioration (uh meel yuh RAY shuhn) _n._ act of making something better or less painful

amenable (uh MEH nuh buhl) _adj._ agreeable

amiably (AY mee uh blee) _adv._ pleasantly

annihilate (uh NY uh layt) _v._ destroy completely

antiquity (an TIHK wuh tee) _n._ very great age

appeasement (uh PEEZ muhnt) _n._ giving in to demands in order to keep peace

articulate (ahr TIHK yuh liht) _adj._ spoken clearly; distinct; (ahr TIHK yuh layt) _v._ clearly express

artifact (AHR tuh fakt) _n._ object made, modified, or used by people

asphyxiation (uhs fihk see AY shuhn) _n._ state of being unable to breathe

asunder (uh SUHN duhr) _adv._ divided; torn into separate pieces

attribute (A truh byoot) _n._ quality or characteristic; (uh TRIHB yoot) _v._ think of as belonging to; to think of as caused by

avarice (AV uh rihs) _n._ great greed

aversion (uh VUR zhuhn) _n._ strong dislike

B

background music (BAK grownd) (MYOO zihk) _n._ music that is not the focus of a show but is added for effect

bar graph (bahr) (graf) _n._ representation of data points using rectangular bars

beachhead (BEECH hehd) _n._ secure starting point; foothold

beguiling (bih GY lihng) _adj._ influencing through charm

belaboring (bih LAY buhr ihng) _v._ focusing on something too much

beneficent (buh NEHF uh suhnt) _adj._ kind and good

bigotry (BIHG uh tree) _n._ intolerance; prejudice

blessings (BLEHS ihngz) _n._ things that benefit or bring happiness

burnished (BUR nihsht) _adj._ shiny; polished to a shine

C

cartilage (KAHR tuh lihj) _n._ firm, flexible tissue almost as hard as bone

chronicle (KRON uh kuhl) _n._ recorded history; narrative _v._ write the history of

clench (klehnch) _v._ close tightly

close-up shot (KLOS uhp) (shot) _n._ close-range view of the subject

GLOSSARY: ACADEMIC / CONCEPT VOCABULARY

cognitive (KOG nuh tihv) *adj.* relating to the process of thinking

commentators (KOM uhn tay tuhrz) *n.* people who discuss or write about events for film, television, radio, or newspapers

communal (kuh MYOON uhl) *adj.* belonging to all in a community or group

composition (kom puh ZIHSH uhn) *n.* arrangement of the parts of a photograph

contentious (kuhn TEHN shuhs) *adj.* fond of arguing; quarrelsome; controversial

context (KON tehkst) *n.* position and immediate surroundings of an artifact or other feature in the location where it is found

contradict (kon truh DIHKT) *v.* do, say, or mean the opposite of; disagree with

current (KUR uhnt) *n.* flow of liquid, air, electricity, etc.

D

decree (dih KREE) *n.* decision made by an authority

deduce (dih DOOS) *v.* reach a conclusion by reasoning

delineate (dih LIHN ee ayt) *v.* trace an outline; draw or sketch out; describe

delusions (dih LOO zhuhnz) *n.* false beliefs

demarcate (DEE mahr kayt) *v.* set the limits of

democracy (dih MOK ruh see) *n.* government that is run by the people

democratic (dehm uh KRAT ihk) *adj.* belonging to a democracy; of, by, and for the people

desperate (DEHS puhr iht) *adj.* extremely bad; reckless; without hope

despoiled (dih SPOYLD) *v.* robbed; stripped of possessions

dimension (duh MEHN shuhn) *n.* measurement of length, width, or depth; quality or part

disarmament (dihs AHR muh muhnt) *n.* limiting or getting rid of weapons

dissolution (dihs uh LOO shuhn) *n.* ending or downfall

dissonance (DIHS uh nuhns) *n.* lack of agreement or harmony

distress (dihs TREHS) *n.* unhappiness or pain

doctrine (DOK truhn) *n.* set of principles or beliefs

dominating (DOM uh nay ting) *adj.* rising high above; towering over

E

edicts (EE dihkts) *n.* commands from a public authority

editing (EHD iht ihng) *v.* taking pieces of film or video and putting them together in a new way.

Egyptology (ee jihp TOL uh jee) *n.* study of the language, culture, and history of ancient Egypt

elemental (ehl uh MEHN tuhl) *adj.* basic; necessary; as found in nature

entitled (ehn TY tuhld) *adj.* having the rights to something; having privileges

entreating (ehn TREET ihng) *adj.* asking; pleading

enunciation (ih nuhn see AY shuhn) *n.* manner in which a speaker pronounces words

envoy (EHN voy) *n.* messenger

ethereal (ih THIHR ee uhl) *adj.* extremely delicate and light in a way that seems too perfect for this world

exquisite (EHKS kwihz iht) *adj.* very beautiful or lovely

F

fissure (FIHSH uhr) *n.* long, narrow crack or opening

flurry (FLUR ee) *n.* sudden burst of activity or excitement

fundamental (fuhn duh MEHN tuhl) *adj.* basic; essential; most important

G

gallantries (GAL uhn treez) *n.* acts of polite attention to the needs of women

gesture (JEHS chuhr) *n.* movement of the body that conveys meaning

gilded (GIHLD ihd) *v.* covered in a thin layer of gold; *adj.* golden

gregarious (gruh GAIR ee uhs) *adj.* sociable

H

heir (air) *n.* person who is legally entitled to inherit

hierarchy (HY uh rahr kee) *n.* people or things organized in higher and lower ranks or classes

homage (OM ihj) *n.* something done to honor someone

hounded (HOWN dihd) *v.* chased; hunted; urged

I

iconography (y kuh NOG ruh fee) *n.* system of symbolic images that conveys a subject, worldview, or concept

ideologies (y dee OL uh jeez) *n.* sets of beliefs of a people, groups, or cultures

implore (ihm PLAWR) *v.* beg or plead

incite (ihn SYT) *v.* strongly encourage

incoherent (ihn koh HIHR uhnt) *adj.* not understandable; confused

indomitable (ihn DOM uh tuh buhl) *adj.* bravely or stubbornly unyielding

industrious (ihn DUHS tree uhs) *adj.* hard-working

inestimable (ihn EHS tuh muh buhl) *adj.* too great to count or measure

inexorable (ihn EHK suhr uh buhl) *adj.* impossible to prevent or stop

inflection (ihn FLEHK shuhn) *n.* changes to pitch or volume within a single word or between words

influence (IHN floo uhns) *n.* dishonest persuasion; bribery

infographic (ihn foh GRAF ihk) *n.* display that combines text with visual elements and design to represent data

initiative (ih NIHSH ee uh tihv) *n.* readiness and abillity to start something; lead

integrate (IHN tuh grayt) *v.* make public facilities availabe to people of all races; bring parts together to make a whole

intemperate (ihn TEHM puhr iht) *adj.* lacking self-control; excessive

interactions (ihn tuhr AK shuhnz) *n.* actions with each other

intercept (ihn tuhr SEHPT) *v.* stop or seize something before it gets to its destination

interdependence (ihn tuhr dih PEHN duhns) *n.* reliance on each other

invective (ihn VEHK tihv) *n.* negative, aggressive language that seeks to harm

invoke (ihn VOHK) *v.* call on

invulnerable (in VUHL nuhr uh buhl) *adj.* incapable of being harmed

L

lead-in (LEED ihn) *n.* in a newscast, the short preliminary section that is used to set up the main story or interview

legacy (LEHG uh see) *n.* something handed down from an ancestor or prior generation

lighting and color (LYT ihng) (KUHL uhr) *n.* use of light, shadow, and color in a photograph

line graph (lyn) (graf) *n.* representation of data points using a line that connects points

listlessly (LIHST lihs lee) *adv.* without energy or interest

location (loh KAY shuhn) *n.* place or scene in which a photograph is taken

luminous (LOO muh nuhs) *adj.* glowing; shining with its own light

lustrous (LUHS truhs) *adj.* shiny; brilliant

M

mail (mayl) *n.* flexible armor

manipulate (muh NIHP yuh layt) *v.* handle or operate; unfairly influence or change

marauding (muh RAW dihng) *adj.* killing and using violence to steal precious items

marginalize (MAHR juh nuh lyz) *v.* treat as unimportant

marvel (MAHR vuhl) *n.* astonishment; used poetically as an adjective meaning "astonished" or "full of wonder"

merciful (MUR sih fuhl) *adj.* showing kindness

motivate (MOH tuh vayt) *v.* provide with an incentive

muffled (MUH fuhld) *adj.* difficult to hear because something is covering and softening the sound

N

navigating (NAV uh gayt ihng) *n.* finding one's way

needy (NEE dee) *adj.* very poor; requiring help

negate (nih GAYT) *v.* make invalid; deny the truth of

O

obdurate (OB duhr iht) *adj.* stubborn; unyielding

objection (uhb JEHK shuhn) *n.* reason or argument against something

obscure (uhb SKYAWR) *adj.* not well-known

opportune (op uhr TOON) *adj.* very favorable

oracles (AWR uh kuhlz) *n.* people who deliver messages from the gods

ore (awr) *n.* any type of mineral, rock, or metal found in the earth

P

pacification (pas uh fuh KAY shuhn) *n.* state of peace put in place through diplomacy, or political negotiation; also, use of force to suppress a hostile or resistent population

paradox (PAR uh doks) *n.* seeming contradiction

pardon (PAHR duhn) *v.* forgive

pariah (puh RY uh) *n.* someone who is despised; social outcast

penitent (PEHN uh tuhnt) *adj.* sorry for one's wrongdoing

perfidious (puhr FIHD ee uhs) *adj.* unfaithful and dishonest

periphery (puh RIHF uhr ee) *n.* outer boundary; edge

perplexity (puhr PLEHK suh tee) *n.* confusion; being in a puzzled state

perspective (puhr SPEHK tihv) *n.* particular way of looking at something; point of view

perspective or angle (puhr SPEHK tihv) (ANG guhl) *n.* vantage point from which a photograph is taken

pie chart (py) (chahrt) *n.* representation of data points using a circle cut into segments

primary (PRY mehr ee) *adj.* first in importance

proclamation (prok luh MAY shuhn) *n.* official announcement

propaganda (prop uh GAN duh) *n.* information, often of a false or misleading nature, used to promote a cause

prophecy (PROF uh see) *n.* prediction about the future

psychological (sy kuh LOJ uh kuhl) *adj.* of the mind

R

recessed (rih SEHST) *adj.* remote; set back

reclusive (rih KLOO sihv) *adj.* solitary; avoiding the company of others

rectify (REHK tuh fy) *v.* correct

refinement (rih FYN muhnt) *n.* politeness; good manners

rending (REHN dihng) *n.* violent or forceful pulling apart of something

resplendent (rih SPLEHN duhnt) *adj.* dazzling; gorgeous

revolution (rehv uh LOO shuhn) *n.* overthrow of a government that is replaced by a new system

S

sabotage (SAB uh tozh) *v.* intentionally ruin or destroy

scarred (skahrd) *adj.* marked by healed wounds

shunned (shuhnd) *v.* rejected; avoided

silhouette (sihl uh WEHT) *n.* dark figure that is seen as a filled-in shape against a light background

sinister (SIHN uh stuhr) *adj.* giving the impression that something harmful or evil is happening or will happen

slant (slant) *n.* attitude or opinion that a reporter takes toward a story

sliver (SLIHV uhr) *n.* small, slender piece of a hard material

sneered (sneerd) *v.* showed dislike with a mean smile

spacious (SPAY shuhs) *adj.* large; roomy

spitefully (SPYT fuhl ee) *adv.* in a way that purposely harms someone or something

stimulus (STIHM yoo luhs) *n.* something that causes a response or reaction

stock footage (stok) (FUT ihj) *n.* film or video that has been shot for one purpose and is available for use in other projects

stoical (STOH ih kuhl) *adj.* keeping strong emotions in check

subject (SUHB jehkt) *n.* primary figure(s), object(s), or other content in a photograph

subversive (suhb VUR sihv) *adj.* causing ruin; destructive

succession (suhk SEHSH uhn) *n.* process by which one is entitled to a privilege, rank or inheritance

supplant (suh PLANT) *v.* replace by unethical means

suppleness (SUHP uhl nihs) *n.* smoothness; fluidity; ability to adapt easily to different situations

surrender (suh REHN duhr) *n.* act of giving up

swollen (SWOH luhn) *adj.* puffed up

T

target (TAHR giht) *n.* object to be hit or shot at

tolerate (TOL uh rayt) *v.* endure; allow to happen without interference

tone (tohn) *n.* sound of a voice with respect to pitch, volume, and overall quality

totalitarian (toh tal uh TAIR ee uhn) *adj.* ruled or governed by a single person or group

transcend (tran SEHND) *v.* go beyond the limits of; be higher or greater than

travail (truh VAYL) *n.* difficult situation or work

traversed (truh VURST) *v.* crossed; traveled across; moved sideways

treacherous (TREHCH uhr uhs) *adj.* not trustworthy

treachery (TREHCH uhr ee) *n.* act of betrayal

trill (trihl) *n.* high-pitched vibrating sound

tumultuous (too MUHL choo uhs) *adj.* loud, excited, and emotional

tyranny (TEER uh nee) *n.* harsh rule over a nation or people

U

unconquerable (uhn KAHNG kuh ruh buhl) *adj.* unable to be defeated

unvoiced (uhn VOYST) *adj.* not spoken out loud or expressed

usurp (yoo ZURP) *v.* take over without having authority

V

valiant (VAL yuhnt) *adj.* brave; courageous

valor (VAL uhr) *n.* personal fortitude or bravery

vehement (VEE uh muhnt) *adj.* showing stong feeling; passionate

verify (VEHR uh fy) *v.* prove to be true

vestibule (VEHS tuh byool) *n.* entrance room

vigilance (VIHJ uh luhns) *n.* watchfulness

vivid (VIHV ihd) *adj.* bright and brilliant; strong and distinct; very intense

volition (voh LIHSH uhn) *n.* act of choosing

vulnerable (VUHL nuhr uh buhl) *adj.* able to be wounded or hurt

W

welt (wehlt) *n.* ridge on the skin caused by a blow

windfall (WIHND fawl) *n.* unexpected good fortune

VOCABULARIO ACADÉMICO/ VOCABULARIO DE CONCEPTOS

El vocabulario académico está en **letra azul**.

A

advocate / abogar *v.* representar o apoyar públicamente

allocate / asignar *v.* apartar; repartir o dividir

allusion / alusión *s.* referencia indirecta

altercation / altercado *s.* disputa; pelea

amelioration / mejoramiento *s.* acto de mejorar algo, o de hacerlo menos doloroso

amenable / dispuesto *adj.* agradable

amiably / amablemente *adv.* cordialmente, afablemente

annihilate / aniquilar *v.* destruir por completo

antiquity / antigüedad *s.* de muchos años; de hace mucho tiempo

appeasement / apaciguamiento *s.* el acto de aceptar exigencias con el fin de mantener la paz

articulate / articular *v.* expresar claramente

articulate / elocuente *adj.* claramente expresado

artifacts / artefactos *s.* objetos de interés histórico hechos por los seres humanos

asphyxiation / asfixia *s.* estado en el que resulta imposible respirar

asunder / dividido *adj.* separado; desarmado en distintas partes

attribute / atribuir *v.* pensar que algo es de la competencia de alguien o algo, o que fue causado por esa persona o hecho

avarice / avaricia *s.* avidez o codicia desmedida

aversion / aversión *s.* fuerte rechazo

B

background music / música de fondo *s.* música que no es el centro de un espectáculo, pero que se incluye para producir un efecto

bar chart / gráfica de barras *s.* representación de datos en la que se usa barras rectangulares

beachhead / cabeza de puente *s.* posición militar; asidero o punto de apoyo

beguiling / encantador *adj.* que influye por medio de su encanto

belaboring / concentrarse *v.* centrarse en algo con mucha intensidad

benificent / bienhechor *adj.* amable, bueno, caritativo

bigotry / intolerancia *s.* prejuicio; fanatismo

blessings / bendiciones *s.* cosas que benefician o que producen felicidad

burnished / bruñido *adj.* brilloso; pulido

C

caption / pie de foto *s.* texto breve que acompaña a una imagen

cartilage / cartílago *s.* tejido fuerte y flexible, casi tan duro como un hueso

chronicle / crónica *s.* relato histórico; narración

clench / apretar *v.* cerrar con fuerza

close-up shot / toma de primer plano *s.* imagen del sujeto tomada muy de cerca

cognitive / cognitivo *adj.* relacionado con el proceso de pensar

commentators / comentaristas *s.* personas que comentan o escriben sobre ciertos eventos para el cine, la televisión, la radio o los periódicos

communal / comunal *adj.* que pertenece a todos los miembros de una comunidad o grupo

composition / composición *s.* distribución o arreglo de las partes de una fotografía

contentious / peleador *adj.* que le gusta discutir o buscar pelea

context / contexto *s.* posición y entorno inmediato de un artefacto u otro elemento en el lugar donde es encontrado

contradict / contradecir *v.* negar que un enunciado sea cierto; discrepar

current / corriente *s.* flujo de líquido, aire, electricidad, etc; *adj.* actual, relativo al tiempo presente

D

decree / decreto *s.* decisión tomada por una autoridad

deduce / deducir *v.* llegar a una conclusión a través del razonamiento

delineate / delinear *v.* trazar un bosquejo; dibujar o esbozar; describir

delusions / delirios *s.* creencias falsas; engaños, ilusiones

demarcate / demarcar *v.* establecer los límites de algo

democracy / democracia *s.* gobierno conducido por el pueblo

democratic / democrático *adj.* que pertenece a una democracia; que es de, por y para el pueblo

desperate / desesperado *adj.* extremadamente mal; sin esperanza

despoiled / depojado *adj.* robado; privado de sus posesiones

dimension / dimensión *s.* medición de la longitud, el ancho o la profundidad; una cualidad o parte

disarmament / desarme *s.* acción de limitar o eliminar las armas

dissolution / disolución *s.* final o ruina

dissonance / disonancia *s.* falta de acuerdo o de armonía

distress / aflicción *s.* infelicidad o dolor

doctrine / doctrina *s.* conjunto de principios o creencias

dominating / dominante *adj.* que se alza por encima; que se destaca de los demás

E

edicts / edictos *s.* mandatos

editing / editar *v.* tomar partes de una película o video y volver a juntarlas de otra manera

Egyptology / egiptología *s.* estudio del lenguaje, la cultura y la historia del Egipto antiguo

elemental / elemental *adj.* básico; necesario; como se encuentra en la naturaleza

entitled / autorizado *adj.* que tiene el derecho a algo; que tiene ciertos privilegios

entreating / suplicante *adj.* que pide o ruega

enunciation / enunciación *s.* la manera en que un hablante expone las palabras

envoy / enviado *s.* mensajero

ethereal / etéreo *adj.* sumamente delicado y ligero

exquisite / exquisito *adj.* muy bello o agradable

F

fissure / fisura *s.* abertura o grieta larga y estrecha

flurry / frenesí *s.* explosión repentina de actividad o entusiasmo

fundamental / fundamental *adj.* que forma el fundamento o base; parte esencial

G

gallantries / galanterías *s.* gestos corteses de atención hacia las mujeres

gesture / gesto *s.* movimiento del cuerpo que transmite un mensaje

gilded / dorado *adj.* cubierto con una ligera capa de oro; de color oro

gregarious / gregario *adj.* sociable

H

heir / heredero *s.* persona que está legalmente autorizada a heredar determinados bienes

hierarchy / jerarquía *s.* personas o cosas organizadas en rangos o clases, del más alto al más bajo

homage / homenaje *s.* algo que se hace para honrar a una persona

hounded / acosado *adj.* perseguido; urgido

I

iconography / iconografía *s.* sistema de imágenes simbólicas que representa a un personaje, tema, visión del mundo o concepto

ideologies / ideologías *s.* conjuntos de creencias de una persona, un grupo o una cultura

implore / implorar *v.* rogar, suplicar

incite / incitar *v.* estimular con firmeza a alguien para que haga algo

incoherent / incoherente *adj.* confuso; difícil de entender

indomitable / indomable *adj.* difícil de dominar, bravío; inflexible

industrious / industrioso *adj.* trabajador

inestimable / inestimable *adj.* tan importante que no se puede estimar o medir

inexorable / inexorable *adj.* imposible de prever o impedir

inflection / inflección *s.* cambios en el tono o volumen dentro de una misma palabra o entre palabras

influence / influencia *s.* persuasión, a veces deshonesta, como cuando se usa de "enchufe" o "palanca", es decir, como contacto para lograr algo

infographic / infografía *s.* representación gráfica de información que incluye símbolos, fotos, mapas, textos y elementos de diseño visuales

initiative / iniciativa *s.* disponibilidad o habilidad para iniciar algo

integrate / integrar *v.* hacer los servicios públicos accesibles a todas las razas; unir las partes de un todo

intemperate / desmedido *adj.* descontrolado; excesivo

interactions / interacciones *s.* acciones de unos con otros

intercept / interceptar *v.* detener o apropiarse de algo antes de que llegue a su destino

interdependence / interdependencia *s.* dependencia o confianza mutua

invective / invectiva *s.* discurso negativo y agresivo que intenta herir

invoke / invocar *v.* llamar, convocar

invulnerable / invulnerable *adj.* que no se puede dañar

L

lead-in / entradilla *s.* introducción a una noticia o entrevista

legacy / legado *s.* algo que se transmite o pasa de un ancestro a sus descendientes, o de una generación a otra

lighting and color / luz y color *s.* modo de usar las luces, las sombras y los colores en una fotografía

line graph / gráfica de líneas s. representación de datos mediante una línea para conectar puntos

listlessly / lánguidamente adv. sin energía ni interés

location / ubicación s. lugar donde se toma una fotografía

luminous / luminoso adj. brillante; que brilla con su propia luz

lustrous / lustroso adj. brilloso, brillante

M

mail / cota de malla s. armadura flexible

manipulate / manipular v. manejar u operar; cambiar o influir de manera injusta

marauding / saqueador adj. que mata y usa la violencia para robar objetos de valor

marginalize / marginalizar v. tratar a alguien como si no fuera importante

marvel / maravilla / maravillarse s. algo asombroso; v. estar sumamente asombrado

merciful / compasivo adj. clemente, misericordioso

motivate / motivar v. proporcionar un incentivo para que alguien se interese en algo

muffled / sofocado adj. difícil de oír porque algo cubre y suaviza el sonido

N

navigating / navegar v. dirigir, guiar

needy / necesitado adj. muy pobre; que precisa ayuda

negate / negar v. invalidar; negarle razón a algo

O

obdurate / obstinado adj. terco; inflexible

objection / objeción s. razón o argumento contra algo

obscure / oscuro adj. desconocido

opportune / oportuno adj. muy conveniente; que sucede en el momento apropiado

oracle / oráculo s. persona que da mensajes de los dioses

ore / mineral s. cualquier tipo de sustancia inorgánica sólida, piedra o metal que se encuentra en la tierra

P

pacification / pacificación s. estado de calma o paz como resultado de la acción de la diplomacia o de la negociación política

paradox / paradoja s. enunciado, dato o situación inconsistente con las creencias aceptadas

pardon / perdonar v. disculpar

pariah / paria s. alguien que es despreciado; un marginado

penitent / penitente adj. alguien que se arrepiente de sus malas acciones

perfidious / pérfido adj. infiel y deshonesto

periphery / periferia s. límite exterior; borde

perplexity / perplejidad s. confusión; estado de desconcierto

perspective / perspectiva s. punto de vista

perspective / perspectiva s. en un cuadro o foto, la ilusión o efecto de profundidad

perspective or angle / perspectiva o ángulo s. punto o lugar desde el cual se toma una fotografía

photojournalism / fotoperiodismo s. tipo de periodismo en el que las fotos constituyen gran parte del artículo

pie chart / gráfico circular s. representación de los datos mediante un círculo dividido en segmentos

portrait / retrato s. imagen de una persona o de un grupo de personas

primary / primario / primarias adj. primero en importancia; s. elección en la que se escoge el candidato de un partido político

proclamation / proclamación s. anuncio oficia

propaganda / propaganda s. información, por lo general falsa, que se usa para promover una causa

prophecy / profecía s. predicción acerca del futuro

psychological / psicológico adj. relativo a la mente

R

recessed / retirado adj. lejano; oculto

reclusive / aislado adj. solitario; que evita la compañía de otros

rectify / rectificar v. corregir

refinement / refinamiento s. gentileza; buenas maneras

rending / desgarrar v. rasgar o romper algo con violencia o por la fuerza

resplendent / resplandeciente adj. deslumbrante; espléndido

revolution / revolución s. derrocamiento de un gobierno con el fin de reemplazarlo por otro sistema

S

sabotage / sabotear v. arruinar; hacer daño

scarred / marcado adj. que tiene cicatrices de antiguas heridas

shun / evitar v. rechazar; rehuir

silhouette / silueta s. figura oscura que se ve como un recorte contra un fondo claro

sinister / siniestro adj. malévolo; amenazador

slant / sesgo (ideológico) s. actitud u opinión del reportero acerca de una noticia

sliver / astilla s. trozo pequeño y fino de un material duro

sneered / se burló v. mostró disgusto haciendo una mueca

social documentary / foto documental s. género fotográfico que muestra a la gente en su entorno habitual

spacious / espacioso adj. grande; amplio

spitefully / maliciosamente *adv.* con el propósito de hacerle daño a alguien o algo

stimulus / estímulo *s.* algo que provoca una respuesta o reacción

stock footage / filmación de archivo *s.* película o video que se ha grabado con un propósito y está disponible para usarse en otros proyectos

stoical / estoico *adj.* de manera que controla las emociones fuertes

subject / sujeto *s.* figura(s), objeto(s) u otro contenido de una fotografía

subversive / subversivo *adj.* que intenta cambiar el orden establecido; destructivo o causante de ruina

succession / sucesión *s.* proceso por el cual una persona adquiere el derecho a un privilegio, rango o herencia

supplant / suplantar *v.* reemplazar a alguien por medios ilegítimos o poco éticos

suppleness / flexibilidad *s.* la habilidad de adaptarse con facilidad a distintas situaciones

surrender / rendirse *s.* darse por vencido

swollen / inflamado *adj.* hinchado

T

target / blanco *s.* objeto al que se debe disparar o tirar

tolerate / tolerar *v.* soportar; permitir que algo suceda, sin interferir

tone / tono *s.* sonido de una voz con respecto a la modulación, volumen y timbre general

totalitarian / totalitario *adj.* dominado o gobernado por un solo grupo o persona

transcend / trascender *v.* traspasar los límites de algo; ser más alto o más grande que algo

travail / esfuerzo *s.* trabajo o situación difícil

traversed / atravesado *adj.* cruzado; recorrido; que se movió de lado

treacherous / traicionero *adj.* que no es digno de confianza

treachery / traición *s.* acción desleal

trill / gorjeo *s.* sonido muy alto y vibrante; *v.* gorjear, producir un sonido muy alto y vibrante

tumultuous / tumultuoso *adj.* fuerte, alterado y emocional

tyranny / tiranía *s.* gobierno cruel de un pueblo o nación

U

unconquerable / inconquistable *adj.* que no puede ser vencido

unvoiced / tácito *adj.* no dicho, implícito

usurp / usurpar *v.* tomar algo por la fuerza, sin tener autoridad para hacerlo

V

valiant / valiente *adj.* bravo; aguerrido

valor / valor *s.* valentía o fortaleza personal

vehement / vehemente *adj.* que demuestra tener sentimientos intensos; apasionado

verify / verificar *v.* comprobar que algo es cierto

vestibule / vestíbulo *s.* entrada o recibidor

vigilance / vigilancia *s.* supervisión, custodia, alerta

vivid / vívido *adj.* luminoso y brillante; fuerte y distinto; muy intenso

volition / volición *s.* acto o capacidad de escoger

vulnerable / vulnerable *adj.* que puede ser herido o dañado

W

welt / verdugón *s.* marca en la piel causada por un golpe

windfall / ganancia inesperada *s.* golpe de suerte; beneficios caídos del cielo

LITERARY TERMS HANDBOOK

ABSURDISM *Absurdism*, or *absurdist literature*, is a form of modernism that includes fantastic or dreamlike elements that blur the boundary between what is real and unreal.

ALLITERATION *Alliteration* is the repetition of initial consonant sounds. Writers use alliteration to give emphasis to words, to imitate sounds, and to create musical effects.

ALLUSION An *allusion* is a reference to a well-known person, place, event, literary work, or work of art.

ANALOGY An *analogy* makes a comparison between two or more things that are similar in some ways but otherwise unalike.

ANAPHORA *Anaphora* is a type of parallel structure in which a word or phrase is repeated at the beginning of successive clauses for emphasis.

ANECDOTE An *anecdote* is a brief story told to entertain or to make a point.

ANTAGONIST An *antagonist* is a character or force in conflict with a main character, or protagonist.

APOSTROPHE An *apostrophe* is a figure of speech in which a speaker directly addresses an absent person or a personified quality, object, or idea.

APPEAL An *appeal* is a rhetorical device used in argumentative writing to persuade an audience.

An appeal to ethics (Ethos) shows that an argument is just or fair.

An appeal to logic (Logos)shows that an argument is well reasoned.

An appeal to authority shows that a higher power supports the ideas.

An appeal to emotion (Pathos) is designed to influence readers.

ARGUMENT An *argument* is writing or speech that attempts to convince a reader to think or act in a particular way. An argument is a logical way of presenting a belief, conclusion, or stance. A good argument is supported with reasoning and evidence.

ASIDE An *aside* is a short speech delivered by a character in a play in order to express his or her thoughts and feelings. Traditionally, the aside is directed to the audience and is presumed not to be heard by the other characters.

AUTOBIOGRAPHY An *autobiography* is a form of nonfiction in which a writer tells his or her own life story. An autobiography may tell about the person's whole life or only a part of it.

BIOGRAPHY A *biography* is a form of nonfiction in which a writer tells the life story of another person.

Biographies have been written about many famous people, historical and contemporary, but they can also be written about "ordinary" people.

BLANK VERSE *Blank verse* is poetry written in unrhymed iambic pentameter lines. This verse form was widely used by William Shakespeare.

CHARACTER A *character* is a person or an animal who takes part in the action of a literary work. The main character, or protagonist, is the most important character in a story. This character often changes in some important way as a result of the story's events.

Characters are sometimes classified as round or flat, dynamic or static. A *round character* shows many different traits—faults as well as virtues. A *flat character* shows only one trait. A *dynamic character* develops and grows during the course of the story; a *static character* does not change.

CHARACTERIZATION *Characterization* is the act of creating and developing a character. In *direct characterization*, the author directly states a character's traits.

In *indirect characterization*, an author gives clues about a character by describing what a character looks like, does, and says, as well as how other characters react to him or her. It is up to the reader to draw conclusions about the character based on this indirect information.

The most effective indirect characterizations usually result from showing characters acting or speaking.

CLIMAX The *climax* of a story, novel, or play is the high point of interest or suspense. The events that make up the rising action lead up to the climax. The events that make up the falling action follow the climax.

COMEDY A *comedy* is a literary work, especially a play, that has a happy ending. Comedies often show ordinary characters in conflict with society. These conflicts are introduced through misunderstandings, deceptions, and concealed identities. When the conflict is resolved, the result is the correction of moral faults or social wrongs. Types of comedy include *romantic comedy*, which involves problems among lovers, and the *comedy of manners*, which satirically challenges the social customs of a sophisticated society. Comedy is often contrasted with tragedy, in which the protagonist meets an unfortunate end.

COMIC RELIEF *Comic relief* is a technique that is used to interrupt a serious part of a literary work by introducing a humorous character or situation.

CONFLICT A *conflict* is a struggle between opposing forces. Characters in conflict form the basis of stories, novels, and plays.

There are two kinds of conflict: **external** and **internal**. In an external conflict, the main character struggles against an outside force. The outside force may be nature itself.

An *internal conflict* involves a character in conflict with himself or herself.

CONNOTATION The *connotation* of a word is the set of ideas associated with it in addition to its explicit meaning.

CONSONANCE *Consonance* is the repetition of final consonant sounds in stressed syllables with different vowel sounds, as in *hat* and *sit*.

COUPLET A *couplet* is a pair of rhyming lines, usually of the same length and meter.

DENOTATION The *denotation* of a word is its dictionary meaning, independent of other associations that the word may have. The denotation of the word *lake*, for example, is "an inland body of water."

DESCRIPTION A *description* is a portrait in words of a person, place, or object. Descriptive writing uses sensory details, those that appeal to the senses: sight, hearing, taste, smell, and touch. Description can be found in all types of writing.

DIALECT *Dialect* is a special form of a language, spoken by people in a particular region or group. It may involve changes to the pronunciation, vocabulary, and sentence structure of the standard form of the language. Rudyard Kipling's "Danny Deever" is a poem written in the Cockney dialect of English, used by working-class Londoners.

DIALOGUE A *dialogue* is a conversation between characters that may reveal their traits and advance the action of a narrative. In fiction or nonfiction, quotation marks indicate a speaker's exact words, and a new paragraph usually indicates a change of speaker.

Quotation marks are not used in *script*, the printed copy of a play. Instead, the dialogue follows the name of the speaker:

DICTION *Diction* refers to an author's choice of words, especially with regard to range of vocabulary, use of slang and colloquial language, and level of formality.

DRAMA A *drama* is a story written to be performed by actors. The script of a drama is made up of *dialogue*—the words the actors say—and *stage directions,* which are descriptions of how and where action happens.

The drama's *setting* is the time and place in which the action occurs. It is indicated by one or more sets, including furniture and backdrops, that suggest interior or exterior scenes. *Props* are objects, such as a sword or a cup of tea, that are used onstage.

At the beginning of most plays, a brief *exposition* gives the audience some background information about the characters and the situation. Just as in a story or novel, the plot of a drama is built around characters in conflict.

Dramas are divided into large units called *acts*, which are divided into smaller units called *scenes*. A long play may include many sets that change with the scenes, or it may indicate a change of scene with lighting.

ESSAY An *essay* is a short nonfiction work about a particular subject. While classification is difficult, five types of essays are sometimes identified.

A *descriptive essay* seeks to convey an impression about a person, place, or object.

An *explanatory essay* describes and summarizes information gathered from a number of sources on a concept.

A *narrative essay* tells a true story. An autobiographical essay is a narrative essay in which the writer tells a story from his or her own life.

A *persuasive essay* tries to convince readers to do something or to accept the writer's point of view.

EXPOSITION *Exposition* is writing or speech that explains a process or presents information. In the plot of a story or drama, the exposition is the part of the work that introduces the characters, the setting, and the basic situation.

EXTENDED METAPHOR In an *extended metaphor,* as in regular metaphor, a writer speaks or writes of a subject as though it were something else. An extended metaphor sustains the comparison for several lines or for an entire poem.

FANTASY A *fantasy* is a work of highly imaginative writing that contains elements not found in real life. Examples of fantasy include stories that involve supernatural elements, such as fairy tales, and stories that deal with imaginary places and creatures.

FICTION *Fiction* is prose writing that tells about imaginary characters and events. The term is usually used for novels and short stories, but it also applies to dramas and narrative poetry. Some writers rely on their imaginations alone to create their works of fiction. Others base their fiction on actual events and people, to which they add invented characters, dialogue, and plot situations.

FIGURATIVE LANGUAGE *Figurative language* is writing or speech not meant to be interpreted literally. It is often used to create vivid impressions by setting up comparisons between dissimilar things.

Some frequently used figures of speech are *metaphor, simile,* and *personification.*

FLASHBACK A *flashback* is a means by which authors present material that occurred earlier than the present time of the narrative. Authors may include this material in the form of a characters' memories, dreams, or accounts of past events, or they may simply shift their narrative back to the earlier time.

FORESHADOWING *Foreshadowing* is the use in a literary work of clues that suggest events that have yet to occur. This technique helps to create suspense, keeping readers wondering about what will happen next.

FREE VERSE *Free verse* is poetry not written in a regular pattern of meter or rhyme.

GENRE A *genre* is a category or form of literature. Literature is commonly divided into three major types of writing: poetry, prose, and drama. For each type, there are several distinct genres, as follows:
1. **Poetry:** Lyric Poetry, Concrete Poetry, Dramatic Poetry, Narrative Poetry, and Epic Poetry
2. **Prose**: Fiction (Novels and Short Stories) and Nonfiction (Biography, Autobiography, Letters, Essays, and Reports)
3. **Drama:** Serious Drama and Tragedy, Comedy, Melodrama, and Farce

GOTHIC LITERATURE A genre that began in England in the late 1700s, *Gothic literature* features bleak or remote settings, characters in psychological torment, plots that include violence or the supernatural, strongly dramatic and intensely descriptive language, and a gloomy, melancholy, or eerie mood.

HYPERBOLE A *hyperbole* is a deliberate exaggeration or overstatement. Hyperboles are often used for comic effect.

IMAGERY *Imagery* is the descriptive or figurative language used in literature to create word pictures for the reader. These pictures, or images, are created by details of sight, sound, taste, touch, smell, or movement.

INFORMATIONAL GRAPHICS *Informational graphics* or *infographics* use images, symbols, graphs, and text to explain and depict the complexities of a topic in a clear and engaging way.

INTERVIEW An *interview* is a structured conversation between two people. In an interview, one person is trying to gain information from another in a question and answer format.

IRONY *Irony* is the general term for literary techniques that portray differences between appearance and reality, or expectation and result. In *verbal irony,* words are used to suggest the opposite of what is meant. In *dramatic irony,* there is a contradiction between what a character thinks and what the reader or audience knows to be true. In *irony of situation,* an event occurs that directly contradicts readers' expectations.

JUXTAPOSITION *Juxtaposition* is setting ideas or details side by side. This effectively helps readers analyze the similarities and differences between two ideas.

LITERARY NONFICTION *Literary nonfiction* is writing that employs many of the same literary devices as fiction while still remaining factual. It may develop a plot, use sensory details, incorporate dialogue, and even use figurative language. Memoirs, autobiographies, speeches, and lectures are often considered literary nonfiction.

LYRIC POEM A *lyric poem* is a poem written in highly musical language that expresses the thoughts, observations, and feelings of a single speaker.

MAGICAL REALISM *Magical realism* incorporates elements of fantasy and myth into otherwise realistic narratives.

METAPHOR A *metaphor* is a figure of speech in which one thing is spoken of as though it were something else. Unlike a simile, which compares two things using *like* or *as,* a metaphor implies a comparison between them.

METER The *meter* of a poem is its rhythmical pattern. This pattern is determined by the number and arrangements of stressed syllables, or beats, in each line. To describe the meter of a poem, you must scan its lines. Scanning involves marking the stressed and unstressed syllables:

Each stressed syllable is marked with a slanted line (´) and each unstressed syllable with a horseshoe symbol (˘). The stressed and unstressed syllables are then divided by vertical lines (|) into groups called *feet.* The following types of feet are common in English poetry:
1. *Iamb:* a foot with one unstressed syllable followed by a stressed syllable, as in the word "again"
2. *Trochee:* a foot with one stressed syllable followed by an unstressed syllable, as in the word "wonder"
3. *Anapest:* a foot with two unstressed syllables followed by one strong stress, as in the phrase "on the beach"
4. *Dactyl:* a foot with one strong stress followed by two unstressed syllables, as in the word "wonderful"
5. *Spondee:* a foot with two strong stresses, as in the word "spacewalk"

Depending on the type of foot that is most common in them, lines of poetry are described as *iambic, trochaic, anapestic,* and so forth.

Lines are also described in terms of the number of feet that occur in them, as follows:
1. *Monometer:* verse written in one-foot lines
2. *Dimeter:* verse written in two-foot lines
3. *Trimeter:* verse written in three-foot lines
4. *Tetrameter:* verse written in four-foot lines
5. *Pentameter:* verse written in five-foot lines
6. *Hexameter:* verse written in six-foot lines
7. *Heptameter:* verse written in seven-foot lines

Blank verse is poetry written in unrhymed iambic pentameter.

Free verse is poetry that does not follow a regular pattern of meter and rhyme.

MODERNISM *Modernism* is a form of creative expression that developed during the early twentieth century. Modernism developed in response to the rapid rise of industry, the shift from rural to urban societies, and the horrors or war. Ambiguity, blurred boundaries between reality and fantasy, and themes of alienation are elements of modernism.

MONOLOGUE A *monologue* in a play is a long speech by one character that, unlike a soliloquy, is addressed to another character or characters.

MOOD *Mood,* or *atmosphere,* is the feeling created in the reader by a literary work or passage. The mood is often suggested by descriptive details. Often the mood can be described in a single word, such as *lighthearted, frightening,* or *despairing.*

NARRATION *Narration* is writing that tells a story. The act of telling a story in speech is also called *narration.* Novels and short stories are fictional narratives. Nonfiction works—such as news stories, biographies, and autobiographies—are also narratives. A narrative poem tells a story in verse.

NARRATIVE A *narrative* is a story told in fiction, nonfiction, poetry, or drama.

NARRATIVE POEM A *narrative poem* is one that tells a story.

NARRATOR A *narrator* is a speaker or character who tells a story. The writer's choice of narrator determines the story's *point of view,* or the perspective from which the story is told. By using a consistent point of view, a writer controls the amount and type of information revealed to the reader.

When a character in the story tells the story, that character is a *first-person narrator.* This narrator may be a major character, a minor character, or just a witness. Readers see only what this character sees, hear only what he or she hears, and so on. Viewing unfolding events from this character's perspective, the reader shares in his discoveries and feels more suspense than another point of view would provide.

When a voice outside the story narrates, the story has a *third-person narrator.* An *omniscient,* or all-knowing, third-person narrator can tell readers what any character thinks and feels. A *limited third-person narrator* sees the world through one character's eyes and reveals only that character's thoughts.

NONFICTION *Nonfiction* is prose writing that presents and explains ideas or that tells about real people, places, ideas, or events. To be classified as nonfiction, a work must be true.

NOVEL A *novel* is a long work of fiction. It has a plot that explores characters in conflict. A novel may also have one or more subplots, or minor stories, and several themes.

ONOMATOPOEIA *Onomatopoeia* is the use of words that imitate sounds. *Whirr, thud, sizzle,* and *hiss* are typical examples. Writers can deliberately choose words that contribute to a desired sound effect.

OXYMORON An *oxymoron* is a combination of words that contradict each other. Examples are "deafening silence," "honest thief," "wise fool," and "bittersweet." This device is effective when the apparent contradiction reveals a deeper truth.

PERSONIFICATION *Personification* is a type of figurative language in which a nonhuman subject is given human characteristics: *The moss embraced the tree.*

PERSUASION *Persuasion* is writing or speech that attempts to convince the reader to adopt a particular opinion or course of action.

An *argument* is a logical way of presenting a belief, conclusion, or stance. A good argument is supported with reasoning and evidence.

PLOT *Plot* is the sequence of events in a literary work. In most novels, dramas, short stories, and narrative poems, the plot involves both characters and a central conflict. The plot usually begins with an **exposition** that introduces the setting, the characters, and the basic situation. This is followed by the *inciting incident,* which introduces the central conflict. The conflict then increases during the *development* until it reaches a high point of interest or suspense, the **climax.** All the events leading up to the climax make up the *rising action.* The climax is followed by the *falling action,* which leads to the *denouement,* or *resolution,* in which the conflict is resolved and in which a general insight may be conveyed.

POETIC STRUCTURE The basic structures of poetry are lines and stanzas. A *line* is a group of words arranged in a row. A line of poetry may break, or end, in different ways. Varied *line lengths* can create unpredictable rhythms.

An *end-stopped line* is one in which both the grammatical structure and sense are complete at the end of the line.

A *run-on,* or *enjambed, line* is one in which both the grammatical structure and sense continue past the end of the line.

POETRY *Poetry* is one of the three major types of literature, the others being prose and drama. Most poems make use of highly concise, musical, and emotionally charged language. Many also make use of imagery, figurative language, and special devices of sound such as rhyme. Poems are often divided into lines and stanzas and often employ regular rhythmical patterns, or meters. Poetry that does not follow a regular metrical pattern is called *free verse.*

POINT OF VIEW *Point of view* is the perspective, or vantage point, from which a story is told. By using a consistent point of view, a writer controls the amount and type of information revealed to the reader. When a character in the story tells the story, that character is a **first-person narrator** and has a **limited point of view.** When a voice outside the story narrates and is all-knowing, the story has an **omniscient point of view.** A narrator that uses the **third-person point of view** sees the world through one character's eyes and reveals only that character's thoughts.

PROSE *Prose* is the ordinary form of written language. Most writing that is not poetry, drama, or song is considered prose. Prose is one of the major categories of literature and occurs in two forms: fiction and nonfiction.

PROSE POEM A **prose poem** is a poetic form that looks like prose, or a non-poetic work, but reads like poetry. Prose poems lack the line breaks most often found in poetry, but they contain other poetic techniques such as repetition or rhyme.

REPETITION *Repetition* is the use of any element of language—a sound, a word, a phrase, a clause, or a sentence—more than once within a passage of text.

Poets use many kinds of repetition. *Alliteration, assonance, consonance, rhyme,* and *rhythm* are repetitions of certain sounds and sound patterns. A *refrain* is a repeated line or group of lines. In both prose and poetry, repetition is used for musical effects and for emphasis.

RHETORICAL DEVICES Rhetorical devices are special patterns of words and ideas that create emphasis and stir emotion, especially in speeches or other oral presentations. *Parallelism,* for example, is the repetition of a grammatical structure in order to create a rhythm and make words more memorable.

Other common rhetorical devices include:
analogy: drawing comparisons between two unlike things
charged language: words that appeal to the emotions
concession: an acknowledgment of the opposition's argument
humor: use of language and details that make characters or situations funny
paradox: statement that seems to contradict but actually presents a truth
restatement: an expression of the same idea in different words
rhetorical questions: questions not meant to be answered because the answers are obvious. For example, *Is freedom a basic human right?* is a rhetorical question.
tone: the author's attitude toward the topic

RHYME *Rhyme* is the repetition of sounds at the end of words. End rhyme occurs when the rhyming words come at the ends of lines.

Internal rhyme occurs when one of the rhyming words appears within a line.

Exact rhyme involves the repetition of the same final vowel and consonant sounds in words like *ball* and *hall. Slant*

rhyme involves the repetition of words that sound alike but do not rhyme exactly, like *grove* and *love.*

RHYME SCHEME A **rhyme scheme** is a regular pattern of rhyming words in a poem. The rhyme scheme of a poem is indicated by using different letters of the alphabet for each new rhyme. In an *aabb* stanza, for example, line 1 rhymes with line 2 and line 3 rhymes with line 4.

Many poems use the same pattern of rhymes, though not the same rhymes, in each stanza.

SATIRE A **satire** is a literary work that ridicules the foolishness and faults of individuals, an institution, society, or even humanity in general.

SENSORY LANGUAGE *Sensory language* is writing or speech that appeals to one or more of the senses.

SEQUENCE OF EVENTS Authors often use **sequence of events,** or the order in which things happened, to structure nonfiction pieces that describe historical events or explain a change over time. Authors frequently describe important events in **chronological order,** or time order.

SETTING The **setting** of a literary work is the time and place of the action. Time can include not only the historical period—past, present, or future—but also a specific year, season, or time of day. Place may involve not only the geographical place—a region, country, state, or town—but also the social, economic, or cultural environment.

In some stories, setting serves merely as a backdrop for action, a context in which the characters move and speak. In others, however, setting is a crucial element.

SHORT STORY A **short story** is a brief work of fiction. In most short stories, one main character faces a conflict that is resolved in the plot of the story. Great craftsmanship must go into the writing of a good story, for it has to accomplish its purpose in relatively few words.

SIMILE A **simile** is a figure of speech in which the words like or as are used to compare two apparently dissimilar items. The comparison, however, surprises the reader into a fresh perception by finding an unexpected likeness.

SOCIAL COMMENTARY In works of **social commentary**, an author seeks to highlight, usually in a critical way, an aspect of society. Social commentary is often the point of **satire**, in which the author points out the absurdity of a practice, custom, or institution.

SOLILOQUY A **soliloquy** is a long speech expressing the thoughts of a character alone on stage.

SONNET A **sonnet** is a fourteen-line lyric poem, usually written in rhymed iambic pentameter. The *English,* or *Shakespearean,* sonnet consists of three quatrains (four-line stanzas) and a couplet (two lines), usually rhyming *abab cdcd efef gg.* The couplet usually comments on the ideas contained in the preceding twelve lines. The sonnet is usually not printed with the stanzas divided, but a reader can see distinct ideas in each.

The *Italian*, or *Petrarchan*, sonnet consists of an octave (eight-line stanza) and a sestet (six-line stanza). Often, the octave rhymes *abbaabba* and the sestet rhymes *cdecde*. The octave states a theme or asks a question. The sestet comments on the theme or answers the question.

SPEAKER The *speaker* is the imaginary voice assumed by the writer of a poem. In many poems, the speaker is not identified by name. When reading a poem, remember that the speaker of a poem may be a person, an animal, a thing, or an abstraction.

STAGE DIRECTIONS *Stage directions* are notes included in a drama to describe how the work is to be performed or staged. These instructions are printed in italics and are not spoken aloud. They are used to describe sets, lighting, sound effects, and the appearance, personalities, and movements of characters.

STANZA A *stanza* is a repeated grouping of two or more lines in a poem that often share a pattern of rhythm and rhyme. Stanzas are sometimes named according to the number of lines they have—for example, a *couplet*, two lines; a *quatrain*, four lines; a *sestet*, six lines; and an *octave*, eight lines.

STYLE *Style* refers to an author's unique way of writing. Elements determining style include diction; tone; characteristic use of figurative language, dialect, or rhythmic devices; and typical grammatical structures and patterns.

SURPRISE ENDING A *surprise ending* is a conclusion that violates the expectations of the reader but in a way that is both logical and believable.

SYMBOL A *symbol* is a character, place, thing or event that stands for something else, often an abstract idea. For example, a flag is a piece of cloth, but it also represents the idea of a country. Writers sometimes use conventional symbols like flags. Frequently, however, they create symbols of their own through emphasis or repetition.

SYNTAX *Syntax* is the structure of sentences.

THEME A *theme* is a central message or insight into life revealed through a literary work.

The theme of a literary work may be stated directly or implied. When the theme of a work is implied, readers infer what the work suggests about people or life.

Archetypal themes are those that occur in folklore and literature across the world and throughout history.

TONE The *tone* of a literary work is the writer's attitude toward his or her audience and subject. The tone can often be described by a single adjective, such as *formal* or *informal*, *serious* or *playful*, *bitter* or *ironic*.

TRAGEDY A *tragedy* is a work of literature, especially a play, that tells of a catastrophe, a disaster or great misfortune, for the main character. In ancient Greek drama, the main character was always a significant person—a king or a hero—and the cause of the tragedy was often a tragic flaw, or weakness, in his or her character. In modern drama, the main character can be an ordinary person, and the cause of the tragedy can be some evil in society itself. Tragedy not only arouses fear and pity in the audience, but also, in some cases, conveys a sense of the grandeur and nobility of the human spirit.

VOICE *Voice* is a writer's distinctive "sound" or way of "speaking" on the page. It is related to such elements as word choice, sentence structure, and tone. It is similar to an individual's speech style and can be described in the same way—fast, slow, blunt, meandering, breathless, and so on.

Voice resembles *style*, an author's typical way of writing, but style usually refers to a quality that can be found throughout an author's body of work, while an author's voice may sometimes vary from work to work.

MANUAL DE TÉRMINOS LITERARIOS

ABSURDISM / LITERATURA DEL ABSURDO La *literatura del absurdo* es un tipo de *modernismo* que incluye elementos de fantasía o surreales que borran el límite entre lo real y lo irreal.

ALLITERATION / ALITERACIÓN La *aliteración* es la repetición de los sonidos consonantes iniciales. Los escritores usan la aliteración para dar énfasis a las palabras, para imitar sonidos y para crear efectos de musicalidad.

ALLUSION / ALUSIÓN Una *alusión* es una referencia a una persona, lugar, hecho, obra literaria u obra de arte muy conocida.

ANALOGY / ANALOGÍA Una *analogía* establece una comparación entre dos o más cosas que son parecidas en algunos aspectos pero se diferencian en otros.

ANAPHORA / ANÁFORA La *anáfora* es un tipo de paralelismo en el que una palabra o frase se repite al principio de varias cláusulas para hacer énfasis.

ANECDOTE / ANÉCDOTA Una *anécdota* es un relato breve que se narra con el fin de entretener o decir algo importante.

ANTAGONIST / ANTAGONISTA Un *antagonista* es un personaje o fuerza en conflicto con el personaje principal o protagonista.

APOSTROPHE / APÓSTROFE El *apóstrofe* es una figura retórica en la que el hablante se dirige directante a una persona ausente o a una idea, objeto o cualidad personificada.

APPEAL / APELACIÓN Una *apelación* es un recurso retórico que se usa en los escritos de argumentación para persuadir al público. Una apelación a la ética (Ethos) muestra que un argumento es justo. Una apelación a la lógica (Logos) muestra que un argumento está bien razonado. Una apelación a la autoridad muestra que las ideas que se presentan están respaldadas por un poder más alto. Una apelación a las emociones (Pathos) se usa con el propósito de influir en los lectores.

ARGUMENT / ARGUMENTO Un *argumento* es un escrito o discurso que trata de convencer al lector para que siga una acción o adopte una opinión en particular. Un argumento es una manera lógica de presentar una creencia, una conclusión, o una postura. Un buen argumento se respalda con razonamientos y pruebas.

ASIDE / APARTE Un *aparte* es un parlamento breve en boca de un personaje en una obra de teatro, en el que expresa sus verdaderos pensamientos y sentimientos. Tradicionalmente, los apartes se dirigen a la audiencia y se suponen inaudibles a los otros personajes.

AUTOBIOGRAPHY / AUTOBIOGRAFÍA Una *autobiografía* es una forma de no-ficción en la que el escritor cuenta su propia vida. Una autobiografía puede contar toda la vida de una persona o solo una parte de ella.

BIOGRAPHY / BIOGRAFÍA Una *biografía* es una forma de no-ficción en la que un escritor cuenta la vida de otra persona. Se han escrito biografías de muchas personas famosas, ya de la historia o del mundo contemporáneo, pero también pueden escribirse biografías de personas comunes.

BLANK VERSE / VERSO BLANCO El *verso blanco* es poesía escrita en líneas de pentámetros yámbicos sin rima. Esta forma de verso fue muy utilizada por William Shakespeare.

CHARACTER / PERSONAJE Un *personaje* es una persona o animal que participa de la acción en una obra literaria. El personaje principal, o protagonista, es el personaje más importante del relato. Este personaje a menudo cambia de una manera importante como resultado de los eventos que se suceden en el cuento.

Los personajes a veces son clasificados como complejos o chatos, dinámicos o estáticos. Un *personaje complejo* muestra muchos rasgos diferentes, tanto faltas como virtudes. *Un personaje chato* muestra solo un rasgo. Un *personaje dinámico* se desarrolla y crece en el curso del relato; mientras que un *personaje estático* no cambia.

CHARACTERIZATION / CARACTERIZACIÓN La *caracterización* es el acto de crear y desarrollar un personaje. En una *caracterización directa,* el autor expresa explícitamente los rasgos de un personaje. En una *caracterización indirecta,* el autor proporciona claves sobre el personaje, describiendo el aspecto del personaje, qué hace, qué dice, así como la manera en que otros personajes lo ven y reaccionan a él. Depende del lector qué conclusiones saque sobre los personajes basándose en información indirecta.

La caracterización indirecta más efectiva resulta por lo general de mostrar cómo hablan y actúan los personajes.

CLIMAX / CLÍMAX El *clímax* de un relato, de una novela o de un drama es el punto de mayor interés o suspenso. Los sucesos que forman el desarrollo de la acción anteceden al clímax. Los sucesos que conducen al desenlace son posteriores al clímax.

COMEDY / COMEDIA Una *comedia* es una obra literaria, por lo general una obra de teatro, que tiene un final feliz. Las comedias a menudo presentan personajes comunes en conflicto con la sociedad. Estos conflictos se producen a partir de malentendidos, engaños y falsas identidades. Cuando el conflicto se resuelve, el resultado es la corrección de fallas morales o de injusticias sociales. Entre los distintos tipos de comedia, se distinguen: *la comedia romántica*, que gira alrededor de problemas entre enamorados o amantes, y *la comedia de costumbres*, que satiriza las costumbres sociales. La comedia suele oponerse a la tragedia, en la cual el protagonista tiene un final desafortunado.

COMIC RELIEF / ALIVIO CÓMICO El *alivio cómico* es una técnica que se usa para interrumpir una parte seria de una obra literaria introduciendo una situación o personaje gracioso.

CONFLICT / CONFLICTO Un *conflicto* es una lucha entre fuerzas opuestas. Los personajes en conflicto forman la base de cuentos, novelas y obras de teatro.

Hay dos tipos de conflicto: *externos* e *internos.* En un *conflicto externo*, el personaje principal lugar contra una fuerza externa.

Un *conflicto interno* atañe a un personaje que entra en conflicto consigo mismo.

CONNOTATION / CONNOTACIÓN La *connotación* de una palabra es el conjunto de ideas que se asocian a ella, además de su significado explícito.

CONSONANCE / CONSONANCIA La *consonancia* es la repetición de los sonidos consonantes finales de sílabas acentuadas con distintos sonidos vocálicos, como en *hat* and *sit*.

COUPLET / PAREADO Un *dístico* o *pareado* es un par de versos rimados, por lo general de la misma extensión y metro.

DENOTATION / DENOTACIÓN La *denotación* de una palabra es su significado en un diccionario, independiente-mente de otras asociaciones que la palabra suscita. Por ejemplo, la denotación de la palabra "lago" es "masa de agua acumulada en medio de un terreno".

DESCRIPTION / DESCRIPCIÓN Una *descripción* es un retrato en palabras de una persona, un lugar o un objeto. La escritura descriptiva utiliza detalles sensoriales, es decir, aquellos que apelan a los sentidos: la vista, el oído, el gusto, el olfato y el tacto. La descripción puede encontrarse en todo tipo de escritos.

DIALECT / DIALECTO El *dialecto* es la forma de un lenguaje hablado por la gente en una región o grupo particular. Puede incluir diferencias en la pronunciación, el vocabulario y la estructura de la oración, con respecto a la forma estandarizada de esa lengua. "Danny Deever", de Rudyard Kipling, es un poema escrito en el dialecto *cockney* del inglés, usado por las clases trabajadoras de Londres.

DIALOGUE / DIÁLOGO Un *diálogo* es una conver-sación entre personajes que puede revelar sus rasgos y hacer progresar la acción de un relato. Ya sea en un género de ficción o de no ficción —en inglés— las comillas repro-ducen las palabras exactas de un personaje, y un nuevo párrafo indica un cambio de personaje. En un guión, es decir, en la versión impresa de una obra de teatro, no se usan comillas, sino que cada parlamento va introducido por el nombre del personaje que debe pronunciarlo.

DICTION / DICCIÓN La *dicción* comprende la elección de palabras que hace el autor, especialmente en relación al vocabulario, al uso de un lenguaje coloquial o jerga y al nivel de formalidad.

DRAMA / DRAMA Un *drama* es una historia escrita para ser representada por actores. El guión de un drama está consituido por *diálogo* —las palabras que dicen los actores— y por *acotaciones*, que son los comentarios acerca de cómo y dónde se sitúa la acción.

La *ambientación* es la época y el lugar donde sucede la acción. Se indica a través de una o varias escenografías, que incluyen el mobiliario y el fondo, o telón de fondo, que sugieren si las escenas son interiores o exteriores. La *tramoya* o *utilería* son los objetos, tales como una espada o una taza de té, que se usan en escena.

Al principio de la mayoría de los dramas, una breve *exposición* le da a la audiencia cierta información de contexto sobre los personajes y la situación. Al igual que en un cuento o una novela, el argumento o trama de una obra dramática se construye a partir de personajes en conflicto.

Los dramas se dividen a grandes unidades llamadas *actos*, que a su vez se dividen en unidades más breves llamadas *escenas*. Un drama de cierta extensión puede incluir muchas escenografías que cambian con las escenas, o pueden indicar un cambio de escena por medio de la iluminación.

ESSAY / ENSAYO Un *ensayo* es una obra breve de no-ficción sobre un tema en particular. Si bien es difícil llegar a una clasificación, suelen diferenciarse cinco tipos de ensayos.

El *ensayo descriptivo* se propone transmitir una impresión acerca de una persona, un lugar o un objeto.

El *ensayo explicativo* describe y resume información sobre un determinado concepto recogida de cierto número de fuentes.

El *ensayo narrativo* narra una historia real.

El *ensayo persuasivo* intenta convencer a los lectores de que hagan algo o que acepten el punto de vista del escritor.

EXPOSITION / EXPOSICIÓN Una *exposición* es un escrito o un discurso que explica un proceso o presenta información. En un cuento o un drama, la exposición es la parte donde se presenta a los personajes, la ambientación y la situación básica.

EXTENDED METAPHOR / METÁFORA EXTENDIDA En una *metáfora extendida*, al igual que en una metáfora habitual, el escritor escribe o habla de algo como si fuera otra cosa. Una metáfora extendida prolonga la comparación a lo largo de varias líneas o de un poema entero.

FANTASY / RELATO FANTÁSTICO Un *relato fantás-tico* es una obra altamente imaginativa que contiene ele-mentos que no se encuentran en la vida real. Ejemplos de relatos fantásticos son los cuentos que incluyen elementos sobrenaturales, tales como los cuentos de hadas, y cuentos que tratan sobre lugares y criaturas imaginarias.

FICTION / FICCIÓN Una obra de *ficción* es un escrito en prosa que cuenta algo sobre personajes y hechos imaginarios. El término se usa por lo general para referirse a novelas y cuentos, pero también se aplica a dramas y poemas narrativos. Algunos escritores se basan solamente en su imaginación para crear sus obras de ficción. Otros basan su ficción en hechos y personas reales, a las que agregan personajes, diálogos y situaciones de su propia invención.

FIGURATIVE LANGUAGE / LENGUAJE FIGURADO El *lenguaje figurado* es un escrito o discurso que no se debe interpretar literalmente. A menudo se usa para crear impresiones vívidas, estableciendo comparaciones entre cosas disímiles.

Algunas de las formas más usadas del lenguaje figurado son la *metáfora*, el *símil* y la *personificación*.

FLASHBACK / FLASHBACK Un *flashback* o *escena retrospectiva* es una de las maneras a través de las que los autores presentan materiales, que ocurrieron antes del tiempo presente del relato. Los autores pueden incluir estos materiales, como los recuerdos o sueños de un personaje, o narrar directamente hechos anteriores al momento en que empezó el relato.

FORESHADOWING / PREFIGURACIÓN La *prefiguración* es el uso, en una obra literaria, de claves que sugieren hechos que van a suceder. Esta técnica ayuda a crear suspenso, manteniendo a los lectores interesados preguntándose qué sucederá.

FREE VERSE / VERSO LIBRE El *verso libre* es una forma poética en la que no se sigue un patrón regular o metro o de rima.

GENRE / GÉNERO Un *género* es una categoría o tipo de literatura. La literatura se divide por lo general en tres géneros principales: poesía, prosa y drama. Cada uno de estos géneros principales se divide a su vez en géneros más pequeños. Por ejemplo:

1. **Poesía:** Poesía lírica, Poesía concreta, Poesía dramática, Poesía narrativa y Poesía épica.
2. **Prosa:** Ficción (Novelas y Cuentos) y No-ficción (Biografía, Autobiografía, Cartas, Ensayos, Artículos).
3. **Drama:** Drama serio y Tragedia, Comedia, Melodrama y Farsa.

GOTHIC LITERATURE / LITERATURA GÓTICA La *literatura gótica* es un género que comenzó en Inglaterra a finales del siglo XVIII. Algunas de las características de esta literatura son: ambientaciones en lugares sombríos y remotos, personajes atormentados psicológicamente, trama que incluye violencia o lo supernatural, lenguaje altamente descriptivo e intenso y una atmósfera pesimista, melancólica o fantasmal.

HYPERBOLE / HIPÉRBOLE Una *hipérbole* es una exageración o magnificación deliberada. Las hipérboles se usan a menudo para lograr efectos cómicos.

IMAGERY / IMÁGENES Las *imágenes* son el lenguaje figurado o descriptivo que se usa en la literatura para crear una descripción verbal para los lectores. Estas descripciones verbales, o imágenes, se crean mediante el uso de detalles visuales, auditivos, gustativos, táctiles, olfativos o de movimiento.

INFORMATIONAL GRAPHICS / INFOGRAFÍAS Las *infografías* usan imágenes, símbolos, gráficas y texto para explicar y presentar las partes más complejas de un tema de manera clara y atractiva.

INTERVIEW / ENTREVISTA Una *entrevista* es una conversación entre dos personas estructurada en forma de preguntas y respuestas, en la cual una persona trata de obtener información de la otra persona.

IRONY / IRONÍA *Ironía* es un término general para distintas técnicas literarias que subrayan las diferencias entre apariencia y realidad, o entre expectativas y resultado. En una *ironía verbal*, las palabras se usan para sugerir lo opuesto a lo que se dice. En la *ironía dramática* hay una contradicción entre lo que el personaje piensa y lo que el lector o la audiencia sabe que es verdad. En una *ironía situacional*, ocurre un suceso que contradice directamente las expectativas de los personajes, o del lector o la audiencia.

JUXTAPOSITION / YUXTAPOSICIÓN La *yuxtaposición* es una manera de exponer ideas o detalles uno al lado del otro, lo que ayuda a que los lectores puedan analizar las semejanzas y las diferencias entre dos ideas.

LITERARY NONFICTION / LITERATURA DE NO-FICCIÓN La *literatura de no-ficción* es un texto que emplea muchos de los recursos literarios de la ficción, pero presenta hechos y datos reales. Puede tener una trama, usar detalles sensoriales, incorporar diálogo e, incluso, lenguaje figurado. Las memorias, las autobiografías, los discursos y las conferencias se suelen considerar literatura de no-ficción.

LYRIC POEM / POEMA LÍRICO Un *poema lírico* es una sucesión de versos de mucha musicalidad que expresan los pensamientos, observaciones y sentimientos de un único hablante.

MAGICAL REALISM / REALISMO MÁGICO El *realismo mágico* incorpora elementos de fantasía y mito en una narrativa que es, por lo demás, realista.

METAPHOR / METÁFORA Una *metáfora* es una figura literaria en la que algo se describe como si fuera otra cosa. A diferencia del símil, que compara dos cosas usando el conector *como*, la metáfora establece la comparación entre ellas de modo implícito.

METER / METRO El *metro* de un poema es el patrón rítmico que sigue. Este patrón está determinado por el número y disposición de las sílabas acentuadas en cada verso. Para describir el metro de un poema hay que escandir los versos. Escandir significa marcar las sílabas acentuadas y no acentuadas.

Cada sílaba acentuada se marca con un ('), y cada sílaba no acentuada se marca con un (˘). Las sílabas acentuadas y no acentuadas se dividen luego con líneas verticales (|) en grupos llamados *pies*. En la poesía en inglés algunos de los pies más frecuentes son:

1. el *yambo:* un pie con una sílaba no acentuada seguida por una sílaba acentuada, como en la palabra "again"

2. el *troqueo:* un pie con una sílaba acentuada seguida por una sílaba no acentuada, como en la palabra "wonder"

3. el *anapesto:* un pie con dos sílabas no acentuadas seguidas por un acento fuerte, como en la frase "on the beach"

4. el *dáctilo*: un pie con un acento fuerte seguido por dos sílabas no acentuadas, como en la palabra "wonderful"

5. el *espondeo:* un pie con dos acentos fuertes, como en la palabra "spacewalk"

Según el tipo de pie más frecuente en ellos, los versos de un poema se describen como *yámbicos, trocaicos, anapésticos,* etc.

Los versos también se describen según el número de pies que los formen. Por ejemplo:

1. *monómetro:* verso de un solo pie

2. *dímetro:* verso de dos pies

3. *trímetro:* verso de tres pies

4. *tetrámetro:* verso de cuatro pies

5. *pentámetro:* verso de cinco pies

6. *hexámetro:* verso de seis pies

7. *heptámetro:* verso de siete pies

Verso blanco: se dice de la poesía escrita en pentámetros yámbicos sin rima.

Verso libre: se dice de la poesía que no sigue un patrón métrico ni rímico regular.

MODERNISM / MODERNISMO NORTEAMERICANO
El *modernismo norteamericano* es una forma de expresión creativa que se desarrolló a principios del siglo XX en respuesta al rápido crecimiento de la industria, el paso de las sociedades rurales a las urbanas y los horrores de la guerra. La ambigüedad, la desaparición de límites claros entre realidad y fantasía, y los temas de la enajenación del ser humano moderno son algunos de los elementos típicos de este movimiento.

MONOLOGUE / MONÓLOGO
Un *monólogo* en una obra de teatro es un parlamento por parte de un personaje que, a diferencia del *soliloquio*, se dirige a otro u otros personajes.

MOOD / ATMÓSFERA
La *atmósfera* es la sensación que un pasaje u obra literaria crea en el lector. Por lo general, la atmósfera se crea a través de detalles descriptivos. A menudo puede ser descrita con una sola palabra, tal como *desenfadado, aterrador* o *desesperante.*

NARRATION / NARRACIÓN
Una *narración* es un escrito que cuenta una historia. El acto de contar una historia de forma oral también se llama narración. Las novelas y los cuentos son obras narrativas de ficción. Las obras de no-ficción, como las noticias, las biografías y las autobiografías, también son narrativas. Un poema narrativo cuenta una historia en verso.

NARRATIVE / RELATO
Se llama *relato* a la historia que se narra en una obra de ficción, obra de de no-ficción, en un poema o en un drama.

NARRRATIVE POEM / POEMA NARRATIVO
Un *poema narrativo* es un poema que cuenta una historia.

NARRATOR / NARRADOR
Un *narrador* es el hablante o el personaje que cuenta una historia. La elección del narrador por parte del autor determina el *punto de vista* desde el que se va a narrar la historia, lo que determina el tipo y la cantidad de información que se revelará.

Cuando el que cuenta la historia es uno de los personajes, a ese personaje se lo llama *narrador en primera persona*. Este narrador puede ser uno de los personajes principales, un personaje menor, o solo un testigo. Los lectores ven solo lo que este personaje ve, oyen solo lo que este personaje oye, etc. Al ver cómo se desarrollan los sucesos desde la perspectiva de este personaje, el lector comparte sus descubrimientos y experimenta mayor suspenso que el que producen narraciones desde otros puntos de vista.

Cuando la que cuenta la historia es una voz exterior a la historia, hablamos de un *narrador en tercera persona*. Un narrador en tercera persona, *omnisciente* —es decir, que todo lo sabe— puede decirles a los lectores lo que cualquier personaje piensa o siente. Un narrador en tercera persona *limitado* ve el mundo a través de los ojos de un solo personaje y revela solo los pensamientos de ese personaje.

NONFICTION / NO-FICCIÓN
La *no-ficción* es un escrito en prosa que presenta y explica ideas o cuenta algo acerca de personas, lugares, ideas o hechos reales. Para ser clasificado como no-ficción un escrito debe ser verdadero.

NOVEL / NOVELA
Una *novela* es una obra extensa de ficción. Tiene una trama que explora los personajes en conflicto. Una novela también puede tener una o más tramas secundarias —es decir, historias de menor importancia—, así como tocar varios temas.

ONOMATOPOEIA / ONOMATOPEYA
La *onomatopeya* es el uso de palabras que imitan sonidos, tales como *pío-pío, tic-tac* o *susurro*. Los escritores pueden escoger palabras deliberadamente con el fin de producir el efecto sonoro deseado.

OXYMORON / OXÍMORON
Un *oxímoron* es una combinación de palabras que se contradicen mutuamente. Por ejemplo, "un silencio ensordecedor", "un ladrón honesto", "la música callada". Este recurso es especialmente efectivo cuando la aparente contradicción revela una verdad más profunda.

PERSONIFICATION / PERSONIFICACIÓN
La *personificación* es un tipo de figura retórica en la que se dota a

una instancia no humana de rasgos y actitudes humanas: *El musgo se abrazaba al árbol.*

PERSUASION / PERSUASIÓN La *persuasión* es un recurso escrito u oral por el que se intenta convencer al lector de que adopte una opinión o actúe de determinada manera. Un *argumento* es una manera lógica de presentar una creencia, una conclusión o una postura. Un buen argumento se respalda con razones y evidencias.

PLOT / TRAMA o ARGUMENTO La *trama* o *argumento* es la secuencia de los hechos que se suceden en una obra literaria. En la mayoría de las novelas, dramas, cuentos y poemas narrativos, la trama implica tanto a los personajes como al conflicto central. La trama por lo general empieza con una *exposición* que introduce la ambientación, los personajes y la situación básica. A ello le sigue el *suceso desencadenante*, que introduce el conflicto central. Este conflicto aumenta durante el *desarrollo* hasta que alcanza el punto más alto de interés o suspenso, llamado *clímax*. Todos los sucesos que conducen al clímax contribuyen a la *acción dramática creciente*. Al clímax le sigue la *acción dramática decreciente* que conduce al *desenlace*, o *resolución*, en el que se resuelve el conflicto y en el que puede darse a entender cierta idea o percepción más amplia acerca de la situación tratada.

POETIC STRUCTURE / ESTRUCTURA POÉTICA Las *estructuras poéticas* básicas son los versos y las estrofas. Un *verso* es un grupo de palabras ordenadas en un mismo renglón. Un verso puede terminar, o cortarse, de distintas maneras. Versos de distinta extensión pueden crear ritmos imprevistos.

En un *verso no encabalgado* la estructura gramatical y el sentido se completan al final de esa línea.

En un *verso encabalgado* tanto la estructura gramatical como el sentido de un verso continúan en el verso que sigue.

POETRY / POESÍA La *poesía* es uno de los tres géneros literarios más importantes. Los otros dos son la prosa y el drama. La mayoría de los poemas están escritos en un lenguaje altamente conciso, musical y emocionalmente rico. Muchos también hacen uso de imágenes, de figuras retóricas y de recursos sonoros especiales, tales como la rima. Los poemas a menudo se dividen en versos y estrofas, y emplean patrones rítmicos regulares, llamados metros. Los poemas que no siguen un metro regular están escritos en *verso libre*.

POINT OF VIEW / PUNTO DE VISTA El *punto de vista* es la perspectiva desde la cual se narran o describen los hechos. Al usar un punto de vista constante, el escritor controla la cantidad y tipo de información que quiere revelarle al lector. Cuando quien cuenta la historia es uno de los personajes, ese personaje es el *narrador en primera persona* y tiene un *punto de vista limitado*. Cuando quien narra la historia es una voz exterior al relato que sabe y ve todo lo que ocurre, el relato está escrito desde un *punto de vista omnisciente*. El *relato en tercera persona* presenta el mundo desde la perspectiva de un solo personaje y revela solo lo que piensa ese personaje.

PROSE / PROSA La *prosa* es la forma más común del lenguaje escrito. La mayoría de los escritos que no son poesía, ni drama, ni canciones, se consideran prosa. La prosa es uno de los géneros literarios más importantes y puede ser de dos formas: de ficción y de no-ficción.

PROSE POEM / POEMA EN PROSA Un *poema en prosa* es una forma poética que se ve como si fuera prosa, pero que tiene las características propias de la poesía. Los poemas en prosa no tienen los cortes de verso que suelen encontrarse en la poesía, pero tienen otros elementos de la poesía tales como la repetición y el ritmo.

REPETITION / REPETICIÓN La *repetición* es el uso de cualquier elemento del lenguaje —un sonido, una palabra, una frase, una cláusula, o una oración— más de una vez en un mismo pasaje del texto.

Los poetas usan muchos tipos de repeticiones. La *aliteración*, la *asonancia*, la *consonancia*, la *rima* y el *ritmo* son repeticiones de ciertos sonidos o patrones sonoros. Un *estribillo* es un verso o grupo de versos que se repiten. Tanto en prosa como en poesía, la repetición se usa tanto para lograr efectos de musicalidad como para enfatizar algo.

RHETORICAL DEVICES / FIGURAS RETÓRICAS Las *figuras retóricas* son patrones especiales de palabras e ideas que dan énfasis y producen emoción, especialmente en discursos y otras presentaciones orales. El *paralelismo*, por ejemplo, es la repetición de una estructura gramatical con el propósito de crear un ritmo y hacer que las palabras resulten más memorables.

Otras figuras retóricas muy frecuentes son:

la *analogía*: establece una comparación entre dos cosas diferentes

el *lenguaje emocionalmente cargado*: las palabras apelan a las emociones

la *concesión*: un reconocimiento del argumento del contrario

el *humor*: uso del lenguaje y detalles que hacen que los personajes y las situaciones resulten graciosos

la *paradoja*: un enunciado que parece contradecirse, pero que en realidad presenta una verdad

la *reafirmación*: expresa la misma idea con distintas palabras

las *preguntas retóricas*: preguntas que no se hacen para contestarse porque las respuestas son obvias. Por ejemplo, *¿Es la libertad un derecho esencial del ser humano?* es una pregunta retórica.

el *tono*: la actitud del autor hacia el tema

RHYME / RIMA La *rima* es la repetición de los sonidos finales de las palabras. Se llama *rima de final de verso* a la rima entre las palabras finales de dos o más versos. La *rima interna* se produce cuando una de las palabras que riman está situada en el interior de un verso. En la *rima perfecta (o consonante)* todas las vocales y las consonantes que siguen a la vocal acentuada son iguales, como en *ball* y *hall*. Se llama *rima falsa* a la que se da entre palabras que suenan de modo parecido pero que en realidad no riman, como *grove* y *love*.

RHYME SCHEME / ESQUEMA DE RIMA Un *esquema de rima* es el patrón de las palabras que riman en un poema. El esquema de rima de un poema se indica con distintas letras del alfabeto para cada tipo de rima. En una estrofa aabb, por ejemplo, el verso 1 rima con el verso 2 y el verso 3 rima con el verso 4. Muchos poemas siguen el mismo patrón de rimas, aunque no las mismas rimas, en cada estrofa.

SATIRE / SÁTIRA Una *sátira* es una obra literaria que ridiculiza las tonterías y fallas de ciertos individuos o instituciones, de la sociedad o incluso de la humanidad.

SENSORY LANGUAGE / LENGUAJE SENSORIAL El *lenguaje sensorial* es un escrito o discurso que incluye detalles que apelan a uno o más de los sentidos.

SEQUENCE OF EVENTS / SECUENCIA DE SUCESOS Los autores usan a menudo la *secuencia de sucesos*, es decir, el orden en que suceden los hechos, para estructurar textos de no-ficción que tratan sobre hechos históricos o que explican un cambio que se produjo a lo largo del tiempo. Con frecuencia los escritores presentan los hechos en **orden cronológico**, es decir, en el orden en que se sucedieron.

SETTING / AMBIENTACIÓN La *ambientación* de una obra literaria es la época y el lugar en el que se desarrolla la acción. La época incluye no solo el período histórico —pasado, presente o futuro —, sino también el año específico, la estación, la hora del día. El lugar puede incluir no solo el espacio geográfico —una región, un país, un estado, un pueblo— sino también el entorno social, económico o cultural.

En algunos cuentos, la ambientación sirve solo como un telón de fondo para la acción, un contexto en el que los personajes se mueven y hablan. En otros casos, en cambio, la ambientación es un elemento crucial.

SHORT STORY / CUENTO Un *cuento* es una obra breve de ficción. En la mayoría de los cuentos, un personaje principal se enfrenta a un conflicto que se resuelve a lo largo de la trama. Para escribir un buen cuento se necesita mucho dominio técnico, porque el cuento debe cumplir su cometido en relativamente pocas palabras.

SIMILE / SÍMIL Un *símil* es una figura retórica en la que se usa la palabra *como* para establecer una comparación entre dos cosas aparentemente disímiles. La comparación sorprende al lector ofreciéndole una nueva percepción que se deriva de descubrir una semejanza inesperada.

SOCIAL COMMENTARY / COMENTARIO SOCIAL En las obras de **comentario social** el autor tiene como objetivo resaltar, generalmente de forma crítica, un aspecto de la sociedad. El comentario social suele ser el objetivo de la *sátira*, en la que el autor señala lo absurdo de una práctica, costumbre o institución.

SOLILOQUY / SOLILOQUIO Un *soliloquio* es un largo parlamento en el que un personaje, solo en escena, expresa sus sentimientos.

SONNET / SONETO Un *soneto* es un poema lírico de catorce versos, por lo general escritos en pentámetros yámbicos rimados. El *soneto inglés o shakesperiano* consiste en tres cuartetas (estrofas de cuatro versos) y un pareado (estrofa de dos versos), por lo general con rima *abab cdcd efef gg*. El pareado suele consistir en un comentario sobre las ideas expuestas en los doce versos que lo preceden. El soneto inglés no se suele imprimir con la división interestrófica, pero el lector puede identificar las distintas ideas que se presentan en cada estrofa.

El *soneto italiano o petrarquista* consiste en una octava (una estrofa de ocho versos) y una sextina (una estrofa de seis versos). A menudo, las octavas riman *abbaabba* y las sextinas riman *cdecde*. La octava expone el tema y propone una pregunta. La sextina comenta el tema o responde la pregunta que se planteó en las estrofas anteriores.

SPEAKER / HABLANTE El *hablante* es la voz imaginaria que asume el escritor en un poema. En muchos poemas, el hablante no se identifica con un nombre. Al leer un poema, recuerda que el hablante puede ser una persona, un animal un objeto o una abstracción.

STAGE DIRECTIONS / ACOTACIONES Las *acotaciones* son notas que se incluyen en una obra de teatro para describir cómo debe ser actuada o puesta en escena. Estas instrucciones aparecen en itálicas y no se pronuncian durante la representación. Se usan para describir decorados, la iluminación, los efectos sonoros y el aspecto, la personalidad y los movimientos de los personajes.

STANZA / ESTROFA Una *estrofa* es un grupo de dos o más versos cuya estructura se repite. Las distintas estrofas de un poema suelen seguir un mismo patrón de ritmo y de rima. Las estrofas a menudo reciben su nombre del número de versos que las componen. Por ejemplo, un *dístico* o *pareado* (dos versos), una *cuarteta* (cuatro versos), una *sextina* (seis versos), y una *octavilla* (ocho versos).

STYLE / ESTILO El *estilo* es la manera particular en que escribe un autor. Los elementos que determinan el estilo son: la dicción, el tono; el uso característico de ciertas figuras retóricas, del dialecto, o de los recursos rítmicos; y la sintaxis, es decir, los patrones y estructuras gramaticales que usa con más frecuencia.

SURPRISE ENDING / FINAL SORPRESIVO Un *final sorpresivo* es una conclusión que no responde a las expectativas del lector, pero que de todos modos resulta lógica y verosímil.

SYMBOL / SÍMBOLO Un *símbolo* es algo que representa otra cosa. Además de tener su propio significado y realidad, un símbolo también representa ideas abstractas. Por ejemplo, una bandera es un trozo de tela, pero también representa la idea de un país. Los escritores a veces usan símbolos convencionales como las banderas. Con frecuencia, sin embargo, crean sus propios símbolos, a veces a través del énfasis o la repetición.

SYNTAX / SINTAXIS La *sintaxis* es la estructura de las oraciones.

THEME / TEMA Un *tema* es el mensaje central o la concepción de la vida que revela una obra literaria.

El tema de una obra literaria puede estar implícito o bien puede expresarse directamente. Cuando el tema de una obra está implícito, los lectores hacen inferencias sobre lo que sugiere la obra acerca de la vida o la gente.

Los *temas arquetípicos* son aquellos que aparecen en el folklore y en la literatura de todo el mundo y a lo largo de toda la historia.

TONE / TONO El *tono* de una obra literaria es la actitud del escritor hacia su tema y su audiencia. A menudo puede describirse con un solo adjetivo, tal como *formal* o *informal*, *serio* o *jocoso*, *amargo* o *irónico*.

TRAGEDY / TRAGEDIA Una *tragedia* es una obra literaria, por lo general una obra de teatro, que termina en una catástrofe, un desastre o un gran infortunio para el personaje principal. En el drama de la antigua Grecia, el personaje principal siempre era una persona importante —un rey o un héroe— y la causa de la tragedia era un *error trágico*, una debilidad de su carácter. En el drama moderno, el personaje principal puede ser una persona común, y la causa de la tragedia puede ser algún problema de la sociedad misma. La tragedia no solo despierta miedo y compasión en la audiencia, sino también, en algunos casos, le hace tomar conciencia de la majestuosidad y la nobleza del espíritu humano.

VOICE / VOZ La *voz* es el "sonido" distintivo de un escritor, o la manera en que "habla" en la página. Se relaciona a elementos tales como la elección del vocabulario, la estructura de las oraciones y el tono. Es similar al estilo en que habla un individuo y puede describirse de la misma manera: rápida, lenta, directa, dispersa, jadeante, etc.

La voz se parece al *estilo*, es decir, a la manera típica en que escribe un autor, pero el estilo por lo general se refiere a una cualidad que puede encontrarse a lo largo de toda la obra de un autor, mientras que la voz de un autor puede variar de una obra a otra.

PARTS OF SPEECH

Every English word, depending on its meaning and its use in a sentence, can be identified as one of the eight parts of speech. These are nouns, pronouns, verbs, adjectives, adverbs, prepositions, conjunctions, and interjections. Understanding the parts of speech will help you learn the rules of English grammar and usage.

Nouns A **noun** names a person, place, or thing. A **common noun** names any one of a class of persons, places, or things. A **proper noun** names a specific person, place, or thing.

Common Noun	Proper Noun
writer, country, novel	Charles Dickens, Great Britain, *Hard Times*

Pronouns A **pronoun** is a word that stands for one or more nouns. The word to which a pronoun refers (whose place it takes) is the **antecedent** of the pronoun.

A **personal pronoun** refers to the person speaking (first person); the person spoken to (second person); or the person, place, or thing spoken about (third person).

	Singular	Plural
First Person	I, me, my, mine	we, us, our, ours
Second Person	you, your, yours	you, your, yours
Third Person	he, him, his, she, her, hers, it, its	they, them, their, theirs

A **reflexive pronoun** reflects the action of a verb back on its subject. It indicates that the person or thing performing the action also is receiving the action.

I keep *myself* fit by taking a walk every day.

An **intensive pronoun** adds emphasis to a noun or pronoun.

It took the work of the president *himself* to pass the law.

A **demonstrative** pronoun points out a specific person(s), place(s), or thing(s).

this, that, these, those

A **relative pronoun** begins a subordinate clause and connects it to another idea in the sentence.

that, which, who, whom, whose

An **interrogative pronoun** begins a question.

what, which, who, whom, whose

An **indefinite pronoun** refers to a person, place, or thing that may or may not be specifically named.

all, another, any, both, each, everyone, few, most, none, no one, somebody

Verbs A **verb** expresses action or the existence of a state or condition.

An **action verb** tells what action someone or something is performing.

gather, read, work, jump, imagine, analyze, conclude

A **linking verb** connects the subject with another word that identifies or describes the subject. The most common linking verb is *be*.

appear, be, become, feel, look, remain, seem, smell, sound, stay, taste

A **helping verb**, or **auxiliary verb**, is added to a main verb to make a verb phrase.

be, do, have, should, can, could, may, might, must, will, would

Adjectives An **adjective** modifies a noun or pronoun by describing it or giving it a more specific meaning. An adjective answers the questions:

What kind?	*purple* hat, *happy* face, *loud* sound,
Which one?	*this* bowl
How many?	*three* cars
How much?	*enough* food

The articles *the, a,* and *an* are adjectives.

A **proper adjective** is an adjective derived from a proper noun.

French, Shakespearean

Adverbs An **adverb** modifies a verb, an adjective, or another adverb by telling *where, when, how,* or *to what extent*.

will answer *soon, extremely* sad, calls *more* often

Prepositions A **preposition** relates a noun or pronoun that appears with it to another word in the sentence.

Dad made a meal *for* us. We talked *till* dusk. Bo missed school *because of* his illness.

Conjunctions A **conjunction** connects words or groups of words. A **coordinating conjunction** joins words or groups of words of equal rank.

bread *and* cheese, brief *but* powerful

Correlative conjunctions are used in pairs to connect words or groups of words of equal importance.

both Luis *and* Rosa, *neither* you *nor* I

Subordinating conjunctions indicate the connection between two ideas by placing one below the other in rank or importance. A subordinating conjunction introduces a subordinate, or dependent, clause.

We will miss her *if* she leaves. Hank shrieked *when* he slipped on the ice.

Interjections An **interjection** expresses feeling or emotion. It is not related to other words in the sentence.

ah, hey, ouch, well, yippee

PHRASES AND CLAUSES

Phrases A **phrase** is a group of words that does not have both a subject and a verb and that functions as one part of speech. A phrase expresses an idea but cannot stand alone.

Prepositional Phrases A **prepositional phrase** is a group of words that begins with a preposition and ends with a noun or pronoun that is the **object of the preposition.**

before dawn   as a result of the rain

An **adjective phrase** is a prepositional phrase that modifies a noun or pronoun.

Eliza appreciates the beauty **of a well-crafted poem.**

An **adverb phrase** is a prepositional phrase that modifies a verb, an adjective, or an adverb.

She reads Spenser's sonnets **with great pleasure.**

Appositive Phrases An **appositive** is a noun or pronoun placed next to another noun or pronoun to add information about it. An **appositive phrase** consists of an appositive and its modifiers.

Mr. Roth, **my music teacher,** is sick.

Verbal Phrases A **verbal** is a verb form that functions as a different part of speech (not as a verb) in a sentence. **Participles, gerunds,** and **infinitives** are verbals.

A **verbal phrase** includes a verbal and any modifiers or complements it may have. Verbal phrases may function as nouns, as adjectives, or as adverbs.

A **participle** is a verb form that can act as an adjective. Present participles end in *-ing;* past participles of regular verbs end in *-ed.*

A **participial phrase** consists of a participle and its modifiers or complements. The entire phrase acts as an adjective.

Jenna's backpack, **loaded with equipment,** was heavy.

Barking incessantly, the dogs chased the squirrels out of sight.

A **gerund** is a verb form that ends in *-ing* and is used as a noun.

A **gerund phrase** consists of a gerund with any modifiers or complements, all acting together as a noun.

Taking photographs of wildlife is her main hobby. [acts as subject]

We always enjoy **listening to live music.** [acts as object]

An **infinitive** is a verb form, usually preceded by *to,* that can act as a noun, an adjective, or an adverb.

An **infinitive phrase** consists of an infinitive and its modifiers or complements, and sometimes its subject, all acting together as a single part of speech.

She tries **to get out into the wilderness often.** [acts as a noun; direct object of *tries*]

The Tigers are the team **to beat.** [acts as an adjective; describes *team*]

I drove twenty miles **to witness the event.** [acts as an adverb; tells why I drove]

Clauses A **clause** is a group of words with its own subject and verb.

Independent Clauses An independent clause can stand by itself as a complete sentence.

George Orwell wrote with extraordinary insight.

Subordinate Clauses A subordinate clause, also called a dependent clause, cannot stand by itself as a complete sentence. Subordinate clauses always appear connected in some way with one or more independent clauses.

George Orwell, **who wrote with extraordinary insight,** produced many politically relevant works.

An **adjective clause** is a subordinate clause that acts as an adjective. It modifies a noun or a pronoun by telling *what kind* or *which one.* Also called relative clauses, adjective clauses usually begin with a **relative pronoun:** *who, which, that, whom,* or *whose.*

"The Lamb" is the poem **that I memorized for class.**

An **adverb clause** is a subordinate clause that, like an adverb, modifies a verb, an adjective, or an adverb. An adverb clause tells *where, when, in what way, to what extent, under what condition,* or *why.*

The students will read another poetry collection **if their schedule allows.**

When I recited the poem, Mr. Lopez was impressed.

A **noun clause** is a subordinate clause that acts as a noun.

William Blake survived on **whatever he made as an engraver.**

SENTENCE STRUCTURE

Subject and Predicate A **sentence** is a group of words that expresses a complete thought. A sentence has two main parts: a *subject* and a *predicate*.

A **fragment** is a group of words that does not express a complete thought. It lacks an independent clause.

The **subject** tells *whom* or *what* the sentence is about. The **predicate** tells what the subject of the sentence does or is.

A subject or a predicate can consist of a single word or of many words. All the words in the subject make up the **complete subject.** All the words in the predicate make up the **complete predicate.**

Complete Subject	Complete Predicate
Both of those girls	have already read *Macbeth*.

The **simple subject** is the essential noun, pronoun, or group of words acting as a noun that cannot be left out of the complete subject. The **simple predicate** is the essential verb or verb phrase that cannot be left out of the complete predicate.

Both of those girls | **have** already **read** *Macbeth*.
[Simple subject: *Both;* simple predicate: *have read*]

A **compound subject** is two or more subjects that have the same verb and are joined by a conjunction.
Neither the horse nor the driver looked tired.

A **compound predicate** is two or more verbs that have the same subject and are joined by a conjunction.
She *sneezed and coughed* throughout the trip.

Complements A **complement** is a word or word group that completes the meaning of the predicate. There are four kinds of complements: *direct objects, indirect objects, objective complements,* and *subject complements.*

A **direct object** is a noun, a pronoun, or a group of words acting as a noun that receives the action of a transitive verb.
We watched the **liftoff.**
She drove **Zach** to the launch site.

An **indirect object** is a noun or pronoun that appears with a direct object and names the person or thing to which or for which something is done.
He sold the **family** a mirror. [The direct object is *mirror.*]

An **objective complement** is an adjective or noun that appears with a direct object and describes or renames it.
The decision made her **unhappy.**
[The direct object is *her.*]
Many consider Shakespeare the greatest **playwright.** [The direct object is *Shakespeare.*]

A **subject complement** follows a linking verb and tells something about the subject. There are two kinds: *predicate nominatives* and *predicate adjectives.*

A **predicate nominative** is a noun or pronoun that follows a linking verb and identifies or renames the subject.
"A Modest Proposal" is a **pamphlet.**

A **predicate adjective** is an adjective that follows a linking verb and describes the subject of the sentence.
"A Modest Proposal" is **satirical.**

Classifying Sentences by Structure

Sentences can be classified according to the kind and number of clauses they contain. The four basic sentence structures are *simple, compound, complex,* and *compound-complex.*

A **simple sentence** consists of one independent clause.
Terrence enjoys modern British literature.

A **compound sentence** consists of two or more independent clauses. The clauses are joined by a conjunction or a semicolon.
Terrence enjoys modern British literature, but his brother prefers the classics.

A **complex sentence** consists of one independent clause and one or more subordinate clauses.
Terrence, who reads voraciously, enjoys modern British literature.

A **compound-complex sentence** consists of two or more independent clauses and one or more subordinate clauses.
Terrence, who reads voraciously, enjoys modern British literature, but his brother prefers the classics.

Classifying Sentences by Function

Sentences can be classified according to their function or purpose. The four types are *declarative, interrogative, imperative,* and *exclamatory.*

A **declarative sentence** states an idea and ends with a period.

An **interrogative sentence** asks a question and ends with a question mark.

An **imperative sentence** gives an order or a direction and ends with either a period or an exclamation mark.

An **exclamatory sentence** conveys a strong emotion and ends with an exclamation mark.

PARAGRAPH STRUCTURE

An effective paragraph is organized around one **main idea,** which is often stated in a **topic sentence.** The other sentences support the main idea. To give the paragraph **unity,** make sure the connection between each sentence and the main idea is clear.

Unnecessary Shift in Person

Do not change needlessly from one grammatical person to another. Keep the person consistent in your sentences.

Max went to the bakery, but **you** can't buy mints there. [shift from third person to second person]

Max went to the bakery, but **he** can't buy mints there. [consistent]

Unnecessary Shift in Voice

Do not change needlessly from active voice to passive voice in your use of verbs.

Elena and I **searched** the trail for evidence, but no clues **were found.** [shift from active voice to passive voice]

Elena and I **searched** the trail for evidence, but we **found** no clues. [consistent]

AGREEMENT

Subject and Verb Agreement

A singular subject must have a singular verb. A plural subject must have a plural verb.

Dr. Boone uses a telescope to view the night sky.

The **students use** a telescope to view the night sky.

A phrase or clause that comes between a subject and verb does not affect subject-verb agreement.

His **theory,** as well as his claims, **lacks** support.

Two subjects joined by *and* usually take a plural verb.

The **dog** and the **cat are** healthy.

Two singular subjects joined by *or* or *nor* take a singular verb.

The **dog** or the **cat is** hiding.

Two plural subjects joined by *or* or *nor* take a plural verb.

The **dogs** or the **cats are** coming home with us.

When a singular and a plural subject are joined by *or* or *nor,* the verb agrees with the closer subject.

Either the **dogs** or the **cat is** behind the door.

Either the **cat** or the **dogs are** behind the door.

Pronoun and Antecedent Agreement

Pronouns must agree with their antecedents in number and gender. Use singular pronouns with singular antecedents and plural pronouns with plural antecedents.

Doris Lessing uses **her** writing to challenge ideas about women's roles.

Writers often use **their** skills to promote social change.

Use a singular pronoun when the antecedent is a singular indefinite pronoun such as *anybody, each, either, everybody, neither, no one, one,* or *someone.*

Judge **each** of the articles on **its** merits.

Use a plural pronoun when the antecedent is a plural indefinite pronoun such as *both, few, many,* or *several.*

Both of the articles have **their** flaws.

The indefinite pronouns *all, any, more, most, none,* and *some* can be singular or plural depending on the number of the word to which they refer.

Most of the *books* are in **their** proper places.

Most of the *book* has been torn from **its** binding.

Principal Parts of Regular and Irregular Verbs

A verb has four principal parts:

Present	Present Participle	Past	Past Participle
learn	learning	learned	learned
discuss	discussing	discussed	discussed
stand	standing	stood	stood
begin	beginning	began	begun

Regular verbs such as *learn* and *discuss* form the past and past participle by adding *-ed* to the present form. **Irregular verbs** such as *stand* and *begin* form the past and past participle in other ways. If you are in doubt about the principal parts of an irregular verb, check a dictionary.

The Tenses of Verbs

The different tenses of verbs indicate the time an action or condition occurred.

The **present tense** expresses an action that happens regularly or states a general truth.

> Tourists **flock** to the site yearly.

Daily exercise **is** good for your heallth.

The **past tense** expresses a completed action or a condition that is no longer true.

> The squirrel **dropped** the nut and **ran** up the tree.
> I **was** very tired last night by 9:00.

The **future tense** indicates an action that will happen in the future or a condition that will be true.

> The Glazers **will visit** us tomorrow.
> They **will be** glad to arrive from their long journey.

The **present perfect tense** expresses an action that happened at an indefinite time in the past or an action that began in the past and continues into the present.

> Someone **has cleaned** the trash from the park.
> The puppy **has been** under the bed all day.

The **past perfect tense** shows an action that was completed before another action in the past.

> Gerard **had revised** his essay before he turned it in.

The **future perfect tense** indicates an action that will have been completed before another action takes place.

> Mimi **will have painted** the kitchen by the time we finish the shutters.

Degrees of Comparison

Adjectives and adverbs take different forms to show the three degrees of comparison: the *positive*, the *comparative*, and the *superlative.*

Positive	Comparative	Superlative
fast	faster	fastest
crafty	craftier	craftiest
abruptly	more abruptly	most abruptly
badly	worse	worst
much	more	most

Using Comparative and Superlative Adjectives and Adverbs

Use comparative adjectives and adverbs to compare two things. Use superlative adjectives and adverbs to compare three or more things.

> This season's weather was **drier** than last year's.
> This season has been one of the **driest** on record.
> Jake practices **more often** than Jamal.
> Of everyone in the band, Jake practices **most often.**

Pronoun Case

The **case** of a pronoun is the form it takes to show its function in a sentence. There are three pronoun cases: *nominative, objective,* and *possessive.*

Nominative	Objective	Possessive
I, you, he, she, it, we, you, they	me, you, him, her, it, us, you, them	my, your, yours, his, her, hers, its, our, ours, their, theirs

Use the **nominative case** when a pronoun functions as a *subject* or as a *predicate nominative.*

> **They** are going to the movies. [subject]
> The biggest movie fan is **she.** [predicate nominative]

Use the **objective case** for a pronoun acting as a *direct object,* an *indirect object,* or the *object of a preposition.*

> The ending of the play surprised **me.** [direct object]
> Mary gave **us** two tickets to the play. [indirect object]
> The audience cheered for **him.** [object of preposition]

Use the **possessive case** to show ownership.

> The red suitcase is **hers.** [belongs to her]

Diction The words you choose contribute to the overall effectiveness of your writing. **Diction** refers to word choice and to the clearness and correctness of those words. You can improve one aspect of your diction by choosing carefully between commonly confused words, such as the pairs listed below.

accept, except

Accept is a verb that means "to receive" or "to agree to." *Except* is a preposition that means "other than" or "leaving out."

> Please **accept** my offer to buy you lunch this weekend.

> He is busy every day **except** the weekends.

affect, effect

Affect is normally a verb meaning "to influence" or "to bring about a change in." *Effect* is usually a noun meaning "result."

> The distractions outside **affect** Steven's ability to concentrate.

> The teacher's remedies had a positive **effect** on Steven's ability to concentrate.

among, between

Among is usually used with three or more items, and it emphasizes collective relationships or indicates distribution. *Between* is generally used with only two items, but it can be used with more than two if the emphasis is on individual (one-to-one) relationships within the group.

> I had to choose a snack **among** the various vegetables.

> He handed out the booklets **among** the conference participants.

> Our school is **between** a park and an old barn.

> The tournament included matches **between** France, Spain, Mexico, and the United States.

amount, number

Amount refers to overall quantity and is mainly used with mass nouns (those that can't be counted). *Number* refers to individual items that can be counted.

> The **amount** of attention that great writers have paid to Shakespeare is remarkable.

> A **number** of important English writers have been fascinated by the legend of King Arthur.

assure, ensure, insure

Assure means "to convince [someone of something]; to guarantee." *Ensure* means "to make certain [that something happens]." *Insure* means "to arrange for payment in case of loss."

> The attorney **assured** us we'd win the case.

> The rules **ensure** that no one gets treated unfairly.

> Many professional musicians **insure** their valuable instruments.

bad, badly

Use the adjective *bad* before a noun or after linking verbs such as *feel, look,* and *seem.* Use *badly* whenever an adverb is required.

> The situation may seem **bad**, but it will improve over time.

> Though I **badly** mismanaged my time, I might be able to recover over the weekend.

beside, besides

Beside means "at the side of" or "close to." *Besides* means "in addition to."

> The stapler sits **beside** the pencil sharpener in our classroom.

> **Besides** being very clean, the classroom is also very organized.

can, may

The helping verb *can* generally refers to the ability to do something. The helping verb *may* generally refers to permission to do something.

> I **can** run one mile in six minutes.

> **May** we have a race during recess?

complement, compliment

The verb *complement* means "to enhance"; the verb *compliment* means "to praise."

> Online exercises **complement** the textbook lessons.

> Ms. Lewis **complimented** our team on our excellent debate.

compose, comprise

Compose means "to make up; constitute." *Comprise* means "to include or contain." Remember that the whole comprises its parts or is composed of its parts, and the parts compose the whole.

> The assignment **comprises** three different tasks.

> The assignment is **composed** of three different tasks.

> Three different tasks **compose** the assignment.

different from, different than

Different from is generally preferred over *different than,* but *different than* can be used before a clause. Always use *different from* before a noun or pronoun.

> Your point of view is so **different from** mine.

> His idea was so **different from** [or **different than**] what we had expected.

farther, further

Use *farther* when you refer to distance. Use *further* when you mean "to a greater degree or extent" or "additional."

> Stephon has traveled **farther** than anybody else in the class.

> If I want **further** details about his travels, I can read his blog.

fewer, less

Use *fewer* for things that can be counted. Use *less* for amounts or quantities that cannot be counted. *Fewer* must be followed by a plural noun.

> **Fewer** students drive to school since the weather improved.
> There is **less** noise outside in the mornings.

good, well

Use the adjective *good* before a noun or after a linking verb. Use *well* whenever an adverb is required, such as when modifying a verb.

> I feel **good** after sleeping for eight hours.
> I did **well** on my test, and my soccer team played **well** in that afternoon's game. It was a **good** day!

its, it's

The word *its* with no apostrophe is a possessive pronoun. The word *it's* is a contraction of "it is."

> Angelica will try to fix the computer and **its** keyboard.
> **It's** a difficult job, but she can do it.

lay, lie

Lay is a transitive verb meaning "to set or put something down." Its principal parts are *lay, laying, laid, laid*. *Lie* is an intransitive verb meaning "to recline" or "to exist in a certain place." Its principal parts are *lie, lying, lay, lain*.

> Please **lay** that box down and help me with the sofa.
> When we are done moving, I am going to **lie** down.
> My hometown **lies** sixty miles north of here.

like, as

Like is a preposition that usually means "similar to" and precedes a noun or pronoun. The conjunction *as* means "in the way that" and usually precedes a clause.

> **Like** the other students, I was prepared for a quiz.
> **As** I said yesterday, we expect to finish before noon.

Use **such as,** not **like,** before a series of examples.

> Foods **such as** apples, nuts, and pretzels make good snacks.

of, have

Do not use *of* in place of *have* after auxiliary verbs such as *would, could, should, may, might,* or *must.* The contraction of *have* is formed by adding *-ve* after these verbs.

> I **would have** stayed after school today, but I had to help cook at home.
> Mom **must've** called while I was still in the gym.

principal, principle

Principal can be an adjective meaning "main; most important." It can also be a noun meaning "chief officer of a school." *Principle* is a noun meaning "moral rule" or "fundamental truth."

> His strange behavior was the **principal** reason for our concern.
> Democratic **principles** form the basis of our country's laws.

raise, rise

Raise is a transitive verb that usually takes a direct object. *Rise* is intransitive and never takes a direct object.

> Iliana and Josef **raise** the flag every morning.
> They **rise** from their seats and volunteer immediately whenever help is needed.

than, then

The conjunction *than* is used to connect the two parts of a comparison. The adverb *then* usually refers to time.

> My backpack is heavier **than** hers.
> I will finish my homework and **then** meet my friends at the park.

that, which, who

Use the relative pronoun *that* to refer to things or people. Use *which* only for things and *who* only for people.

That introduces a restrictive phrase or clause, that is, one that is essential to the meaning of the sentence. *Which* introduces a nonrestrictive phrase or clause—one that adds information but could be deleted from the sentence—and is preceded by a comma.

> Ben ran to the park **that** just reopened.
> The park, **which** just reopened, has many attractions.
> The man **who** built the park loves to see people smiling.

when, where, why

Do not use *when, where,* or *why* directly after a linking verb, such as *is.* Reword the sentence.

> *Incorrect:* The morning is when he left for the beach.
> *Correct:* He left for the beach in the morning.

who, whom

In formal writing, use *who* only as a subject in clauses and sentences. Use *whom* only as the object of a verb or of a preposition.

> **Who** paid for the tickets?
> **Whom** should I pay for the tickets?
> I can't recall to **whom** I gave the money for the tickets.

your, you're

Your is a possessive pronoun expressing ownership. *You're* is the contraction of "you are."

> Have you finished writing **your** informative essay?
> **You're** supposed to turn it in tomorrow. If **you're** late, **your** grade will be affected.

Capitalization

First Words

Capitalize the first word of a sentence.

Stories about knights and their deeds interest me.

Capitalize the first word of direct speech.

Sharon asked, "**D**o you like stories about knights?"

Capitalize the first word of a quotation that is a complete sentence.

Einstein said, "**A**nyone who has never made a mistake has never tried anything new."

Proper Nouns and Proper Adjectives

Capitalize all proper nouns, including geographical names, historical events and periods, and names of organizations.

Thames **R**iver   **J**ohn **K**eats   the **R**enaissance

United **N**ations   **W**orld **W**ar II   **S**ierra **N**evada

Capitalize all proper adjectives.

Shakespearean play   **B**ritish invaision

American citizen   **L**atin **A**merican literature

Academic Course Names

Capitalize course names only if they are language courses, are followed by a number, or are preceded by a proper noun or adjective.

Spanish   **H**onors **C**hemistry   **H**istory 101

geology   **a**lgebra   **s**ocial **s**tudies

Titles

Capitalize personal titles when followed by the person's name.

Ms. Hughes   **D**r. Perez   **K**ing George

Capitalize titles showing family relationships when they are followed by a specific person's name, unless they are preceded by a possessive noun or pronoun.

Uncle Oscar   Mangan's **s**ister   his **a**unt Tessa

Capitalize the first word and all other key words in the titles of books, stories, songs, and other works of art.

Frankenstein   "**S**hooting an **E**lephant"

Punctuation

End Marks

Use a **period** to end a declarative sentence or an imperative sentence.

We are studying the structure of sonnets.

Read the biography of Mary Shelley.

Use periods with initials and abbreviations.

D. H. Lawrence   Mrs. Browning

Mt. Everest   Maple St.

Use a **question mark** to end an interrogative sentence.

What is Macbeth's fatal flaw?

Use an **exclamation mark** after an exclamatory sentence or a forceful imperative sentence.

That's a beautiful painting!   Let me go now!

Commas

Use a **comma** before a coordinating conjunction to separate two independent clauses in a compound sentence.

The game was very close, but we were victorious.

Use commas to separate three or more words, phrases, or clauses in a series.

William Blake was a writer, artist, and printer.

Use commas to separate coordinate adjectives.

It was a witty, amusing novel.

Use a comma after an introductory word, phrase, or clause.

When the novelist finished his book, he celebrated with his family.

Use commas to set off nonessential expressions.

Old English, of course, requires translation.

Use commas with places and dates.

Coventry, England   September 1, 1939

Semicolons

Use a **semicolon** to join closely related independent clauses that are not already joined by a conjunction.

Tanya likes to write poetry; Heather prefers prose.

Use semicolons to avoid confusion when items in a series contain commas.

They traveled to London, England; Madrid, Spain; and Rome, Italy.

Colons

Use a **colon** before a list of items following an independent clause.

Notable Victorian poets include the following: Tennyson, Arnold, Housman, and Hopkins.

Use a colon to introduce information that summarizes or explains the independent clause before it.

She just wanted to do one thing: rest.

Malcolm loves volunteering: He reads to sick children every Saturday afternoon.

Quotation Marks

Use **quotation marks** to enclose a direct quotation.

"Short stories," Ms. Hildebrand said, "should have rich, well-developed characters."

An **indirect quotation** does not require quotation marks.

Ms. Hildebrand said that short stories should have well-developed characters.

Use quotation marks around the titles of short written works, episodes in a series, songs, and works mentioned as parts of collections.

"The Lagoon"   "Boswell Meets Johnson"

Italics

Italicize the titles of long written works, movies, television and radio shows, lengthy works of music, paintings, and sculptures.

Howards End　　　*60 Minutes*　　　*Guernica*

For handwritten material, you can use underlining instead of italics.

The Princess Bride　　　Mona Lisa

Dashes

Use **dashes** to indicate an abrupt change of thought, a dramatic interrupting idea, or a summary statement.

> I read the entire first act of *Macbeth*—you won't believe what happens next.
>
> The director—what's her name again?—attended the movie premiere.

Hyphens

Use a **hyphen** with certain numbers, after certain prefixes, with two or more words used as one word, and with a compound modifier that comes before a noun.

> seventy-two
> self-esteem
> well-being
> five-year contract

Parentheses

Use **parentheses** to set off asides and explanations when the material is not essential or when it consists of one or more sentences. When the sentence in parentheses interrupts the larger sentence, it does not have a capital letter or a period.

> He listened intently (it was too dark to see who was speaking) to try to identify the voices.

When a sentence in parentheses falls between two other complete sentences, it should start with a capital letter and end with a period.

> The quarterback threw three touchdown passes. (We knew he could do it.) Our team won the game by two points.

Apostrophes

Add an **apostrophe** and an *s* to show the possessive case of most singular nouns and of plural nouns that do not end in -*s* or -*es*.

> Blake's poems　　　the mice's whiskers

Names ending in *s* form their possessives in the same way, except for classical and biblical names, which add only an apostrophe to form the possessive.

> Dickens's　　　Hercules'

Add an apostrophe to show the possessive case of plural nouns ending in -*s* and -*es*.

> the girls' songs　　　the Ortizes' car

Use an apostrophe in a contraction to indicate the position of the missing letter or letters.

> She's never read a Coleridge poem she didn't like.

Brackets

Use **brackets** to enclose clarifying information inserted within a quotation.

> Columbus's journal entry from October 21, 1492, begins as follows: "At 10 o'clock, we arrived at a cape of the island [San Salvador], and anchored, the other vessels in company."

Ellipses

Use three ellipsis points, also known as an **ellipsis,** to indicate where you have omitted words from quoted material.

> Wollestonecraft wrote, "The education of women has of late been more attended to than formerly; yet they are still . . . ridiculed or pitied . . . ."

In the example above, the four dots at the end of the sentence are the three ellipsis points plus the period from the original sentence.

Use an ellipsis to indicate a pause or interruption in speech.

> "When he told me the news," said the coach, "I was . . . I was shocked . . . completely shocked."

Spelling

Spelling Rules

Learning the rules of English spelling will help you make **generalizations** about how to spell words.

Word Parts

The three word parts that can combine to form a word are roots, prefixes, and suffixes. Many of these word parts come from the Greek, Latin, and Anglo-Saxon languages.

The **root word** carries a word's basic meaning.

Root and Origin	Meaning	Examples
-leg- (-log-) [Gr.]	to say, speak	*legal, logic*
-pon- (-pos-) [L.]	to put, place	*postpone, deposit*

A **prefix** is one or more syllables added to the beginning of a word that alter the meaning of the root.

Prefix and Origin	Meaning	Examples
anti- [Gr.]	against	*antipathy*
inter- [L.]	between	*international*
mis- [A.S.]	wrong	*misplace*

A **suffix** is a letter or group of letters added to the end of a root word that changes the word's meaning or part of speech.

Suffix and Origin	Meaning	Part of Speech
-ful [A.S.]	full of: *scornful*	adjective
-ity [L.]	state of being: *adversity*	noun
-ize (-ise) [Gr.]	to make: *idolize*	verb
-ly [A.S.]	in a manner: *calmly*	adverb

Rules for Adding Suffixes to Root Words

When adding a suffix to a root word ending in *y* preceded by a consonant, change *y* to *i* unless the suffix begins with *i*.

ply + -able = pliable   happy + -ness = happiness
defy + -ing = defying   cry + -ing = crying

For a root word ending in *e*, drop the *e* when adding a suffix beginning with a vowel.

drive + -ing = driving   move + -able = movable
SOME EXCEPTIONS: traceable, seeing, dyeing

For root words ending with a consonant + vowel + consonant in a stressed syllable, double the final consonant when adding a suffix that begins with a vowel.

mud + -y = muddy   submit + -ed = submitted
SOME EXCEPTIONS: mixing, fixed

Rules for Adding Prefixes to Root Words

When a prefix is added to a root word, the spelling of the root remains the same.

un- + certain = uncertain   mis- + spell = misspell

With some prefixes, the spelling of the prefix changes when joined to the root to make the pronunciation easier.

in- + mortal = immortal   ad- + vert = avert

Orthographic Patterns

Certain letter combinations in English make certain sounds. For instance, *ph* sounds like *f*, *eigh* usually makes a long *a* sound, and the *k* before an *n* is often silent.

pharmacy   n**eigh**bor   **k**nowledge

Understanding **orthographic patterns** such as these can help you improve your spelling.

Forming Plurals

The plural form of most nouns is formed by adding -*s* to the singular.

computer**s**   gadget**s**   Washington**s**

For words ending in *s*, *ss*, *x*, *z*, *sh*, or *ch*, add -*es*.

circus**es**   tax**es**   wish**es**   bench**es**

For words ending in *y* or *o* preceded by a vowel, add -*s*.

key**s**   patio**s**

For words ending in *y* preceded by a consonant, change the *y* to an *i* and add -*es*.

cit**ies**   enem**ies**   troph**ies**

For most words ending in *o* preceded by a consonant, add -*es*.

echo**es**   tomato**es**

Some words form the plural in irregular ways.

women   oxen   children   teeth   deer

Foreign Words Used in English

Some words used in English are actually foreign words that have been adopted. Learning to spell these words requires memorization. When in doubt, check a dictionary.

sushi   enchilada   au pair   fiancé
laissez faire   croissant

Analyzing Text

Analyze, 32, 44, 56, 278, 382, 406, 583, 611, 699, 722

  essential question, 32, 44, 56, 78, 96, 110, 180, 188, 208, 220, 228, 242, 278, 288, 296, 315, 332, 340, 382, 426, 438, 457, 465, 476, 569, 583, 598, 611, 630, 640, 722, 742, 754, 782, 798

  media

    essential question, 296, 321, 348, 406

    present and discuss, 88, 321, 348

    review and clarify, 348

    review and synthesize, 88, 321

  prepare to compare, 48

  present and discuss, 78, 96, 110, 208, 220, 228, 242, 315, 332, 340, 426, 438, 457, 465, 476, 630, 640, 742, 754, 782, 798

  review and clarify, 78, 96, 110, 208, 220, 228, 242, 315, 332, 340, 426, 438, 457, 465, 476, 630, 640, 742, 754, 782, 798

  writing to compare, 292, 322, 468, 612

Argument, 225

Argument model, 130, 496

Assess, 551

Author's style

  apostrophe, 632

  author's choices, 467, 784

  character development, 80, 399

  descriptive details, 61

  details, 334

  diction, 98, 210

  Greek Chorus, 701

  information integration, 301

  motifs, 585

  pace, 784

  parallelism, 230, 725

  paraphrase, 617

  poetic form, 222

  poetic language, 440

  poetic structure, 467, 601

  point of view, 112

  quotations, 617

  repetition, 585

  rhetorical devices, 291

  scientific and technical diction, 98

  sentence variety, 478

  sound devices, 440

  syntax, 210

  transitions, 193

  word choice, 342, 428, 553

  word choice and meaning, 756

Characterization, 80

Cite textual evidence, 32, 44, 45, 78, 79, 96, 97, 110, 111, 180, 181, 208, 209, 220, 221, 228, 229, 242, 243, 278, 279, 288, 289, 296, 315, 316, 332, 333, 340, 341, 382, 383, 397, 426, 427, 438, 439, 457, 458, 465, 466, 476, 477, 531, 532, 551, 552, 569, 583, 584, 598, 599, 611, 630, 631, 640, 641, 699, 700, 722, 723, 742, 743, 754, 782, 783, 798, 799

Classify, 699

Close read, 531, 551, 569, 583, 699

  annotate, 32, 44, 78, 96, 110, 119, 180, 208, 220, 228, 242, 251, 278, 288, 355, 382, 396, 476, 485, 509, 598, 630, 640, 649, 722, 742, 754, 782, 798, 807

  close-read guide, 119, 251, 355, 485, 649, 807

  conclude, 32, 44, 78, 96, 110, 119, 180, 208, 220, 228, 242, 251, 278, 288, 315, 332, 339, 355, 382, 396, 426, 438, 457, 465, 476, 485, 509, 598, 611, 630, 640, 649, 722, 742, 754, 782, 798, 807

  question, 32, 44, 78, 96, 110, 119, 180, 208, 220, 228, 242, 251, 278, 288, 315, 332, 339, 355, 382, 396, 426, 438, 457, 465, 476, 485, 509, 598, 611, 630, 640, 649, 722, 742, 754, 782, 798, 807

Close review

  conclude, 56, 88, 188, 296, 321, 348, 406

  question, 56, 188, 296, 321, 348, 406

  synthesize, 88

Compare and contrast, 44, 180, 288, 382, 406, 583, 699

Compare texts, 12, 36, 268, 282, 308, 442, 604

Compare texts to media, 318

Connect, 32, 44, 278, 296, 531, 551, 699

Contrast, 188

Craft and Structure

  author's choices, 221, 333, 439, 466, 743

author's claims, 97

author's purpose, 316

development of ideas, 799

dramatic structure

  aside, 584

  monologue, 584

  plot, 570

  soliloquy, 584

  subplot, 570

drama types

  comedy, 532

  romance, 532

  tragedy, 532

emotional appeals, 289

evidence, 316

  credibility, 229

  relevance, 229

  variety, 229

feature story

  body, 477

  conclusion, 477

  introduction, 477

  title, 477

figurative language

  analogy, 755

  extended metaphor, 333

  hyperbole, 743

  metaphor, 333, 743

  personification, 743

  simile, 333, 743

  theme, 755

Greek play structure

  exodos, 700

  odes, 700

  parados, 700

  prologue, 700

  verse drama, 700

Greek tragedy

  antagonist, 723

  dramatic irony, 723

  hamartia, 723

  protagonist, 723

  tragic hero, 723

literary devices

  irony, 383

  situational irony, 383

  surprise ending, 383

literary nonfiction

  conclusion, 243

  discussion, 243

INDEX OF SKILLS

INDEX OF SKILLS

INDEX OF SKILLS

Writing

INDEX OF AUTHORS AND TITLES

The following authors and titles appear in the print and online versions of *my*Perspectives.

ADDITIONAL SELECTIONS: AUTHOR AND TITLE INDEX

The following authors and titles appear in the Interactive Student Edition only.

ACKNOWLEDGMENTS AND CREDITS

Acknowledgments

The following selections appear in Grade 10 of *my*Perspectives. Some selections appear online only.

ABC News - Permissions Dept. Spooky Business: American Economy ©ABC News; Diane Sawyer Sits Down With the Inspirational Malala Yousafzai ©ABC News; 14-Year-Old Teaches Family the 'Power of Half' ©ABC News; Dr. Geoffrey Tabin Helps Blind Ethiopians Gain Sight ©ABC News.

American Folklore. "What We Plant, We Will Eat" by S. E. Schlosser; Used with permission from S.E. Schlosser and American Folklore. Copyright 2015. All rights reserved.

American Foundation for the Blind. "The Empire State Building" by Helen Keller, originally appeared in *New York Times*, January 17, 1932. Courtesy of the American Foundation for the Blind, Helen Keller Archives.

Amnesty International UK. Everybody—we are all born free ©Amnesty International UK.

Anchor Books. "The Sun Parlor" from *The Richer, The Poorer* by Dorothy West, copyright ©1995 by Dorothy West. Used by permission of Doubleday, an imprint of the Knopf Doubleday Publishing Group, a division of Penguin Random House LLC. All rights reserved. Any third party use of this material, outside of this publication, is prohibited. Interested parties must apply directly to Penguin Random House LLC for permission.

Arte Publico Press. "Fences" is reprinted with permission from the publisher of *Communion,* by Pat Mora ©1991 Arte Publico Press—University of Houston.

Atlantic Monthly. "Why Do Some Dreams Enjoy Fear?" ©2013 The Atlantic Media Co., as first published in *The Atlantic Magazine*. All rights reserved. Distributed by Tribune Content Agency, LLC.

BBC News Online. "How Your Eyes Trick Your Mind," from BBC; Used with permission.

BBC Worldwide Americas, Inc. *Franz Kafka and Metamorphosis* ©BBC Worldwide Learning; Socrates ©BBC Worldwide Learning; Episode 1: Rock the Ship ©BBC Worldwide Learning; Blind Teen ©BBC Worldwide Learning; How Your Eyes Trick Your Mind ©BBC Worldwide Learning.

Black Moon Theatre Company. Kafka's *The Metamorphosis* ©Black Moon Theatre Company.

Bowers, Jai. "By Any Other Name" from *Gifts of Passage* by Santha Rama Rau. Copyright ©Santha Rama Rau. Reprinted by permission of the author's estate.

Cambridge University Press - US – Journals. "A Dose of What the Doctor Never Orders," from *The Japanese Family Storehouse* by Ihara Saikaku, translated by G. W. Sargent. Copyright ©1959 Cambridge University Press. Reprinted with the permission of Cambridge University Press.

Carmen Balcells Agencia Literaria. Julio Cortazar, "House Taken Over," *Blow-Up and Other Stories* ©The Estate of Julio Cortazar, 1967.

Curtis Brown, Ltd. (UK). "They are hostile nations" from *Power Politics* by Margaret Atwood. Copyright ©1976 by Margaret Atwood. Used with permission.

Dancing Bear, J. P. "Caliban," Copyright ©J. P. Dancing Bear. Used with permission of the author.

Farrar, Straus and Giroux. "Avarice" from *Talking Dirty to the Gods* by Yusef Komunyakaa. Copyright ©2000 by Yusef Komunyakaa. Reprinted by permission of Farrar, Straus and Giroux, LLC. CAUTION: Users are warned that this work is protected under copyright laws and downloading is strictly prohibited. The right to reproduce or transfer the work via any medium must be secured with Farrar, Straus and Giroux, LLC.

Forgiveness Project. "The Forgiveness Project: Eric Lomax," ©The Forgiveness Project.

Freedom House. "Harsh Laws and Violence Drive Global Decline," Freedom of the Press 2015. By permission of Freedom House.

Frost, Adam. Adapted from "How to tell you're reading a gothic novel—in pictures" by Adam Frost and Zhenia Vasiliev, from *The Guardian,* May 9, 2014.

Getty Images. JFK Inaugural Address ©MediaRecall Holdings/Archive ED/Getty Images.

Gibbons, Reginald. "Money" copyright by Reginald Gibbons. Reprinted by permission of the author.

Goldsmith, Margie. "The Thrill of the Chase" by Margie Goldsmith, from *Hemispheres Magazine,* January 2013. Copyright ©2013 by Margie Goldsmith. Used with permission of the author.

Graywolf Press. Tracy K. Smith, "The Good Life" from *Life on Mars.* Copyright ©2011 by Tracy K. Smith. Reprinted with the permission of The Permissions Company, Inc., on behalf of Graywolf Press, Minneapolis, Minnesota.

Guardian News and Media Limited. "Stone Age man's terrors still stalk modern nightmares," Copyright Guardian News & Media Ltd 2015; "A Dish Best Served Cold," Copyright Guardian News & Media Ltd 2015; "Experience: I first saw my wife 10 years after we married," Copyright Guardian News & Media Ltd 2015.

Hanging Loose Press. "Sonnet With Bird," reprinted from *What I've Stolen, What I've Earned* ©2014 by Sherman Alexie, by permission of Hanging Loose Press.

HarperCollins Publishers. "Harrison Bergeron" from *Welcome to the Monkey House* (audio) by Kurt Vonnegut. Copyright © 1950, 1951, 1953, 1954, 1955, 1956, 1958, 1960, 1961, 1962, 1964, 1966, 1968 by Kurt Vonnegut Jr. (p) & © 2006 HarperCollins Publishers. Used by permission of HarperCollins Publishers.

HarperCollins Publishers Ltd. (UK). "Windigo" from Jacklight by Louise Erdrich. Reprinted by permission of HarperCollins Publishers Ltd ©1984 Louise Erdrich

Houghton Mifflin Harcourt. "They are Hostile Nations" from *Selected Poems I:* 1965–1975 by Margaret Atwood. Copyright ©1976 by Margaret Atwood. Reprinted with permission of Houghton Mifflin Harcourt Publishing Company. All rights reserved.

Houghton Mifflin Harcourt Publishing Co. Excerpt from *Blindness* by Jose Saramago, translated from the Portuguese by Giovanni Pontiero. Copyright ©1995 by Jose Saramago and Editorial Caminho, SA. English translation copyright ©1997 by Juan Sager. Reprinted by permission of Houghton Mifflin Harcourt Publishing Company. All rights reserved.

Ivan R. Dee, Publisher. *Oedipus the King.* Copyright ©2000 by Ivan R. Dee, Inc. Translation copyright ©2000 by Nicholas Rudall. All rights reserved.

© Pearson Education, Inc., or its affiliates. All rights reserved.

Acknowledgments **R77**

prohibited. Interested parties must apply directly to Penguin Random House LLC for permission; "Civil Peace" from *Girls at War: And Other Stories* by Chinua Achebe, copyright ©1972, 1973 by Chinua Achebe. Used by permission of Doubleday, an imprint of the Knopf Doubleday Publishing Group, a division of Penguin Random House LLC. All rights reserved. Any third party use of this material, outside of this publication, is prohibited. Interested parties must apply directly to Penguin Random House LLC for permission; "Civil Peace" from *Girls at War* by Chinua Achebe, copyright © 1972, 1973 by Chinua Achebe. Used by permission of Doubleday, an imprint of the Knopf Doubleday Publishing Group, a division of Penguin Random House LLC. All rights reserved; "The Blind Seer of Ambon" from *Travels* by W.S. Merwin, copyright ©1992 by W.S. Merwin. Used by permission of Alfred A. Knopf, an imprint of the Knopf Doubleday Publishing Group, a division of Penguin Random House LLC. All rights reserved. Any third party use of this material, outside of this publication, is prohibited. Interested parties must apply directly to Penguin Random House LLC for permission.

Robbins, Alexandra. "Revenge of the Geeks," by Alexandra Robins, author of *The Geeks Shall Inherit the Earth: Popularity, Quick Theory, and Why Outsiders Thrive After High School*. "Revenge of the Geeks" from *LA Times,* May 28, 2011.

Simmons, Anne. "King Midas" by Howard Moss, from *Poetry Magazine* (May 1957). Used with permission of the Estate of Howard Moss.

Tutu, Desmond. "Let South Africa Show the World How to Forgive," Copyright ©2000 by Desmond M. Tutu, used with permission. All rights reserved.

Unger, David. "The Censors," ©David Unger, 1982.

United Nations Publications. From "The Universal Declaration of Human Rights" ©United Nations. Reprinted with the permission of the United Nations.

University of California Press. "Elliptical," republished with permission of University of California Press, "Elliptical" from *Sleeping with the Dictionary* by Harryette Mullen, 2002; permission conveyed through Copyright Clearance Center, Inc.

University of Chicago Press. From *Shakespeare & the French Poet* by Yves Bonnefoy. Copyright ©2004 by the University of Chicago. Reprinted with permission of the publisher, University of Chicago Press.

University of Illinois Press. "En El Jardin, de los Espejos Quebrados, Caliban Catches a Glimpse of His Reflection," From *Guide to the Blue Tongue: Poems.* Copyright2002 by Virgil Suárez. Used with permission of the University of Illinois Press.

University of Texas Press, Books. "The Feather Pillow" from *The Decapitated Chicken and Other Stories* by Horacio Quiroga, translated by Margaret Sayers Peden. Copyright ©1976 by the University of Texas Press. By permission of the University of Texas Press.

Vasiliev, Zhenia. Adapted from "How to tell you're reading a gothic novel—in pictures" by Adam Frost and Zhenia Vasiliev, from *The Guardian,* May 9, 2014.

Virginia Polytechnic Institute and State University. "Fleeing to Dismal Swamp, Slaves and Outcasts Found Freedom," by Sandy Hausman, as appeared on NPR, December 28, 2014. ©WVTF; Fleeing To Dismal Swamp, Slaves And Outcasts Found Freedom (audio) ©WVTF.

Visual Capitalist. "The Gold Series," ©Visual Capitalist

W. W. Norton & Co. "Under One Small Star," "Under a Certain Little Star," from *Miracle Fair* by Wislawa Szymborska, translated by Joanna Trzeciak. Copyright ©2012 by Joanna Trzeciak. Used by permission of W.W. Norton & Company, Inc.

WGBH Media Library & Archives. "Understanding Forgiveness," from *This Emotional Life, Understanding Forgiveness* ©2009 WGBH Educational Foundation and Vulcan Productions, Inc.

Wylie Agency. "Windigo" from *Jacklight* by Louise Erdrich. Copyright ©1984 by Louise Erdrich, used by permission of The Wylie Agency LLC.; "Civil Peace" from *Girls at War and Other Stories* by Chinua Achebe. Copyright ©1972, 1973 by Chinua Achebe, used by permission of The Wylie Agency LLC.; "The Blind Seer of Ambon" by W. S. Merwin, collected in *Travels.* Copyright ©1992 by W. S. Merwin, used by permission of The Wylie Agency LLC.

YGS Group. "Heirlooms' value shifts from sentiment to cash" by Rosa Salter Rodriguez. June 15, 2014. ©Associated Press, Reprinted by permission of the YGS Group.

Credits

vi Larry Lilac/Alamy; viii Michael Blann/Stone/Getty Images; x Alexey U/Shutterstock; xii Abdul Aziz Apu Bangladesh/Ocean/Corbis; xiv Glowimages/Getty Images; 2 Larry Lilac/Alamy; 3 (BC) Alexsvirid/Shutterstock, (BCR) Rachel K. Turner/Alamy, (BL) Sfam_photo/Shutterstock, (BR) Zbramwell/Shutterstock, (CT) Arthur Tress copyright 2015; (CTL) Blackwaterimages/E+/Getty Images, (CTR) Bonciutoma/Fotolia, (T) Quavondo/Vetta/Getty Images, (TC) Pixforfun/Getty Images, (TL) Mary Evans Picture Library/ARTHUR RACKHAM, (TR) Hung Chung Chih/Shutterstock; 6 Quavondo/Vetta/Getty Images; 11 (C) Blackwaterimages/E+/Getty Images, (T) Mary Evans Picture Library/ARTHUR RACKHAM; 12 (B) Everett Historical/Shutterstock, (TL) Mary Evans Picture Library/ARTHUR RACKHAM, (TR) Blackwaterimages/E+/Getty Images; 13, 32, 34, 36 (TL), 48 (T) Mary Evans Picture Library/ARTHUR RACKHAM; 18 Tom Tom/Shutterstock; 25 Frozenstarro/Fotolia; 26 Perseo Medusa/Shutterstock; 36 (B) Ulf Andersen/Getty Images, (TR) Blackwaterimages/E+/Getty Images; 37, 44, 46, 48 (B) Blackwaterimages/E+/Getty Images; 50 (B) ZheniaVasiliev, (T) © Adam Frost; 65 (B) Sfam_photo/Shutterstock, (BC) Alexsvirid/Shutterstock, (T) Pixforfun/Getty Images, (TC) Arthur Tress copyright 2015; 68 Francois Durand/Getty Images; 69 Pixforfun/Getty Images; 74 Ken Tannenbaum/Shutterstock; 78 Pixforfun/Getty Images; 80 Pixforfun/Getty Images; 82 Arthur Tress copyright 2015; 83–88 Arthur Tress copyright 2015; 90 Allegra Ringo; 91, 96, 98 Alexsvirid/Shutterstock; 100 Sfam_photo/Shutterstock; 101 (B) Chris Felver/Archive Photos/Getty Images, (C) Everett Historical/Shutterstock, (T) Drew Altizer/Sipa USA/Newscom; 102 Sfam_photo/Shutterstock; 104 SlavaGerj/Shutterstock; 108 Chris Clor/Blend Images/Corbis; 126 Michael Blann/Stone/Getty Images; 127 (BC) Arina P Habich/Shutterstock, (BCR) Sam Steinberg, (BL) Nick Fox/Shutterstock, (BR) Subos/Shutterstock, (C) Tntphototravis/Shutterstock, (CR) V.S.Anandhakrishna/Shutterstock, (T) When They Were Young Benjamin Franklin, Jackson, Peter (1922–2003)/Private Collection/Look and Learn/Bridgeman Art Library, (TL) MarishaSha/Shutterstock, (TR) Aleksey Stemmer/Shutterstock; 130,190 When They Were Young Benjamin Franklin, Jackson, Peter (1922–2003)/Private Collection/Look and Learn/Bridgeman Art Library; 135 (B) BBC Worldwide Learning, (T) MarishaSha/Shutterstock; 136 Lebrecht Music and Arts Photo Library/Alamy; 137 MarishaSha/Shutterstock; 141 Fasphotographic/Shutterstock; 146 Madeleine Forsberg/Shutterstock; 150 VasilyevAlexandr/Shutterstock; 158 Jan Faukner/Shutterstock; 165 Michael ZittelSerr/Shutterstock; 170 Alenavlad/Shutterstock; 180 MarishaSha/Shutterstock; 182 MarishaSha/Shutterstock; 184 MarishaSha/Shutterstock; 187 BBC Worldwide Learning; 197 (BC) Arina P Habich/Shutterstock, (TC) Tntphototravis/Shutterstock; 200 Lebrecht Music and Arts Photo Library/Alamy; 212 Tntphototravis/Shutterstock; 213 (B) © Pat Mora, (C) © Judy Natal 2015 www.judynatal.com, (T) Ulf Andersen/Getty Images; 214 Tntphototravis/Shutterstock; 216 Isaravut/Shutterstock; 218 AlexandrOzerov/Fotolia; 224 David Robbins; 225, 230 Arina P Habich/Shutterstock; 228 Arina P Habich/Shutterstock; 232 S(TR)/AFP/Getty Images; 233 Nick Fox/Shutterstock; 237 Geogphotos/Alamy; 242, 244 Nick Fox/Shutterstock; 258 Alexey U/Shutterstock; 259 (BC) Ub foto/Shutterstock, (BCR) Atlantis Films Limited/Everett Collection, (BL) Andipantz/Vetta/Getty Images, (BR) Art4all/Shutterstock, (T) Hine, Lewis Wickes/Library of Congress, (TC) Fareed Khan/AP Images, (TCL) Bettmann/Corbis; (TCR) Soe Zeya Tun/Reuters, (TL) AP Images, (TR) AC Rider/Shutterstock; 262 Hine, Lewis Wickes/Library of Congress; 267 (B) MediaRecall Holdings/Archive ED/Getty Images, (C) Bettmann/Corbis, (T) AP Images; 268 (B) Fine Art/Corbis, (TL) AP Images, (TR) Bettmann/Corbis; 269 AP Images; 273 BrooklynScribe/Shutterstock; 278, 280, 282 (TL) AP Images; 282 (B), 294 National Archives/Getty Images; 282 (TR), 283, 288, 290, 292, 295, 297 Bettmann/Corbis; 298 Hine, Lewis Wickes/Library of Congress; 305 (BR) Andipantz/Vetta/Getty Images, (C) Ub foto/Shutterstock, (T) Fareed Khan/AP Images, (TR) ABC News; 308 (B) Dpa picture alliance/Alamy,(TL) Fareed Khan/AP Images, (TR) ABC News; 309 Fareed Khan/AP Images; 311 Epaeuropeanpressphoto agency b.v./Alamy; 315,316,318 (TL), 322 (T) Fareed Khan/AP Images; 318 (B) Everett Collection Inc/Alamy; 318 (TR), 319, 321, 322 (B) ABC News; 324,326 Ub foto/Shutterstock; 325 (B) Ozkok/Sipa/Newscom, (T) Ken

Charnock/Getty Images; 328 Cunaplus/Shutterstock; 336 Abdel Meza Notimex/Newscom; 337, 340 Andipantz/Vetta/Getty Images; 342 Andipantz/Vetta/Getty Images; 362 Abdul Aziz Apu Bangladesh/Ocean/Corbis; 363 (BC) Arthur Rackman/Mary Evans Picture Library/The Image Works, (BCR) Joy Brown/Shutterstock, (BL) Addison Doty,363 (BR) LiliGraphie/Shutterstock, (CB) Wiktord/Shutterstock, (CBL) Michael Snell/Alamy Stock Photo/Alamy, (CBR) Sagar Singh Bisht/EyeEm/Getty Images, (CT) Alexskopje/Shutterstock, (CTL) Natasha Owen/Fotolia, (CTR) Ollyy/Shutterstock, (T) Melpomene/Fotolia, (TC) Jan Sochor/Alamy, (TL) Pamela Moore/E+/Getty Images; 366 Melpomene/Fotolia; 371 (B) Michael Snell/Alamy Stock Photo/Alamy, (C) Natasha Owen/Fotolia, 371 (T), 373, 382, 384, 386 Pamela Moore/E+/Getty Images; 372 Culture Club/Hulton Archive/Getty Images; 388 Eamonn McCabe/Hulton Archive/Getty Images; 389 Natasha Owen/Fotolia; 393 Doug McKinlay/Lonely Planet Images/Getty Images; 396, 398, 400 Natasha Owen/Fotolia; 402 Wael Hamdan/Alamy Stock Photo/Alamy; 403 Everett Collection/Newscom; 404 (T) Brendan McDermid/EPA/Newscom, (B) Images of Africa Photobank/Alamy Stock Photo/Alamy; 405 (T) Frank Trapper/Corbis, (B) Michael Snell/Alamy Stock Photo/Alamy; 407 Michael Snell/Alamy Stock Photo/Alamy; 408 Melpomene/Fotolia; 415 (B) Addison Doty, (BL) Arthur Rackman/Mary Evans Picture Library/The Image Works, (C) Wiktord/Shutterstock, (T) Jan Sochor/Alamy, (TL) Alexskopje/Shutterstock; 418 Julia Ewan/The Washington Post/Getty Images; 419, 426, 428 Jan Sochor/Alamy; 423 Heritage Image Partnership Ltd/Alamy; 430 Alexskopje/Shutterstock; 431 (B) Cornelia Spelman, (C) Jason DeCrow/AP Images, (T) Beowulf Sheehan/ZUMA Press/Newscom; 432 Alexskopje/Shutterstock; 434 Daniel Schweinert/Shutterstock; 435 Nina Leen/The Life Picture Collection/Getty Images; 442 (B) Lebrecht Music and Arts Photo Library/Alamy, (TL) Wiktord/Shutterstock, (TR) Arthur Rackman/Mary Evans Picture Library/The Image Works; 443, 457, 458, 460 (TL), 468 (T) Wiktord/Shutterstock; 447 Determined/Fotolia; 451 Lana Langlois/Shutterstock; 460 (B) Oscar White/Corbis; 460 (TR), 461, 465, 466, 468 (B) Arthur Rackman/Mary Evans Picture Library/The Image Works; 470 Margie Goldsmith; 471, 476, 478 Addison Doty; 492 Glowimages/Getty Images; 493 (BCL) Warongdech/Shutterstock, (BCR) Ingram Publishing/Newscom, (BL) sherwood/Shutterstock, (BR) Elena Ray, (C) The Guardian/Alamy, (CBR) Quint & Lox/akg images, (CR) Robert Hoetink/Shutterstock, (CTL) Melinda Sue Gordon/Touchstone Pictures/Everett Collection, (CTR) Infuksc 02/Stockpix/INFphoto/Newscom, (T) 'The Tempest', c.1790 (oil on canvas),Hamilton,William (1751–801)/Royal Pavilion, Libraries & Museums, Brighton & Hove/Bridgeman Art Library, (TC) Prudkov/Shutterstock, (TL) GeorgiosKollidas/Shutterstock, (TR) Robert Walker Macbeth/Hulton Fine Art Collection/Getty Images; 496 'The Tempest', c.1790 (oil on canvas), Hamilton,William (1751–1801)/Royal Pavilion, Libraries & Museums, Brighton & Hove/Bridgeman Art Library; 501(BCL), (BL), (CTL), (CTR), (TL) Melinda Sue Gordon/Touchstone Pictures/Everett Collection, (BCR) sherwood/Shutterstock, (BR) Warongdech/Shutterstock, (CL) AF archive/Alamy, (T) GeorgiosKollidas/Shutterstock; 502 (TL) Elizabeth I, Armada Portrait, c.1588 (oil on panel), Gower, George (1540–96) (attr. to)/Woburn Abbey, Bedfordshire, UK/Bridgeman Art Library,(BCL) World History Archive/Alamy, (BCR) Pantheon/Superstock, (BL) The Print Collector/Alamy, (BR) IanDagnall Computing/Alamy, (T) Elizabeth I (1533–1603) (colourlitho), Oliver, Isaac (c.1565–1617) (after)/Private Collection/Ken Welsh/Bridgeman Art Library; 503 (BL) Pantheon/Superstock,(BR) © IanDagnall Computing / Alamy Stock Photo; 504 Mary Evans Picture Library/The Image Works; 505 Travel Pictures/Alamy; 506 Steve Vidler/Superstock; 508 Stocksnapper/Shutterstock; 510, 534, 554, 572, 587 Georgios Kollidas/Shutterstock; 511 Matt Mawson/Corbis; 512, 520, 525, 531, 532, 535, 541, 552, 557, 564–565, 579, 583, 585, 598, 600, 602, 604 (L), 612 (B) Melinda Sue Gordon/Touchstone Pictures/Everett Collection; 569, 571, 596 AF archive/Alamy; 572, 586 Georgios Kollidas/Shutterstock; 597 Victor Schrager; 604 (R), 606 (Bkgd), 612 (B) Warongdech/Shutterstock; 605 © J. P. Dancing Bear; 606, 611, 612(Bkgd) sherwood/Shutterstock; 608, 611 SasinT/Shutterstock; 614 'The Tempest', c.1790 (oil on canvas), Hamilton,William (1751–1801)/Royal Pavilion, Libraries & Museums, Brighton & Hove/Bridgeman Art Library; 621 (B) The Guardian/Alamy, (T) Prudkov/Shutterstock; 624 Prudkov/Shutterstock; 625 (B) Polish Press Agency (PAP), (T)

ImehAkpanudosen/Getty Images; **626** Prudkov/Shutterstock; **628** SandratskyDmitriy/Shutterstock; **634** Jennifer Bruce/AFP/Getty Images; **635, 640, 642** The Guardian/Alamy; **656** Bruce Rolff/Shutterstock, **657** (BC) GalynaAndrushko/Shutterstock, (BCL) Neil Hanna/ZUMA Press/ Newscom, (BCR) Diana Ong/SuperStock/Getty Images, (BL) Vkara/Fotolia, (BR) Divgradcurl/Shutterstock, (CBR) Stocksnapper/Alamy, (CT) Bphillips/ Getty Images, (CTL) Popperfoto/Getty Images, (TC) Everett Collection Historical/Alamy, (TCL) Hercules Milas/Alamy, (TCR) Chanase,Dane (1894–1975)/Private Collection/Photo Christie's Images/Bridgeman Art Library, (TL) Tomgigabite/Shutterstock, (TR) Akg images, (Bkgd) Tomgigabite/Shutterstock; **665** (B) Neil Hanna/ZUMA Press/ Newscom, (C) Popperfoto/Getty Images, (T) Hercules Milas/Alamy; **666** Cardaf/Shutterstock, (TL) Hercules Milas/Alamy; **668** FedorSelivanov/ Shutterstock; **669** Khirman Vladimir/Shutterstock; **670** Alfredo DagliOrti/ The Art Archive/Art Resource, New York; **671** Ingres,JeanAuguste Dominique (1780–1867)/Musee des Beaux Arts, Angers, France/ Bridgeman Art Library; **672** Universal Images Group/Getty Images; **673** Ariy/Shutterstock; **674** Popperfoto/Getty Images; **678** akg images/ Newscom; **682** Flaxman,John (1755–1826)/York Museums Trust (York Art Gallery),UK/Bridgeman Art Library; **685, 694** Merlyn Severn/Picture Post/ Getty Images; **690–691** Neil Hanna/ZUMA Press/Newscom; **699, 701** Popperfoto/Getty Images; **702** Universal Images Group/Getty Images; **703** Neil Hanna/ZUMA Press/Newscom; **709** Eileen Darby/The LIFE Images Collection/Getty Images; **716** John Vickers/ University of Bristol Theatre Collection/ArenaPal/The Image Works; **719** Lebrecht Music and Arts Photo Library/Alamy; **722, 724, 726** Neil Hanna/ZUMA Press/Newscom; **728** (L) Tomgigabite/Shutterstock, (R) Akg images; **735** (B) Vkara/Fotolia, (BC) GalynaAndrushko/Shutterstock, (T) Everett Collection Historical/ Alamy, (TC) Bphillips/Getty Images; **738** GraphicaArtis/Getty Images; **739, 742,744** Everett Collection Historical/Alamy; **746** Bphillips/Getty Images; **747** (B) Clement/AFP/Getty Images, (C) Don Tormey/Los Angeles Times/ Getty Images, (T) AL Youm AL Saabi/Reuters/Reuters; **748** Bphillips/Getty Images; **750** MerkushevVasiliy/Shutterstock; **752** Sophie Bassouls/Sygma/ Corbis; **759** GalynaAndrushko/Shutterstock; **764** LenarMusin/ Shutterstock; **770** Saraporn/Shutterstock; **777** Nina B/Shutterstock; **782** GalynaAndrushko/Shutterstock; **786** Rosemary Mahoney; **787, 798, 800** Vkara/Fotolia; **793** Wu Hong/EPA/Newscom.

Credits for Images in Interactive Student Edition Only

Unit 1

Colin McPherson/Corbis; Lopris/Shutterstock; Oronoz/Album/SuperStock; Virunja/Shutterstock

Unit 2

© Earl Wilson; © Sarah Cramer; Kevin Day/Shutterstock

Unit 3

Epa european pressphoto agency b.v./Alamy; Oliver Morris/Hulton Archive/Getty Images

Unit 4

Jeff Desjardins; Mark Higgins/Shutterstock; Olivier Le Queinec/ Shutterstock; Rose Salter Rodriguez; Russel Belk

Unit 5

Brooks Kraft/Sygma/Corbis; Louis Monier/Gamma-Rapho/Getty Images; The Forgiveness Project/Brian Moody;

Unit 6

Stocksnapper/Alamy; Chanase,Dane (1894–1975)/Private Collection/Photo Christie's Images/Bridgeman Art Library; Apoorva Mandavilli; Hulton Archive/Handout/Getty Images; Hulton Archive/Stringer/Getty Images; Melissa Hogenboom; Sasha/Stringer/Hulton Archive/Getty Images; Shander Herian; Ulf Andersen/Getty Images